The journal of a self injurer

    I'm at the hospital. The place where everyone knows to go when they're sick. I'm not just at any place in the hospital though. People don't come here because their back hurts or they can't stop coughing. They come here because they see or hear things that keep them from telling what's real from what's not. They come here because their mood changes so fast that it scares the people they love. They come here because they starve themselves out of pure hatred for a body that they are convinced is ugly, no matter how beautiful they may be. The people here can be loud. They can be afraid. They can be so sad that they do nothing but cry as they fall asleep. Some of us come here by our own will, while others are forced to come by those who are stronger. But whether by will or by force, none of us are permitted to leave unless freedom is granted.

    I am afraid, I am sad, and I am anxious. Let me tell you how I got here.

Friday, May 23

The medical clinic was one floor up from the pharmacy. I didn't have an appointment, so I had to wait my turn in the afternoon.

I looked to see who would be responsible for the walk-in-patients for that day, but I didn't recognize the name in the slot. I was disappointed because every time I went to the clinic, I got someone new. I had no idea what kind of person I was about to meet.

I had to tell my story from the start once again to a new and unfamiliar man. The doctor from my previous visit had seemed so disinterested and didn't even bother reading my file. He prescribed an anti-depressant called Citalopram.

Months later, Citalopram was the very drug that I had come back to complain about.

I was called to room three. I waited in an office chair that was on the side of a desk for the doctor to arrive. I usually took advantage of my time alone in the examination room to explore all the trinkets and gadgets on the tables and walls, but this time I just sat down, rested my head against the wall, and closed my eyes.

When the doctor came in the room, he shut the door.

"Hello," Dr Stone greeted me as he walked over and shook my hand.

"Hello," I replied nervously. I was never at ease in a medical clinic, but then again, I was rarely at ease at all.

Dr Stone was a tall man with curly grey hair. His hair may have been grey, but his face was young; maybe in his forties. He had a warm personality and a French, European accent in his speech. "What can I do for you?" he inquired as he took his seat at the desk next to my chair.

"I was given anti-depressants for my anxiety the last time I came," I explained. "For the first few weeks they made me really nauseous, but now I find that they make me really depressed. They make me so sad that it physically hurts. I'm often on the verge of tears for no reason. I wasn't like this before."

I had begun thinking that my medication was evil. I found myself feeling like I was dying or like I wasn't real. I walked around and wondered if I was alive. Perhaps all I was, was a consciousness floating through the world without a body. Maybe no one heard me speak because the words I spoke were as unreal as I was. My chest hurt and it was hard to breathe. I wondered how the air got so thick. I wondered how I had come to hurt so badly.

"Where does it hurt?" Dr Stone asked.

I didn't say the words. I simply motioned to my chest with my hand.

"What kinds of things make you that anxious?" he wanted to know.

I hesitated for a moment. Some words were harder to say. "My father is an alcoholic, but I cut off contact with him. I haven't seen him in years." I confided. "I was also sexually abused in my early teens by the father of one of my friends."

"What makes you anxious now?"

"Memories," I stated. "Nightmares are bad. When my father comes to town, I'm a mess. He was here recently. He was at my workplace and I had to make sure to leave before he got there. It was a close call. Since then I have an anxiety attack every time I go to work. Every time I stand where I know he stood, it's too much for me. I usually start freaking out without thinking about why. It's become automatic now," I paused. "Oh, and going to the dentist is pretty bad too. Having to lay there, with him hovering over me. Even just laying down on the chair is hard." I pointed to the examining table in front of me because it reminded me of the one at the dentists office. I was silent as the memories came back. "The last time I went to the dentist, I bit his hand. I was so anxious that when it was done and I got up to go, I nearly passed out. I was so dizzy that I clung to the wall. The dentist got me to sit back down in the same chair that caused my panic in the first place."

"That couldn't have been helpful," the doctor observed.

"No, it wasn't."

I remembered trying to get out of the chair and being pushed back down. The dentist and his assistant put wet paper towels on my forehead. I was angered by the memory of the dentist telling me that I had to eat. I wasn't anorexic. I wasn't dizzy because I hadn't eaten; I was dizzy because I was practically hyperventilating for an hour. Hadn't he noticed me panicking the entire time I was in his chair? I was angered, but I didn't correct him. I didn't have the courage to explain the post traumatic stress I was living.

I needed medication for times like that; times where I needed to scream, but couldn't; times where I struggled to breathe, but found no way to calm down. I needed my medication, but the ones I was on made me hurt so deeply and in so many ways.

"What about sleep? Do you sleep well?" The doctor inquired.

"No. Last night it took me two hours to fall asleep, then I woke up with my heart pounding in the middle of the night. It took me another hour to fall back to sleep. Sleep hasn't been good. So, can I get off of this medication and onto something else?" I asked hopefully. I was sure the answer would be yes. I couldn't imagine that he would leave me like that.

"No, Im going to have you continue on these, but I'm going to give you something to help you sleep. If you can sleep better, your medication should help you more," Dr Stone explained.

I was disappointed. I was really looking forward to getting off of that medication, but I assumed that the doctor knew what he was talking about. I trusted that sleep had to be the cure.

There was silence in the room as a prescription was being written.

It took a lot of courage to ask a question that I was unsure of whether to bring up at all, but I didn't want to lose the opportunity. I watched as the doctor scribbled several sideways words that were meant for the pharmacist. What was the right time to ask? When he was done writing? I wasn't sure if I should interrupt. If I waited too long, he would be assuming it was time for good-byes and I wouldn't have the guts to bring it up. I had to really push myself, but finally I just said it. "I was wondering if there's some kind of vitamins or whatever that could help compensate for the fact that my blood is incredibly thick. I read that thick blood can be really bad for the heart. It makes it pump harder."

Dr Stone didn't look up from his notes as he scribbled them. "Where are you getting that from?"

"Huh?" I was confused.

"What brought you to that conclusion?" The doctor asked his question once again without looking away from his paper.

"You mean, how do I know that my blood is thick?" I asked for him to specify.

"Yes."

I hesitated for a moment as my prescription continued to be filled. The answer to his question wasn't something that I brought up much. In fact, I had paid good money to keep it a secret, even from my family. I was embarrassed, ashamed, and afraid. I was alone in a world of darkness that I kept from the light. What would happen if people saw my world? Would they still be able to look at my face, or would they turn away from it like I had? How would a girl like me know that her own blood was thick?

I took a deep breath. "I self-mutilate."

I barely had the courage to look over and see what kind of reaction my words had evoked. I turned my eyes, but not my head to see his face.

First, Dr Stone looked upwards at the wall in front of his desk. I watched the word *mutilate* form silently on his lips. It was like he was letting the meaning of my word register in his mind, then he turned his chair, leaned towards me and asked, "Where do you do this?"

"My lower leg," I admitted shyly.

"Show me," he requested as he tapped my leg and got up to close the second door of the office; the one that led to the secretaries desks.

The words *show me* instilled a kind of fear in me. I wasn't proud of what I had done to myself and I wasn't accustomed to letting anyone see the results of my self destruction.

The Doctor noticed my uneasiness. "You don't have to," he reassured me.

I thought about it for a second. What did I have to lose? Would my darkness grow deeper? Would the light leave me forever?

I raised my right leg so that my foot could rest on the chair I was sitting on, then I pulled up my pant-leg and lowered my knee high socks. I always made sure to keep my secrets well concealed, so I had made my lower leg as layered as possible.

The doctor sat down in his chair and took my exposed leg so he could look more closely. He ran his hand over my scars and wounds that were as recent as the day before.

He looked at my mess for an uncomfortably long time. I was sure that he must have thought that I was crazy and disgusting; A creature.

I pulled my pant-leg down and the doctor rubbed my leg sympathetically. I was not used to that kind of behavior. It struck me as both comforting and odd. I saw that it was his way of letting me know that he cared.

"What are we going to do about this?" he asked as he still held onto my leg, but looked into my eyes. When I didn't answer, he said, "Hmm? What do we do about this?"

"I don't know. I don't know how to stop." I tried to think of a good answer to give him, but I was still at a loss.

"Have you ever told a doctor about this before?" he asked.

"Yes."

"And what did he say?"

"He asked if I had scars. I said that I did. The conversation ended there." I thought back to that day. I hadn't been disappointed that no further help was offered because I hadn't expected any. I never had any help before.

"Well, I think that under the circumstances, you shouldn't take any blood thinners or you'll have trouble making the bleeding stop."

That made sense, but I was grateful that at least a blood test was ordered so I could know what was going on.

"At least I don't cut where there's a lot of veins," I told him in reference to my lower leg.

"Yes, I thought it was an interesting place that you chose. There's a place in Africa where it's a tradition to cut their lower legs for scarification. They find it attractive," the doctor informed me.

"Really?" I was surprised. "I should go to Africa. At least then I could wear shorts," I remarked with a smile.

I liked that he told me about people cutting their legs at the same place as me in some far away place. It made me feel less strange and morbid.

"Tell me about your anxiety," Dr Stone requested. "What are your symptoms?"

"It gets hard to breathe," I told him. "The pain in my chest is so strong. It's like a huge weight pressing down on me. It feels like a heart attack. I remember having to lean against a table and close my eyes and let the worst of it pass. My heart races so quickly; I feel like I'm going to choke on it."

If I was around people when I had an attack, I would hide in a hallway or a small room where I would pretend to scream. I wanted to kick the walls, but I couldn't or someone would hear and know something was wrong. If I couldn't hide, I had to pretend I was fine. If it got too strong when I was in the presence of others, I would bury my face in my hands and cringe really hard without explaining why.

Dr Stone got up and walked to the other side of me so he could kneel at my side. "Show me how you breathe," he requested.

I wasn't completely sure what he meant. "How do I do that?"

"Sit up straight. Im going to put my hands on you," he warned me politely.

The doctor put one hand on my lower back and the other right below my neck. I was supposed to close my eyes, and breathe deeply while moving forward and back.

After breathing in several times, he asked calmly, "What is the first thing that comes to your mind?"

The doctors hands were still resting on me, and it was hard to think of anything else. I felt his presence intensely as he knelt next to me. I thought about his question, but I didn't want to give the answer because I was afraid it might be rude.

"What is the first thing that comes to your mind?" he asked again, so I answered.

"Where your hands are," I let him know.

"Where my hands are? That's what comes to your mind?"

"Yes."

The doctor pulled away. "You don't like to be touched?"

"No," I admitted. I was embarrassed to say so. There was nothing wrong with the way he was touching me. I was an adult. I shouldn't have been bothered by something so trivial.

Dr Stone got up and tapped my knee in a comforting way and said, "I understand."

Instead of literally feeling how I was breathing, he sat in his chair and coached me on what to do. "Let's do it at the same time," the doctor invited and closed his eyes. "I'm not looking at you. We're just breathing."

I watched this tall, distinguished man breathe in deeply with his eyes closed and with one hand on his chest. I had never seen anyone be so comfortable with themselves.

Dr Stone asked his question once again. "What comes to your mind when you think of the pain in your chest?"

My mind came up empty. I felt like this was something that I was supposed to know. I didn't like being asked questions that I didn't know the answers to. I finally said the most logical thing that came to my mind. "It just reminds me of all the other times I've felt this way. It's a familiar pain."

"Pain is a good thing because it lets us know that something is wrong," the doctor pointed out.

I didn't believe him. Pain wasn't a good thing. Pain made me exhausted and I didn't know how to cope with it in a healthy way.

Pain took my strength and my sanity and twisted them into knots. Pain wasn't something that I allowed myself to feel if I had the power to take it away.

"We need to take care of your anxiety, but the thing that really worries me is that you are doing this," the doctor pointed to my leg and I knew that he was referring to the cuts. I didn't say anything, so he continued, "I can arrange for you to see a psychiatrist. They will be able to evaluate you and figure out what kind of therapy you need. The waiting list depends on the severity of the case, but with you, I don't think the wait will be long."

I had never seen a psychiatrist before and the idea struck me as strange. The only thing I knew about them was what I had seen on television. The thought of seeing a psychiatrist made me nervous, but it was also reassuring. Maybe something was finally going to change for me.

Dr Stone made the phone call to put me on the waiting list, and when he hung up, he offered me something more. "I would be ready to follow your case regularly," he told me.

I got exited about what he had offered and I finally felt myself smile. "You mean that I won't have to see a different doctor each time?"

"Is there someone that you feel particularly comfortable with that you would like as a family doctor?" Dr Stone asked.

My excitement lowered when I thought that maybe he was rethinking the idea of following my case. I wondered why I was being passed off onto someone else so soon after he offered to see me himself. Did he regret his offer? If I said that I wanted him to be my doctor, would that be out of the question?

I thought of all the doctors I had seen at the clinic. I hadn't come to know any of them very well. The first one I saw was a woman. She was nice, so I thought I would offer her name.

"I think her name was….Melissa….or something," I suggested. I remembered that there was a doctor with the same name as mine, and I was sure that she was the one I saw.

"Melissa Turner?"

"Yeah," I agreed as the name was familiar to me.

I watched and waited as this kind man called up his colleague and asked her if she would be my doctor.

Dr turner agreed to follow my case.

I was grateful for everything that was done for me, but when I left the clinic and went home, I regretted that Dr Stone wasn't going to be my doctor. When he asked if I knew who I wanted to have as my doctor, why didn't I say, "*Yeah, you?*" I hadn't seen Dr Melissa Turner in over a year, and I was very satisfied with my visit with Dr Stone. He was the first person to offer to help me.

I thought back to when he asked me, "What are we going to do about this?"

I really liked that question. The question not only implied that there could be a solution, but also that I wasn't the only one looking for one. It was like a weight off my shoulders.

Dr Stone was the kindest of all the doctors I had seen so far. He saw that I had a problem and he not only cared, but he did something about it.

I wanted a doctor that did something about it.

~ ~ ~ ~

I had been cutting a lot that week. The day that I met Dr Stone was the sixth time that I had cut in just a few days. I was cutting everyday, sometimes twice a day. I was cutting, bleeding and laughing afterwards because I felt so much better for a while. I could find the mess in front of me to be one of the funniest things I had ever encountered. It was a bright, liquid insanity. Whatever troubles could have stayed with me past that cut, rose in the air and disappeared with my laughter.

So many days had come with bleeding in bathrooms or on living room floors. So much stupidity. Why couldn't I just learn to deal with negative emotion? If I felt like I was going to cry, why didn't I just cry? All evening I felt like I wanted to cry, but I didn't. I would hurt myself to keep from doing so.

I tried to avoid cutting by snapping a rubber band on my wrist. It would create pain, but it wouldn't break the skin. It worked; sometimes.

I felt sick. I felt like my heart was being squeezed and my breathing got hard.

I knew that I had to be careful not to lose too much blood or I would be in trouble.

The anxiety twisted around in my stomach and made me feel like I was going to throw up.

I didn't know what I was doing or what was happening.

I was torn between wanting to make it all right again, and being too scared to stop what I was doing. I felt like I needed the cutting and a big part of me didn't want to give it up.

I knew that I couldn't keep going on that way.

I knew that I had to do something about how deeply broken I was feeling, so I did the only thing that I found was in my power to do.

I called the clinic Monday morning to see if I could trade doctors, but it wasn't even registered in the computer systems that I even had a doctor at all.

I waited as the woman on the phone checked my file. It turned out that it was in fact written that Dr Turner was my doctor. There was also a written request that an appointment be made with me. There was a time slot for me to go in on the sixth of June.

I didn't want that appointment though. I didn't want to talk to this doctor that I barely remembered.

"Would it be possible to ask Dr Stone if he could be my doctor?" I asked.

The woman on the phone sounded blunt. "None of our doctors are accepting new patients. If you decide not to see Dr Turner, you wont have any doctor at all."

I was always so nervous on the phone and I so rarely defended the things I needed. I didn't feel like explaining my somewhat special circumstances that made it so that I got a doctor when no one else could.

I didn't argue with the woman and we both hung up.

I was very disappointed.

Monday, May 26

By Monday night it occurred to me that I should look at the old prescription bottle that the lady doctor had given me the year before. I wanted to be sure that the woman who just became my family doctor was in fact the same one I had met on my first visit to the clinic.

The name on the bottle wasn't Dr Melissa Turner at all; it was Dr Susan Alder.

I was disappointed and stunned to learn that my new family doctor was a complete stranger. I knew nothing about her. Was she nice? Would she be respectful of me despite my self injury? Would she be freaked out by my habit?

The next day when I saw my therapist, I told her that I had accidentally found myself with a family doctor that I had never met. That was the first time that I had ever seen this psychologist with a shocked expression. It didn't last long though, and I wondered why she worked so hard to hide her emotions from me.

I decided to bounce my ideas off of my psychologist. "At first I figured that this new doctor had to be pretty nice and that everything would be fine. Then I worried about how I really don't know what this woman is like or how she will react to my issues. That's when I started to get really anxious about it."

"And how did you deal with your anxiety?" The young woman crossed her legs under a knee length grey skirt.

"I freaked out," I confessed. "I couldn't leave things that way. I called the medical clinic back this morning, but this time, a different secretary answered. I explained what had happened and that I wanted to change doctors. I wanted Dr Stone."

"And what did she say?" She encouraged me to continue.

"She told me the same thing that the other secretary said to me yesterday. She said that neither of the doctors I mentioned are accepting new patients."

I was proud of my own social courage when I mentioned the next part of my story. "I stood up for my request and this time I told her that Dr Stone had offered to be my family doctor," I smiled. "So they called him."

I remembered that shortly afterwards the girl left and came back on the line to say, "Yes, Dr Stone wants to have you as a patient."

"Whoopee!" I cried out and the girl on the phone laughed at my excitement.

Then someone else came on the line; a woman with a much deeper voice. "Is it you that had an appointment with Dr Turner?"

The woman sounded moody.

"Yes,"

As scary as that woman was, she managed to get my appointment switched over to Dr Stones patient list.

I had an appointment for June fifth.

I wasn't sure why I needed an appointment though.

"What is the appointment for?" I inquired. " Are you sure that Dr Stone wants to see me so soon? The other appointment was requested of me when I was supposed to meet Dr Turner. Dr Stone may not have the same request to meet with me."

The secretary didn't understand my question. "Are you saying that you wish to return to Dr Turner?"

"No! No!" I cried out. "That's not what I want."

I explained myself again.

"Wait a minute," the secretary said before she left and then came back moments later. "Okay, It's fine for you to return with Dr Turner."

"What?!" I exclaimed with eyes wide. "No, I don't want that."

I explained myself again. "I wanted Dr Stone, but was he requesting a meeting with me?"

The secretary clearly still didn't understand. "If you want a gynecology appointment, then you have to be with Dr Turner because Dr Stone doesn't give them." That fact was specified a few times because the secretary felt that I had not understood.

I rolled my eyes and took a deep breath. Oh boy. "That's fine Lady," I thought, "I don't want one."

I couldn't make the secretary understand my question, and the sad thing was that she thought I was the one who couldn't be made to understand.

"I can explain it to you again if you need," the secretary offered. "I don't mind."

I couldn't help but laugh.

I gave up.

I kept my appointment and hung up.

My psychologist startled me back to reality as I recounted my story. "So you got the appointment that you wanted."

"Yes," I confirmed.

I always felt strange after I was done talking with my therapist. Talking so much about myself was something new to me. Often times it even scared me, so every Tuesday after therapy I would walk it off. I walked where it was calm and I felt like I could put my thoughts back together.

It usually felt like my mind was racing and I couldn't catch up. A racing mind made me anxious, and anxiety made me desperate, and desperation made resort to hurting myself. It became automatic after a few years of cutting. At first I would only resort to it once in a while, but as time passed and I grew more accustomed to my habit, nearly every problem I had would lead to cutting.

I felt like I must have been insane, because being upset about the fact that I wanted to cut was making me want to cut even more.

I was trying to change things for myself. I had ordered a punching bag and set it up in the extra room. I thought that I could use it to vent my anger at the bag instead of at myself. The only thing that was missing was to paint the room. I picked out a burgundy color and only managed to do the contours of the walls. My mood was so bad that I couldn't bring myself to finish it.

With all the times that I had cut that day and the days before, I was feeling pretty drained; metaphorically and literally.

Two days earlier when I had cut on the washroom floor, my violent means of coping didn't make me feel any better. I was too worried that my brother would show up at my apartment and catch me in the act. I lived alone, but my family had the key. It was the fist time that cutting had not provided a relief. Yet, still, two days later, I dared to sit on the living room floor with a blade in my hand. Blood was stained down my leg and onto the floor. Red fluids smeared a small piece of steel and coated my hands.

The phone rang and I looked immediately up at the white receiver that was screaming on the shelf in front of me.

I felt my heart being squeezed again.

"Crap," I thought. "Not now. Please, not now."

I stood up and stepped past the blood on the floor as the phone rang a second time. I put the blade down and studied my fingers to find which ones were the cleanest. I would use those fingers to pick up the receiver. I was terrified to allow myself to speak to someone when I was such a psychotic mess.

I took a deep breath and tried to act natural.

"Hello?" I spoke into the phone that I held carefully with two mostly clean fingers.

It was my sister Marie.

I pretended like nothing was going on.

I can't even remember what we talked about. All I could think about during our whole conversation was of the blood that surrounded me; the blood that I could never allow her to see.

I hung up the phone, then I walked down the hallway to the washroom where I lifted my right leg to put it in the sink, and then rinsed off the blood from three of my limbs.

I felt sick to my stomach.

I had done it again, and it was disgusting.

LADY INJURY

I had so much regret, and once again, cutting hadn't made me feel any better. The anxiety from talking on the phone had taken it all away. It took away the feeling of peace that came with cutting.

That wasn't the way that it was supposed to go. Cutting was supposed to help; It was supposed to take the hurt away.

How was I going to face my friend Lisa the next day? Lisa and I had made up some code words that we could use around our family and friends. If I were to cut or if she were to purge her meal, that would be what we called a Russian. We made a deal one day that neither of us would be seeing any Russians. I had even told her at some point that I hadn't seen any Russians in four weeks. I hadn't cut in four weeks. That was true at the time, but in the last week I had completely lost control.

What should I have told her if she had asked if I'd seen any Russians?

Maybe I could I have used a reassuring smile and the words, "Don't worry. I'm fine."

Would that really have been lying?

When I finally saw Lisa, I hugged her so hard and told her that if I didn't let go, I was going to start to cry; so she hugged me again.

I hadn't cried in a long time. For a while, I thought myself incapable. If I felt like crying, I would hurt myself to keep the tears away. It worked, and I didn't cry. It felt like the tears I had kept away had been gathered up and were ready to overflow. I grew tired of keeping it all in, and I sensed that tears would come soon.

I had to sit because with the anxiety and the blood loss, I wasn't feeling so well. Lisa and I then went downstairs to her room and sat on the floor.

When I checked to see if my wounds were still bleeding, I allowed my friend to see what I had done.

"Do they need stitches?" Lisa looked closely. "Almost, but not quite."

We talked for a while. It felt good to see her. We both shared our struggles with each other like it was a release. I talked about how hard it was not to cut and how hard it was when I did end up cutting. She would talk about how hard it was to eat and keep her food down. We both knew what it was like to hurt our bodies. It's a strange reason to be bonded to someone, but I think we both needed to feel understood, and even though we couldn't love ourselves, we could love each other.

Wednesday, May 28

On the Wednesday after, I had cut three different times. A large part of my motivation was to prove to myself that cutting was still an effective way to make me feel better; and it was. The pain on my flesh made the hurt I felt inside fade away.

I even cut myself when I was at my workplace. Three times a week I would clean a grocery store that was a half an hour from my place. After closing time, I had the store all to myself. I would usually sit on the bathroom floor with my back against the door. I would cut and let the blood run onto some pieces of paper.

Work was intolerable for me, but it wasn't the job itself that I found difficult.

Working on my own gave me too much time to think, and when I did too much thinking, my heart would race and I would have anxiety attacks. I would think about my past, my present, and my future, but I found none of those things to be settling. I thought of the dangers around me. I thought of the people who could hurt me and had hurt me before.

My father was not a good man; or maybe he was. I do believe that good people can do bad things. Was there a part in all of us that stayed as good as the day of our coming into innocence? I didn't know, but I liked to think that there was.

To be blunt, my father was a drunk who spent his evenings sulking in the basement; either in his office or by the fireplace. He was a man who pitied himself greatly. He spoke of how he didn't matter and nor did I. We meant nothing to the world. Whether we lived or we died, it changed nothing because we were nothing. He told me that nobody cared about us. He spoke badly of my sister and three brothers. He even asked my siblings why they couldn't be more like me. I don't know what was so special about me that they had to imitate. Maybe it was because I listened to his late night madness. Maybe it was because of how hard I tried to fix him, and to make him stop saying that things were so bad. I wanted him to see the good, but instead he stared into a fireplace and watched his life burn.

When I was thirteen, the man that I was born to be loved by, announced that he was no longer my father or the father of my siblings. He would be nothing to us as a parent. Truthfully, he never really did much as a parent, but having him say those words was cruel and they lay cold on my heart. I felt guilty for all the days that followed because I knew he abandoned his relationship with his children because of me. My siblings lost their father because of me. I had just told him that I hated him for hitting me and so he resigned.

I grew to be a woman, and he grew to be a man that I could never call father. He smelled of alcohol and screamed at his children. He staggered and turned red with rage as he knocked down my door just so he could hit me out of punishment. He hit us if we were too quiet and he hit us if we cried.

I often refused to cry. I refused out of anger and spite for his punishments. I could handle a lot. I was most proud of myself when I could tolerate the pain, because it meant that a part of me had won. A part of me hadn't given up and that's what I clung to. I could win if he was unsatisfied with my reaction.

I practiced pain even as a small child. I would bruise myself with blunt objects. The more pain I could tolerate the better and more confident I felt. I refused to be the one who got hit and walked away crying. I felt that I had to be stronger than that.

I couldn't blame all of my state on alcoholic parenting. When I was 14 I made the mistake of accepting a ride home from the father of a friend. He ended up parking in a remote area where he forced himself on me. I never went to his home again.

I had grown to be a woman that they called beautiful, though I struggled to see that in myself. What I saw when I looked in the mirror was something completely different. I saw someone dark and ugly. I saw someone disgusting that could never become clean. On her skin I saw the hands that were born out of acts of darkness. I saw the places that a man had allowed himself to touch when the night had no eyes to look upon his sins.

The girl in the mirror had a name. I called her Stupid Girl. I gave her all the responsibility. She was the one who was part of something bad. She was the one who was dirty and guilty and sad. She was angry and torn inside. She was guilty of allowing herself to be touched for fear of resisting and therefore being offensive to another.

I cursed this Stupid Girl and she cursed me back. She thought constantly of bleeding and choosing the places where she would make her own blood rise.

I thought of all these things when I was at my work place. I pushed large machines around that washed the floors. I had walked up and down those aisles so many times that I had memorized all the foods that stocked the shelves. I liked my job, but it was my thoughts that plagued me. Over and over, it was my thoughts that grew so deep that they weighed on my chest until it hurt. My leg was sore from the cuts, but I tried to focus on that pain instead of the stories in my head. I told myself that soon it would be over and I would be able to sleep.

One night, I returned home to find my sister, Marie, sleeping in my bed. I didn't wake her, but I went to the extra room to get some blankets for myself. When I turned the light on, I was pleasantly and happily surprised. All the walls were painted red the way that I had been meaning to do for so long. My sister had given me the gift of finishing the room that I had begun using as a refuge and a place to let out my anger. It was an act of love on her part.

I hadn't been able to paint the room, so she did it for me. I was quite touched.

I woke Marie up to thank her. She was disappointed that she hadn't been awake to see my reaction to the finished room, so I decided to re-enact the event. I left my bedroom, and re-entered with a similar expression to the one I had when I discovered her gift. The problem with my acting was that I felt very self conscious and broke down laughing.

I thanked my sister so many times. She gave me a really nice end to a really bad day.

Thursday, May 29

For the two days following, I didn't hurt myself. I think a large part of it was because I was still freaked out from the two times that I cut and it didn't help. Remembering myself washing away all that blood and seeing how bad the wounds were had really affected me. I remembered being near tears instead of the laughter and relief that usually came with cutting.

I didn't want to cut again. I wanted to quit.

I wasn't going to try and quit for somebody else the way I had tried before; I was going to stop for me.

I had a kit that I kept all my blades and sharps and scissors in. It also had medical equipment so I could care for the resulting injuries. I kept this kit near me at all times in case I would need it. I took the kit from its usual place in the living room and I buried it under a dresser drawer in my bedroom. I hoped to never use that tool kit again. I hoped to bury it and find it years later. I would remember how things had been but would never be again.

Not hurting myself wasn't too hard for most of the week. I barely even wanted to do it, so fighting the urge was easy. I was proud of how well I was doing and I was determined to keep it up.

The problem was that as the days passed, I grew less disgusted with the idea of cutting again, and soon, the thought became appealing.

I had reached ten days without cutting, but by then the urge to hurt myself was so strong and my resolve was too weak. I managed ten days, but that was all I had accomplished before falling back into old habits. I would quit and restart cutting over and over again, like a light that flickers before it burns out.

I even punched my arm until it bruised. I hoped that it would become big and ugly with lots of colors.

I was still wondering if the anti-depressants I had been on for the last few months were making me even more depressed. I was sad beforehand, but that felt different from the bad moods that came after I started the medicine.

At the same time, I wondered if this would have happened anyways. Would I still have had this drastic mood change without the anti-depressants? I wasn't sure if I should see a doctor or ride it out to see if it would pass.

I began thinking of cutting my wrists. I don't mean the veins. I mean that I wanted to cut the spaces between my veins.

I had actually bought several kinds of wide wristbands. I wanted to be prepared for the possibility that I might have to hide if I acted on my impulses.

I had a second job. Or technically it was my first job. I had worked there the longest. I worked at an old age home. I was responsible for fourteen elderly people for twelve hours, three times a week. I would make them toast and coffee. I would put drops in their eyes and give them their medication. I was there for their needs and in case of emergencies. I was responsible for their lives when something went wrong. I would call my boss and an ambulance and I would take care of the person until the medics arrived. I was their security and their safety net.

I had to stay calm with them and pretend things were okay. I would smile and talk to them about anything from the weather to simply joking around. They thought I was happy. They even said so.

I had gotten to know them so well that they were like family. I was the favorite of all the employees. I knew it because everyone said so, even my boss. I liked being the favorite. I liked being cared about. I liked feeling special.

I had two good jobs that I liked. I could be on my own in a grocery store, or I could be taking care of people at an old age home. I felt satisfied with what I was doing.

I should have been happy. I should have been, but I wasn't.

One night when I was working at the old age home, I was serving drinks to the ladies in the living room. I remembered standing there and looking longingly towards the stove top in the kitchen. I thought about turning the burner on and setting my wrist against it.

That was the first time I had any real thoughts about burning myself. It occurred to me that burning could be more painful than cutting. I knew that was the kind of thought that should scare a person, and it certainly did scare me.

I didn't burn myself with the stove top that night. I didn't burn myself the next day either when I dreamed of using my car's cigarette lighter.

In the evenings I was lucky that I had to be responsible and of service to the residents at my job. I was safe from myself when I was there. I couldn't allow myself to bleed there because if I got called to help someone while I was like that, I would be a mess. In an emergency I couldn't allow my disturbing habits to keep me restrained from helping them.

Burning however, would not be messy. I could have burned my wrists and have nothing to clean up. If someone called, I would still be ready to help them. It was a convenient form of self harm that I found brilliant and intended to use when necessary.

Saturday, May 31

A few days later, to my own self disgust, I found that I didn't have the courage to burn myself.

I stood over a stove top that grew red and hot. I managed to hold my wrist only half an inch away from being scorched, but I couldn't bring myself to touch the burner. The pain was intense even when I simply approached the heat. This realization made me afraid of the pain that an actual burn would bring.

I tried for a long time to work up the courage to go that final half an inch and burn myself on the stove top.

I couldn't do it.

I was very upset with myself over this failure. I called myself a big baby. I couldn't allow myself to be afraid of pain. I felt that I was weak and cowardly.

I didn't lack the courage to cut myself, so why couldn't I bring myself to burn? It should have been easy.

Tuesday, June 3

It took me four days before I grew the courage to cross that line of self infliction.

All the old ladies at work were in the living room, chatting and drinking the juice that I served them. I knew that from where they were sitting, they couldn't see me at the kitchen stove.

I turned the burner on and paced a bit, back and forth in front of the stove as I waited for it to grow hot enough. I grabbed a knife from the silverware drawer and held the metal end of it against the red burner. When the knife was hot enough, I held it against my wrist and let it burn in a few different places. The pain was intense, but that feeling faded fast.

The burns were obvious. At first they were white, but soon they turned red and filled with water. After the water was released, the wounds would turn to scabs. It wasn't attractive. It was an ugly form of self-infliction.

I wasn't accustomed to that kind of injury, but I was glad that I had conquered my fear and found a way to cope with my anxieties while I was at work.

In the end though, it didn't matter how hard I tried, I still felt terrible. Tears were often so close, but the idea of letting them come seemed awful and like too much pain for me to deal with. I felt that crying meant being defeated.

I refused to stop trying to make things better. I was too stubborn to stop.

Thursday, June 5

It was time for my appointment with my new family doctor. I was nervous and didn't know what to expect. I hoped that Dr Stone would have something to say because I had nothing new that I felt I needed to address with him. I didn't want to waste his time.

I was called to room number 5. It was a different room from the last times I had visited.

When I entered the doctors office, he shook my hand and closed the door.

"I didn't expect to see you so soon," he admitted.

I felt awkward; like I wasn't supposed to be there. I didn't know what to say, but we both sat down on chairs facing each other and with a large brown desk between us. There was another room attached to the office that had all the medical supplies and an examining table. There were a lot of certificates on the walls, but none of them belonged to Dr Stone, so I assumed that he was borrowing the office.

"Have you hurt yourself since we last saw each other?" Dr Stone inquired.

I was embarrassed, but I admitted what I had done.

The doctor got up and walked to my side of the desk to see for himself. I pulled off the arm warmer that I was using to hide my burns and showed him the damage. Apparently they were second degree burns, though I wasn't quite sure what that meant.

I asked about my blood test results. Apparently they were perfect. My blood was fine. Everything in it was well balanced and it wasn't too thick.

I was confused because my blood looked incredibly thick to me. "But if it's not too thick, why is it that I can pick it up in gobs?"

The doctor shrugged his shoulders. "Maybe you have alien blood," he suggested jokingly.

I smiled at his joke, but I still longed to understand the mystery.

Dr Stone spoke up, "You know that what you are doing to yourself is a kind of suicide." His sentence was more of a statement than a question.

I grew defensive and narrowed my eyes. "No it isn't," I argued. "I'm not trying to die. I can hurt myself and have it heal, and then Im fine."

"It's still a kind of suicide."

"I disagree."

"When you hurt yourself you are killing the cells in your body," the doctor explained.

"Well, sure," I thought. "But I survive just fine."

"It's called para-suicide," the doctor continued. "That includes anything that people do to purposefully damage themselves."

I refused to accept his point of view, but I didn't argue my side of it anymore.

I later understood that the doctor was trying to get a feel for how far at risk I was in committing anything life threatening.

There was a silence as we both considered what we would say.

Dr Stone was the first to speak. "What do you think you need?"

I was puzzled by the question. I didn't know how to answer. I knew I needed help, but I didn't know what that help was supposed to be.

"I don't know," I answered.

"How would you feel about going to the hospital for a few days?" Dr Stone suggested.

I didn't answer. I only blinked.

Dr Stone continued. "We could arrange for you to be supervised at the hospital and there will be people to help you in times of crisis.

When you feel like you are in trouble, you will have someone to talk to."

The offer scared me. Staying at the hospital seemed like an intimidating idea. I thought of impersonal hallways and sick people and being under someone else's authority. I thought of how disarming it would be to be in a place where I would have to give up my habits.

Going inpatient? Was he serious?

Apparently he was, because he wanted me to go right away. He wanted me to go straight from the clinic to the hospital without going home. He didn't want me to have a chance to go home and do something stupid before checking myself in. He didn't call it *doing something stupid*, but I knew that if I did it, it would be.

"But I have a job. I have to go to work tonight. I have responsibilities," I worried.

"Can you ask to be replaced for a few days?"

I was silent for a moment. I wasn't sure if I could agree to this. I knew that I needed something drastic to happen for things to change, but the idea of going to the hospital made my heart race. I was afraid, and fear was not something that I handled well.

"They're going to take my tools away," I stated with insecurity.

"Tools?"

"The things I use to hurt myself," I explained.

"Oh," the doctor understood. "Yes, they would have to take them away. You can't have them at the hospital."

It took me a few moments of thinking in silence, but in the end I agreed to go. I was reassured that I could leave the hospital whenever I wanted.

So Dr Stone called someone who worked in the psychiatric unit of the hospital. I was then given a paper that I was supposed to hand to the nurses in the emergency room.

I got up to leave the office and breathed deeply to calm myself down.

Dr Stone was sympathetic and made certain to reassure me before I left. "Hey. Give me your hands," he requested as he held his own hands out for mine.

I reached out and for a moment, he held both my hands in his as he spoke calmly. "It's going to be okay. They will take care of you there. Would you like me to go and visit you to make sure everything is okay?"

I nodded my head to say, yes.

I then tried to take my hands back, but he still held them tightly. "It's going to be okay," Dr Stone repeated because he saw that I was still very nervous.

After that I was able to leave the office and the clinic, but I didn't do quite what I was asked.

I wasn't supposed to go home, but I wanted to leave my car at my place instead of paying for parking at the hospital. I lived close enough that I could walk. There was something that I needed to take out of my purse and leave at home. I couldn't bring my self injury kit to the hospital. I was afraid that they would take it away and never give it back. I also wanted to make sure that I had all the things that I needed with me. I needed a hair brush, a toothbrush, a change of socks and underwear, and most importantly, I needed my journal so I could write about everything that was going on.

After I got to the hospital and gave them the paper notice provided by Dr Stone, I was led into the back of the emergency room. I walked passed several patients sleeping in cots that surrounded an office. I entered a rectangular room with about five cots in it. All the beds were side by side, creating a row of beds.

A stocky man with white hair who looked to be in his early fifties was in charge of the psychiatric section of the emergency room. He introduced himself as Roger.

"You have to put this on," Roger told me as he picked up an ugly, sickly green hospital gown covered in snow flakes that had been laying at the end of a cot.

I was afraid that he meant that I had to change right in front of him, so my response was a bit loud. "You've got to be kidding!"

"It's no joke. You need to put this on and put all your clothes in a bag," Roger instructed as a large plastic bag was provided for me.

"You can change in there," he pointed to a bathroom that was right next to us.

I was relieved that I got to change in private. I put on the gown, but kept my underwear and my socks. I was wearing knee high socks so I could pull them all the way up and hide my cuts and scars from my lower leg.

I got comfortable in my cot. I sat cross legged in the middle of it and laid the blanket over my legs.

I asked if I could have my journal and a pen and the guard accepted, so I got to unload a lot of my fears onto paper. I couldn't believe that I was writing in my journal from a place I would call the crazy house.

A woman came into the room and interrupted me as I was writing. She had long, brown, curly hair. I hadn't quite understood what her function was at the hospital, but she stood beside my cot with a clip board in her hands.

"I need to know if there is someone I can call to get some information on you," the woman told me.

I felt trapped. I didn't want anybody to know that I was at the hospital. Very few people knew that I was cutting, especially not my family. I had some of my friends who knew, but they were long distance. Who could I tell her to call?

"I can give you whatever information you need," I told her in the hopes of avoiding the inclusion of anyone else.

She shook her head. "I need someone to tell me what kind of changes in mood they may have noticed in you."

"But not many people know that I even have a problem, and those that do don't live anywhere near here," I stopped to think about it. I knew of someone that I had thought many times about revealing my secrets to. There was a woman who was a sister, a mother, and a friend to me. I had known her for a long time and I found it easy to confide in her. "There is one person that you might be able to call. She's a friend. I'll get you her number."

After the woman left, I asked if I could use the phone so I could call my friend and warn her that she was going to get a phone call.

I was given a phone with a long cord that I unravelled and plugged into the wall next to my cot. I dialed the numbers and waited nervously for my friend to pick up.

"Shy-Anne?" I spoke her name into the receiver. "It's Melissa."

"Hi Melissa. How are you doing?"

I paused and swallowed my fears. "I'm at the hospital."

"What happened?"

I paused again. I was near tears. "Shy-Anne, would you come and see me?"

"I'll be there right away," Shy-Anne told me and we both hung up the phone.

I had seen my friend Shy-Anne the night before. When she saw the black lace wristband on my arm, she asked, "Do you have a booboo?"

In an effort to answer without lying, I said jokingly, "Yes, a big booboo."

I knew that if I said it with a smile, I wouldn't be taken seriously and it wouldn't be a lie. We had laughed it off and nothing more was said.

When Shy-Anne got to the hospital, I stood up and gave her a long hug.

"What's wrong?" she asked as we broke our hug and she brushed my hair from my face.

"I lied to you," I admitted with tears in my eyes.

We sat down on my cot and Shy-Anne put her arm over my shoulder.

"Last night you asked if I was wearing a wristband because I had been hurt. I pretended like I wasn't, but the truth is that I was. I had wounds, but I'm the one that caused them."

"Yeah," Shy-Anne acknowledged as she passed her fingers through my hair. "That's what I thought when you told me that you were at the hospital. I put two and two together because of the wristband. I want you to know that I don't judge you and that I understand. I know that you have been through so much in your life and this is your way of dealing with it."

I was grateful and I wasn't sure what else to say, but soon I was filling Shy-Anne in on some of the details of my secret life. It was a life that I had worked so hard to hide, but it felt like telling someone new was like releasing pressure.

"I have to go," Shy-Anne told me. "But I'm coming back to see you again today. Is there something that you want me to bring back for you?"

I was pleased at the opportunity to get some comforting goodies. I asked for some of my favorite chocolate and an Ice tea.

That was at noon. Shy-Anne came back at 4:00 pm.

She had brought me an ice tea, a chocolate bar, four dried fruit strips, a bag of four cheese sticks and a bag of sliced apples. Oh! I can't forget about how she brought me a short red rose with babies breath in a green papered vase.

It was beautiful. I had never been given hospital flowers before, but then again, I didn't remember having been hospitalized before that day either.

Shy-Anne told me that she would come back and see me the next day. I found that both kind and discouraging at the same time. I wanted to see my friend again, but hoped that I wouldn't still be there by the next day.

While Shy-Anne wasn't with me, there was a woman two beds away from me that was very lively and interesting. Her name was Charlotte. She had been wheeled into the room on an ambulance gurney. On her right hand she was wearing a purple rubber glove that she took from the paramedics as a souvenir.

From what I understood, Charlotte wasn't at the hospital by her own will, but was brought there by legal force.

I found this woman hard to understand at times. She talked a lot about numbers and what they meant in our lives. She said that everything was connected by numbers. One number was indicative of something in particular, and if you doubled the number, it's meaning was related to whatever the definition was at half that. If you didn't understand that, it's likely because I didn't either. It's hard to describe something that I couldn't comprehend. I pretended to know what she was talking about though. All I had to do was nod.

Charlotte's mood would change dramatically. She was oddly happy and animated when she first arrived, but soon she was crying.

I tried not to stare and make her feel self conscious, so I concentrated on writing my thoughts down in my journal. Everything was new, and as anxious as I was about being in the hospital, I was also fascinated by the experience.

I never thought that I would be a psychiatric patient in a room with a mildly eccentric woman and a guard at the door.

There was always a guy sitting at a little desk on wheels in the doorway. I knew that the guard was there for security purposes, but whose security was he protecting? I wasn't violent, so they couldn't have been protecting the rest of the hospital from me, but then, why did I have to stay in that room?

The guard named Roger was sitting comfortably in his chair.

I rose from my bed and walked up to where Roger was sitting in the doorway.

"If I try to make a run for it, will you have to chase after me?" I asked with a curious smile.

"Yes," Roger answered simply.

"Okay. Let me drink some water so that I can get some energy and make a real good go of it."

I was trying to bring humor into my situation, but Roger barely reacted, so I boldly inched around his table to see what he would do.

Roger gave me a serious look and moved his table over a bit so he could block my way.

I laughed and backed away.

I found it funny, but at the same time it bothered me that I had no choice but to stay there. I was so used to being free and independent. I didn't like being restricted.

I went back to my cot and soon supper was being served.

Everything I had heard on television about hospital food made the stuff sound pretty bad, but it tasted fine to me. Any free food was good food.

Charlotte laughed and said how cute it was that I was writing everything that was going on.

I was a writer. Telling stories was what I did. I couldn't imagine living any other way.

I wrote in detail. I even talked about how good the grape flavored jello was and that I should have it more often. I'll never forget that I dropped some of that jello on the floor. I won't forget because I wrote it down.

It was when I wasn't writing, or when I would stop to think that I would get in trouble. I tried cutting my arm on the bottom of my small dinner table on wheels. I didn't want to be found out. If they found out, they might take my table away. If I didn't have my table, where would I put my stuff?

It wasn't long before I abandoned using the table as a tool and moved on to something that I found had more potential. I used the plastic dinner knife that I had on my tray. I was disappointed with how ineffective of a tool it was. I had created a few red lines, but none of them bled.

I thought about asking that I not be given a knife in the future. I clearly couldn't be trusted with one.

Anxiety began to rise high within me. I set my knife and my journal aside and tried to calm down.

The next time I picked up my journal was to confess yet another act of self injury. I had hurt myself with the small piece of aluminum foil from off the box of ice tea that Shy-Anne had given me.

I felt like I had betrayed my friend. I was sorry that I had used something that she had given me, but I still managed to convince myself that I really needed it. I folded the aluminum so it was more layered and could be stronger. I used it to scratch hundreds of lines around my wrist.

I felt badly about hurting myself with four other people in the room, but they had no idea. I made sure that no one saw.

A new patient that had been recently admitted was sleeping at the far side of the room. Charlotte was having a conversation with a male visitor and the guard was listening to them speak, so no one noticed what I was doing under the cover of my blanket.

When I was done scratching my wrist, I kept the aluminum and put it in the pages of my journal. I hid the scratches under my wristband.

A guilty conscience suggested that I confess and give up the aluminum, but I did neither.

~ ~ ~ ~

It was 8:00 pm by the time I was called to meet with the psychiatrist. He was a man in his sixties with thick framed glasses. His appearance was scattered and he looked like he should be the psychiatric patient and not the doctor.

I was in the psychiatrists office for quite a while. It was at least an hour.

I was confused by a lot of the questions he asked, as I didn't see how they related to my case. I was grateful though when he decided to change my medication.

The doctor also arranged for me to see a psychologist in my own town. I liked the idea of not having to drive half an hour to get to an appointment. Gas wouldn't be so costly and the therapy would be free.

I hoped that a different psychologist could help me more. I had grown unsatisfied with a therapist that never answered my questions and constantly asked me how things made me feel. I thought of daring her to say "How does that make you feel?" three times fast without pissing herself off.

I had told the doctor that I wished to work on my problem and that hurting myself wasn't a life that I wanted to continue.

I was happy with the changes being made, but I was still unsure of whether I would be kept at the hospital, or let go.

After leaving the psychiatrists office, I was led back to the room in the back of the ER where I waited for decisions to be made.

I chewed on bits of candy that Shy-Anne had given me until a nurse came to inform me that I had permission to leave. I was allowed to go as long as someone came to get me, so I called Shy-Anne.

By the time that my friend arrived, my papers hadn't been ready yet.

I scratched my arms with my finger nails when I retreated to the bathroom to put my own clothes back on.

A bad feeling settled over me. I was anxious enough that I knew exactly what I would do when I got home. I knew because I had been there so many times before.

I sat on my cot and crumpled to the pillow. Shy-Anne sat next to me.

I admitted that it may not be such a good idea for me to go home.

"You're afraid to go home?" Shy-Anne asked.

"No. I'm afraid of me."

I remember hearing Charlotte say, "Poor little thing."

Shy-Anne ignored my neighbor and asked me a question. "Why is that?"

"Because I know what I'm going to do," I answered simply and with discouragement.

"What?" she asked. "What will you do?"

I was silent and tears followed. Normally I would have hurt myself to keep the tears away, but that wasn't an option at the time. "I hurt myself while I was here," I admitted.

My friend reached for my arm and lifted my wrist band where under it she found all the scratches and the cuts from the knife and the aluminum.

"You're hurting yourself," Shy-Anne spoke with tears in her voice and she hugged me for a long time. She wiped tears from her face and I wiped tears from mine. "What did you use?" she asked after pulling away from our hug.

"They gave me a knife with my dinner, but that's not all I used."

"What then? Not with something that I brought?"

I let the silence answer her question, then I pulled the aluminum from my journal and gave it to her.

I hadn't wanted to hurt her by using something she brought.

"I'm sorry," I apologized with much guilt.

Not surprisingly, Shy-Anne didn't want to give the aluminum back to me, but when the psychiatrist entered the room, she gave it to him instead.

"She cut herself," Shy-Anne informed the doctor.

"You did this here?" The doctor asked me.

I nodded, yes.

The doctor was silent, then turned around and left. Soon after my nurse was telling me that I would be staying and that I had to get back into the ugly hospital gown.

I had confessed what I had done, so it was my choice to stay, but I wouldn't get to leave until permission was given.

I was going to be transferred to the psychiatric unit on the eighth floor. Everyone knew what it meant when we referred to the eighth floor, because there was only one building in my town that went eight floors up. It was commonly known through the culture of my town that if you were eight floors up, you were crazy. Many would joke about it, but for me, on that day, it wasn't a joke.

I had to wait a few hours for a place to be available upstairs. In the meantime, I was put on 24 hour watch. They moved my cot closer to the guard so I could be under constant surveillance. I was only allowed to have my pen when I was using it, and they took my wristband away so they could see if I were to make any new cuts.

I hated having my wounds exposed. It was humiliating. I was grateful that I was allowed to keep my leg warmers so my other wounds were hidden.

By 11:00 pm, I was escorted upstairs by three men. One of them carried my things, and I carried the rose that Shy-Anne gave me. I felt like a criminal being marched to her cell. Did they really need that much security?

The elevator door opened up to show some desks and offices where about four people were sitting and working. There were two desks with windows surrounding them, and there were five desks out in the open.

The man at the front desk stood up and accepted my things. I was then guided to a room right next to the desks where they could keep an eye on me. I was pleased to find that my room only had one bed in it. I was too nervous and shy to deal with a room mate.

I was made to change into a different gown. Apparently all the floors had their own colors for gowns. I much preferred the eighth floor one as they were brown and not a pale, ugly green. I liked earthy tones.

The part I didn't like was when they took away my watch and my bra. I felt uneasy without them and tried to resist giving them up, but in the end the nurses left with them both.

I was told that I would be allowed to have my clothes and my things after I was evaluated by my on site doctor and trusted with the privilege.

One of the men that had escorted me upstairs stayed with me while the other two left. He was a stocky middle aged man with receding brown hair.

I was surprised to see the man be given a chair and small desk on wheels so he could sit in my doorway and watch me. I felt more self conscious than I had downstairs because I was the only one in the room being watched.

I had to fall asleep with his attention on me at all times. He needed to make sure that I wouldn't hurt myself.

I managed to sleep well through the night, and tried to forget the guards constant watchful eyes.

Friday, June 6

I woke up early in the morning when the lights were being turned on. I didn't feel like sleeping anymore so I sat up at the head of the bed with my back against the wall.

The guard stood up and spoke to me for the first time that morning. "You can't sit there. You have to be where I can see you well at all times."

I sighed at the strict code and at being told what to do. I had the head of the bed raised so I was able to sit while also being in the view of the guard.

I sat silently while listening to the dull sounds of the staff talking and moving around the offices outside my room.

A few minutes passed before two men in the same brown gowns as mine walked by my doorway. One of the guys slowed down when he saw me and immediately began calling out to the other patient. "Ooh! Did you see the pretty girl? Did you see? Beautiful creature."

The strange patient continued on about me and even passed by my room a few more times so he could look at me. Soon, both men were stealing glances into my room. I hadn't expected to have an audience, but I managed to find it funny. I liked being able to smile about something when I was so nervous at my new surroundings.

I didn't think that I was all that beautiful, but my hair was blond and my eyes were blue just like so many poster girls.

I had the same guard until 8:00 that morning. That seemed to be time for the shift change and a new guard took his place.

The new guard was young and pleasantly attractive. He was around twenty years old with dark hair. His name was Carl.

I grew increasingly nervous when I was told that it was time to go to the cafeteria for breakfast. I didn't want to leave the safety of my room. I knew my room and what to expect, but I didn't know the halls and the people outside my door.

I looked down at my bare wrist with all its cuts and burns and felt exposed. How was I supposed to leave the room with nothing to hide my wrist?

I tried hiding my arm in my gown, but that was awkward. The best thing I could think of was to pull one of my navy blue knee high socks over my hand and arm. I would have one less hand for eating breakfast, but at least I would have something to cover my humiliatingly disfigured wrist.

The young guard followed me to the cafeteria where I had to make my own breakfast. There were coffee machines, toasters, and cereal boxes at our disposal.

I walked into a crowd that was waiting for their turns at the toasters and my anxiety grew. Several of them were wearing hospital gowns, but most were wearing their own clothes. I was in a room full of strangers. I loved people, but I had a hard time relaxing around anyone new.

The guys in brown gowns who were outside my door that morning approached me and asked me my name.

"Melissa," I told them.

I was on display again when one of the men, who was a patient in his forties, spoke about me to what seemed to be his friend. "Just look at her face; And now look at mine."

I got the impression that he was complementing both me and himself. His expression indicated that he was perfection itself.

I fixed myself two peanut butter toasts and ate them as quickly as I could. It was a bit complicated preparing my food with a sock over my left hand, but I managed well enough.

The guard stood nearby and watched until I got up to leave and he followed me back to my room.

My bed was my hiding place. I crawled under the covers and laid still while trying to catch up with my own thoughts.

For everything I did, there were notes being taken about me. Every fifteen minutes my guard would have to write what I was doing at the time. If I was laying down, sitting, talking, writing, or even going to the bathroom, he would have to write it down.

I had no mirror in my room so I couldn't see if I looked like a mess. I was unaccustomed to skipping the visual part of my morning grooming.

Oh, and let me tell you the worst part. Apparently, I wasn't allowed to pee with the door completely closed. It had to be a few inches open so my guard could stand next to it and listen in to know if I was doing anything to hurt myself while I was there. It was humiliating to say the least.

I must have been laying there for half an hour by the time a young man who presented himself as my nurse came to take my blood pressure. His name was Ashton. He was shorter than me, but I found him very cute. He ran my blood pressure two times. The first one was while I was laying down, and the second was while I stood up.

While I was laying down, Ashton asked if I was okay.

"Yes," I replied unconvincingly.

"Really?"

"No."

"That's what I thought. I didn't believe your *yes*," Ashton told me. "So what's wrong?"

"Anxiety, but I'll be fine," I said to reassure both him and myself.

Thankfully the psychiatrist I had seen downstairs had prescribed me some lorazepam for the anxiety. My nurse brought me the medication with a glass of water. After swallowing the medicine, I asked Ashton if I could have my wristband back because I had spent half the morning with my knee high sock on my arm.

Ashton promised to find out about it and soon returned. He said that he couldn't find the armband among my personal things.

When I explained that it was the nurse girl from the night before that had taken the armband away, he was able to locate where it would have been placed.

Ashton handed me the five inch wide, black lace armband. "I'm going to let you have it, but we have to make a compromise. You can wear it, but you also have to have bandages under it because of the wounds on your wrist."

I was rather embarrassed to hold out my wrist for this kind young man to bandage up. My breathing grew deeper as my anxiety got worse, but I was grateful to be able to take my sock off my arm and put it back on my foot.

I spent much of the morning sulking under my covers before the cute young guard told me that I was allowed to leave the room. I suspected that he was hinting at me because he found it boring to stay in one place for so long.

I was allowed to leave, but did I really want to? For the sake of how bored the guard was, I decided to get up and bravely venture forth into the halls of the psychiatric ward. There were several different games in the cafeteria. Dozens of boxes of puzzles were piled up on a windowsill. There were rocking chairs in front of a television. There was an air hockey table and a game of pockets, and there was even a ping-pong table.

I remembered having a ping-pong table in the basement of my old house, but it had been years since I played and I was no longer familiar with the game.

"I'm no good at this," I told my guard as I picked up a red paddle.

While I was holding the paddle, one of the patients walked in and asked me if I would play with him. I had recognized him from earlier that morning when he had walked by my door and called to his friend about a beautiful creature. He introduced himself as Joseph. At that point, Joseph was out of the gown and in his own clothes.

I agreed to play, but I warned Joseph that I hadn't done so in at least ten years.

We paddled the ball pack and forth without counting points. I was surprised at how easily I was able to hit the ball and aim it across the table to the other side of the net. It was like riding a bike. I never really forgot how to do it.

"Looks like you can play this game after all," my guard remarked.

"I guess so."

After the game I returned to my room to write in my journal. I'd had to beg my nurse Ashton to let me have my journal back and give me a pen. Nobody wanted to give me a pen because I might hurt myself with it. Finally, I was given one. Well, half of one. Ashton pulled off the outside shell of the pen and left me the floppy ink stick. It was difficult to write with it, but I managed.

I was warned that it was written on my file that I had the pen and that if I didn't return it, they would know.

I was informed that the doctor that was assigned to me in the psychiatric unit wouldn't be visiting until Monday. It was Friday at the time and I didn't like thinking of three more days in that place.

I freaked out a few times that morning. I was too anxious to allow myself to go back to the cafeteria for lunch time where I would have to shyly search for a place to sit among strangers. I sat in a chair next to my bed that was in a hidden corner of my room and I waited there. I would have preferred to go hungry than to go out and face a crowd. I stood my ground and I refused to leave no matter who asked me to.

I stayed in that chair until Dr Stone showed up and sat on my bed next to my chair.

"Are you all right?" he asked.

"I've had better days."

Dr Stone reassured me that I was doing a good thing by going to the hospital. "Are you usually like this?" the doctor asked. "This is the first time I've seen you so tense."

"I'm like this a lot," I admitted. "But I usually hide when I feel this way so no one sees me."

Dr Stone placed his hand over mine to comfort me. "It's good that we can share moments like this."

I tried to smile to be polite but wasn't able. The panic was too high in me.

I explained to my visiting doctor why I was in my room and not the cafeteria. I was relieved when he ordered for me to get some anti-anxiety medication and to have my lunch served to me in my room.

Dr Stone left and my meal was brought to me on a small rolling table. The table was placed where the guard would be able to watch me eat. Carl had to watch me take every mouthful. It was a very self conscious meal.

Later that afternoon I played ping-pong again with Joseph. Practice made both of us better, and Joseph was a good player. He told me that he was glad to find someone who could keep up with him.

We both grew tired of playing after several games and so we parted ways. Joseph went back to his room while I began walking around the halls with my guard Carl at my side.

The halls were shaped like a ladder with four steps. There were the two main halls where the patients rooms and doctors offices were. Then there were the four small halls that made the larger ones join together. The farthest one had a room with a scale in it for weighing the patients. Across the hall from that room was the laundry room that was kept locked unless it was in use. The second hall had two main elevators on one side and desks and offices for the nurses and orderlies on the other side. The third hall also had two elevators, but they were only to be used by staff and were only able to be opened with a key. No patient could go through them. Across from those elevators was a small kitchen that was also kept locked. The fourth hall was more of a large room that was used as the cafeteria, a living room and a game room.

I met up with one of the patients that had introduced himself that morning. It was the man who compared his face to mine. His name was Jed and his interest in me hadn't faded. He offered me gum and different kinds of candy, but I turned down all his offers. Beyond offering gifts, Jed said nothing to me.

Carl and I would walk in figure eights inside the hallways. We looked out windows that showed us large parts of the city and hillsides. I curiously peeked into bedrooms in the main halls. Most of the rooms had two beds in each.

Soon, curiosity wasn't enough to entertain me and I was distracted by my own anxiety. My heart was racing quickly and I wanted so badly to hurt myself. I started digging my fingernails into the walls as I walked by them. I focused on the sensation at the end of my fingertips and on the noise that it created.

Carl asked me if I had an obsession with walls.

I answered, yes. What else could I say?

When I couldn't take it anymore, I went to my room and laid down until I was calm enough to walk again.

When we resumed our walk, I told Carl that it was better for me to hurt the walls than it was to hurt myself.

He agreed. My guard also advised me to talk to my nurse when I was feeling like that.

I danced around the idea of asking for help, but had a hard time getting the courage to walk up to one of the nurses. Finally, I took a deep breath and walked up to the front desk where Ashton was standing on the other side of it. I waited until Ashton was done speaking with a patient.

I told my nurse about how I was feeling and asked what I should do in that situation.

Ashton suggested that I could go and talk to him about what was going on so I could get past it, or I could ask for medication to help me calm down.

I wasn't comfortable with talking and I had already received medication, so I thanked my nurse and left.

Time passed slowly as I made more figure eights around the halls. At some point while I was walking with Carl, I snapped my rubber band on my wrist.

"Hey!" my guard protested.

"What?" I asked. "I can't do that either?"

"No."

I sighed and handed him my rubber band. "I want that back after," I told him pointedly with a serious expression. "You know what? I miss it already. Can I have it back?"

"No."

"Well don't lose it or leave with it. I like that one."

The rubber band I was wearing was the first one I'd ever used. It was orange and I had found it on the floor of the grocery store that I worked at. I liked that it was orange because that was the color that represented self injury.

My expression was of shocked surprise when I heard Carl tell my nurse that I had used a rubber band in front of him.

Tattle tale….

Ashton shook his head in recognition and said, "They like those because they can do this." Ashton made a gesture to pretend to snap a rubber band on his wrist. "They can do a lot of damage with those."

They were familiar with those tricks at the hospital.

When Roger was going through my things earlier that day, he found a little container of make-up powder among my toothpaste and deodorant. "Is this a mirror in here?" Roger asked as he held up my make-up container.

"Yeah," I confirmed. "So?" But then I figured out that I could break the mirror and use it to cut. "Oh," I realized.

Ashton had been standing next to Roger and he said, "Yeah, we've done this before." Clearly they had, because I wasn't getting away with much.

~ ~ ~ ~

By 4:00 pm, there was a shift change. I got a new guard and a new nurse.

By that evening, all I wanted to do was cry. I couldn't believe that I had gotten myself into that place. I couldn't believe that I had a guard watching me 24/7 just to keep me from hurting myself. I couldn't believe that I was writing in my journal with a gutted pen so I wouldn't stab myself with it. I couldn't believe this was me. It was unreal and couldn't be my life.

I actually considered begging my nurse to give me something sharp; or at least my rubber band. Couldn't I at least have my rubber band?

I tried writing in my journal, but my guard was very chatty and didn't give me much of a chance.

Jed came by my doorway. He stood next to my guard and offered me a chocolate bar. By that time, Jed was out of his hospital gown and was allowed to wear his regular clothes. I knew he was just trying to impress me with gift offerings. He was trying to win me over, but I had a weakness, and that was chocolate. I couldn't refuse chocolate.

When Jed left, my guard warned me to be careful. "That guy has a plan attached to his chocolate." But the guard also told me that I was safe because he wasn't going to let Jed near me.

Eating chocolate made me feel a bit better and cheered my melodrama.

Another good thing was that Shy-Anne came to visit me that night, but she and my very talkative guard were the ones to have the main conversation.

Visiting hours were over by 8:30 pm, and by 9:00 pm it was time for everyone to take their medication.

I learned that there was a routine at the hospital where all the patients would gather at the main desks and wait in line to see their respective nurses.

I didn't get in line at first, but instead I leaned against the wall next to the elevators. I was feeling so sad and upset at my situation that I just closed my eyes and tried to drown everything out. That's when I met Jolene. She was a heavy set middle aged woman with short red hair. She was wearing pajamas, so I knew she was given the right to wear her own clothes.

Jolene came up to me and put her hand on my shoulder in a motherly way. She told me that she was going to look out for me and that it was going to be okay. She was the first real friend I had met there.

When the line up was empty, my nurse called me over to have me take my turn. My nurse was a man in his forties with curly black hair. His name was Carson.

I took my pills and went to leave with them, but I was then informed that I had to take them in front of my nurse. I had begun feeling like a child under her father's thumb and sensed my independence slipping away.

I swallowed my pills in front of my nurse as I was told, then I retired to my room where I crawled under my covers and into my hiding place.

Saturday, June 7

I woke up many times that night, but I never knew the time because I still wasn't allowed to have my watch. I could have nothing that could potentially be used to harm myself.

I took my shower, and yeah, I had to keep the door partially open so that my guard, who was an awkward looking kid, could listen to what I was doing.

I was also disappointed that the room where I took a shower didn't have a mirror either. I needed to see my reflection in order to put my make-up on. How was a girl supposed to fix herself up in the morning?

In the end I had to resort to putting some make-up on without the use of a mirror, so it may have looked strange, but I never found out.

When I was walking around I had noticed that all the other rooms had mirrors in them. Why not in mine too? Why did I have to be the extra crazy chick who needed a guard, no mirror, and no bra? I could have nothing that a normal person would have used responsibly, but that I might not. I was the only one who had someone watch her eat, and sleep, and scratch her face.

Latter that morning I sat on my bed and wrote in detail into my journal.

My guard was a black man from the Congo named Cedric. He had moved to Canada just three years before. He had been married seventeen years and had four kids.

Cedric was falling asleep in his chair next to my bed. His arms were crossed and his eyes were closed. Once in a while his head would rise a bit as if he were fighting to stay awake, but his eyes didn't open.

I looked up at Cedric once in a while as I thought about what to write in my journal. Yeah, he was either falling asleep or he was sleeping.

I could totally have been hurting myself right then and he would get into so much trouble, but then again, so would I. I would have to stay longer and who knows what else. Don't worry. I wasn't going to tell on him.

I looked at a room across the way from mine. It was empty except for a bed. There was a small opening and closing slot that covered a window near the top of the large wooden door. A slot in the door would be able to be pushed over so there was no more window. It was clearly so the staff could look in on whoever was in the room and have the option of making it so that the patient wouldn't see out. It was creepy and made me feel like I was in a movie. This was not something I was supposed to be a part of. I was supposed to be one of the normal people on the outside.

The really scary part was when I realized that my door was just like the one across the way. I could be made to be all alone in a locked room with strangers looking in on me through a tiny window.

Most of the other doors weren't like that. The other doors were normal. There was something else that I noticed was different though. Most of the rooms had two beds to a room.

What made me so different? Was I the craziest of the crazies? Was there something especially wrong with me? I felt like a freak. A freak among those strange and hidden away.

Ashton came to see me in my room, and I was glad because his was a face that I recognized.

"I thought I would be your nurse today as well, but I am assigned to different patients of the ward."

"Oh," I was disappointed. I didn't like getting shifted around from nurse to nurse. I wanted someone that I recognized. I wanted to have enough of a basis with them for me to feel comfortable talking and asking for what I needed.

Ashton may have read my thoughts when he said, "You can still come to me though. I'm available if you want to talk."

I was relieved. Ashton's offer made the world of crazy-town just a little less scary.

By lunch time I found a seat in the cafeteria. Jed came and sat across from me the way he had that morning and the day before. I wasn't used to that much concentrated attention.

Jed had actually asked me if I would invite him to eat with me.

I said, "Of course."

After having set his tray down, Jed asked curiously, "Why are they keeping you alone in that room?"

I wasn't sure of the proper response. Should I lie? No. I hated lies.

I could say that I didn't want to answer, but what for? Every one of these patients were there because they had a mental health problem serious enough to be admitted. We were all in it together.

"Because I have a tendency to hurt myself," I answered bravely.

"What's a pretty young girl like you doing that for? Someone hurt you, right?" Jed inquired perceptively.

"Yeah."

The conversation had become even more uncomfortable, but soon the subject changed. Jed would brag about how he was the boss of everyone on the ward. He was proud of his alpha male position.

Jed would talk a lot about strange theories that I couldn't make sense of.

He also said that I reminded him of his first love from when he was fourteen. He repeated it in several conversations that I reminded him of her. It made me uncomfortable because he seemed to expect something from me.

Jed was very sweet with me. He would tell me how nice and pretty I was, but he was actually a complete jerk with everyone else. Maybe his highly abusive past made him angry at the world. Jed confided much of his life to me. He told me about his childhood and the people who hurt him.

I was honored to be confided in, but I also felt that I needed to be careful.

After finishing my meal I excused myself and was able to get up to go.

I spent a while walking around the hallways with my guard Cedric. I tried not to let it bother me when I saw mirrors in most of the other rooms. I wished I was a more normal form of crazy so I could be like the rest of them.

During one of our walks around the hallways, we met up with Saffron who was playing ping-pong in the cafeteria game room. Saffron had a strong character. She was slim with long, beautiful, brown and curly hair. I hadn't spoken with her before, but I had heard her talking with the other patients, which made her a bit less of a stranger in a strange land.

Saffron found the fact that I had a guard following me to be laughable.

Saffron spoke to my guard. "What are you doing watching a docile little thing like her? She's so small and quiet. It's not like she's a threat to us. Ooh, wow, she looks so dangerous." Saffron mocked sarcastically.

My guard didn't answer her, but in my head I thought, "He's not protecting you from me. He's protecting me from myself."

About a half an hour later, I had an uncomfortable conversation with Saffron. She was sitting in a rocking chair in front of the television. I thought it might be nice if I got to know her a little bit. Maybe she needed a friend too.

I asked her a question that was common on the ward. "So how long have you been here?"

"I'm really tired of your blah blah blah," Saffron said in an annoyed and offended tone.

"I'm annoying?" I asked feeling embarrassed. I was surprised to hear her react that way, and sorry to have bothered her. This was the first conversation that I'd had with Saffron and she was already tired of me.

"No, you're not annoying," Saffron corrected herself. "I was just trying to be as polite as possible. Don't try to get to know me."

"I'm sorry," I apologized. "I was just trying to be polite."

I had wanted to make sure that Saffron felt included, but it turned out that she didn't want to be.

I continued my walk with Cedric while I played with my hospital bracelet very nervously. It was loose enough that I was able to slip it off my hand whenever I wanted. I was spinning my bracelet around and around when a few nurses noticed and they warned me that I wasn't supposed to take it off. I was disappointed and slipped it back over my hand. I would forget sometimes and slip the bracelet off to fiddle with it out of nervousness. When I was nervous, I needed something to play with, so I got warned several times that I wasn't to take it off.

The bracelet I was wearing was confiscated and another one was put on me at a tighter notch, but I was still able to take it off.

I continued my walk, but eventually I felt so suffocated by my anxiety. I got up the courage to go talk to Ashton who was working at the front desk of the office.

"I would like to either have a rubber band, or a lorazepam," I stated to Ashton as he looked up at me from the papers he was working on.

"No rubber bands," Ashton answered. "And I'd rather we talk about what is making you anxious before resorting to medication."

Did I want to talk? Talking about my problems was still very new and scary to me. I knew how to live in secret. Should I really defy that?

I had to think hard because I didn't know what to say.

"I could try to talk, but I can't guarantee that I'll say anything," I told him and he got up from his desk and started to walk around the halls with me.

I talked a bit about how anxious being at the hospital was making me.

Once in a while I would nervously play with my hospital bracelet by twirling it around my fingers, so I was often finding myself saying, "Oops, I'm not supposed to do that."

I put my bracelet back on my wrist and asked once again for my rubber band.

I needed so badly to hurt myself and my usual methods weren't an option, so I thought wildly about getting my rubber band.

"I'd like to give it to you, but I can't," Ashton answered, but then took his words back, "Well no. I wouldn't give it to you because I know what you would do with it."

"But it doesn't break the skin," I protested. "It only creates pain."

"That's why you can't have it. There are better ways to deal with things, like talking. You can come and talk to me when you need," Ashton offered.

"Okay."

"How many times would you snap your rubber band if you had it?" Ashton wondered.

"Well, it could be two times, or fifty times...." I saw Ashton's expression and realized that if I was negotiating for a rubber band, I would have to soften my answer. "Or, um....just two times," I said while hoping that my correction would win me my rubber band.

"You aren't going to be able to twist your way into getting it back," Ashton informed me with a smile.

"Oh well, a girl's gotta try."

"You are really fixated on that rubber band," he observed.

"Yeah," I agreed. "I think about it a lot."

I didn't get my rubber band, but I was pleased to be allowed to write again. I was given a floppy, danger free pen and headed straight to my room where I picked up my journal and sat comfortably on my bed. So there I was, trying to write my way into feeling calm again.

I did start feeling better. Writing helped, but it was also good to be hidden away from the less strict bedrooms in the halls.

I wrote all about my day. I didn't want to spare any important details, so I was very thorough.

I was called to meet with a woman that I didn't recognize, so I handed my pen in to the office and met with a brunette in her early forties. She seemed welcoming, but I was very nervous. Everything was so new. I didn't know how to react.

LADY INJURY

My guard was asked to wait in the hall as I followed the woman into an office and sat in a chair at a desk across from her. I felt very intimidated. The room was big and painted in a deep blue. I wondered why this office was better taken care of than the rest of the ward. The walls were clean and bright instead of cracked and faded.

I had thought that the woman I was meeting with was a doctor, but she turned out to be a nurse from another hospital who came to evaluate me.

It was up to her to decide if I could be trusted to go without a guard. I was very motivated into convincing her that I could.

I was asked to show the cuts on my leg, and then the burns on my wrist, so I removed my arm warmer and the bandages. I found that my wounds were gross and mushy because the bandages had been soaked from when I took a shower.

"I'll tell your nurse to re-bandage this," Nurse Fowel informed me.

I saw this as the perfect opportunity to complain. "Can it be made clear that my bandages should be done in the privacy of my room? I find it really embarrassing to have to do it at the offices where anyone can see."

My request was accepted.

"Do you feel that you can be trusted now to go without a guard?" the nurse asked.

I thought hard about my answer because I found it important to be honest. "Yes," I replied.

So it was decided that I would be left without a guard and only checked on by my nurse every 15 minutes. I was allowed to be on my own, but still on high surveillance.

I had even talked to the woman about being allowed to have my rubber band. She said that I couldn't have it, but she would go see the rubber band in question.

"Thank-you. Can I have my own clothes now?" I asked hopefully.

"No," she answered. "You can have your clothes when you are trusted with a lower lever of surveillance."

I was disappointed, but I didn't give up on everything. "What about my bra and my watch? I feel really uncomfortable without my underwear."

"You can have those back," the nurse granted me my wish.

I was so relieved. I happily accepted my underwear. I was also pleased that I would be able to pee and shower with the door closed. There are so many things that I hadn't appreciated until they were taken away.

I was a few steps closer to normal. Well, as normal as one could be on a psychiatric ward.

I still had to wear a gown, and I was still alone in a room with no mirror, but things were looking up.

I immediately went to my room to put my underwear on. My clothes were like a trophy that I'd had to win, even if it was one piece at a time.

It felt good to be able to close my bedroom door and change without a guard nearby. I liked the taste of freedom that I was given.

I wasn't allowed to leave my door closed at all times though because I had to be watched by the staff.

After re-opening my door, the nurse who gave me my review came to see me with her left hand held out.

"I tested your rubber band out on myself," Nurse Fowel told me as she pointed to her wrist. "Look what it did."

There was a noticeable red line on her wrist where the rubber snapped against it.

"It really hurt," the nurse complained. "It didn't feel good at all."

I smiled at her distaste for something I longed for.

"Well, it's good for me," I told her.

After I was done speaking to nurse Fowel I was able to walk to the cafeteria alone for the first time. The ping-pong table had been pulled out and Joseph and John were in the middle of a game. They asked if I wanted to play. I did. So I was told that I would play the winner.

The winner was John. He was a good player. I found it funny though because when the game was over, John walked over to my side of the table to thank me for playing and he shook my hand.

I retired from ping-pong for a while and decided to walk around in the halls. I liked that I could walk without a guard, but it was a bit scary at first to have to face the hospital world by myself.

I soon met up with Shanny on my walk. Shanny was a friend that I had made at the hospital. She was nineteen years old with shoulder length, dark hair. Shanny had a very positive and talkative personality.

"Hey," Shanny welcomed me cheerily. "There's a guy over there that has such a crush on you."

I was taken by surprise. "Who?"

"John."

"How do you know?"

"Because of the way he looks at you and follows you around," Shanny explained.

"Oh." I thought about it and realized that may have been why he shook my hand after the game.

"There's one who likes me too," she gossiped with a smile. "It's Joseph."

Joseph may well have liked her, but I didn't notice.

I didn't question Shanny's theories any further and we moved on to talking about other things.

When the topic was brought up, my new friend told me that she had cut her wrist once a long time before. She even showed me the scar.

We talked about our reasons behind self injury. Shanny admitted to being attacked and then living with post traumatic stress disorder.

"I have post traumatic stress too," I told her.

We went on to talk about less intense things, like school. Shanny was taking a course to become a secretary.

"Really?" I was curious. "My sister Marie is studying to be a secretary. Do you know her?"

Shanny paused. "Oh yeah. She's the one that everyone goes to when they need help. She knows the subject so well."

I thought that was cool and felt proud of my sister. Then I thought about how small the world was that this girl should know Marie. Soon I became very nervous at the possibility that Shanny might mention to

Marie that she had met me, and where she met me. So far, only Shy-Anne knew that I was at the hospital. I wanted for it to stay that way.

Shanny left to go sit at the rocking chairs in the cafeteria.

I thought a lot about how to keep my secrets a secret. I decided that when I got the opportunity to talk to Shanny alone again, I would ask her to keep her knowledge of me to herself.

I must have looked rather anxious, because Ashton came to join me as I walked through the hallway and he asked if I was okay.

"Well, not really," I admitted and then asked about something that had been on my mind. "What's the big consequence if I do it?"

"Do what? Play with that?" he asked while pointing at my medical bracelet that I was still incessantly playing with.

"No. I mean if I hurt myself," I clarified. "What's the big scary thing?"

"Well," he began. "It depends. You could be locked up in your room except for thirty minutes in the morning, afternoon and evening. Or we would have to tie you down."

That's when my eyes got really wide.

Ashton nodded with a smile that said, "Yeah, sounds like fun, huh?" After the nod and smile he said, "We could put you in an isolation room and tie you to the bed like this," he said as he demonstrated by standing with his legs apart and his hands up. "You'll be laying there in a star position."

"Oh boy. I'm really looking forward to that!" I spoke sarcastically.

While we were walking and talking, Joseph came up and asked if I would play ping-pong. So the conversation with Ashton was over and I was back with the games.

We played ping-pong and a few different card games. I struggled to learn the rules to games that I had never heard of before.

~ ~ ~ ~

There was drama in the ward later that afternoon when Shanny's advances had been turned down by Joseph. Joseph explained to her about a girl that he had already been seeing and may have had a chance at seeing again. Her name was Betty and she was much younger than Joseph. Joseph was 32 and Betty was 18. He said that he loved her and that she was very pretty.

Joseph said that he didn't want a girlfriend at that time in his life despite the fact that Shanny had basically begged him to be with her. It was sad, and I felt badly for her.

Shanny also later argued that Joseph was being rude and insensitive by saying that he liked blondes best. She felt that he should have said that he liked brunettes because she was a brunette.

It turned out that Shanny had it backwards. Joseph didn't have a crush on Shanny. It was the other way around. She clearly liked him.

When Shanny and I were sitting alone on the two rocking chairs at the end of the hallway, she spoke about her feelings for Joseph. "He's so cute, and he has a nice butt."

I have to edit out much of what Shanny said because she had a habit of talking repeatedly and at length about sex. I wondered how her life could be so centered around it and how she was able to be so open about it. I had always been quiet about most personal things.

I listened to Shanny as she went through the pains of having been rejected.

"I can't believe he told me that he prefers blonds," Shanny complained. "Maybe I should talk to him again about dating."

I felt that things had gotten a little obsessive and I wasn't sure why it was so dramatic when she had only met the guy a few days before. It must have been lust at first sight.

I didn't have a guard, but I was finding that I wasn't alone. I had made a nice group of friends like Joseph, John, Shanny, Jolene and even a girl named Stacy. Stacy reminded me so much of a girl I had seen in a movie. She had very long brown hair and similar facial features. Stacy was twenty-five years old and had a four year old son that she liked to talk about.

At supper time, the kitchen forgot again that I needed a vegetarian meal, so I had to wait for them to prepare another one and send it up.

That was the first time I had sat next to Stacy. I told her that she looked like someone I had seen in a science-fiction movie.

When we stopped talking, I sat there silently waiting for my food. I had gotten so lost in a place in my head that was too dark and I just wanted to cry. I was sure that I was going to lose it in the cafeteria.

Roy was an older man with a bit of a hunchback. He was wearing the same brown gown as I was. Wearing our own clothes was a privilege that had to be earned.

As I sat there waiting, I heard Roy say to the nurse, "That girl is very nice."

I realized that he was referring to me. I remembered speaking kindly to him earlier that day. I hadn't reacted to Roy's comment because I simply didn't care about it much. I had too much weighing down on me.

Only minutes later, little old Roy got up from his seat and came towards me saying, "Kiss on the lips. Kiss on the lips."

Roy took my head between his hands and leaned in close to kiss my lips, but I turned my face in time and he started sucking on my cheek like a human vacuum. I thought for a second that my head would get sucked right into his.

I sat there stunned for a moment, but soon my bad mood was gone and I broke out laughing really hard.

"I really needed that," I laughed as I looked over at Stacy.

I had been in such a bad place. I was so zoned out. A real unexpected and intense smooch from an old man like that was just what I needed to wake up.

About five minutes later, Roy came back and did the same thing again; a vacuum kiss.

When I moved over by one chair to get away, the old man moved over too. There was no escape.

I noticed that Stacy was looking really sad. I guessed that she was thinking of her four year old son who had to see her being driven away in an ambulance.

"Do you need a kiss from Roy to cheer you up?" I asked Stacy and she smiled.

After supper a group of us got together and played some card games. By that time my bad mood had returned and I was too distracted by my own hurt to learn the game.

Stacy noticed my mood and asked me the same question that I had asked her. "Do you need a kiss to wake you up?"

I managed to smile. "At least it's not a very wet kiss," I told her. "But there are a lot of whiskers."

~ ~ ~ ~

There was a new nurse assigned to me that evening. He was a tall, nice looking young man with brown hair. I wondered where all those attractive nurses came from. His name was Daniel.

Daniel let me have a few of my things so I could brush my teeth. He told me that I should go see him later on so he could re-bandage my wrist.

I agreed, but I waited for him to tell me that he was ready. I played ping-pong until my name was called on the microphone. I was hoping that my name was being called because someone came to visit, but it was Daniel who was waiting for me and ready to do my bandages.

I was grateful that my bandages were done in my room with the door closed so no one could see.

I sat on my bed and Daniel stood in front of me with his supplies. He slowly pulled off the bandages that I already had. I could tell he was working hard to not hurt me. I laughed at his caution and told him that he could just rip it off.

"I'm not afraid of pain," I told him.

"Do you still have the desire to do this kind of damage?" Daniel asked.

I hesitated. "My answer depends on the consequence."

"What do you mean?"

"If the answer is bad, will there be a consequence?" I clarified.

"There's no consequence," Daniel reassured me.

"Yeah. I've been doing this kind of thing long enough that I still want to do this. It's always on my mind."

"That's good," Daniel said.

I was confused. "That's good?!" I repeated his words.

"Really? You find pleasure in doing this to yourself?" Daniel's expression was of shock and surprise.

"Of course not," I told him. "I meant that it was funny when you said that it was good that I wanted to hurt myself."

"Oh no," Daniel corrected. "That's not what I meant. I have a habit of saying, *that's good*, but it's good that you are honest."

I accepted his explanation.

"Does the hospital staff make you nervous?" Daniel asked me.

"No," I answered simply.

"And what about the patients?"

"Mostly no," I told him. "There are some weird ones." I told him about what happened at supper time with Roy. "I don't think he is a danger," I theorized.

Daniel wasn't so sure that what Roy did was okay. "Roy can be dangerous. You should tell us when that happens."

After my young nurse left, I found a rubber band wrapped around a cup holder over my sink. I took it off and studied it like I had just found gold. I put it on my wrist and snapped it several times.

I had a big decision to make. Would I hide the rubber band and take it out when I needed it? Would I risk the possibility of being caught, or would I admit to finding it and give it to the nurse?

I stood in my doorway for a long while, just watching the nurses at their desks and struggling to decide what to do. I couldn't find an answer that I liked. If I kept it, I was breaking the rules and taking a risk, but if I gave it to Daniel, I would have lost my treasure and would have nothing to calm me.

I thought about what I would do without the rubber band. I remembered that banging my wrist against the windowsill had proven helpful. Yes, this was the kind of stupidity that I came up with when I was left unsupervised.

My dilemma was interrupted when Joseph came and asked me to play cards with him. I was grateful for the distraction.

We played a game called Eight. It was an ironic game to be playing considering where we were.

Joseph was really looking forward to Monday when he could meet with his doctor and ask for more privileges.

"Forget more privileges," I said to Joseph. "I'm asking to get out of here on Monday!"

Joseph made a face like he found the idea ridiculous. "We get our privileges gradually," he informed me. "And how many guards did you have watching you?"

Joseph's reaction took me by surprise.

"Five guards," I answered. Five guards! I'd had five guards in the course of two days and I was expecting to leave just a few days later?

"You might make it out of here the Monday after that," Joseph guessed.

I was floored and I was terrified. I couldn't stand the idea of staying there for so long. My levels of anxiety and depression rose and I began to panic.

After the card game, it was time to get in line for medication. I felt like a mess, and I guess that I looked like one too because Jolene came over and tried to comfort me.

"You're one of my kids here, you know?" Jolene told me. "I take care of my kids because I know they really need it."

I leaned against the wall like I had done the night before. I felt so sad and broken.

When everyone had their medication and had left, I went up to get mine.

"Is your bandage comfortable?" Daniel asked.

"It is," I replied and then held out my prized rubber band for him to see. "I found this in my room, but I'm not supposed to have it."

Daniel took the rubber band and put it in his shirt pocket.

"Can I have that back when I leave here?" I asked.

"Okay."

I was still in a daze when he handed me my medication. It was hard to pretend like I was fine. How could I be fine when I was trapped in the crazy house with all my responsibilities waiting for me on the outside? How could I stop from breaking? Why was I always breaking? Couldn't I just have been fine?

After swallowing my pills, I asked if I could have some lorazepam for my anxiety. I must have looked messed up enough because he didn't even ask me any questions, he just gave me the lorazepam.

I was glad that he gave it to me. I don't think that I could have fallen asleep without it. It took a while before the medication stopped my heart from thumping violently into my pillow.

That was one more night that I fell asleep crying.

Sunday, June 8

I woke up around 6:30 on Sunday morning. Just as I did the day before, I went and asked the nurse at the desks if I could have something for my migraine.

I was given two extra strength pain killers and then took what was my first shower with the door completely closed.

I had gotten lucky that morning because I was able to make a deal with Jolene. She got to take some of my body wash, and in exchange, I got to use her make-up and the mirror in her room. Although, on the day before I made an exciting discovery. I could see my reflection rather well in the electrical panel for plug in razors next to my sink. I could see myself well enough to put some cover-up for the circles under my eyes.

After my shower I went to the desks and found both Ashton and Daniel sitting there.

"Could my bandages be changed?" I asked. "They're all wet."

"We don't have time right now," Ashton said. "It's the shift change."

I didn't want soggy wounds like the days before. "Can I just take them off then?"

"No," they both said.

I sighed and thought, "Whatever."

My nurse that day was Natasha, just like the day before.

As usual, I walked around the halls that morning while fidgeting nervously after my hospital bracelet.

"You aren't supposed to play with that," Natasha warned. "It has to stay on your wrist."

"Why?"

"Because it's procedure," she explained.

"Why?"

"Because it's procedure," she repeated, but still hadn't truly answered my question.

"Why is it procedure?" I asked more specifically.

"You might hurt yourself by doing that."

I should have dared her to show me where it was written in procedure to not let the patients play with their bracelets.

"This doesn't hurt me," I told her.

"You can't do it anyway."

In my mind I growled at her pushiness that lacked logic.

I was anxious and I didn't have my rubber band. What did they expect me to do with my anxiety if I couldn't even do something as trivial as fiddle around with a bracelet?

Natasha and I talked a bit as we walked. From the way she was talking to me, I gathered that she was trying to calm me down, but she wasn't very good at it.

My nurse left briefly and then came back saying that she had to take my bracelet away, and then she cut it off of my wrist with a pair of scissors.

What?! How was I supposed to hurt myself with a strip of plastic with no sharp edges? I felt irritated about the distrust and ridiculous over-protection.

I was grateful however, that although Natasha removed my bracelet, she also gave me some lorazepam.

I played with my watch as I waited for the medication to kick in.

When I was calm again, I played some cards with Joseph.

Ashton even came to join the game for a little while. He said that he liked being able to spend some time with his patients. I didn't like being called a patient. I didn't like the whole concept of being a patient.

The game ended and my name was called over the microphone. This time someone really did come to see me.

I got to talk to Shy-Anne for a long time that evening. I let her know some things about my past that we hadn't discussed before.

Shy-Anne offered that we could go meet with a Spanish friend of hers once a week and then go for milkshakes, that way I wouldn't be alone as much.

While both Shy-Anne and I were sitting comfortably on my bed, Joseph came to my room to say, "Hi."

"Hey Joseph. This is the friend who gave me the flower," I told him.

"Yeah? Nice," After Joseph greeted my friend, he had something new to tell me. "I've decided to accept to go out with Shanny after all. I didn't realize it at first, but I like her and find her interesting."

Joseph began to leave and I called out, "Hey!"

So Joseph peeked his head back into my doorway and asked, "What?"

"Tell her that you used to like blonds best, but since you met her, you like brunettes," I instructed, thinking of how romantic it would be.

Joseph smiled and left. I wondered how this story would end.

Shy-Anne left shortly afterwards. We made arrangements that if I was still hospitalized passed Monday, she would use the key to my apartment to go get some of my clothing. I didn't know how I would have made it through without my friend. I don't just mean gratitude for the clothing, but mostly for the love and support.

You'll never guess what I did after Shy-Anne left. I started walking. I know, it's unoriginal, but there wasn't much else to do and walking had become an outlet for my emotions. It helped me stay busy and kept me from being alone in my room.

Jed past by without looking at me, but he said, "You, Melissa, I'm not talking to you anymore."

Jed was gone before I got a chance to respond.

A few minutes later, I saw Jed near the cafeteria and I asked, "Hi Jed. Why aren't you talking to me?"

Jed didn't reply. He didn't even slow down.

I found his behavior strange and wondered what I had done to make him react that way.

I wasn't used to being around so many different people and I wasn't sure how to act. Was I doing everything wrong?

I forgot about my encounter with Jed by the time I met up with Joseph in the halls. I was eager to hear how his new romance unfolded.

"Tell me what happened," I instructed eagerly.

"Shanny changed her mind," Joseph spoke solemnly. "She doesn't want to date me after all."

"What?!" I couldn't believe it. How did things change so fast?

"How could she have played with my emotions like that?" Joseph asked, but I had no answer. This behavior puzzled me as well.

During our walk through the halls, Joseph and I ended up in the cafeteria where Shanny was sitting at one of the small, round tables.

Instead of talking to Shanny, Joseph directed his thoughts to me for her to hear. "Tell her that it wasn't okay for her to do that."

I didn't like being stuck in the middle. I did stop to talk to Shanny though while Joseph continued on.

I didn't tell Shanny that what she did wasn't okay. I asked her, "What's going on?"

"I don't know. I don't know what happened or what I want," Shanny struggled to find an explanation.

I wasn't sure what to say or to suggest.

I was taken off guard when Shanny threw her next words at me. "You are just so self centered and manipulative, and you have no love for people," Shanny spoke coldly and with eyes full of an emotion that I didn't understand. "You live too much in your head," she said.

I couldn't believe what was happening. I wasn't used to having people be hostile towards me. "That's not true," I told her while trying to stay calm. "I have a lot of love for others. So much so that it hurts."

"Not enough love," Shanny said flatly.

"You've known me for two days. You have no idea what I'm like," I spoke defensively, but calmly.

"Yes, I do," Shanny disagreed. "I see things in people that other people don't. I know you are manipulative and have no love for people."

I didn't want a fight. I didn't want an attack. "Why are you saying these things?"

"Because I've had enough of being messed with," Shanny explained simply.

"What you are saying to me is really mean," I stated. "I am none of those things and you are being really mean."

That's when I stood up and left.

I wasn't going to attack her in return. I couldn't. I didn't understand how anyone could do that.

I went to my room and sat in the chair in the corner. I stayed there until Joseph came over and asked how it went.

I just sat there in silent tears, almost unable to say what happened. Though the words were difficult, I told him what Shanny said.

Joseph comforted me and said that I wasn't like that at all, then he offered that we play cards.

I accepted.

We went to the cafeteria and started playing the game called Eight. I didn't really like the game, but Joseph did, so I played.

We were alone in the room until Shanny came in and sat in one of the rocking chairs in front of the television. Her presence was uncomfortable, but I said nothing about it.

Barely a minute had passed before Shanny began turning towards us in continued hostility. "You know that Joseph only wants to be your friend so he can get in your pants. All he does is use people to get what he wants and then he hurts them."

Joseph and I looked at each other briefly, just as if to say that we had heard her but wouldn't respond. We stayed quiet, even though I was getting increasingly upset, and we continued to play Eight.

Shanny left the room, but came back only moments later. She had re-entered the room at the same time as the nurse that I had been assigned to for that evening.

"I want to be friends again," Shanny said as she walked up to our table. "I don't want to leave things like this, and I forgive you."

I looked at her like I couldn't believe her words. She forgave *us*? What was she forgiving us for? For listening to her cold-hearted and unprovoked lectures?

"It's not forgiveness I need to hear, it's an apology." I was surprised that I had just stood up for myself. It wasn't something I commonly found myself doing. Even more surprising was the fact that I had done it in front of my nurse who was then standing right next to Shanny.

My nurse was a young woman in her twenties. She was tall and a bit stalky with shoulder length brown hair. Her name was Michelle. She was looking at the tense expressions on all our faces while trying to figure out what was going on.

"Okay, I'm sorry," Shanny told us mockingly with a smile. Was this a joke?

"I'd rather a sincere apology," I specified.

"Okay, I'm really, really, really sorry," Shanny apologized, but still with a hint of a smile. "I'm okay with the fact that you are self centered. I was self centered too."

"That doesn't sound sincere." I continued to stand my ground.

"She looks sincere," Joseph added. "I can always forgive."

I was disappointed that he didn't back me up. I was a very forgiving person, but only if the person was sorry. This girl was not sorry.

Shanny took Joseph's words as an invitation to rejoin our group and she sat down at the table with us. I wasn't accepting of her re-immersion. Shanny had really hurt me and her apology didn't go very far.

I tried reasoning with myself in my head. I had to remember that Shanny was bipolar and that could cause her to say bad things sometimes. I pushed myself to be understanding.

My nurse Michelle was the next to speak. "I don't know what's going on here, but I can tell there is tension."

Joseph answered, "No, we're okay."

"But it doesn't look like Melissa is okay," Michelle observed. "I can tell by her expression."

Michelle was right. I was really upset and mad, I couldn't even think about sitting there playing card games next to Shanny while pretending everything was okay. Things were not okay.

I got up and left to go to my room. I didn't know how to react to a situation like that.

I sat alone in my room for about ten minutes before Michelle came in to see if I was all right and find out what happened.

I told her the story through anxiety and tears. I worried that I was overreacting and tried to be understanding considering Shanny's mental health condition.

"I think she will be all right," I said to Michelle.

"You don't have to worry about her. You just worry about you," Michelle guided. "Would you like some meds to help you calm down?"

I accepted.

The medicine was supposed to help me calm down, but that's around when something occurred to me that really made me worry. I remembered that Shanny knew my sister Marie at school. If Shanny was mad at me and behaving the way she was, would she tell my sister that she met me and why I was at the hospital? Would she do that out of spite?

Fear rose high within me and I didn't know what to do with it.

Should I tell Marie about self injuring and being in the hospital before Shanny did?

Should I patch things up with Shanny just to gain back her loyalty and keep her from telling on me?

There was so much to think about. I was also worried about my responsibilities that were waiting for me on the outside. I had my job at the old age home. If I couldn't go, I would have to inform my boss. I wanted to cover my bases, so I decided to tell my boss that I probably wouldn't be able to go to work for the next week.

"Why?" Tory asked with concern. "Is there a family emergency?"

Could I use a family emergency as an excuse? Well, I was part of my family, and I had an emergency, so technically that was the truth.

"Yeah, a family emergency," I agreed.

"What's going on?" she inquired. "Is it your mothers cancer again?"

"No," I told her. "I actually can't talk about the reason."

"Okay," she accepted. "Just take care of yourself, okay?"

"Yes," I agreed. "Thank-you."

After hanging up with Tory, I had another call to make. I had my ferrets, kitten and hedgehog that needed to be fed and cared for. I had thought that I would only be gone a few days, so I loaded up their dishes with food and assumed it would be enough, but by then it would be proving to be lacking.

I decided to call my brother to ask him to drop by my place when he would pass through town. I could talk to him about the animals at the same time as I called him to say that I probably wouldn't be able to make it to work for Tuesday night. My brother was my boss when it came to the grocery store.

Devon seemed quite lost when I told him I couldn't work. He wasn't able to do the job himself and there was no one else to ask. It was just the two of us.

I didn't know what solution to offer and felt really guilty for putting him in that position. I wasn't used to backing out on work. I had always been so reliable. I didn't know how to handle being out of the game.

I said nothing to Devon about where I was or why I couldn't be there to clean the grocery store. I just told him I couldn't make it, and he didn't ask any questions. I was thankful for that. I don't know how I would have handled it if he had asked.

Before we hung up, my brother had a message for me. "Lisa has been looking for you. She passed by your place and you weren't there. She seems really worried about you."

I didn't know that Lisa was in town again. Of course she would be worried. She knew things were getting bad with me and she didn't know where I was.

After talking with Devon, I called Lisa to let her know what happened and asked if she would come and see me. I was pleased when my friend showed up just fifteen minutes later.

I waited near the elevators and smiled as my friend arrived. I saw her familiar wild red hair and small frame and I immediately went to hug her. I always loved being able to hug Lisa. It seemed that we could really feel each others loving friendship passing through us. It seemed that nobody could hug like she could.

Lisa gave me a teddy bear book mark that I put in my journal and then she offered to go get some of my things for me.

Lisa already had a key to my apartment. I had given it to her so she would always have somewhere safe to go, even if I wasn't there.

All my belongings that Lisa brought back had to pass through inspection by Roger the orderly. He had to make sure I didn't get anything that I could hurt myself with.

All of my pants and tops were put into my closet and locked in so I couldn't have access to them until I was allowed my own clothes.

Lisa couldn't stay long because visiting hours ended at 8:30 pm, but she said that she would come back the next day. She was going to bring me some slippers because the staff had been getting after me for walking around in stockings or barefoot.

I had already gotten my shoes back, but I found them too noisy when I walked and I didn't want to use them.

After Lisa left, my nurse Michelle came to talk to me. I wasn't sure why at first, but it seemed she just wanted to give me a chance to vent and express myself.

She asked about the reasons why I was self injuring.

We didn't talk long because our conversation was cut short when she was called away, but she said that she would be back on Wednesday night.

"I don't like to think that I will still be here on Wednesday night," I told Michelle.

"It's better for you if you stay," Michelle told me.

"But there's the money issue," I confided. "I'm not earning rent money by staying here."

"I'll make a note at the desk to see if something can be arranged for your finances," Michelle offered.

"Thank-you."

Medication was at the same time every night, and I went to bed right afterwards. I had nothing to stay up for.

I had barely begun hiding under my covers when I heard Jed whisper my name in the doorway. I got up and went to meet him because the male patients weren't allowed to come in. I was actually grateful for that.

"Yes?" I asked as I saw Jed standing there in his grey pajamas. I wasn't sure what it was, but there was something frightening about Jed. He had this menacing presence even when he was being polite. His facial features were very hard. I'm not sure how to explain that. Could I say chiseled? His cheekbones and forehead were very pronounced and his eyes seemed pale but shadowed.

"I'm sorry for what I said to you earlier," Jed apologized. "Things get messed up in my head sometimes. I thought that you lied to me about something, but I like to buy you things."

I knew that Jed had to have some confusing things going on in his mind. I had been told that he was schizophrenic.

"Thank-you for the apology. I'm sorry if I said anything to offend you," I extended my own apologies. "I know you have a big heart and I was worried about you."

That's when Jed left, and I slept.

Monday, June 9

I was pleased to get up the next morning and shower once again with the door closed. Although for each shower, someone would knock on the door and ask who was there. They had to check regularly to make sure that every patient on the ward was accounted for.

My nurse for that day was named Charlotte. She was a rather skinny middle aged woman with really short brown hair. She took my blood pressure and later she changed my bandages and applied some cream to my wrist that was meant especially for burns.

When Charlotte pulled my old bandage off, one of my raw burns began to bleed. One of the scabs had peeled off with the bandage. I could see little white holes all over the red wound.

"Cool, there are holes in it," I spoke with fascination as I studied the wound.

"You think that's cool?" she asked with a frown. "That's too bad."

I realized I had made a mistake by saying that it was cool. It was just that I had never seen anything like that before. If I had seen it on someone else, I would have thought that it was gross.

When Charlotte left, I was free to walk around as I pleased.

I met Shanny in the little hallway by the laundry room. I didn't want to leave things with her the way they had been the night before. I didn't just want to patch things up to keep her from ratting me out to my sister, but also because I had liked having her as a friend.

"I'm sorry about last night," I apologized. "I wasn't very quick to forgive."

"No," Shanny corrected. "It was me that was in the wrong. I said things from my heart that I shouldn't have."

With just a short conversation, Shanny and I were friends again. We played cards and talked about how confused Shanny was about Joseph. She still felt that she shouldn't be with him.

Little old Roy gave me another vacuum kiss that day. I had lost count of how many kisses he had given me. One of the staff had witnessed the kiss and warned Roy to be respectful of peoples boundaries the way she had told him to.

Roy wanted to eat with me that day the way he had the day before, but all the seats were taken. He was clearly disappointed.

Roy liked to give me things from his tray. He just took random things and put them in front of me. That day he gave me his soup, some cheese from the fridge, and another kiss.

"You're my favorite," Roy told me.

After lunch, Joseph found a paper clip on the floor. He asked the staff at the desks about where he should put it. He didn't get an answer, so Joseph offered me the paper clip as a simplistic gift.

"I can't have that. I'll get in trouble," I told Joseph as he held the clip up to me, but I guess he didn't understand because he continued to hold it out, so I took it.

Right around the corner, Ashton appeared with his blood pressure monitor attached to a long metal rod on wheels.

I held the clip out to Ashton. "Look how nice my friends are. They give me things like these."

Joseph cooed, "Ooh," as he realized why I shouldn't have it.

Ashton made a serious face, as if to say, "Oh, that's not good. You can't have that."

I had a big smile on my face, so Ashton said, "I can already see you planning things with that. You can't have it."

I knew that I would have to give it up, that's why I had shown the clip, but I still squirmed around with the idea of letting it go. I gave it to Ashton and he put it in his shirt pocket.

"I miss it already," I stated solemnly.

Joseph walked away, but Ashton stayed behind to talk with me.

"Are you still having thoughts of hurting yourself?" he asked.

"Yes."

"Well, you can have things like this and rubber bands when you are dressed like this," Ashton told me as he looked down at his shirt and pants.

"I don't know how to deal with my emotions without hurting myself," I admitted.

"Because you're trying to forget your past?" Ashton asked.

"Yes."

"Well we would like it if you didn't feel like that anymore. You can come and talk to me when you like," he offered kindly.

I was glad that someone cared to come and talk to me. I never would have initiated the conversation because I was just too scared and too shy.

We had a nap time on the ward. We didn't have to actually sleep, but all the patients had to be in their rooms quietly from 12:45 pm to 1:30 pm every day. I used that time to write in detail into my journal. The pages were filling fast.

That was Monday afternoon. After the nap, I got to meet the doctor that was assigned to me. Her name was Dr Knoll and she would be taking charge of my case for the duration of my stay.

We met in the same big blue office as I had with the nurse a few days before. I sat in the same seat, and in the same brown gown.

I was looking forward to leaving, so I asked when she thought I would be able to go.

"I find it troubling that you are concerned with leaving," Dr Knoll told me.

My internal red alert went off as I remembered a conversation with Ashton. He told me that if we showed that we were too interested in leaving, it could indicate that we weren't concerned enough with getting better and could therefore be kept longer.

I quickly jumped in to try and correct my mistake. "I am well aware that I need help. I need help and so far I haven't been able to get out of this on my own. I couldn't stop for my loved ones and I couldn't stop for me. I have responsibilities on the outside though. I have to work. I need money to pay my rent. If you asked me to stay a month, that would seem like a long time, but I can do a little while."

The doctor seemed to accept my answer and proceeded to ask me a series of strange psychologically based questions.

She wanted to know if I ever heard voices or felt that people were out to get me.

"No."

She wanted to know if I ever starved myself or made myself throw up.

"No."

She wanted to know if I saw things in black and white. Was I usually thinking that a friend was great at one moment, but terrible in the next?

"No."

I didn't fit in with any of the things that she was talking about, until she asked if I ever felt like more than one person.

"I realize you may be referring to dissociative identity disorder, but I feel like that in another way," I told Dr Knoll. "I often find that I split myself into more than one person. When I look in the mirror, I see the person staring back at me to be someone else. She is all the bad things that happened to me and all the bad things I do. I hate her and often find myself unable to look in the mirror for fear that I would hurt her. I know she is me, but that's how I see her. I call her Stupid Girl. That's her name."

The doctor didn't seem troubled by what I said. Maybe what I was feeling wasn't so unusual.

"What is that from?" Dr Knoll asked in reference to the large multi colored bruise on the back of my arm.

I was at the hospital and there was no secret that I was hurting myself, so I felt that I could be honest. "I beat it repeatedly with a metal wrench while I was at work," I admitted as I remembered the violence behind my bruise.

Dr knoll seemed disturbed, but I wasn't sure what that was supposed to mean.

I was then asked to show her the cuts on my leg. Once my cuts were inspected, I was asked to show her the other leg.

"I never hurt that leg. Only this one," I told her as I pointed to my right leg.

"Show me," the doctor insisted.

It bothered me that she didn't believe me and that I was asked to prove it, but I complied and pulled down my leg warmer to show her underneath.

When Dr Knoll was satisfied that I hadn't mutilated a second leg, she returned to her chair on her side of the desk.

I was relieved to be able to hide again when I pulled my leg warmers back up.

I was asked a few questions about my childhood, as well as about my history with anxiety and self injury.

"When did you start hurting yourself?" Dr Knoll asked.

I told the doctor about being five years old and hiding in the play room to hurt myself. "I needed to teach myself to tolerate pain," I explained. "I practiced pain so that when my father would hit me, I wouldn't react. It worked. After he hit me, my expression was always blank, but that would make him angrier. He would then hit me harder just to make me cry. I felt that as long as I didn't cry, I won."

"And where was it that you would hurt yourself?" Dr Knoll asked.

"My tummy," I said as I laid my hand over my stomach. "There are no marks. I didn't do it bad enough back then to leave a lasting impression."

The doctor stood up and told me to show her my stomach.

I was hesitant. "I don't hurt myself there anymore."

"Show me."

I was insulted once again that she didn't take my word for it. I was also very shy because I was only wearing my underwear under my hospital gown. I didn't feel comfortable lifting the gown up when I wasn't wearing pants. I had always been very private and conservative about showing my body. I was also very bad at saying, *no*, so I lifted my gown and showed her my stomach.

The doctor looked at my stomach briefly. She saw nothing there, but noticed some bruised on my thighs. She thought that I had done that to myself, but I told her that I hadn't. I could tell that she didn't believe me. Had I given reason to be taken for a liar?

It was such a cold attitude and it made me feel smaller.

"Have you been making friends?" Dr Knoll wanted to know.

"Yes, several, especially Shanny and Joseph," I told her.

The doctor then made a strange disapproving face. "You need to be careful with him."

I was taken by surprise. Was Joseph dangerous?

"He's just a friend," I told her.

"It's best if you keep your distance," Dr Knoll warned.

I wasn't sure what to think, but her words did make me nervous. I understood that she couldn't actually tell me the reasons behind her warning. She couldn't discuss another patients case, so I didn't ask.

I knew that Joseph was admitted because he was taking speed and he was hyperactive, but he seemed harmless.

I decided to move onto other matters until I figured things out. "May I ask how long I will be kept here?"

"How does next Monday sound?" she asked.

I tried not to show it, but I felt my heart sink. Would I have to survive that place for a total of two weeks? Joseph was right. After having a guard for a few days, there was no way that they would let me leave right away.

"Monday sounds okay." I tried to act like it didn't bother me, but it sounded awful and it frightened me.

I tried to forget about my disappointment and see what things could be made better during my stay.

I asked if I could get some stronger medication for my migraines because what they had been giving me wasn't nearly enough. I was then prescribed some extra strength Ibuprofen.

My next question was one that I looked very forward to asking. "Can I wear my own clothes now?"

"That depends," Dr Knoll answered. "Do you think that you can be trusted not to hurt yourself?"

"Well," I began. "I had the chance to use a rubber band and a paper clip, but I turned them both down at great emotional cost."

"Okay then. Yes, you can have your clothes," the doctor granted.

In my head I was leaping for joy. I couldn't wait to get out of that hospital gown.

After my meeting with the doctor, my closet was unlocked and I was allowed to choose some of my own clothing. I pulled out some black pants and a green top and eagerly put them on.

After throwing my hospital gown into the laundry hamper, I went over to my friends and excitedly said, "Ta da!" I was on a happy high.

There was a new guy that arrived that day. His name was Parker and he was wearing the same brown gown that I had just escaped. He was sitting alone, so I asked him if he wanted to play cards. He accepted and joined our group.

Parker was a man in his early twenties. He had black hair and a slightly unshaven look.

Most often, we played a game called *Janitor*. It was a nice way to pass the time, although, we had to take breaks often so Parker and Joseph could go get their cigarettes and light them up in the smoke room.

I got a visit from Lisa that afternoon and she joined our card game. I liked her attitude when she played. She was very animated and it felt good to see her smile.

After the game, Lisa and I went to my room just to talk. We stood at the window and looked down at the cars in the parking lot.

"This was my room when I was admitted to the hospital last year," Lisa told me. "I used to look out the window and count the cars in the parking lot."

Lisa had been admitted many times to the children's ward for her eating disorders, but when she turned eighteen, she was with the other adults in the psych ward.

She told me about being at her college and having her teacher call an ambulance for her because she was extremely underweight and still refusing to eat. It took eight people to catch her when she tried to run away and then she fought them off until they tied her to the gurney.

She talked about smuggling piles of cookies into her room so she could binge and purge with them at night. She talked about trying to escape out the window, but getting stuck and then getting caught.

We both shared our stories until Lisa had to go, but said that she would come back after supper.

Daniel and Michelle were both on staff that evening, but neither of them were my nurse. A young woman in her twenties named Sara was in charge of me. She had long blond hair that she kept tied back, but left some of her long bangs out to fall over her face. There was something unique about Sara's face that I can't quite describe, but I found her appearance fascinating.

I hadn't gotten to talk to Sara, but I was uneasy with having so many different people take care of me. I just started to get to know a few of them and then I got someone else and had to start all over.

When Lisa came back that evening, she brought me a hot chocolate in a thermos. I thought it was really sweet of her.

My friend also smuggled me in a few pain killers because the hospital rules were rigid, and I couldn't have more medication for my migraines until a certain time had passed. The dosage that was prescribed to me still wasn't enough.

Lisa and I were still chatting when the announcement passed that it was 8:30 pm and that all visitors had to leave. We were both disappointed, but Lisa decided to defy the rules and stay longer.

It wasn't until about 9:20 that evening that Michelle came in during the rounds and found that I still had a visitor. We got in a bit of trouble for that.

"Why do you still have a visitor?" Michelle wanted to know.

I hadn't planned on what I would say when we got caught. I hesitated, then explained. "Lisa lives over two hours away and she is going home tomorrow. We won't get another chance to see each other for at least a few weeks."

"Well it's still too late right now," Michelle reprimanded. "We don't want the other patients to get jealous and say they want company for longer too."

"But it was therapeutic for me to talk with her," I argued, though my words did not sway her.

Lisa decided that she would drop by the next day right before she would leave to go home. She would bring me a few more of my things, including another journal for me to write in for when my first was full.

After Lisa left, I stayed up for a while so I could write about my day, but I had to stop at 10:30 pm when it was lights out.

Tuesday, June 10

I noticed three times in the night when someone came in with a flashlight and shone it in my face. They were doing regular rounds to make sure everyone was there and safe. I would cover my eyes with my hands to hide them from the light, then seconds later the flashlight would disappear and I could sleep again.

Breakfast that morning was my regular peanut butter and jam toast. The cafeteria felt a bit empty because Jolene had gotten released the day before. She was going to a hospital called Ste-Marguerite's that was only for psychiatric patients. It was an outpatient facility, but also a long term inpatient facility. If someone still needed care after a few months on the eighth floor of the hospital, then they were sent to stay at Ste-Marguerite's.

I felt a bit sad because I was one of Jolene's kids. She had taken me under her wing, and so then someone I had gotten to know in that strange place was gone.

I noticed that Saffron was missing as well. I wondered if she had been released.

When I saw Dr Knoll that morning I got in trouble for not respecting the rules of visiting hours the night before. I was also reproached for having another patient in my room that morning. It was Joseph that had come to my doorway to greet me and gave me a hug. We were warned that it was inappropriate. I didn't mind the reproach for that because I didn't feel comfortable with Joseph hugging me anyways.

Dr knoll gave me a small checkup. She listened to my heart while having me breathe deeply several times.

Afterwards I asked her if I could have some time away from the hospital so I could check on my animals and get some more of my things.

I was granted permission for a two hour leave everyday, as long as I had someone with me.

I decided to call Lisa and she took the short walk with me from the hospital to my apartment just down the road. I was able to gather my MP3 player, some books to read, and some more arm warmers to hide my wrists. After checking my emails, I was walked back to the hospital and escorted directly to the eighth floor.

Upon my return, my nurse came to chat with me briefly, just to talk about how I was. She told me that I was so sweet and nice that she couldn't imagine me hurting myself. Our conversation was cut short by a woman who turned out to be a psychologist.

The psychologist was shorter than I was. She had thick blond hair and she looked to be in her fifties. Her name was Mabel Werthers.

Mabel's office was on the opposite side of the building to where I had met with Dr Knoll. Her office didn't look as neat as the doctors though. It was very cluttered and had several chairs that didn't match.

"Where do I sit?" I asked Mable.

"Wherever you want," she answered.

Mable didn't sit behind a big desk. She chose a chair across from me so we were facing each other. There was no furniture between us.

I spent about an hour in her office. She had me talk about my self injury and my reasons behind it. We talked about being raised by an abusive alcoholic. We talked about my unwanted sexual encounter when I was 14. Mabel asked me to tell her about it.

"I had just turned 14," I began my story. "I had stayed late at school and missed the bus. I tried to catch the city bus after that, but I just missed it and would have to wait another hour. I was so tired and discouraged that when the father of a friend of mine saw me and offered me a ride, I didn't turn him away. At first he just smiled and waved as he passed by in his car. I hadn't recognized him to begin with because I had only seen him once before. I would say that he was older than my own father. When the man passed a second time, he stopped and rolled down the drivers side window and told me to get in. I didn't like being rude and turning people down, so I got into the car without question. He asked me where I wanted to go, and he said that he would take me there. I thought that I shouldn't worry. People took rides from strangers all the time, and this man wasn't quite a stranger.

Things didn't go quite as he said they would when he told me that we had to take a detour. The man said that he had to see some of his employees that were working in the woods. I knew it sounded bad right then. I remember the slow gulp when he placed his hand under my chin and asked if my sister had blue eyes like mine.

We drove at least ten minutes into the woods when he parked down a short dirt road. Trent got out of the car and told me to wait a moment. He walked a short ways down the road and pretended to check for some of his employees, but there was no one there. He came back to the car only seconds later," I paused to breathe. "He cupped his hand under my chin again and asked if I would let him fondle me a little. He even offered me money. I'll never forget that look in his eyes. The desire."

I stopped my story there. I didn't feel that I needed to tell the rest and I rarely did. The words didn't feel right in my mouth and they made me panic.

I was then asked to read several phrases on a long list. I had to identify which ones applied to me when I was having a flashback of being abused.

I picked out words like, powerless and helpless.

Then, while keeping certain memories in mind, I was supposed to follow Mabel's finger as she waved it back and forth in front of her.

I had to describe how I felt. "Anxious and guilty," I told her.

At the end I was supposed to imagine a safe place in my mind so the session could end in a less emotionally difficult way. I imagined a park with a library, and with my family outside. There was a large squeaky toy penguin that was bigger than me and a fence made of chocolate.

After the appointment I wasn't feeling too badly. It was as some time went by that I was feeling increasingly freaked out and anxious. Bad memories were swirling around my head and old feelings resurfaced.

I spent some time in my room, but I spent it by going over a list of ways that were at my disposal for me to hurt myself.

I could burn myself with the hot water from the sink.

I could use the uneven piece of metal under the bed frame to scratch myself.

There was a strange thing protruding from the wall that I could do some damage with.

There was also the windowsill that I could beat my wrist on and make bruises.

I was so tempted to hurt myself that I decided to stand in my doorway as a preventative measure. I thought that if I was where people could see me, I wouldn't hurt myself.

I waited there a long time with my head against the doorframe. My anxiety was rising, but I said nothing about it. I imagined that no one would care.

When I saw that no one was looking, I would bang my head against the door frame.

Eventually I got desperate enough to ask for help. I walked up to the desks and asked Daniel if he knew who my nurse was that day.

"Why?" he asked.

"Because I would like some lorazepam please," I answered nervously.

Daniel brought me my anti-anxiety medication. I wasn't breathing very well and I felt really dizzy. I took deep breaths as I got my water and took my pill.

Shanny was nearby at the desks with her mother. She gave me a concerned look and an awkward wave.

I thanked Daniel for the help and returned to my room where I laid down in my bed. I beat my hand against the mattress in a rhythmic fashion. I needed some way to release my anxiety.

Eventually I got down on the floor and inspected the uneven piece of bed frame and came very close to using it. It took an enormous amount of self control.

I stopped inspecting for ways to hurt myself and just sat there with my knees against my cheek. I rocked back and forth.

I ignored the calls for me to come to supper. I didn't want to go. I didn't want to eat.

They even called my name on the loud speakers, but I just stayed there, rocking on the floor with a mess of long blond hair in front of my face.

Roger came in and asked if I was going to come to eat.

I answered, "No."

Roger opened my door further so he could see in better. That's when my nurse came in to see how I was. I hadn't seen her before. I had no idea who she was.

The nurse pushed the hair away from my face.

"I'm fine," I told her.

"You don't look fine," she said. "Poor little thing."

"I'm fine," I repeated.

"You want to hurt yourself," she observed.

I said nothing.

"But don't you know that you're pretty?" she asked.

Silence.

"Don't you know that you are pretty and you are a really sweet girl?" the nurse looked at me with concerned eyes.

"I don't see what my appearance has to do with anything," I told her.

Her insinuation bothered me. I could have been the nicest and prettiest person in the world, but that still wouldn't make me incapable of cutting myself. We are all just people who break in different ways.

In an effort to get me to express myself, the nurse suggested that I write a poem and to show it to her. I said that I would.

There was a poem that I had previously written, but knew by heart. I thought that I could write it out for her. It was about being a broken doll that got tossed aside, then started tearing herself apart.

The nurse left and I spent my time looking at the spots on the floor tiles and imagining that they were bubbles of blood rising. Then I sat back on the bed and stared at a crack in the wall and pictured it bleeding.

The nurses could do nothing to make my urges go away. I had to hurt myself and there was nothing that helped.

I was shaken from my obsession with bleeding when I got two visitors. Tory and Gene had come to see me. Tory was my boss, and Gene was the cook that took care of the residents at the old age home during the day. I couldn't believe it.

I gave both Tory and Gene a big hug. I had been working at the old age home for several years, so I knew them well and cared about them both.

"How did you guys know I was here?" I asked while feeling both pleased and embarrassed.

"You weren't fooling me on the phone the other day," Tory said with a comforting smile. "I figured you must have been here. You've been having a hard time and I know what that's like."

"These are for you," Gene told me as she handed me a chocolate bar and some sour candy.

"But you have to eat it right away," Tory added. "The nurses said you can't keep it in your room when we are gone."

"Yummy," I marveled at the chocolate and unwrapped it right away.

I was also given two cards. One was signed by everyone at the old age home. The cooks had signed it and so did all the residents. I got to read a little note from all of them. There was also money in the envelope.

"Wow," I was in amazement as one hundred dollars fell into my hand. I looked up at them with such appreciation. "Oh my goodness. Thank-you. I was so worried about money. You guys are really saving me."

"I thought you would be worried about that." Gene seemed proud of her intuition.

"Don't worry about everyone knowing you are here," Tory reassured me. "I told them that you have pneumonia. They think you are tired and overworked and that's why you got pneumonia."

I smiled at the covert operation they planned.

The second card I received was from Mme Poplin. She was an elderly lady that lived on the top floor of the home. She was always very cheery and sentimental. She wrote me a nice note, and even put twenty dollars in the envelope. I had a total of one hundred and twenty dollars. It helped alleviate some stress.

"I'm really grateful," I told them with a lot of sentiment, then I gave them both another hug.

They didn't stay long, but I enjoyed their visit. When they had arrived, I felt like crying, but when they left and I was all full of chocolate and the merriment of good company, I felt better.

I got to share my sour candy with Joseph and Shanny while we played a crossword puzzle board game. They found the candy just as addicting as I had.

My good mood didn't last long. It left not long after my company did. By the time we were supposed to be in bed, I still wanted to hurt myself. I wondered what to do with it. Would I be able to just sleep?

I had already dug my fingernails into my wrist several times. I didn't want anyone to know in case they would make me stay longer on account of it. I couldn't let that happen.

I slipped my arms under the blankets so they could hide with me, and I fell asleep.

Wednesday, June 11

I was woken up the next morning by two men and a woman who took a bit of blood for testing. The woman drew my blood while the men just watched. It was really weird and I wondered why she needed the escorts.

The test was taken because Dr Knoll wanted to make sure that my anxiety and depression weren't part of some other condition.

After breakfast, I went to bed listening to the music on my MP3 player. I stayed there until my nurse came to take my blood pressure. The nurse was worried because my pulse was 92. Apparently that meant it was fast, but it didn't worry me. I just fell back to sleep.

I woke up in a bad way. I had a nightmare that could just as well have been a memory. It reminded me so much of the past.

I felt suddenly tense and through the darkness, I saw an arm and a hand moving over my chest. I could have sworn that I felt it happen.

I tried to scream for help, but no sound came. I couldn't even open my mouth, but inside my head I was screaming desperately. It was useless though, because no one could hear the sounds that I couldn't make.

The moment I managed to wake up I went to get help to calm down, but the nurse didn't seem to understand what I meant when I said that I had a flashback. I explained that it's when we relive a traumatic event.

After talking with the nurse, I stood in my door frame again to make sure I wasn't alone and in a place where I could hurt myself. I started banging my head, but no one noticed.

My nurse asked me if I was feeling better.

"No."

The conversation was left at that.

I sat on the floor, but someone came and warned me that I wasn't allowed to do that. "It's a hospital," they would say. "The floors are full of germs."

I was disappointed that I was making an actual effort to not hurt myself and it didn't matter. What help could they offer me? None. They told me to come and talk, but the urge was still there. They offered me Lorazepam, but the urge was still there.

I approached the desks and asked my nurse if there was anything they could offer that could take away my need to hurt myself.

"You've waited long enough for your Lorazepam to kick in, so I can give you some Quetiapine," my nurse informed me.

I was given some anti-psychotics to slow my racing thoughts of self injury. Quetiapine was a drug usually prescribed for the symptoms of schizophrenia, but was sometimes given for depression and suicidal tendencies.

That was the first time that I had received any Quetiapine.

At least Shanny gave me a hug when I told her that I had a flashback. She knew what it was because she got them too.

The medication I was given worked really well. I didn't feel like crying or cutting anymore. I had found my miracle drug.

During nap time, I hadn't had time to fall asleep before Dr Stone paid me a visit. I heard a knock at the door and I groggily rose from under my sheets. By that time the anti-psychotics had made me so sleepy and I had a hard time understanding what was going on.

"How are you doing?" Dr Stone asked as he took a seat next to my bed. "You are looking better than the last time I came."

I told him about the visit with the psychologist and about the flashback.

Dr Stone then spoke about a lot of things, but I couldn't possibly say what they were because I understood none of them. I couldn't figure out what he was saying and my eyelids were weighing down on me.

"I'm really sorry," I apologized. "But I don't understand what you are saying. They gave me something to keep me from hurting myself and now I'm all confused."

"That's okay," my doctor told me. "I think you got the gist of it."

I really hadn't gotten the gist of it.

"Would you like me to come back?" Dr Stone asked.

I liked the idea of seeing another familiar face. "Yes," I answered.

Then he helped to cover me up with my blanket and I drifted to sleep.

When I woke up again, my mind was much clearer. I was tired, but I could think right.

I soon got a visit from Helen. She was Lisa's mother. Helen knew I was at the hospital because I passed by her place with Lisa when I was allowed two hours out.

I liked Helen. She was always kind and compassionate and wanting to know what she could do to help.

Helen was able to accompany me on my two hour leave. We got a few things done and even ate at a restaurant where we had submarine sandwiches. It was nice.

After I was accompanied upstairs, I hugged Helen goodbye.

Things were a bit more active after Helen left. Apparently I had to change rooms. I couldn't stay in room 861 anymore, but I wasn't told why. They put all my things on my bed and rolled it out the door and down the hall to room 856.

As they rolled my bed down the hall towards the more normal people rooms, I asked if this move meant that I was less crazy, or that the next person was more crazy.

I was told that I shouldn't talk like that. Then I wondered if I had been reprimanded because I had been insulting to myself or to the person who would be taking my place.

There were two beds in the new room, but nobody else was staying there. I wondered how long I would be alone.

I finally had a mirror in my room. I was happy about that.

Another good thing was that I was down the hall instead of right next to the office where everyone could keep a constant eye on me.

There must have been someone else in my old room. I guessed that they were being isolated, because the door was closed. My other theory was that the room was empty and they just thought it was time for me to move on.

I spent my time after that playing ping-pong and watching the television.

I showed my new friends some drawings that I had made in a sketch book. They were all very impressed.

Later Jed spoke with me and he seemed very sad. "I wanted to see the drawings too, but you didn't bring them to me."

"Oh," I said in realization that Jed felt left out. "I'll go get them for you."

I showed Jed the drawings and he seemed very interested. He especially liked the one of a couple dancing in the rain.

"Thank-you for showing them to me," Jed expressed his gratitude.

"You're welcome."

"I get jealous sometimes," Jed admitted. "I don't like when you talk to other guys. When we ate together today I wanted it to be just us. I got jealous when someone else joined us. I don't like competition."

I wasn't sure how to react to that. It was very intense and I didn't want to hurt his feelings.

Jed ended our conversation the way he usually did. He thanked me for honoring him by having a chat.

Shanny was being awful again that afternoon, but this time she was being angry at the male race in general. "Men are all jealous," she would say.

I got to talk with Shanny after. She didn't seem mad at me, but just with Joseph. She had such a low opinion of him when only days before she was lusting after him and saying how amazing he was. Her behavior reminded me of one of the questions Dr knoll had asked about seeing things in black and white. It was just like Shanny. She loved someone one moment and hated them the next.

Shanny couldn't wait to leave the hospital. She had been told that she might be able to go on Friday.

I played with my MP3 player cord and realized there was a black wire wrapped around it. If I rolled back the black plastic covering, the tiny and sharp tip of the wire came out. I thought about the damage that I could do with it.

"You can't have that," Shanny told me as she leaned forward to see the wire.

"It's mine." I defended my new tool.

"Give it to me," Shanny ordered.

"Nope."

"I'm going to tell the nurses that you have that," she threatened.

"You don't have to do that," I informed her. "I've had opportunities in the last few days to use some things like this, but I always gave them to the nurses. I have the wire, but it doesn't mean I'll use it."

Shanny accepted what I told her and left me with the wire.

I went to my room and sat on my bed with my journal. I set the wire down next to my book as I wrote.

I liked the idea that I could make things better if I had to. I liked to feel that I was in control.

I kept the wire and decided to hide it for the moment and figure out what to do with it the next day. I wrapped the wire around a loop in the top of my pants.

It was time for the night medication and I got in line as I was asked.

"Why do you have an arm warmer on both arms?" the nurse asked.

"Because they match," I told her. "They are a pair. They come together."

"Let me see under the sleeve," she ordered.

I immediately complied and rolled up the sleeve. "See? There's nothing."

I laughed nervously.

"Why are you laughing?" the nurse asked
"Because I'm not used to this," I explained.
"Used to what?"
"Having to show it."

Thursday, June 12

I didn't sleep very well on the night of Wednesday to thursday.

I was constantly waking up because my burns itched so much and the bandage was too thick for me to be able to scratch through it.

I was glad though that a nurse changed my bandages right after my shower that morning, so I didn't have to deal with it being soggy for so long.

At breakfast Roy had me make his toast because he couldn't on his own and the orderly wasn't around to help.

"You're my favorite," he told me as usual.

Jed wanted to eat with me, but there wasn't enough place at the table.

I was actually disappointed that Jed couldn't sit with me. Despite how intense a conversation with Jed would have been, it still would have been better than sitting between Joseph and Shanny as they fought bitterly. There was a sweet old lady that had the misfortune of sitting with us and had to quietly endure the hostility.

When I was asked for my opinion, I told Shanny that I wasn't taking sides.

Poor Naomi was looking sad as usual. She was an elderly lady with short white hair. I would often see her in the halls during visiting hours walking hand in hand with her husband. I had told Naomi how beautiful I thought it was when I saw them together. It was beautiful, but it was also sad because she was often crying as they walked.

I played a crossword puzzle board game after breakfast, but there were some words I found in my letters that I didn't have the courage to put on the board, like, cut and slit.

I got to play ping-pong with little old Roy afterwards. He was a terrible player, but he was determined and didn't seem to mind that he could rarely hit the ball even if I was passing it to him really slowly.

Roy thanked me about a dozen times for having made his toast that morning, and when I took a break to go walk, Roy came with me. Shortly after we started walking, Roy put his arm around my shoulder.

I called out, "Hello!" to the nurses in the hopes that they would tell Roy to respect my personal boundaries, but nobody said a thing.

John laughed when he saw me with Roy and he warned Joseph that there were other guys after me. That was the point where Joseph gave me a kiss on the cheek. It made me uncomfortable because although I liked Joseph as a friend, I didn't want him to think we had more than that.

Not long afterwards, I noticed that the nurses were gathering Roy's clothes. I thought that it was because he had only recently gotten his own wardrobe instead of the gown.

When I was standing in front of the elevators, Roy came up and said, "Kiss on the cheek," right before he leaned in to kiss me.

I was sorry that I turned my head and told him, "No," because I hadn't realized that he was trying to say goodbye.

I noticed that a lot of people had been leaving, and others had been coming in to take their place.

Roy was leaving. Jolene was gone to Ste-Marguerite's. Stacy had left the day before to stay with her sister. Joseph was given permission to leave that afternoon, and Shanny may have been leaving the next day.

I had been wrong about Saffron though. She was still there and staying in the room next to mine.

Shanny was upset that Joseph had left that day without saying goodbye. She didn't like that things finished on such bad terms. I wondered why she behaved the way she did if she was worried about how things would end.

Joseph did say goodbye to me though. He even told me that he would come and see me on Saturday. He said he wanted to be close like brother and sister forever. I still wasn't sure what to do about that. Dr Knoll had warned me twice that I should be careful with him. She made it sound so serious.

When Joseph left, I still had a ping-pong partner. I played with Parker, who I thought of as the new guy.

Parker asked me why I was there and I admitted that I had been hurting myself. That's when Parker told me that he had also done so once before, but never since. He even showed me the scar on his arm.

Parker couldn't understand how it was that I was hurting myself. "I can't believe that a girl like you could do that," he said as we were sending the ball back and forth.

I wondered what that meant exactly. A girl like me? Was that another reference to my appearance? That was the third time in a matter of days that I had been given a comment like that. Was a girl like me supposed to have it all? Should I have had it easy? Could no one have hurt me?

"All kinds of people are capable of anything," I told Parker in response to his insinuation.

My name was called on the loud speakers and we had to stop the game.

I was being called for another meeting with Dr Knoll.

Once I sat down in the chair of that familiar blue office, Dr Knoll opened my file and pulled out the poem that I had given to the nurse the night before. The poem was on the top of the pile.

"Your poem is very revealing," Dr Knoll told me.

"Is that bad?" I asked nervously. Had I done something wrong in writing that poem?

"No, it just lets us know how you feel," Dr Knoll explained. "You refer to yourself as a doll?"

"Yes," I confirmed. "My father used to call me, daddy's little dolly. The poem was inspired from that."

I wondered if she believed that I thought of myself as an actual doll. When that occurred to me I found the idea funny. If that was what she thought, it would only have made me sound more interesting.

When the subject of the poem was put to rest, Dr Knoll granted me another hour of leave per day. I always respected the time that I was allowed out and returned when I was supposed to, although I hadn't gone out at all that day.

My meeting with Dr Knoll was short, but that suited me fine because I found her presence uncomfortable.

I was in a relatively good mood, although I did have some interesting encounters with Jed.

I had been walking with Sally, a blond, older woman who had once worked as a ballerina.

When Sally and I had reached the part of the hallway that was near my door, we saw Jed sitting in one of the rocking chairs by the window at the end of the hall. Jed called out to me saying that he liked my arm warmers.

"Thank-you," I said with a smile. "I like them too. Having different colors makes for a nice variety."

Sally and I made one more tour around the halls and passed Jed once again who was still in the rocking chair. This time, Jed's attitude was very different.

"You're a horrible person Melissa!" Jed called out with anger in his tone. "You broke a promise."

I hadn't realized that I had made any promises. "What promise?" I asked with confusion.

Jed either didn't or wouldn't answer, so I just continued walking.

When I saw Jed again at supper, he seemed fine with me again. I offered him the coffee that came with my meal and he accepted. I was glad that things were okay again, but it made me nervous that I couldn't predict how Jed would behave with me. His attitude changed so fast.

I was also disappointed that I was given fish in my meal again. I had to clarify once more that I did not eat fish or any other meat. They knew I was a vegetarian, but they thought I ate fish. Fish was just as much of a corpse as any other animal and I wasn't going to put it in my mouth. I hoped that the kitchen would get my diet right for the next day.

I was feeling well, so that evening was rather uneventful. It was the second night that I would be spending in the 856. I was still alone in the room and hoped it would stay that way.

Friday, June 13

I hadn't slept well that night because my mouth was so dry from the new medication.

I found someone new to sit with for breakfast because some of my friends were gone, and others were still sleeping. I was shy about approaching new people and worried that they wouldn't want me to sit with them. My school years in the cafeteria taught me that I could be rejected by a lot of people.

Ashton was on staff that day and he joined me for a short chat while I was walking. I was glad to talk with someone I already knew.

"How are you doing?" Ashton asked as he fell into step with me.

"Not terrible," I answered.

"Ooh," Ashton cooed. "What does not terrible really mean?"

"That it could be and has been worse," I explained.

"So that means things are okay," Ashton deciphered.

"I'm just anxious. At first I couldn't wait to leave this place but now I'm not so sure," I admitted.

"Why is that?"

"Because I don't know what I'm going to do when I get out," I hinted.

"Do you know when you are getting released?"

"Maybe Monday," I said. "I'm supposed to meet with three people and then I will know for sure, but I'm worried about what I'm going to do when I get out."

"What do you think you are going to do?" Ashton asked.

"Fall into my old habits," I answered simply.

"Oh," he said. "You've made it a habit of hurting yourself."

"Yes," I confirmed. "I once managed to make it to 30 days without hurting myself, but when I started again it was worse than before I had stopped. I was cutting deeper and more often."

"Well, we are going to try and give you enough help so you don't fall back into that," Ashton reassured me. "I would much rather see you walking on the streets than to see you here."

I thought about being well again and walking down the street without fear or hurt. I thought about being someone who didn't hurt herself. I found myself very much wanting that kind of life.

I was glad to have been able to talk about what I was feeling and I thanked Ashton for the conversation. I noticed that I was talking really very quickly and I later asked my nurse to check and see if that was a side-effect of my new medication.

I was finding that there were less and less patients at the hospital that I actually knew and I felt awkward being alone.

Shanny was released before lunch that day. Her parents came to get her. I gave her a goodbye hug, and she was gone.

I did manage to meet one of the new patients. He was an older man with a bummed leg. He had been there two days, but our friendship didn't extend beyond one walk around the halls.

"Do you live far?" the man wanted to know.

"No, I live just a few blocks from here," I told him. "I came here by foot." I smiled. "Sorry, I don't usually talk so fast. I think it's because of my medication."

"It's fine," he reassured me. "I saw you talking with Ashton. He's a good nurse."

"Yeah," I agreed. "People aren't usually as tolerant as Ashton when it comes to the reason I'm here. They often think it's for attention."

"You're here for anxiety, aren't you?"

"I self injure," I told him as I raised my arm to show the wristband.

"Oh, you shouldn't do that," he told me.

"I know, but it's too late."

"You have to be good to yourself," he told me. "You're so young. You shouldn't do that. You have your whole life ahead of you. You're too young to do that."

"A lot of young people hurt themselves," I informed him. "I started hurting myself when I was about five."

"Five years old?" He was surprised. "What did your parents have to say about that?"

"They didn't say anything. They didn't know. No one did."

"Well, don't do that anymore. It's not okay to hurt yourself," he lectured.

"I know, but I get into this place in my head where I'm so desperate and I don't care about anything but making the pain go away. I get in this place where nothing else is important; consequences be damned."

"Yeah, I know," he understood. "I'm here for that too."

"You are?!" I was surprised.

"Yeah," he admitted.

"Ha!" I called out. "You and your *don't do that,* and you did it too!"

"I did. I shot myself."

"No way! You did not!" My eyes grew wide.

"It was after my separation with my wife."

"Does your family know that you did that?" I asked.

"Yes."

"Mine doesn't," I admitted. "They don't even know that I'm here."

"They don't?" It was his turn to be surprised. "Why wouldn't you tell them?"

"If I told them that I was here, I would have to tell them the reason why, and can you imagine me telling my mom that I do this?" I asked in reference to my wrist and my leg.

"Of course not," he agreed. "It would devastate her."

"And that's why I don't tell her."

"You still shouldn't do that," he reprimanded. "I did it, but I'm twice your age."

"Fifty?"

"Forty six. I could be your dad," he told me.

LADY INJURY

We walked a few times around the halls. "I'm leaving soon," he told me and then gently tapped my wrist. "Don't do that anymore."

"I'll try."

~ ~ ~ ~

My nurse was Charlotte that day. It was the second time that she was assigned to me.

Charlotte came to chat with me in my room, but our chat seemed more like a formal interview than a conversation. She asked me several questions about my situation and wrote it all down in a file right in front of me.

"There are much better ways to deal with your problems than to hurt yourself deliberately," Charlotte told me.

Her words felt more like a sermon. Did she think I didn't know that? Did she think I felt that cutting was a good idea? She clearly didn't understand the shame and the guilt I had felt for so long. She didn't understand the reasons behind the years of secrecy. I didn't think that cutting was a good thing. I didn't need her to tell me what I already knew just so she could write in her file that she had said the right thing.

"You are so pretty," Charlotte told me. "Why would you hurt yourself when you are so pretty?"

I was surprised at how many people were asking me that. Did I lose credibility because I had a pretty face? The insinuation continued to agitate me.

"Yeah, I'm pretty and making myself ugly," I remarked in reply.

"That's not what it's about," Charlotte told me.

It wasn't about making a pretty girl ugly. What did it mean though? Did it mean that I had everything it took to be happy? Should I spend my life thinking about how great I had it just based on what I looked like on the outside? Should my appearance have made all my problems go away?

I was facing a lot of opinions that I had never thought of before, but not all of them made any sense to me.

After nap time, I was allowed to leave the hospital for the first time on my own for three hours.

I asked for a bag so I could bring my laundry home and wash it. I was allowed to have a bag, but I wasn't allowed to go to my room alone with it, so Ashton accompanied me.

"Why can't I go alone with a bag?" I asked as we began our walk down the hall to my room.

"It's so you can't do this with it," Ashton said as he demonstrated putting an imaginary bag over his head, then twisting it around so that he chocked on it.

I laughed.

Once in my room, I gathered my clothes and asked Ashton a question that had been on my mind, but that I was afraid to ask. "Psst," I made a small noise to get his attention. "What if all I do is some scratches? What then? How long would I have to stay if it's only scratches?"

"The consequence isn't dependent on the degree of the injury," Ashton informed me. "Do you think that you can control your impulse to do that?"

"I hope so," I sighed.

Ashton had to leave then to give a bath to an annoying old lady. She was constantly asking if she was going to be put into isolation for not eating, or asking and asking about how much time was left before lunch.

I thought for a moment about how I was a bit like the annoying old lady. I was often asking if I could have my rubber band back, and about what the consequences would be if I hurt myself.

I made a mental note about the last question I asked; The consequence is not dependent on the degree of the injury.

I took my laundry and ventured out on my own. I was able to get lots of cleaning done at home. I cleaned out the animals cages and fixed up my place while running the laundry.

I was actually considering telling my brother Devon that I had been cutting. I had prepared this whole speech in my head. I felt that I was getting used to talking to people about my problem and having them see the things that I had done.

I thought that Devon might be at my place to eat and take a nap like he often did Thursday and Friday afternoons. Devon's car wasn't in the parking lot though, and he wasn't in my apartment. I was relieved that he wasn't there because I was terrified at the idea of telling him what had been going on.

I then felt that it wasn't a good idea to tell my family after all and that the secret should continue.

I returned to the hospital 45 minutes early because I really couldn't figure out what else to do with myself.

I was given fish for supper again. Maybe they were trying to starve me by giving me foods I couldn't eat. Even if I did eat fish, I would be so sick of eating it by then because that's all they seemed to send me. I complained about my menu, but I wasn't going to hold my breath that they would get it right on the next day.

Jed was mad at me, though I still couldn't understand why. He had mentioned something about a promise again. He was convinced I had broken a promise.

While I was eating whatever was on my plate that wasn't fish, Jed got up, looked at me and said, "There always has to be at least one girl who won't leave me be!"

I didn't reply. I didn't really have time to say anything though. Jed had made a dramatic exit at the same time as his dramatic statement.

Everyone in the cafeteria had heard, but no one said anything about it. We all just kind of looked at each other and turned back to our meals. We had become accustomed to hearing Jed throw fits. Jed would throw his arms in the air to make himself bigger and more intimidating and he would call out to everyone about how he was the boss. The problem with Jed's statement was that he was the only one who believed it.

After supper I walked over to the other end of the hospital and started beating my wrist against the windowsill. I stopped hurting myself when I heard someone coming. It was John. I decided to leave the window and walk with him. I was glad to have someone to distract me.

Apparently, John had been at the hospital for three weeks. He said that he usually stayed for three months when he was admitted. I didn't see how someone could manage to stay there for so long. I wondered what John was in the hospital for, but I never asked.

John showed me a poem that he wrote and I showed him one of mine. He was a good writer. He showed a lot of emotion.

John didn't walk with me long, but then again, nobody did. I seemed to like walking more than the others and they would usually only join me for a few minutes. I loved walking though. I had always loved walking. It was just too bad that I had to do it for so long in just one place. I was walking around and around the same halls with the same chipped paint.

When John left, Jed came to join me, but this time he was nice again.

"Are you mad at me?" Jed asked with a worried tone and expression.

"I'm not mad," I told him. "I understand that you are human and can lose your cool sometimes."

That's when Jed started confiding in me. He mentioned the girl he was in love with when he was 14. "I can't think of Valerie when I look at you because it messes me up. You're pretty. I can tell you that. You're really pretty."

I had been hearing that a lot since I got to the hospital.

For someone that worked so hard to be intimidating, Jed was actually very raw and hurting. He expressed a lot of sentimental emotion and thoughts.

"I really liked your drawing of a cat," Jed told me. "It reminded me of a cat that I used to have."

I wondered how a black and white drawing of a cartoon cat could remind him of anything. Jed seemed to live a lot in the past.

I was glad that Jed was being nice to me again. I realized though that his attitude could change in the blink of an eye.

Jed thanked me for honoring him with a conversation, then he took a small bow and walked away.

It was hard to know what to expect in that place.

I was still very anxious after having talked with Jed and John; probably even more so. I started banging my wrist on the corners of walls as I walked. Nobody walked around the hall like I did, so I wasn't concerned with being caught. I didn't want to continue that way though, so I went to talk with my nurse.

I waited at the desks until I was noticed.

"Yes?" Michelle asked

"I'm crazy," I stated.

"You're crazy?"

"Yes," I confirmed. "I've been beating my wrist against corners and windowsills. I'm supposed to tell when I get this way."

"Okay."

So Michelle went to get me some Quetiapine and told me that it should start working after half an hour.

"I'll come and see you later," Michelle told me.

I went to sit in a rocking chair by the window at the end of the hallway. I was looking at the new bruises forming on the back of my hand. I wondered how many colors there would be.

I went from thinking of bruises to thinking of the wire I had wrapped around the loop in my pants. I untwisted the wire and pushed the little metal end into the bruise on the back of my hand. I stopped myself from breaking my skin in such an obvious place and I got up to go sit on my bed behind the curtain. I pulled off my right sock and used the wire to scratch my foot at least a hundred times. What started as little white lines turned into red ones, but none of them bled.

When I heard someone knock at my door, I quickly pulled up my sock and acted as if I had just been sitting there. The wire was small and hid easily in my hand.

"Are you feeling any better?" Michelle asked as she pulled the chair that was at the end of my bed a little closer to me and sat down.

"Not really," I admitted.

"What kinds of things are making you anxious?" she asked.

"A few things," I said. "Like that I seriously considered telling my older brother about my cutting. I didn't tell him, but I'm glad I didn't. I don't think I could deal with him knowing and I'm so scared about how my family would react."

"Do you think it would be good to have your family supporting you?" Michelle asked.

"I've been doing fine on my own," I told her. "I don't need to bother them with this. That's not all that's been bothering me though. Jed has been making me really nervous. He's very angry and jealous. Other than that, I'm just anxious for no reason. I'm often anxious without knowing why."

We talked about how I could manage my anxiety, then we talked about how I was allowed to leave the hospital for 3 hours.

"Did you earn your trust well?" Michelle asked. "Did you hurt yourself?"

"I was very good and I didn't hurt myself when I was out," I told her.

"What about when you were here?" Michelle asked when she detected how specific I was about where I hadn't hurt myself.

"Um, well," I began. "I didn't do that either."

"Well, with the way you say that I'm not sure if I can believe you."

I knew she wouldn't believe me. I hated lies.

I showed Michelle the bruise on my hand, but I didn't admit to scratching my foot. If she had asked if I had done something other than the bruise, I would have admitted it, but she didn't ask, so I didn't say.

"I'm not proud of the things I do," I admitted. "But I don't know how to stop. It's so addicting. It's all I can think about."

"Do you think that your case should be treated like that of a drug addict?" my nurse asked. "You would have to stop everything right away."

"That would be really hard, but I like the idea," I told her.

When Michelle left, I put the wire away and didn't look at it again that night.

I had a surprise visitor though.

"Hey! Melissa," I heard the whisper of a familiar voice come from my doorway.

I got up and went to see and it was Joseph. He was wearing a hospital gown, but I didn't understand why because he had been released the day before.

"I wanted to say hi," he told me then left before I had a chance to ask what was going on.

I left my room not long afterwards and did a tour around the halls. I found Joseph sitting in the doorway of isolation room 807. When he saw me, Joseph got up and stepped into the hall, he smiled, and put his arms out.

I was then thinking about how the dork wasn't supposed to be in the halls if he was in isolation.

I walked up to him and he hugged me.

"Hey!" I reproached. "Aren't you going to get in trouble for being out of your room?"

"Oh, that's true," Joseph said as he stepped back in.

"What did you do to get back in here?" I asked with urgent curiosity because I didn't know when the nurses would catch us talking.

"I took speed," he admitted.

"Oh!" I yelled at him. "I should hit you for that!"

That's when Joseph's doctor came to see him and I had to go.

Our conversation ended there, but so did the evening because the medication was making me really sleepy and I had to roll into bed. I felt like a zombie.

Saturday, June 14

I went to get my things for my shower on Saturday morning and the nurse asked me why I was wearing my arm warmers.

"To hide what's underneath," I answered.

"But I need to see under them so we know if you have done any mutilations," the nurse told me. "You need to take them off."

"All you have to do is ask and I will show underneath," I told her. "That's what the other nurses did."

"I still need you to take them off," she insisted.

"No, please," I begged. "It's embarrassing for people to see."

"It's none of their business," the nurse said with an irritated tone. She acted as though she was reasoning with an obstinate child.

"Maybe not, but I still wont feel right," I argued. "Please, please don't take them. All you have to do is ask and I will show you when the other patients aren't looking."

"You could at least take it off at night during my shift," she suggested.

"Okay." I was so relieved. I had been so scared. I didn't know how I could possibly have dealt with having everyone see that I was hiding bandages under my arm warmers. "I can do that. I would be alone in my room and that's okay."

"Okay," she agreed. "So at night you bring the arm warmers here and you can come get them in the morning."

I was grateful to have gotten away with as much as I did, but I started worrying a lot about whether they would take my warmers away during the day.

Breakfast wasn't ready and most of the others weren't up yet, so I used the time to write in my journal about the day before.

When the shift changed at 8:00 am, my nurse came in to talk to me.

"We've discussed it as a group for the last few days and we are going to have to take your arm warmers," Charlotte informed me.

Fear grabbed me by the throat and pinned me against the wall. "I need them!" I tried to defend my hiding places. "I can't have everyone seeing what I've done."

"The fact that you were allowed to wear them in the first place was a mistake," she told me.

I wasn't the type to be defiant. I took my arm warmers off and collected all the other ones that I had in my drawer. I let Charlotte take them and put them in a small brown paper bag.

"Do you understand why we need to take them?" Charlotte asked.

I could have cried. "Yes, but that doesn't make it any less awful."

Charlotte said nothing more and she left, leaving me standing alone and terrified. I looked at one bandaged wrist and another bruised one. To say that I was scared would be an understatement. I was feeling ashamed, humiliated and exposed. I didn't want to leave my room. I couldn't believe this was happening.

I started banging my knuckles together to create pain, then I tried breathing deeply to calm down. Just having to look at what I had done was making me want to self injure. I couldn't see the burns. I saw only the bandages, but just knowing why they were there made it shameful. I didn't just have to hide my wounds from everyone else, I had to hide them from myself as well.

It was summer, but I put a sweater on and promised myself that I would get more clothes with sleeves the next time I went home.

I laid on my bed for a long time. I was feeling so completely sad and out of control. I was an adult and had been making my own decisions for so long, and now I was being ordered around like a child.

My anxiety began to calm, but my depression rose.

I barely even cared when I got a roommate to fill the extra bed beside me. My roommates name was Zelda. She was the patient that got my old room when I cleared out of it. Zelda had had a guard too for a few days. She was at the hospital on a 21 day hold for trying to kill herself. It was court ordered, and even though she applied against the order, her request was denied.

Eventually I motivated myself to get up and walk around. I felt safe from judgement because I had my sweater, but the extra layer made me very hot.

Jed saw me and jumped at the opportunity to come join me. I wasn't in the mood for a conversation, especially with Jed.

"Are you sure that you aren't mad at me for being such a jerk yesterday?" Jed asked as he joined me.

"I'm not mad Jed. It made me nervous, but that's all," I told him. I didn't want to hurt his feelings by saying just how much it had bothered me.

"I really like the way you dress. You have good taste," Jed told me as he looked me over. "I get jealous sometimes."

"I'm not with anyone here," I told him. I wasn't with anybody, including Jed. I didn't understand all the jealousy.

"Yeah, I realized that," Jed admitted. "How are you today?"

"I'm freaking out," I confessed. "The nurses took my arm warmers and it's really making me anxious and depressed. So now I am wearing jackets and sweaters. I hope they don't take those from me as well."

"I like talking with you," Jed told me.

Jed was being sweet, but he still had a menacing presence about him. Jed bowed out and left me to walk on my own.

I noticed that Saffron was in an isolation room. She was in the 862. It was right next to my old room. I guessed the isolation meant that Saffron hadn't been eating. Saffron was on the ward because of her anorexia.

I thought back to the day that Saffron snapped at me for asking her how long she had been there. Maybe she was just embarrassed about her eating disorder and didn't want people to get to know her and find out.

My nurse found me and asked me to go lie down on my bed so she could take my blood pressure. She arrived a few minutes later with her blood pressure monitor on wheels.

"How are you doing with your anxiety this morning?" she asked. "Do you intend to hurt yourself?"

"I had the desire," I admitted.

"But you controlled it?"

"Yes, because I'm at the hospital."

"But if you weren't at the hospital, you would have done it?" she asked.

"Yes."

"So you don't see any improvement since you got here?"

"No."

Being at the hospital didn't make me want to hurt myself less, but at least I didn't do it like I would have if I had been at home. It was a protection for me.

The hospital wasn't much of a place to live, but it had started feeling like a safety net. I still hurt myself when I was there, but the degree of the injury's were far less severe.

I may have been surrounded by strange people, but I was one of them. I had mental health problems and so did they. No matter what our problems were, we were all in the same place. We were all in it together, and we all knew what keeping that secret or facing judgement was all about.

My entire life I had heard and even made jokes about the crazy people on the eighth floor. If a friend was acting silly I would tell them that they belonged on the eighth. I had never been to the eighth though. I didn't know the people there and what they faced. I didn't understand that these people, were just people. They weren't crazy, they were sick or depressed. All of us on the ward, we were really just people who were raw and open, but we didn't bleed any more than anyone else could have.

Jed was certainly not the kind of person I was used to. I didn't see him as crazy though, but just confused.

Jed sat down and ate with me at lunch. I gave him my coffee. At that point his attitude towards me was positive and we had a nice conversation. I never knew when his mood would change, but at least by then, I had seen what kinds of moods that I could expect.

I went out on my own after lunch. I was pleased that I got to leave right after my meal because then I got to miss nap time. Unless I was tired, I found nap time long and boring.

I did as I usually did. I cleaned things up and fed the animals. I riffled through my closet to find some long sleeved shirts that wouldn't be so hot. I checked my phone messages and found one from my sister. She wanted to know if I was going to be going to her place that weekend the way I usually did.

I called Marie. "Hey, do you think you can take some bad news?"

Marie could tell by my tone that what I had to say was serious. "Yes, I'm going out to play sports with some friends so I won't be alone if I freak out."

I took a deep breath and prepared myself for what I would say. "I've been at the hospital all week. I'm there because I have serious problems with anxiety and they are changing my medication. I've been on some anti-anxiety meds for quite a while now, but I didn't tell you because it relates to other things that I'm not ready to talk about. Maybe some day we can talk about it."

There was a knock at my door.

"I have to go," I told Marie and we hung up.

I answered the door and found Shy-Anne standing there. I was really glad to see her. She had tried to find me at the hospital, but I wasn't there, so she came to my place.

Shy-Anne and I barely had time to start a conversation before the phone rang.

It was Marie.

"Have you been hurting yourself?" Marie asked.

My heart fell to the floor. I panicked and wondered how I could word things so that I wasn't lying but also not telling the truth. I didn't want her to know because it would shame me. I also couldn't let her know because she would worry. I was determined to fix things so that Marie didn't know.

"Excuse me?" I tried to sound like I didn't know what she was talking about. "Where did you get that idea? Does it seem like I do?"

"No," Marie said. "But a lot of people who have anxiety disorders hurt themselves."

I couldn't get out of that conversation without lying. I felt trapped. Trapped and afraid. "And what if the answer was yes?" I asked. "How would you deal with that? Would you be okay?"

"Well I'm fine right now, but soon I'll be playing outside," Marie told me. "I'll be able to kick the ball around to get some bad energy out."

At that point I was pretty much busted. I never wanted to have to tell her this over the phone. I never wanted to have to tell her this at all.

"Yes," I confessed. "I hurt myself. I cut myself. I scratch myself. I bruise myself and now I even burn myself," I paused. "How are you? Are you okay?"

"Yeah," she said. "You know how I am. Things never sink in right away. I usually freak out hours later."

"Okay." I tried thinking of what would help Marie if things did go bad. "If you freak out you can call me or go to Lee's place, okay?"

"Yeah," Marie agreed. "I love you."

"I love you too." Our voices were full of emotion.

We hung up and I let Shy-Anne know what had just happened and about how scared I was. I hadn't wanted that. It felt terrible.

A thought suddenly occurred to me and I picked up the phone and called Marie right away. "Marie, are you hurting yourself?" I asked.

"No."

"Then what made you think to ask me that?"

"Because we have a lot of that stuff in our family," Marie explained. "Before I called you back, I had this flash of a memory of a time that you were talking to Lisa on the phone. It sounded like you didn't just sympathize with her, but that you understood her as well."

"Oh yeah." I thought about what Marie said. "Yes, we do understand each other. Lisa and I have a lot in common."

Our conversation was left at that and my attention was turned back to my visiting friend.

It was good that Shy-Anne was there so I could talk about things with her.

Before she left, we shared a long hug and I cried in her arms. Being close to someone I loved made the hurt more intense for some reason.

When Shy-Anne was gone, I left a message on Marie's phone saying that if she wanted to talk to someone about what I told her, she could talk to our youngest brother Andrew, because he already knew and had known for months. I also told her what the hospitals visiting hours were.

I returned to the hospital after an hour and a half. I was planning on taking my 3 hours out in two parts. I wanted to leave again for supper time, but when I asked about it, I was told that I had to use my 3 hours all at once. If I wanted to split my time in two, I would have to have it prescribed by my doctor.

So I had to stay at the hospital, but I didn't use my time well. I hid in my room and used my little wire to scratch my foot about a hundred times again.

I wasn't satisfied with the damage I had done though. I needed it to bleed and to feel the pain as the blade sunk in.

Thankfully I had been given some medication and that made me really tired. My thoughts slowed and I didn't care about wires or bleeding anymore.

It was the end of the afternoon and I used whatever energy I had to go to the phone booth by the office and call Marie.

"Are you okay?" I asked with sincere concern.

"I'm okay at the moment," Marie told me. "But when I called Andrew to tell him you were in the hospital, I broke down crying. Andrew tried consoling me for a bit, but he had to go, so we didn't talk long."

"I'm glad you got to talk to him," I said. "I'm sorry. I didn't want to worry you with this."

"I wish you had told me sooner," Marie said.

"I wasn't ready to tell you," I told her. "This is about me and my own issues. I had to go at my own pace."

I had a major anxiety attack after talking to Marie. It was hard to breathe and I got dizzy. My heart was racing and my chest hurt. I didn't like the reality I was living in. I couldn't stand knowing what Marie knew about me.

I needed the hospital, but it was terrible. I wasn't even my own person there. If I didn't want to do something that they asked of me, they could make me. I was told what to do and where to do it. People I had never met would ask me what I was thinking and why I was thinking it.

It was a lot to handle, and I panicked.

I was given medication to calm down.

I realize now as I look back that medication seemed to be the immediate answer to everything. However I also recognize that without the medicine, I would have dealt with my problems in a much worse way. If I had to chose between hurting myself and taking a little pill, I would take the pill.

Lisa's mother Helen came to see me that night. We got comfortable by sitting in the rocking chairs at the end of the hall.

Jed came up to us and started chatting with me. It was obvious that he was only looking and speaking to me, and ignoring Helen.

I often don't understand most of what Jed tells me, but today I got a sense of what he meant.

"Some people worship useless things," he preached. "Some people have a steak as their god, but my god is the almighty."

Both Helen and I quietly listened to Jed's sermon. When Jed was done, he leaned over and got really close to Helen's face. He spoke very seriously and intensely. "Do you see the color of my eyes?"

And then Jed left. Another dramatic exit to a dramatic moment of deliberate intimidation.

It had been an uncomfortable closeness for Helen.

At first I thought that was just Jed's way, but later I understood what happened.

Jed caught up to me in the halls after Helen left.

"I'm sorry about your friend," Jed apologized. "I did that because I didn't want for her to take away the place I have in your life."

I always felt uncomfortable when Jed talked like that. "I have place for a lot of people in my life," I told him.

"I'm never going to forget you," Jed told me. "Do you think that you will forget me?"

"I won't. I promise," I told him. "I even write everything that goes on into my journal. I wrote about how I met you and even wrote down some of the conversations that we had."

"Really?" Jed looked surprised and then proud. "And do you find our conversations interesting?"

"Of course," I reassured him. "If I didn't find them interesting, I wouldn't have written them down."

"Well thank you for granting me a place in your book," Jed said before he bowed out and walked towards the smoke room.

Sunday, June 15

Nightmares shook me from sleep many times in the night. I dreamt of someone attacking me over and over. I was having that dream when the night nurse came in with a flashlight. I gasped loudly and put my hand over my chest. The nurse came over to me as I breathed deeply and asked me if I wanted some lorazepam.

Medication got passed out a lot at the hospital and I appreciated it. "Yes," I accepted.

Once I was calm, I was able to sleep through the night.

Once I was up I had all kinds of exciting activities that morning. I got new bandages and an elderly lady asked me to clip her toe nails. It was mildly gross, but I liked feeling useful. Notice my sarcasm over the exciting activities.

After lunch I played a board game with Parker.

Parker talked about being right where I was just a few years before. He was in the hospital for hurting himself while his family didn't know. He showed me the scars on his wrist. There were three lines.

"I'm afraid to tell my family," I confided.

Parker understood. "Tell them when it's over."

I thought that made sense. If my problem was over when they found out there would be less worry, but when would it be over?

I had a visitor. Marie had come to see me as soon as visiting hours started at 2:00 in the afternoon. At first Marie joined Parker and I on the board game, but after that the two of us went to my room to chat.

"I've been thinking a lot about certain things that make more sense now that I know you've been hurting yourself," Marie said. "I thought of things like how you wouldn't cry when you were hit as a kid."

"Yeah," I agreed while thinking back. "I used to practice pain so I could put up with that."

It worked too. I didn't want to tell Marie that I felt my goal was successful by using pain. I didn't want to give the impression that I thought self injury was a good thing. I recognized the helpful things that cutting had done for me, but I got those things in a very wrong way.

"I slept at Lee's last night," Marie told me. "I knew that I was going to have an emotional meltdown so I didn't want to be alone."

"And what happened?" I asked anxiously. "Were you okay?"

"Well," Marie began. "My meltdown came this morning. I was crying so much and Lee was trying to console me but she didn't know what was going on."

I felt guilty for causing Marie pain. I never wanted to cause anyone any pain.

The visit was going okay. I felt badly, but I wasn't freaking out.

I took Marie for a walk around the halls of the hospital the way I had done countless times on my own.

I got to introduce Marie to Jed. I was relieved that Jed was polite and didn't make a scene in front of Marie.

I had figured out at that point about how things worked with Jed. If I was alone, he was okay. If I was with anyone else, he was jealous. If I was with someone else when Jed showed up, I had to give my full attention to him until he left.

It was ridiculous but at least I knew what I was dealing with.

Jed had a question before he left. "Would you invite me to eat with you?"

"Of course," I answered. "As long as there is room."

"If there are other people I will be jealous," Jed warned and then left.

I didn't really want to eat with Jed. He was getting too intense, but I didn't want to be mean or offend him by asking him to cool off.

I had a good visit with Marie. She was able to stay for over two and a half hours. We hadn't gotten all teary eyed and I was able to explain things a little better to her.

Marie left not long before supper time. We hugged goodbye and she disappeared behind the elevator door.

I sat down with Jed for supper and he told me a few times, "You are giving me a nice surprise."

It was certainly complimentary, but the degree of attention Jed gave me made me very uncomfortable. I had such a problem with setting boundaries and saying, "No."

After supper I spent the evening playing board games with several people, but none of us actually enjoyed it. The game was drawn on too long and Parker kept leaving and coming back so he could smoke.

I did like the fact that Jolene was playing with us. She had returned to the hospital after a short stay at Ste-Marguerite's, though I never found out why.

Everyone finally admitted how much they really didn't want to be playing and we ended the game.

It was after that game that Parker asked me a question that I didn't want to answer.

"Do you have a phone number?" Parker asked.

"Yes."

"Can I have it?"

"Sure."

Sure?! How could I have said, "Sure?" I knew that he didn't want the number so we could just be friends. I could tell from the way he looked at me that he wanted more.

The problem was that I didn't want to get involved with a guy from the hospital. I actually liked Parker in that way a little, but I knew the kind of problems that he came with and I had enough of my own. I had enough trouble trying to stay afloat with just my own baggage. I couldn't trust just anyone.

"Okay," Parker said. "I'll call you."

I was mad at myself. Why couldn't I just say no when I wanted to say no? It was ridiculous. I was making my life so much more complicated than it needed to be. I was also giving false promises to a guy who just wanted my number.

My problem was that I was terrified of hurting someones feelings in any way. If I had to go out of my way to save someone else's happiness, I would.

I had no courage. Couldn't I at least have specified that it was on the condition that we would just be friends? I barely even knew this guy. He could have been a psycho for all I knew.

Why couldn't I find a normal guy? Why was I so popular with the guys in the psych ward? I wanted someone, but not just anyone.

I hadn't actually given my number at that point, it was just arranged that I would.

I left the cafeteria while kicking myself for messing up and being a coward.

I wasn't alone for long because before I had the chance to get into my room, Jed started talking to me. He was sitting on the floor next to the bathroom while waiting for his turn to take a shower.

"Melissa, Melissa, Melissa," Jed repeated.

"Jed, Jed, Jed," I said in imitation.

Jed had a lot to say. He had more to say than could be understood, at least by me. Jed had a lot of complex theories about the universe. I would try to be polite and agree with what he was saying, but I couldn't understand what it was. He talked about how there were two steps in life, sex and enlightenment.

"I reached enlightenment by the age of 40," Jed informed me. "Now it's not time for me to obey others, it's time for them to obey me. I'm the boss."

"That must be a difficult responsibility," I observed.

Jed shook his head in agreement. "You need to protect yourself."

"Why?"

"People could hurt you and you need to stay safe," Jed explained.

"Okay," I said. "Thanks for the warning."

Jed leaned close to me and spoke with sadness and not intimidation, "Look into my eyes and see the emptiness."

"I'm sorry you are in pain," I told him. "I hope things get better for you."

"You deserve to be cradled by angels," Jed told me.

"Um," I hesitated. "Thank-you."

"Thank you for talking to me," Jed appreciated as he got up and went in for his turn at the shower.

I disappeared into my room after that and pulled out my wire so I could scratch my foot some more. I had only started to do some damage when my roommates nurse came in to see her and I had to quickly hide what I was doing.

I had seen him before. I remembered that he had been my nurse on my first night on the ward. He seemed nice, but I didn't really know.

I twisted my wire back around the loop on my pants. I wanted to make sure it stayed with me and that it wouldn't be found if they searched my things.

I then went to the desks to ask my nurse Michelle for some pain killers.

Michelle gave me the medication, then offered, "Do you need to talk? Headaches are often related to stress."

"Yes, I'll talk." I was comfortable with talking to Michelle because I already knew her and we had talked before.

We walked back and forth down the same hallway while I talked about all the things that were on my mind.

"I had this weird therapy the other day where I had to remember some really awful things from my past while following the ladies finger," I explained.

"Oh, EMDR," Michelle recognized my definition.

"Yeah," I agreed. "I think that's what she called it. It's awful. I've been having resurfacing memories and nightmares ever since."

"Despite all the bad things like anxiety and flashbacks, I think EMDR is a really good thing," Michelle told me. "It helps people a lot to be able to detach negative emotion and leave it behind."

I started feeling a little less down about my therapy and a little more hopeful.

I told Michelle about the way Jed had been behaving with me and how anxious it made me.

"Would you like me to talk to Jed for you?" Michelle offered.

"No," I declined. "Hopefully I wont be here that much longer anyways, and I don't want to make the situation worse, like having Jed get really mad at me."

I felt better after talking to Michelle and was able to go to sleep.

Monday, June 16

Jed wasn't talking to me on Monday morning. I considered that maybe I was being ignored again.

Joseph was still in isolation and still in a gown.

When I walked by, he would say, "Hello my little sister. I love you my little sister."

I wasn't sure how I should respond without being rude. I didn't love Joseph, I barely knew him. All I knew was that he was a nice guy who abused drugs and played ping-pong.

"Be careful," I warned him. "You're going to get yourself in trouble for talking."

The next time I walked passed Joseph's isolation room, he spoke to me again despite my warning. "I Just saw Dr Shire, he says that if it were up to him I would be able to leave the hospital right away. I just have to wait to see the psychiatrist to get permission to leave." Joseph was very exited.

"That's great." I was happy for him. "How come you are in isolation? Do they do that every time you take speed?"

"No," he corrected. "When I was in the emergency room I wouldn't stop singing really loud so they had to sedate me. They put a needle in my butt." Joseph laughed.

"No way!" I exclaimed with a raised brow and an amused smile, then walked away.

I played ping-pong for a short while, but I was interrupted by the psychologist.

"Would you come to my office?" Mabel invited me.

I chose a random chair in the office and Mabel sat across from me as she had done the time before.

We talked about what kinds of things I'd like to do and about the people in my life. I had a lot of friends, but Mabel noticed that I had no man in my life.

"That must be hard," Mabel sympathized.

"Yeah," I agreed. "But I don't want to end up with just anyone. My mom ended up with an alcoholic and I know I can't do that too. I'm careful."

After discussing my personal life, we did another session of EMDR. I had to vividly imagine events from my past. I didn't like it. It made me want to hurt myself. I wanted to stop, but I never said so.

After an hour, the session was over, but the memories followed me out of that room.

I tried to purge the memories from my mind by scratching my foot with my secret wire. When my roommate came in I had to stop, so I got up and went for a walk.

I passed a group of 3 young people that seemed like they worked there, but looked out of place. I assumed they were interns.

There was also a middle aged woman. She was pretty with long, dark, curly hair. I had never seen her before.

"Miss Soyer?" the dark haired woman spoke someone else's name, but she was looking in my direction.

I took a look beside and behind myself to see if there was a Miss Soyer that she was referring to, but there was no one. I was confused.

"Melissa Soyer?" she specified.

"No, Melissa Water," I corrected.

"Oh, I made a mistake with your name," she explained apologetically.

"That's okay."

"Would you mind if the interns did your evaluation for this afternoon?" the woman asked. "One of them would ask the questions while the others watch. I'll be the one to finish the evaluation."

The idea of having my evaluation done by 4 people was highly unwanted. I was very shy and talking to one person at a time was more than enough. I had my age old problem with not being able to say no.

"That would be fine," I accepted but didn't want to.

"Dr Knoll will be the one to see you on Wednesday," the woman informed me.

The word Wednesday caught my attention. "So I'm still going to be here on Wednesday?"

"I don't know. That depends on your doctor," the woman answered then walked away with her interns.

How was I going to find the courage to talk about my self injury with four different people listening?

While playing a board game, I told Parker about my upcoming evaluation and how I felt about it.

"All you have to do is say that you want yours done with only one person," Parker reasoned.

Of course he would see it as that easy. I, on the other hand, saw saying what I really wanted as an insurmountable obstacle.

Our board game was interrupted by a meeting with Dr Knoll. During our meeting, I was informed that I would be able to spend the night at my apartment and come back on the next day. It was a test to see how I would handle the stress of being on the outside. If I was all out of sorts when I returned, they would know that I needed to stay longer.

One meeting was followed by another. When I was done seeing Dr Knoll, the woman with the interns came to get me.

I sat across a desk to one of the young interns. If she told me her name, I don't remember what it was. To the right of me were the three others sitting on chairs against the wall.

"Pretend we aren't here," the older woman instructed. I found out later that she was a psychiatrist. I hadn't been told as much beforehand.

The intern started asking me questions. She seemed nervous. "Are you allowed to leave here by your own choice?" she asked.

"I don't know," I wondered and then turned to the psychiatrist. "Am I?" I was then reminded that I was supposed to ignore them.

I wasn't sure of the answer to that question. Could I leave when I wanted? The way things were being handled it certainly didn't seem that way. I had thought I would be able to leave after two days, but it seemed like Dr Knoll was calling the shots.

I wasn't given an answer to that question. The young intern proceeded to interview me on my situation. She asked about my past and my present.

Most of her questions seemed very familiar. They were the same questions that Dr Knoll had asked me when we first met.

"Do you hear voices?" she asked.

"No.'

"Do you see things that others don't see?"

"No."

"Do you think that people are out to get you?"

"No."

"Do you see yourself as more special than others?"

"No."

"Do you have anyone that you've been friends with for many years?"

"Yes," I said. "Several."

"Do you see things in black and white? Do you think that your friends are great one day and then terrible the next?"

"No."

"Do you have times when you're overly exited and making plans?"

"I do make plans, but I wouldn't call it overly exited," I told her.

I wondered why they bothered to ask me the same questions twice. Didn't they have access to my file?

"Have you hurt yourself since you got here?" the young woman asked.

"That depends on the consequence," I answered with an awkward smile, the same way as I had with the nurse a few days before. We looked at each other in silence for a moment and then I admitted to scratching my foot.

I saw from the corner of my eye that the Psychiatrist was writing something down, then she said, "Why didn't you tell anyone? That's what you are here for."

I wasn't sure what to say. I realized that she was saying that I had done wrong by keeping silent. I knew it was wrong, but I had been afraid to tell.

At the end it was the psychiatrist who finished the interview. Her name turned out to be Dr Fellows. Her questions didn't seem new to me either. The whole interview seemed like a long repeat of the one with Dr Knoll. What I later understood was that the point of the interview was to give the intern some practice.

I was relieved when I was allowed to leave and go back to whatever I was doing. I was really anxious afterwards though, but not as much as I was about to be.

I saw Jed and realized that he still hadn't been talking to me. I wondered if he was okay. "Are you okay Jed? I haven't heard you say anything."

Jed got mad. "Aren't I allowed to stay quiet?"

I didn't like being yelled at, but I answered, "Yes, you are completely allowed."

Not long afterwards, Jed passed me by in the hall and spoke to me angrily. "I have nothing to say to you. Take your side and I'll take mine."

The only thing I could think to say was, "Okay." Then I turned to Naomi and her husband who were walking by, hand in hand. "It's okay," I told them. "He's just like that."

Jed didn't hurt me, but his violent presence still got to me.

I was then called on the loud speakers to take a phone call so I opened the door to the booth and picked up the receiver. It was Marie on the line.

"Hey. How are you?" I asked her.

"Not so good," she admitted. "I had to come home early from school. They sent me home because I couldn't concentrate. I was really anxious and the teacher noticed."

"Is that my fault?" I asked with a guilty conscience.

"Sort of," she answered. "I've been doing lots of research on the internet and finding out about ways that you can use to distract from your cutting. Would going to LaRonde help?"

LaRonde was a theme park in Montreal.

The simplicity of the idea made me laugh. "No, but it would be fun to go."

"I was thinking of that because it says you can be looking for heightened sensations," she explained.

"That's a nice idea," I told her, but I didn't see a roller coaster ride taking away my anxiety.

"There were other suggestions," Marie informed me. "You can use red food coloring to imitate blood instead of actually bleeding. You can melt an ice cube in your hand to create a safer pain, or snap a rubber band on your wrist."

"It's really sweet that you want to help, but I've been dealing with this a long time and I've already heard and read about the things you are talking about," I told her. "I know that it's new for you, but I already know these things."

"It's just that I feel helpless," Marie admitted.

I paused and thought about what she said. "Marie, I own this. This is my fault. I did this. You don't have to carry this burden."

"I know," she said. "This is just how I feel. I need to do something so I don't feel helpless."

I wished I could take things back so Marie didn't know. I wished I could make things better.

"I've got to go Marie," I told her. "I get to spend the night at home tonight and I'm supposed to get my things together."

"I'll come to meet you at your place tomorrow then," Marie informed me. "I saw the school counselor and she thinks it would be a good idea if we spent the day together. I got the day off of school for it."

We said goodbye. When I got out of the phone booth and looked across to the other side of the desks and into isolation room 861, I saw Jed standing inside it while wearing a hospital gown. I smiled to myself while thinking that it served him right.

I went home after supper, but first made a trip to the grocery store. It had made me really nervous to go to a public place after being in at the hospital for a while.

I had thought that I would spend the evening watching television, but I was too nervous to sit still. I spent most of my time cleaning up my apartment. I needed to be occupied.

My thoughts were racing a lot. I was worried about not succeeding at quitting my self injury. I worried about the money I wasn't making by staying away from work. Shy-Anne had suggested that I could take a few months off of work and live on welfare until I got back up on my feet. I wasn't fond of that idea, but I didn't reject it.

My heart was racing and I couldn't slow my mind down, so I took some Quetiapine and that helped me fall asleep.

Tuesday, June 17

I started my morning the same way as I spent my evening; cleaning. Even after Marie got there, she sat and watched television while I ran around getting more stuff done. I couldn't sit still. If I stopped moving I would freak out. I didn't stop moving until I left for the hospital.

I had worried that I may have been put in isolation upon my return because I had admitted to scratching my foot, but nobody said anything.

I walked up to the desks and gave them my things.

Joseph and Parker were there. Joseph was dressed in his own clothes again and Parker was standing there with a bag, ready to leave.

Joseph hadn't been given permission to go, but Parker was headed to a treatment facility that I had never heard of. He said that he was optimistic about it.

"I'll call you," Parker told me. "We can go rollerblading." Then Parker was gone.

I had a new nurse that day. It seemed that she was an intern. She made it clear that she wanted to talk with me. Maybe it was written in my file that someone had to talk to me because she seemed insistent. I had nothing to say though, and I didn't know this girl. I didn't want to talk to her.

At that point I really just wanted to bang my head against something.

I started looking at the spots of color on the floor tiles again and I pictured them bleeding. For a moment, I thought that if I stepped on them, they would smear.

I saw Dr Knoll again. She mentioned nothing about the fact that I had been hurting myself.

It was decided that I would spend the remaining nights until my release at home. Dr Knoll also discussed with Dr Fellows, and they agreed on a treatment plan. They wanted me to attend a program at the outpatient clinic at Ste-Marguerite's. It would be four mornings a week over about a month and a half's time. I realized that it might conflict with my work, but I figured that I could move things around if need be. Going to that program made my heart race, but at least it wasn't a full time thing.

For supper that night, I was sent fish again. Jed was happy about that because he was able to eat the fish from both my plate, and from his own.

Jed was out of isolation and back into his own clothes. He was more polite that day. He even accepted to take my coffee. I didn't want coffee on my tray, but just like the fish, they sent it to me anyways.

"Are you nervous?" Michelle asked me as I was walking around after supper. She was sitting at a desk behind an office window. "I saw you fidgeting with your watch, so I thought you might be nervous."

"I am," I admitted after walking up to the office window.

"Would you like some Lorazepam?" she asked.

"Yes."

Michelle went to get me the Lorazepam and I went to get the water. When I returned, she placed two small, broken pieces of lorazepam in my outstretched hand and asked, "Is there something that's causing your anxiety?"

"Yes," I admitted and was silent as I watched my lorazepam pieces roll around on my palm. I could feel Michelle's eyes on me. "It's just," I paused. "It seems like it's never going to end." I looked from my lorazepam pieces to Michelle, but she said nothing, so I continued. "I mean, I'm going to leave here in a few days and I'm still the same.

Things haven't gotten better. I want to hurt myself every day. I'm going home, and then what will happen?"

The nurse at the back of the office looked over from her papers to talk to me. "You can ask for more time if you want to," she told me.

Then Michelle said, "You can go home for a few hours and if things aren't going well then you can come here for the night."

"Yeah?" I breathed deeply. "Maybe I'll do that," I told her and then swallowed my lorazepam.

"Keep the glass for next time," Michelle told me as I walked away.

Jed found me soon after and asked if he could buy me a chocolate bar.

"No," I declined. "I have some at home and I'm spending the evening there."

Jed looked sad when he said, "I'm sorry about yesterday."

"Apology accepted."

I didn't have trouble forgiving because his apologies were sincere.

It was still hard to picture that man crying the way he said he did at nights. I could tell that the tough way he acted was just a mask.

I left the hospital at nearly 6:00 pm. I figured that I could walk to Shy-Anne's place to say, "Hi", since I had forgotten to call her that afternoon.

I had almost reached her road when Shy-Anne's car pulled up beside me. She was with her dog and headed to buy some exotic soil for her pond.

"Do you want to come?" she asked.

"Yes," I answered and was grateful to have someplace to go.

We searched four stores before we found the right kind of soil.

I told Shy-Anne about what was going on with Jed.

"Is that the guy who was hanging around your door saying that he was protecting you?" she asked.

"That's the one," I confirmed.

I had found a good friend in Shy-Anne. She had a light personality and liked to laugh.

I made fun of myself a lot because the Quetiapine I had taken had slowed my thoughts. I was forgetting really easy words and was having trouble finishing sentences. I wasn't bothered by it though. I knew it was only temporary.

After Shy-Anne dropped me off, I spent more time cleaning up. I was going out of my way to find things that needed fixing. I even rearranged all the stuff on the back porch.

I returned to the hospital at 8:30 pm. I was sure that I was safer from myself if I was at the hospital.

I felt that there was only doom and gloom waiting for me and that there was no way out of my problem. I would be going home for good soon and right back to where I started.

I often looked at the lit up exit signs over the doors and imagined that they were symbolisms for cutting. Cutting was a way out; an exit door so to speak, but what was the way out of cutting?

I was picturing blood in my mind again. I imagined it running from my wrist to my palm, then I would bend my hand back so the imaginary blood could run down and drip from my fingers to the floor.

I saw blood; Blood everywhere.

Jed started walking with me. "Can we talk?"

"Of course," I answered.

"How was your outing?" he asked.

"It went well. I cleaned up and took care of my animals," I told him.

"What kinds of animals?" Jed was curious.

"I have a three month old cat, two ferrets, and a hedgehog," I told him. "Do you have any pets?"

"I used to have a cat."

"Oh, that's right," I remembered. "The one that my drawing reminded you of. When I see an animal at the pet store, I have a hard time leaving it there."

"You are a savior of creatures," Jed observed.

"I guess so," I agreed and liked the title.

Jed was silent but reflective for a moment. "Is it that I'm too old, or you're too young?" Jed asked.

I knew what he was referring to but I wasn't comfortable breaching the subject. I didn't want to hurt his feelings. "That depends on what you are referring to."

"You're intelligent," Jed said. "You know what I mean. Am I too old, or are you too young?"

"Sometimes I think I'm both," I answered, knowing full well what he was talking about. Jed was much older than me and I honestly wasn't interested.

"Would you like to sit down?" Jed asked as he pointed to the two rocking chairs at the end of the hallway.

"Sure," I accepted.

As soon as we sat down, Jed started pouring his heart out. "Sometimes I wish I were your age. I wish I were the person you were looking for. Many times I've cried for it. I cry for a lot of things, but lately I cry for you."

I didn't know what to say. What could I say?

"There's this girl that I need to protect," Jed continued. "I need to make sure that nothing bad ever happens to her. I'm prepared to do five or more years in prison just so nothing happens to her. I'm prepared to do that. I've never felt this way before."

"That's an amazing self sacrifice," I commended him, but it didn't seem that there was anything I could say that could equal what he had said to me. There was nothing I could really say because I simply did not feel the way that he did.

"I admit it," Jed told me. "I wish I were what you were looking for."

"I haven't decided to not be with you because of your character," I told him. "You are intelligent and have an understanding of complex things. If I deny being with you, it's not because of who you are. I'm in a difficult place in my life and I can't handle anything else." I tried letting Jed down nicely.

The loud speaker came on and all patients were asked to report to the desks for their medication.

Jed left and he thanked me for our conversation. I thanked him as well.

Wednesday, June 18

My medication had changed. I used to take Mirtazapine and Orlanzapine, but they stopped the Mirtazapine at night and gave me Venlafaxine in the morning. The change meant that I had to remember to take my medication twice a day.

It was another day where many of the nurses were interns. I wished that there was someone I knew and that I could talk to like Michelle or Ashton.

I had the same intern assigned to me as the day before. Her name was Sandy.

Sandy approached me again about the importance of us having a conversation. I had escaped a conversation the day before, but I wasn't sure if it was likely that I could do it again.

"We need to find the time to talk today," Sandy told me. "It's important."

"I have nothing to say," I replied.

I didn't want to talk to her. I thought that maybe I could exercise free will and just not do it.

I was distracted by a scene that Joseph was causing near the desks. He was yelling and pointing at an older man who looked like he must have worked there. "I don't want that man to be my psychiatrist anymore!" he yelled. "My doctor said I could leave right away, but this jerk wont let me out for several weeks!"

It was clear by the psychiatrists expression that he was trying to ignore Joseph's anger. Pretty soon the orderly was telling Joseph to go calm down in his room.

I then went to the end of the hall and sat in a rocking chair. Jed joined me shortly after. We had an interesting conversation as usual.

"I used to listen to the voices, but now the voices listen to me," Jed told me. "I am suffering. I am the universe. God had many prophets, but now I am the only one. All prophets know not to come because I am here."

I didn't contradict what Jed believed. I didn't see the point. "And what about after you?" I asked. "Will another one come?"

"No," Jed told me. "I am the last of the prophets. If you ask something of your God and He cannot provide, tell Him to send the request to me." Jed was silent for a moment. "You cause me a lot of pain too," he confided. "I see you with two or three people and I don't talk."

"I've made a lot of friends here," I told him. "That doesn't mean that I'm with any of them or with you."

"I know," Jed accepted. "I haven't claimed you."

Our conversation ended there and I headed towards the cafeteria. On my way there, my young nurse told me that she had set 1:30 pm as the time that we would talk.

I used this appointment as a subject of conversation with Joseph and John as we played cards.

"You guys have to give me ideas of what to say to this girl," I pleaded with them.

Joseph was distracted by the music playing in his ears from is MP3 player, so I spoke to John. "Oh, I know! I can talk about you," I told John playfully. "I could say, I know a guy who writes poetry and used to study history at the university. Yup, I'm going to tell her all about you. You can be the subject of conversation."

"Wow. You're on something aren't you?" John teased. "What did you eat?"

"A lot of sugar," I replied with a grin.

I was washing up at the sink in my room when the intern and her teacher came to talk to me. Mostly it was the teacher who talked while Sandy didn't seem to know what to say. The teacher was kind and seemed very practiced at speaking with patients. She told me that I was pretty remarkable for coming out of my situation as well as I did.

I had actually felt bad about how terribly I was handling the things in my life, so I liked the idea that I wasn't a total screw up. I thought, "Thanks Lady."

I was actually saved from my conversation with the intern for a short while because my psychiatrist, Dr Fellows, wanted to see me. One of the uncomfortable parts of the situation was that my young nurse was invited to sit in on the meeting and watch from a chair on the side.

Why did I have to be used to teach these people?

I was asked another series of questions, and once again, the questions seemed much like what I had been asked before. I pointed that out.

"These are similar questions, but in more detail," Dr Fellows explained. "So far I haven't been able to pinpoint any specific mental health disorder based on what you've told me. This makes it hard to know what kind of medication would be best for you."

She made it sound like I should be disappointed that I didn't have a disorder. Although, in a way it was a disappointment. If I had a known disorder, it may have explained my behavior better.

"Don't you find that self-mutilation is immature?" the doctor asked.

I found the question offensive. "I've never thought of it that way."

"It's a childlike behavior," she explained. "Someone taking out their anger on someone else is the same as when they take it out on themselves. It's immature."

"It's not immature; it's desperate," I contradicted.

I felt like I was mildly under attack and wanted to leave the subject behind. Self injury was a lot more complex than just lashing out, but even if it wasn't, should I have been compared to a child for my way of dealing with suffering?

"Your self injury is an abnormal behavior that makes people uncomfortable," Dr Fellows informed me. "That is why Dr Stone sent you to the hospital."

I found her statement upsetting. I made people uncomfortable? I put my doctor in a bad position and made him uncomfortable? I wasn't sure if it was her intention, but all the talk about my abnormal behavior and having a negative impact on others was making me upset and depressed.

"I know that people don't like to hear that I'm hurting myself," I said defensively. "That's why I didn't tell them."

"It's good that you said something now," Dr Fellows told me.

Really? It was good? That's not what it had just sounded like.

"Are you nervous?" Dr Fellows asked. "I can't always tell if someone is nervous if they internalize their anxiety."

"I'm not too bad right now," I told her. "When I'm really nervous I usually play with things, like my watch."

It was a mistake for me to mention that I played with my watch when things were bad, because later on Sandy noticed me doing it and decided we needed to talk again.

I was tired of being interviewed and being made to feel bad in the process. I certainly didn't want another round with someone else.

Sandy came to talk to me in my room and my poor roommate had to leave so we could be in private.

Sandy sat next to me on my bed. "How are you feeling?"

I felt discouraged. "I really don't want to talk to you about it," I told her. "It's not personal. It's just that I don't know you. I didn't want to talk to the other nurses at first either."

"Okay. When you need to talk, you can come and find me," Sandy offered before she left.

The shift changed at 4:00 pm and so did my nurse.

Daniel called me over to see him and had a message for me. "Dr Fellows wants to see you before she leaves tonight."

"I already saw her," I informed him.

"Oh," Daniel hesitated. "That was the note that was left, but I'm going to check that."

Daniel went back to the desks and I continued my walk. I was growing increasingly nervous. Part of it was because of yet another conversation with Jed, and part of it was because of my meeting with Dr Fellows.

I looked everywhere for something sharp or for some place to bang my head when no one was watching. I managed to bang my head against some metal corner covers and knocked my knuckles against the walls. I touched anything that protruded from the walls hoping to find something that would cut my fingertips. Then I thought of looking through my trash can for some kind of usable tool.

I waited until my roommate was finished brushing her teeth and was away from the sink. When she was gone I searched the trash can.

"Bingo!" I thought.

I found a plastic knife that must have been from my roommates lunch. The knife was coated in butter, so I washed it and dried it off. I pressed the teeth of the knife on my fingers and felt the jagged edge against my skin. At last I had found something I could use.

I wanted to cut my leg, but I stopped and asked myself if what I was doing was right. I knew that it wasn't, but how could I not do it? Should I go get help? Medication? An awakening conversation? Or maybe I could just use the knife to saw into my leg.

Dr Fellows had insinuated that I was wrong to keep the fact that I was hurting myself a secret. "That's what you are here for," she had said.

I had to think. I knew what the right thing was, but I was afraid to do it.

I dragged my fingernails along the teeth of the knife, creating a scratching sound. I found that it helped, but it wasn't enough.

I waited until there were no patients around the offices and I walked up to the desk to talk to Daniel who was working on some papers.

Daniel looked up and said, "Yes?"

I just stared ahead for a moment. How could I say what I needed? It was so embarrassing. I wanted to admit to my knife and have him take it away from me, but instead I hung onto it hard and held it where he couldn't see.

"I've been looking for sharp things," I confessed. "What should I take for that? Lorazepam, or Quetiapine?"

"That depends," Daniel said. "Which one do you find works for this?"

"Um....Quetiapine."

"Okay," Daniel accepted and went to get the medication.

While I waited, I found an empty soda can on the front desk. I was very attracted to it and I felt the sharpness on the inside of the hole at the top of the can.

When Daniel came up to me, I had the teeth of the knife pressed against my thumb. I took my pills and let Daniel see my knife.

"I found it in the trash," I told him.

"Yeah, I wondered what I heard you scratching," Daniel remarked as he held his hand out to take my treasured tool.

I knew that I couldn't keep it, but I had longed so much for it.

"They already took my rubber bands and my paper clips," I told him.

"Yeah, but it's better if you give me that." Daniels hand was still extended.

I didn't move. I just stared at my knife and could feel Daniel's eyes on me. Finally, I took a deep breath and handed him my knife.

I left my knife behind but still found myself looking for something sharp. I found my floppy pen on my bed and used it to make several ink dots on the palm of my hand. I tried to concentrate on the movements of my hands and the forming of the stains on my palm.

When Daniel found me, he saw the dots I had made. "Wow. It looks like you've been doing that for quite a while."

"Not that long," I defended my use of the pen.

"Really?" Daniel asked as he started to walk with me. "Because I saw you doing that five minutes ago. Is there something bothering you?"

"No, I'm great." My lie was obvious.

"Yeah," he agreed sarcastically. "It looks like you're having a party."

"I saw the psychiatrist today," I let him know.

"Did she say something that you didn't like?"

"She said that self injury is immature."

"You don't have to believe her," Daniel reasoned. "You have a right to say that it isn't true."

"Yeah," I continued. "She said a lot of things, and I said a lot of things. I don't deal well with conversations about my past."

"Talking about your past made you anxious?"

"Yes," I admitted. "I've talked to a lot of people about this stuff since I got here and I always come out of it all inside out."

"Right," Daniel understood. "And you have to repeat the same things to different people."

"Right."

The conversation ended when Daniel had to go see some patients in the smoke room.

I gathered my things together so I could leave for 6:00 pm.

By the time I signed out and got to the elevator to leave, Daniel was headed for his supper break, so he waited with me. I pushed the button and watched the numbers change on the elevator monitor.

Joseph came up to see me and gave me a kiss on each cheek.

"Hey!" I protested dramatically. "Patients aren't allowed to touch each other here!" I looked over at Daniel and said jokingly, "Put him in isolation!"

Daniel didn't actually do anything aside from give Joseph a playful warning look.

It was pretty cute.

The elevator took forever to reach the eighth floor, but eventually I got on and found my way home.

I wasn't feeling well and I wanted so badly to hurt myself that I decided to sleep through it. I figured that avoiding cutting by sleeping was the only safe plan I had.

And so I slept.

Thursday, June 19

I found the morning at home long because I was running out of things to clean and rearrange. I couldn't seem to sit still like I used to.

Around the noon hour, I called my mom to talk with her for a while.

We chatted about all the normal little things that were going on. All the while I was thinking about how what I was living was not a normal little thing. I felt that some of it didn't have to be a secret any longer.

I actually interrupted something that she was saying. "Mom."

"Yes?"

"I've been at the hospital for the last two weeks," I confessed.

"Why?" I could hear the concerned curiosity in her voice.

"They are changing my medication because the last one made me depressed. So now I'm up on the eighth floor with the schizo's and the bipolar's."

"Like I was," my mother related to her own experience from when she had a breakdown years before.

"Same deal. Different place." I told my mom about all the different medications I had been taking for quite some time. She didn't know about them because I didn't want her to worry. I didn't want anybody to know anything that was related to cutting.

"Oh my daughter," mom sighed.

"But I'm in good hands," I consoled her. "They are taking care of me."

"That's good."

I felt a weight lift from me. I succeeded in telling my mother I was at the hospital. I didn't tell her the whole reason why, but I told her. It was a relief in one way and a source of anxiety in the other. I was so used to keeping secrets that I didn't know what to do with myself when they were out in the open.

By the time I returned to the hospital, it was the beginning of nap time, so I had to stay in my room for 45 minutes. I was so restless that I couldn't lie still for a nap. At first I placed all my things as neatly as I could, then I paced back and forth while trying not to make any noise. My roommate was sleeping and I didn't want to bother her.

I paced until I heard Joseph talking in his room next door.

I knocked lightly on the wall that separated our two rooms. It was a game we had set up the day before so we could communicate through knocks during nap time. Joseph's bed was exactly behind mine, so he should have heard me well. He was supposed to knock back when I knocked, but he didn't.

I knocked again, but there was still no response.

I gave up on him and went to sit on the cabinet sink that was right beside the door. I sat there and dangled my legs rhythmically off the edge.

I heard Joseph's voice grow closer, so I hopped off the cabinet and poked my head out the door and into the hall.

Joseph and I both waved and giggled like school kids who were up to some mischief. We knew that we weren't supposed to be communicating during nap time, but that was what made it so much fun.

"Did you see under your pillow?" Joseph whispered. "Go look!"

"I saw the note, and it was beautiful," I praised. "Thank-you."

Joseph had written me a poem and hidden it under my pillow. He wrote about how he wanted our friendship to be eternal. He mentioned the things he liked about me and that he was proud to be my new big brother. We had made a habit out of calling each other brother and sister. I hadn't expected to get a note though. It was a good thing that he didn't get caught sneaking into another patients room.

"I worked really hard on it," Joseph informed me. "A lot of thought went into it."

"It looks that way," I commended. "I wanted to write you back, but I didn't have a pen."

I backed up into my room and hopped back up on the cabinet.

Joseph snuck partway into the hall to show me what his hair looked like without styling gel. He was insecure about it.

"It looks fine," I told him.

Joseph then noticed that he could see our reflections on the doors across the hall from us because of the light shinning in through our rooms.

"I see you in it," he said. "Do you see me?"

"Yes."

"It's shinny." Joseph liked shinny things, so I nicknamed him Raccoon.

William, the orderly who was often on shift during the day passed by and got after Joseph for talking.

"I was just saying hi to my little sister," Joseph explained himself. "She just got here."

When William disappeared we danced around to see our reflections move. I know it was completely immature, but I didn't care.

When nap time was almost over Sandy the intern came to see me. I was still sitting on the sink.

"How was your outing?" Sandy asked.

"It was fine," I reported. "I was nervous, but I dealt with it without meds or hurting myself." I paused. "Well, I banged my head. Does that count?"

"On what?" she asked.

"First with my hands and then I banged it on the cupboard I was leaning on," I specified.

My legs were dangling and kicking at a very fast pace and by the look on Sandy's face, I could tell that she noticed.

"Sorry," I apologized as I tried to steady my legs.

"It's okay." Sandy smiled.

"Okay." I started kicking my legs again. "I'm really hyper now. It's like I can't sit still. Even at home I couldn't stop long enough to watch TV." I was talking really fast as I kicked. "Could it be my medication doing this?"

"I don't know," she admitted. "Maybe. I'll go look up the side-effects."

So Sandy disappeared and the lights came on in the halls indicating that nap time was over. I jumped off the sink and started walking through the halls.

I eventually found Joseph who was begging Jolene for a smoke.

"I might be leaving today," I informed Jolene.

"Really?" Jolene sounded concerned. "I would wait a few days if I were you. Wait until you are ready. Do you think you are really ready?"

I thought about it. "I don't know. I don't think so. I mean, I was still banging my head yesterday. Does that count?"

Joseph shook his head, "Yes."

"You can ask for a few more days," Jolene told me.

"I can?"

"Yeah," she confirmed. "And you look like you need to."

"Yeah," Joseph agreed. "Just look at her. She can't stop moving."

"She's faking that," Jolene said in reference to my moving from leg to leg.

"No I'm not," I told them. "I think it could be my meds."

I took off to walk around more, but got called to go to the desks.

Dr Knoll was waiting for me.

We sat down in her office and she asked me how my last few days had been.

"Well, um," I stammered.

"Wow. That good, huh?" the doctor kidded with me.

"I had my ups and downs," I told her. "Yesterday I gave a knife I had found to Daniel. I had worked really hard to find it. I really wanted to use it."

"And what about your time at home?" she inquired.

"It was okay, but I was anxious a lot," I told her. "I took my meds when I needed them."

"Did you hurt yourself?"

"No," I answered. I didn't feel that head banging counted for me.

"So everything you did in the last few weeks was done here?" she asked.

"Yes," I confirmed. "Bruising and scratching."

"It sounds like the worst is over then," Dr Knoll noted. "If you are only doing smaller things, that's already better."

"I didn't have anything to do worse things with," I said.

"But at home you could have turned on the stove and burned yourself," Dr Knoll said. "Those scars are going to stay with you for the rest of your life. We want to keep you from getting them."

"It's too late," I told her. "I already have some."

"But we can try and control what comes next," she told me. "You can try other things in the meantime. Hold an ice cube in your hand, but not for too long. Snap your rubber band if you have to. Do you feel that you are ready to leave now?"

I was very uncertain. "I don't know yet if I'm safe from doing anything more. I still want it every day."

"Well, we can't keep you here for a year, and I'm aware that there are times when you're going to slip up," the doctor told me. "I know that will happen because you have been doing this for so long and for so many reasons. This coping mechanism is deep within your habits."

I wanted to contradict her, but she had just said what I had already thought; that I was going to mess up again. I didn't like hearing it. I didn't like having a second opinion saying that I would fail along the way.

Apparently there was a taxi waiting to take me to Ste-Marguerite's. Dr Knoll said that I was lucky because there was a spot open, so I could have an appointment to meet with them right away. I was going to have an interview with one of the leaders of the program.

That was my first taxi ride. A man in a red shirt took me to Ste-Marguerite's.

LADY INJURY

I waited for someone called Miss Reads in a waiting room at the front office. The room was too small for the distance that I needed to walk. I had so much energy that such a small space could not provide for.

After half an hour of pacing and talking about postpartum depression to a lady with a baby, I got to see Miss Reads. She was a psychologist and was younger than I had expected. Probably at the beginning of her career.

It was funny how many times in the last few weeks that I was asked about my sexual history and why.

There were a lot of questions that I didn't understand how they could possibly have been pertinent to the program.

I was given a short tour of the day hospital. It was just a small section of Ste-Marguerite's. There was a room with a large desk where everyone met to do self-evaluating projects and games. There was a relaxation room with a bunch of blue mats to rest on, and there was a room devoted to art projects.

"How is this supposed to help me?" I asked at the end of the tour. I didn't see how any of those things would keep me from cutting again.

"A lot of it is to help with self-esteem," Miss Reads explained. "We get exercise which is important. That's also good for people who are depressed because it gets them outside."

"Oh," I still wasn't sure how that was useful. "I guess I'll understand when I get into it."

"Are you nervous about this program?" she asked.

"I had been," I admitted. "But I think that once I get to that first day I'll be fine."

"Oh, because many people are resistant to work in a group setting," Miss Read told me.

"I think I'll be okay."

Yeah, I wasn't all that fine with the program though. It felt like I was going to kindergarden all over again. Finger paint and nap time; a giant six week waste of time.

At least there were meetings with a psychiatrist regularly during the program. That sounded like it could be useful.

It was arranged that I would start going to the day hospital on the monday after. I still didn't know much about the program though.

Another taxi took me back to the hospital where I found that my bed had been stripped and my things had been put in bags and set next to the chair.

"We need the room because there's another patient coming up," Ashton explained.

I was given my prescription papers and my hospital cards.

Saul, the orderly that was there most evenings, told me to take care of myself. Ashton wished me good luck and told me once again that he would rather see me walking on the street than in the hospital. I hugged my friends goodbye.

I was so nervous that I would have needed some Lorazepam just to leave the hospital.

I got on the elevator and waved goodbye. The door shut and the elevator went down a few flights, then it stopped, and went back up to the eighth floor. I was surprised when the door opened and I saw Saul standing there.

"I thought I was gone and it brought me back up," I said to Saul as he was surprised to see me and he got on the elevator.

"Sometimes it bugs up." Saul smiled.

So I left the building with Saul and he even did the gentlemanly thing by carrying my bags for part of the way.

I walked home with my purse on my shoulder, a large bag in both hands and flowers hanging from my free fingers.

It started to rain outside and the sadness inside me grew. My feelings echoed what the doctor had said. I wasn't going to make it. The harder it rained, the further away my home seemed to be.

I got under shelter at my doorstep and set my bags down around me while I searched for the key. I sat there on the floor, surrounded by my bags and flowers. I was thinking that I had to go back to the hospital, and that I wasn't going to make it on my own.

I could have just given up and cried, but I found my key, picked my stuff up and went through the door. My home smelled of failure and bad things waiting to happen. At least at the hospital I was safer; safe from myself. Now the only person who could keep me safe was me, and I was never good at that.

I was sad, anxious, and restless. I was actually mourning the loss of the hospital and the people in it.

Once I had gotten back into my routine though, it didn't feel so ominous. It felt a little more like home.

Saturday, June 21

I went to visit Joseph on Saturday afternoon. Apparently everyone knew I was on my way because he had been repeating joyfully to everyone that his sister was coming.

John was in his own clothes. I was impressed because he had been in a gown the entirety of my two week stay.

I asked William, if my confiscated rubber bands were at the desks because I hadn't found them among the things that I had been given back.

"They aren't here," William told me after a thorough search.

"Oh no," I mourned. "But I was told that I could get them back when I left."

"Who told you that?" he asked.

"Ashton."

"Then I'll leave a note asking him if he knows where it is," William offered.

"Thanks." I was attached to getting my rubber bands back. The orange one that I gave Ashton was my first one. I was nostalgic about things like that.

I played ping-pong and cards with Joseph. When we weren't playing, he was showing me magic tricks.

I was so glad that I wasn't a patient anymore because I got to wear what I wanted. I was wearing my wide leather wristband to hide my burns.

I didn't mind visiting the hospital, and I was finding it refreshing to not be boxed in with all those rules. I liked being free and independent and the world didn't seem so scary as when I was sheltered from it.

Joseph put a lot of effort into not going to the smoke room while I was there. I didn't smoke and couldn't stand the smell of it so I never went in the smoke room to join him.

"I'm going to quit on August fourth," Joseph told me. "That's my birthday. I'm going to be 33 like Jesus. I'm going to quit smoking on that day. Let's make a deal that we can't be friends anymore if I don't stop smoking. Okay?"

"Yeah you better quit. I can't have friends that smell like exhaust pipes," I joked.

After visiting Joseph I had the chance to go to a large gathering that was organized by friends. The gathering had nothing to do with my release from the hospital, it was just a nice coincidence that I was out on time to attend.

People got a chance to sing karaoke on stage and later there was dancing.

Near the beginning a friend of mine grabbed my arm and studied my leather wristband. She didn't say anything, but she seemed to think it was strange.

Lisa was there. She was so glad to see that I was out of the hospital, and I in turn, was so glad to see her. We shared a warm hug.

"I was planning to go and see you, but you were already out," Lisa told me.

I filled Lisa in on some of what had been going on for the past two weeks.

"Lets go out to lunch tomorrow," Lisa suggested. "We can get a submarine."

I was uneasy about taking my friend to a meal that she was just going to throw up. "Is that a good idea?" I asked over the sound of the music. "Or are you buying a salad?"

"No. A submarine."

"Don't you want to eat something that you're going to keep down?"

"I have to confront my fears sometime," Lisa explained. "I've been eating full meals and keeping them."

My eyes grew wide and I started to scream out of happiness. I gave her a big hug. I was so relieved at my friends progress after years of torment from her bulimia.

"The program I am at is encouraging me to face my fears," Lisa told me. "Today will be the second day that I haven't purged."

Lisa's declaration was followed by more screaming and more happiness.

"Yes!" I cried out. "We are both making progress at the same time."

I let Lisa go talk to her mom and I mingled in with the rest of the group.

One of my friends came up to me and said, "I'm going to give you a kiss. I love you, you know. I should say that more."

That statement sounded suspicious. I thought of asking her if she had heard anything about me lately, but instead I asked, "Are you on something?"

"No," she said. "I just wanted to say that I love you."

"Thank-you."

I thought that was really sweet, but it was out of the ordinary. Somehow she knew I was at the hospital. I didn't know how, but she knew.

A few minutes later another friend came up and said, "I love you, and you're really pretty."

I was taken by surprise. "Wow. What's with people tonight? I'm hearing that a lot."

I went to find Lisa to tell her that it seemed like people knew about my trip to the eighth. I realized that Lisa's father knew because she had told him that she was worried about me. She was trying to get me some help, but a few days later, I was hospitalized. A few more people must have known. Information was leaked and then it spread.

"Does Carl know?" I asked Lisa.

"Yes."

My fears were confirmed. "Then everyone knows."

They knew I was at the hospital, but did they know why?

LADY INJURY

I had enjoyed the party and seeing my friends. I liked the affections they showed me even if it meant that they knew things that I wished they didn't. I liked the dancing and the laughing and the catching up with people I hadn't seen in a long time. I liked the freedom that I appreciated so much more since I knew what it was like to lose it.

Sunday, June 22

On Sunday I went with Lisa to get submarines as we had planned. We both brought our own meat substitutes to put in our subs because we were both vegetarians. Lisa brought her own salad dressing; probably because it was low fat.

The food was great. I was a messy eater though, so I had submarine fillings a little bit all over the place. I was never a classy gal.

Lisa and I talked and laughed. We had so many feelings in common. Lisa could understand losing control. She could understand trying to destroy herself. She understood more than I can say.

I had a bad moment at the end of our lunch though. I don't know if it made me a bad friend or a friend who wasn't afraid to ask important questions.

Lisa had gone to the washroom after our meal, and when she opened the door, I saw her wiping her mouth. I was sure that she had just made herself throw up.

"Did you already lose your lunch?" I asked her.

"No," Lisa answered. "You don't trust me, do you?"

Was it about trust? Maybe. I knew her behaviors really well. I knew what she had done so many times before and could just as well have done again. It wasn't such an offensive assumption, but I believed her when she said that she didn't do it. Lisa had always been honest with me, and I with her.

I walked Lisa home and I hugged her goodbye.

I then got my things together and drove over to visit with my sister as I had traditionally done on weekends.

I found it scary to reenter my regular life while knowing that so much had changed. Reality had shifted. My sister knew about my cutting and I didn't know how to deal with knowing that she knew. It was harder to have a member of my family know. Maybe because I was protective of them. Maybe because I was used to hiding from them. Maybe because my shame was deeper before them.

I got comfortable in Marie's old, grey recliner chair. We started off with small chat, but soon Marie was telling me about the supposedly helpful things that she had been doing for me.

"I asked Paris if she knows anyone who self injures," Marie informed me. "I didn't give your name and I didn't even let on if I was referring to a guy or a girl. At first she thought that I was the one who was cutting. I was like, *No!* And I had to convince her that I don't. She was really impressed, because she said that cutters don't usually tell anyone, but someone confided in me."

"I didn't tell you," I corrected. "You asked and I admitted."

"I know, but that's what she said."

"I already have people that I can talk to about this," I informed her. "I don't need to be connected to someone else."

Marie's kind of help was making me so anxious and fearful. She seemed to think that she was being helpful, but helpful was not the word that I would have used to describe it. I wanted to tell her that I couldn't handle that, but I wasn't sure how to gather the courage.

"I also talked to Debra," Marie informed me. "She is a nurse so I asked her for some information on self injury. She told me about some articles I could read." Marie gave me the references to the articles.

My internal red alert was going wild. Marie had only known for a few days and she had already managed to spread my secret.

"I knew about those articles Marie," I told her with a lot of worry building up inside myself. "I've been dealing with this for a long time. I've done a lot of research. If you wanted to know about where to find articles on self injury, you should have just asked *me*."

Marie seemed surprised. "But she is a nurse, and I didn't tell her that it was you who was cutting."

"I don't care," I was blunt. "She is someone in our social circle. She and Paris may not know who you were talking about now, but what about the next time they see me and I am wearing these?" I raised my hands to show the arm warmers. "They are just going to put two and two together. They will know right away. I can't handle having other people know. I can barely handle having you know."

"I don't think they will say anything," Marie assumed.

"Did you ask them not to say anything?" I asked pointedly. "Even if they say nothing, this still means that they know. That can't happen. I let you know, but I need to be able to trust you with this. I can't do this Marie. It's already so hard. I can barely breathe knowing that you know and now it's being spread. I can't even handle talking to you about this. I used to have self injury as a part of much of my life, but I came here or wherever people didn't know about it and in a way, I got to pretend like it didn't exist. You didn't know and we didn't talk about it and it didn't exist; but now it's filtering in to the rest of my life. It hurts to talk about cutting with you because it hurts that you know. I don't want to remember that you know."

"I'm sorry," Marie apologized.

I took a deep breath and remembered Marie telling me about going into therapy. "The therapy you go to, is it to help you deal with things, or is it also to find out how to help me?"

"It has nothing to do with you."

"Good." I was relieved. "That's what I want. I don't want help."

"Okay."

"Its not that I don't appreciate your efforts."

"You want help from professionals."

"Yeah, but its not like its just you. I don't want help from mom or Devon either. I want help from the doctors and the nurses and the psychiatrists. But, you, you're in a different reality. I don't know if I'm making sense. I mean that this problem I have has always been separate from what we do. We talk and watch movies and thats the way I want it to stay. Do you understand?"

"Yes"

"I don't want you to try and fix me."

"I know. I can't fix you."

"And telling people that you know a cutter is scary to me. Having them know anything at all is scary. Paris was right when she said that cutters don't tell.

I don't tell. You weren't supposed to know. And now things are scary. My realities are colliding. I can't handle this. I'm afraid." I wiped tears from my cheeks. "I'm afraid."

"You don't have to be afraid. I won't tell anyone else. It's not going to happen any more. I promise."

"Okay," I accepted as I got up to get a tissue to dry my eyes. "I like to be able to pretend its not real and that I don't have this problem. When people know its hard to pretend. I don't just hide my legs from everyone else."

"You hide them from yourself too."

I nodded through tears. I got up and went out of Marie's apartment and into the stairway. I needed to calm down before I could go back in and try to pretend like everything was fine.

Marie went outside to see a guy who came to fix her bike tire.

There was spinning in my head.

I couldn't deal with people knowing. Maybe it was a mistake to tell mom as well. I had been planning on telling my whole family so the secrets could just be over. If I couldn't deal with being around Marie when she knew, how could I expect to face mom and Devon?

I was alone inside and too anxious to sit still. I walked through the kitchen to the bathroom and stood in front of the mirror to fix my hair. The flower I had put in it had started to slip. I pulled the white flower out from my hair and then placed it right. Maybe I shouldn't have looked at myself. Maybe I shouldn't have allowed myself to see her; to see that Stupid Girl; to see that part of me that needed pain to calm down.

I pulled the flower back out from my hair and unlatched the pin that made it double as a brooch. I pulled off my wristband and began scratching all around my wrist. Small lines began to cover the back of my wrist and then the front of it around my burns. I winced at the pain as I watched little flakes of skin rise on my arm. The pain was the release that I needed. I looked up at the girl in the mirror as she dragged the pin over her skin. She disgusted me. I couldn't stand to watch her do that. It was the first time that I watched her breaking my skin. I had always been alone with my tools before that.

She made me ashamed to look at her and know that she was me. I was ashamed to have crossed a line for the first time. I hurt myself at my sisters place. I told myself that I wouldn't. I tried to make it seem less important. I told myself that they were only scratches and not cuts. I told myself that I hadn't really cut myself at my sisters home.

At the end of the visit I started walking up the stairwell when Marie stopped me.

"Do you want me to pretend like I don't know? Because I can do that."

"No, I don't want you to pretend. I don't think that we can pretend. You can ask me questions about whatever you want," I said, but I wasn't sure of my answer.

I didn't like to pretend with her and I didn't like to talk about it. I didn't like the fact that she knew anything at all. I wished that I could go back to before Marie knew anything about my cutting. It was too hard dealing with this new reality. If I could go back in time and change it I would. I would go against my principles and lie when she asked if I had been hurting myself.

"It's just that we didn't really talk about how things should be," Marie said.

"I want things to go back to the way they were before. I want us to talk and watch movies and goof around. I'm still the same person I was before, there's just more to me than you knew."

"I know that. I still see you like before. It's just hard as your big sister to know that you're in so much pain," Marie expressed as she choked into tears and walked up by one step. "I love you."

I took a step down to meet her and we hugged.

"I just need for you to take care of you," I told her as we hugged. Then we pulled away from each other and I walked up a few steps.

"I'm not hurting all the time you know. I'm able to have fun too." I said with a weak smile before walking up the rest of the stairs and leaving the building.

Monday, June 23

On Monday I went to Ste-Marguerite's for my first day in the group. There were about ten members.

We had to make personal goals for the week. My goal was to face my fears of talking about my problems. It was hard to keep from panicking when I was supposed to talk to a room full of people.

I was pulled out of the group for a brief meeting with Dr Silk, the psychiatrist. I found that the same questions I had gone through with the other Doctors where being asked once again. I was getting tired of the repetition.

By the end of the morning, the whole group was supposed to lie down on mats in the dark, while listening to a man on the radio who had a really deep voice. I think the idea was that it was supposed to be calming. I didn't find it calming. Lying down in the dark with a bunch of people made me on edge. I never liked to be lying down with people around me. I found it threatening, and it reminded me of when my alcoholic father would come into my room and watch me sleep; at least I pretended to sleep until he went away. I tried to distract myself from my intrusive thoughts by counting the ceiling tiles.

The purpose of the exercise was for me to relax, but I actually left the room more anxious than when I had gone in.

I was glad to leave, but I had to sit in my car for a few minutes so I could calm down before starting the engine. I considered heating up my cars cigarette lighter and burning myself, but I resisted the urge and drove home.

Tuesday, June 24

There was no therapy on Tuesday because it was a holiday.

Joseph called me after lunch. I would answer the phone and he would immediately start talking really fast; so fast that I understood only parts of what he was saying. Joseph had been incredibly revved up ever since I met him. I was told that it was the aftereffects of his abuse of speed.

I had never taken drugs, so I wondered what it was like. There must have been something good about it to keep people coming back to it. Was it really the great trip that others had described? I was curious, but I knew I would never find out, partly because I was personally against it, and partly because I worried that once I got a taste, I could never give it up.

Joseph was asking me to visit him at the hospital again. To be honest, I had only visited him the time before because he asked it of me and I didn't want to hurt his feelings. Joseph was a nice guy, but I still felt that I needed to be careful as Dr Knoll had warned. I wasn't sure as to what I was being warned of.

Joseph waited for me to say if I was going to visit him. I wondered what the right answer was. I liked Joseph. He was a nice friend. He was also sick in ways that not everyone could understand. I liked that we could understand each other in that respect. He was going through something intense at the same time as I was. Joseph needed support too.

"I'll be there in about an hour," I told him.

Joseph and I started off by playing ping-pong. We were both really good at the game by then and were looking for ways to make the game harder and more fun. We tried passing the ball from one side to the other without letting the ball land anywhere. The ball would just get passed from bat to bat. With enough practice, we achieved 18 hits before dropping the ball.

We also played bean bags. It was a noisy game because whenever I would sink the pocket, I would cheer and dance around.

After bean bags, we switched to a more traditional activity by walking around the halls.

"Hey, look," I pointed at room 861. "That's my old room."

"Yeah," Joseph remembered. "The morning I first saw you there, I called out, *Hey, that's not a bad looking girl!* and I told the others to go see."

I smiled at the memory. "I remember."

"You heard that?" Joseph was surprised.

"Well of course I did. I have ears," I confirmed. "You called me a beautiful creature."

Joseph blushed and smiled in embarrassment. "Yeah, beautiful creature."

"So has anyone else come to see you?" I changed the subject.

"No," Joseph replied sadly. "I called my mom but she refuses to come and see me unless I get put into a group home under surveillance."

"Oh, why is that?" I asked nosily.

"She's afraid of me," Joseph replied honestly.

I wondered what was so scary about Joseph. Aside from being kind of wired, I didn't see anything out of the ordinary with him. I had gotten to know Joseph enough that I felt I could ask him, "Why?"

Joseph explained, "Because when I was 16, I was reading the bible really fervently. My mom tried to take the bible from me, but I didn't want her to, so I tried to get it away from her and she fell. It was an accident. I didn't mean to hurt her, but she has been careful of me ever since."

I wasn't sure what to say. I wanted to believe Joseph's side of the story, but I also wanted to be realistic, so I didn't know what to think. That had happened so long ago, and he was just a teenager, should it matter now?

"Do you feel that you've changed since then?" I asked.

"Sure, I'm going to be 33 soon," Joseph informed me. "That's the same age that Jesus was when he died. I'm going to be the same age as Jesus."

I found Joseph's interest in the bible to be admirable because I was also Christian.

"My name is in the bible," Joseph smiled.

"Yes, I know," I concurred. I thought it was cute that he was proud of having his name in the bible, but something struck me as odd. It was almost like he felt the similarities in names meant that he was directly linked with God in some unusual way.

"Betty is supposed to come and see me tomorrow," Joseph bragged.

"Yeah." I remembered hearing him say that before. "She's stopping to see you when she comes to the hospital for her minor operation."

I had heard of Betty many times but I had never seen her. She was supposed to have visited a few times before, but she never showed up.

There was a theory among the other patients that Betty didn't actually exist outside of Joseph's mind. The thought may have started off as a joke, but people really stopped to wonder.

"She had better come this time," Joseph willed. "She said she would come," Joseph paused. "You know, you're prettier than Betty."

I was surprised. "But I thought you said that Betty looked like Shakira."

Shakira was a famous singer that Joseph was obsessed with.

"You're prettier than Shakira."

That was a really sweet thing for him to have said because I had seen pictures and videos of Shakira and knew how beautiful she was. I wondered if it was normal for a male friend to say something like that when there was no romantic interest. I had several guy friends before that, but they all ended with some sweet guy falling for me when I wasn't falling for them. I hadn't experienced a male to female relationship that remained on a friend to friend basis. I believed that it was possible though, and Joseph had made it clear that he wasn't looking for someone.

After a long walk, I said goodbye to Joseph. "Let me know what happens with Betty," I requested.

~ ~ ~ ~

A few hours later I had driven to work at the grocery store. It was my first night of work since the hospital.

I started off in the meat shop as usual. I took the machines apart and cleaned them. I looked at the wrench that I had used several times to beat bruises into my arm. Part of me was horrified at the memory, while the other part was somewhat nostalgic and wondered if another day would come where I would use it again.

Before the store closed, I made sure to buy lots of cookies, and chips and dip. I had gotten into the habit of eating more junk food than usual. I had such a craving for it. I was aware though, that an increased appetite was one of the side-effects of the anti-depressants I was on. I set up my treats in the storage section next to the janitors closet, and ate some chips or cookies every time I got the chance to go back there. Food was comforting.

I was starting to feel terrible and I assumed it was the anxiety, so I took some Lorazepam, but the feeling didn't pass. I stopped to really sense what was going on inside myself and I recognized the feeling. It was the heavy sadness that would lie on my chest and suffocate me. It was the same feeling that made me feel like I was dying or that I didn't really exist. It was the same feeling that brought me to visit the clinic to complain about it.

It shouldn't have been too surprising though, because the pharmacist had told me that the new medication I was on was the same basic thing as the Citalopram that had been increasing my depression.

They hadn't believed me when I said it was making me hurt more and make me more depressed. I was told that depression was not one of the side-effects, but they were wrong. I knew they were wrong because I was living it. I could feel it crawl inside me like roots of a tree smothering the surrounding plants.

Dreams of cutting my arm returned to me. I stopped sweeping once in a while and looked towards the back of the store where the client and employee bathrooms were. I longed to lock myself away and cut the way I wanted, but I didn't allow it. I had been doing that a lot that week. I was dreaming and wishing really hard that I could just give in and do it.

Wednesday, June 25

Wednesday there was art therapy at Ste-Marguerite's. I rummaged through all the cupboards and chose a project. I pulled out all the strings and beads I would need to make some jewelry. I made three bracelets, and had chosen a favorite. It was made of painted wooden beads.

When it was time for the break, most of us went outside on the deck.

Confidentiality in the program was very important and it was clearly stressed that we were not to tell others about what we confided in each other. For this reason, I can't say most of what was done or said.

I can tell you the parts that referred to me though.

One woman sat next to me on a cement wall beside the door. She looked at my wristband and asked me if I was wearing it because I had hurt myself.

"No," I lied and then regretted it. I didn't like lies. "Yes," I corrected myself.

It was an intimidating thing to admit, but there was no scary consequence.

I can also say that they were all surprised when I said that I was working and going to the day hospital at the same time. The others were on paid sick leave, but that was not an option for me. I had been working for long enough to be given the money, but I was working for my own account with most of my cleaning contracts, so I got nothing.

I was used to working a lot anyways. I thought about it, but I really didn't think that I would want to stop working even if I could. I never knew what to do with myself when I wasn't working.

After the break, we made life-sized drawings of ourselves by having a friend trace our contours while we laid on the paper. We were supposed to draw anything that we felt described ourselves.

I was hesitant to draw all the things that came to my mind. I thought of drawing blood and veins and a rock crushing my heart. I thought of drawing the pain I felt, but instead I drew a large broken heart with my family and friends inside it. It represented that I experienced too much emotion and that my family was very important to me.

I drew my wristband and that represented my secrets and what people don't see. I drew my watch because I always had to know the time.

We all had to take turns presenting our drawings.

"And that's my great hair," I said in joke, and in truth, as I pointed to the yellow mess I had scribbled with a marker.

"That's you," one of the therapists agreed.

"Yes, that's me." I stated while thinking that for all the things that were going wrong, at least I had nice hair. I smiled at myself.

I had colored my entire face in red. It represented my dark thoughts, but I didn't tell the group that many of those dark thoughts were thoughts of blood, sadness and anxiety.

Around the red blob that was my face, I made a large yellow circle. The yellow circle was my happiness that would hide the darkness.

One of the members returned to the room after meeting with the psychiatrist. She pointed to the wristband that I had drawn. "I saw her outside and asked her if she had hurt herself and she said, no, but then she said, yes."

I was slightly embarrassed by the story. I didn't like hearing words that implied that I had hurt myself. "Yeah," I confirmed. "I was afraid to say it, but then I thought, *Why not*? it's my goal of the week to talk about my problems, so I did," I paused with anxiety rising. "Yes, I hurt myself, and it wasn't an accident."

"That's okay," a therapists with short red hair told me.

"Not really," I disagreed.

"Are you okay?" she asked. "How are you feeling?"

"Anxious….exposed."

"You usually keep things to yourself," the therapist noted. "You keep it all inside."

"Yeah," I agreed. "I had to hold back from putting all the things that came to my mind into the drawing."

"I noticed that you were pausing a lot when you were drawing," she acknowledged. "It's okay to share here. This is the place for it. Do you think it's helpful to talk about it?"

"I don't know," I hesitated. "I guess so."

"How is it helpful?"

"It could help me get used to opening up," I guessed.

"And has keeping secrets been a negative thing in your life?" she asked.

"In some ways, yes," I admitted. "It makes me lie sometimes. I make excuses for things like about why I don't want to swim; that kind of thing."

"And how do you feel about lying?" she inquired.

"I don't like it," I affirmed. "It's against my principles."

They hadn't been outright lies, but more like diversions from the truth. They felt like lies to me though. My conscience hurt me and made me turn back and admit the real truth.

By that evening I was back at the grocery store cleaning meat machines and floors. Sadness settled inside me and followed me through every step I took. My chest hurt and I recognized it as one of the physical side-effects of my depression. Soon a struggle began between choosing to cut several lines into my wrist, or eating some yummy chocolate sprinkled donuts that I had recently become addicted to.

I had such a deep craving for sugar, but for cutting as well. Which would I choose? Cutting? Or sugar?

Oh....I wanted both so badly, but I had already gained five pounds that week from binging on donuts, cookies and chips. I didn't want to gain five pounds every week. I wasn't fat, but I didn't want to become so either.

With a lot of willpower, I made it through the evening without eating donuts or cutting, but even as I left the grocery store I longed for them.

Thursday, June 26

The medical clinic called me up to make an appointment with Dr Stone on the fourth of July. I wasn't sure what the appointment was for. It was probably just to check in with me, but it made me a bit nervous, because the last time I had went, I also went to the hospital.

Thursday was my first night back to the old age home since the hospital. I was nervous about seeing everyone again considering my absence.

Everyone was so glad to see me. I got so many hugs from these people that I cared about deeply.

It was hot out and everyone was treated with ice cream and juice popsicles. Mme Claymore gave me a cold kiss from her popsicle lips. "I'm so glad you are okay now and that you are back. I always feel safest when you are the one watching us."

I smiled at the nice comment and the warm welcome.

Mme Shore was convinced that the reason I had been so anxious before going to the hospital was because I had the pneumonia coming on. I didn't contradict her. I was just glad that people believed the pneumonia cover story.

"You're going to have to take it easy now," Mme Shore told me. "We don't want you getting sick again."

I reassured her that I would be taking it easy.

When Mr Vaughn saw me, he noticed that I had gained a bit of weight. "Your face looks more round," he told me, then paused. "It looks very nice on you."

I got the feeling that he had said that it looked nice on me only to not make me feel like he wasn't saying that I was fat. It made me very self-conscious. Part of me knew I wasn't fat, but the other part wasn't so sure.

I gave Mr Vaughn his medication and took his order for peanut butter toast on brown bread. He then went back down to his room.

"It's so sad that you had to go through pneumonia," Mme Westmire told me. "I know how awful it is. I went through it recently and I had to be hospitalized for weeks."

I remembered when Mme Westmire got pneumonia. I was there to call for help and watch her get wheeled away to the ambulance.

I prepared coffee and filled glasses of juice for the ladies in the living room. I listened to them talk about what a shame it was for me to get sick when I was so young.

I pulled the coffee table close towards the rocking chairs and set the drinks on it so it was close enough for them to reach. I also got benches and brought them next to those who didn't have a table near them. They thanked me for the kind service. It seemed that I was the only one who would think to do that for them.

Mme Westmire continued to talk about her stay in the hospital months before. "What floor did you stay on?" she asked. "The fourth or the fifth?"

I hadn't expected that question. The first thought that came to mind was that I absolutely could not let them know I was on the eighth floor. I wondered what floor I would have been on if I were sick with pneumonia.

My mind raced to find the right answer. Was I on the fourth or the fifth? Instead of answering, I just said, "Yeah," and walked away.

Saturday, June 28

I went to a Christian based convention in Quebec city. I had known about and looked forward to that weekend for months. Most of my friends would be there, including Lisa. I would get to see the people I loved and I could hear some positive and encouraging points from the bible. My favorite verse was in Isaiah, where it talked about how we didn't have to be afraid because God was holding our right hand. Sometimes I would squeeze my right hand together and pretend that it was God that was holding it.

I looked to God to find strength, but I also hid from him out of shame for what I had been doing to the body he gave me. I didn't feel that I could ask for forgiveness.

I drove to Quebec city on my own. The road was long, but I knew the way. I liked that I could put the volume of my music as loud as I wanted because no one else was there to complain about it. I could relate to so many of the lyrics in the songs I had chosen. The songs were sad, but they understood me. They made me feel less alone and more understood.

I was grateful to be going somewhere good, but inside myself I was still breaking apart. All my worries sat in the same place on my chest.

It was after I had entered the city and started driving down one of the main roads when I looked towards my cigarette lighter with desire. I told myself that burning was not an option and I turned away from it. Only a minute passed before I changed my mind and pushed the lighter in so it could heat.

I nervously took off my green armband so the skin of my wrist was exposed.

The lighter clicked to let me know that it was ready. I pulled it out and saw the red of the heat flaring in the small circle within the lighter. When the car reached a stop light, I used the opportunity to set the lighter against my wrist. I clenched my teeth hard until I pulled the lighter away. The pain was intense but it didn't take long to pass. I put the lighter down and looked at the white circle I had made and noticed parts of it were charred black. I had burned myself worse than I had before. I was getting braver when it came to pain, and although I knew that wasn't a good thing, I felt strangely proud.

I put my armband back on to hide my wrongs and drove into the parking lot of my destination. It didn't take long before my burn had filled with water creating a large bubble. I went into the stadium and immediately hid inside of a bathroom stall so I could take care of my wound.

I later sat with my family in the audience. My sister and my older brother's family were there. During the break I got to visit with a lot of people.

I spoke in a hushed voice to Marie. "Paris knows that I am the cutter that you were talking about."

Marie's expression was of confusion.

"She looked right at my wristband for a few seconds," I told her. "I could see in her eyes that she was realizing it was me."

"Oh," Marie said, but there was nothing that could be done about it. Paris knew and I couldn't take that from her. It was done.

I worked inside my mind at making peace with others knowing about my cutting. I told myself that it didn't really matter.

At the end of Saturdays convention, I made the long drive home. I stopped at a donut shop for some comfort food. I was wanting a chocolate danish that I had tried before, but the shop I went to didn't have any. Their selection was rather limited. Instead of a danish, I chose two donuts and two cookies.

I was driving straight to work at the old age home and planned to eat my treats when I got there.

As I approached my place of work, I was becoming increasingly nervous about eating my much lusted after deserts. I remembered the five pounds I had gained and how my face was getting fat. It had to be true because people had noticed the difference.

I didn't want to get fat off of my donuts, but I had already bought them and I didn't feel right about throwing them out. How could I pass up my donuts though? I wanted so badly to eat them. I was craving sugar wildly. That's when I made a decision. It was a decision that would change my life forever. I thought of a way that I could eat my cookies and donuts without gaining weight. I decided to eat my prized sugar treats and then throw them up.

I remembered one time before that day when I had forced myself to throw up. It was when I was eating a bowl of almonds and realized that there were bugs crawling through them. I knew that I had probably eaten several bugs before noticing that they were there. I had always thought that making myself throw up was something I would never do, but there were bugs inside me and I was too grossed out to allow them to stay there.

When I was grabbing my paper bag of donuts, I thought about the day with the bugs in the almonds. I knew that I was capable of purging my food, and that was what made me feel safe enough to eat again.

I knew it was wrong. I knew that I shouldn't. I knew what it could lead to but didn't worry that it could apply to me.

While all the residents were in their rooms, I sat on the couch and had my treats. After that I made sure that no one was around, and I closed myself into the bathroom to purge.

It was disgusting and much harder to do than I had thought. My stomach would lurch and moments later more food would come up. I gagged and coughed. Tears dripped off my nose and into the water of the toilet that I stared down at. The fingers that I had put in my mouth were coated with vomit and stomach acid, but still I continued to force them down my throat until I was satisfied that I had gotten everything out. I was actually proud when I managed to pull up some of my lunch that I had eaten at least 5 hours before. The whole process must have taken me over twenty minutes.

It was one of the most disgusting things I had ever done and I wondered how Lisa had survived four years of bulimia.

I hoped that I would never do it again, but at the same time, I felt that I had found the perfect way to eat anything that I wanted.

Sunday, June 29

On Sunday I drove to another day of the convention with an old friend of the family. I used to play with her son when I was little.

Part of me was glad that having someone in the car with me was keeping me safe from myself, but another part felt like I was being held back, and I didn't like it.

My mood was terrible. As well as my usual anxiety and depression, I was very bothered by what I had done with my donuts the night before. I worried that I might make a habit of it. I was worried about where I was headed and how I was going to deal with it.

I ran into Lisa at the lunch hour. She was talking with a woman that I didn't know, but I had heard Lisa talk about her several times. She was someone that Lisa felt that she could confide in.

Lisa introduced me to her friend, but I barely reacted. I felt badly for being rude, but I couldn't fake a smile or a hello. I just sort of nodded my head and stared blankly.

Lisa noticed that I was really zoned out, so she followed me to where we could talk alone. I didn't feel ready to admit to purging. "I feel like locking myself into a bathroom stall to cut myself," I confided. "I nearly did, but I changed my mind at the last minute."

"I understand that," Lisa related. "I feel like locking myself into a bathroom stall for a different kind of wrong."

I looked at my friend who was so small and had been through so much. How could I tell her that I had started to do the same thing that was slowly killing her? Lisa's teeth were rotting from the years of stomach acid. Her hair was falling out and getting thin because of the lack of protein in her diet. She was tired and sad. She hated her body.

After everything that she had been through, I couldn't admit that I had purged the night before. I had done the thing that she was so desperately trying to stop.

"I didn't purge today though," Lisa said proudly. "This is the sixth day that I've gone without purging. I've actually gained 10 pounds since I moved away from home."

I finally managed to smile because I was so happy for her. I gave Lisa a congratulatory hug. I was relieved that my friend was doing better. I had worried so much for her when she was bad enough to go to the hospital. Lisa had more weight left to gain, but she was on the right track.

"I've been hurting myself less since my trip to the hospital," I bragged and Lisa was happy for me as well. It felt good to smile.

Tuesday, July 1

I hadn't written in my journal in a long time. I had gotten distracted and forgot about it. I decided to sit down and write about everything that I could remember from the previous month.

Everyday since the convention, I had been throwing up from one, to several times a day. I ate mostly junk food, and so much of it. Chocolate cake with mint ice cream, donuts, cookies and chocolate bars. The list went on.

I bought food, ate it, and then purged it. The temptation to eat in large volumes was overwhelming. It all tasted so good going down, but I went through such misery to make it come back up. It was painful, difficult, and breathless. I had shoved my fingers down my throat so many times until I dry-heaved and there was nothing left inside me. I was only satisfied when I was empty. I liked the pains of hunger because it meant that my stomach was eating itself and I was getting skinnier.

I felt that I had no choice but to continue. I was too fat and had to lose the weight. I had even gained a few more pounds. I decided to become three pounds less than my normal weight just in case I were to gain more weight after. If I gained three pounds after my diet, that would be fine, because that was the weight I was supposed to be at. I had set myself an objective and I was determined to achieve it.

I bought myself a new bathroom scale that was more precise. It showed how much I weighed to the fifth of a pound. I would obsess if I gained even a fraction of a pound and I'd be so happy when I lost anything.

The sad thing about the bathroom scale was that my brother Devon got suspicious after seeing it.

"Do you have a scale to lose weight, or to gain it?" Devon wanted to know.

I was caught by surprise. I wasn't at all prepared to be asked about my new scale. "To stay the same," I answered.

"You're already skinny. Don't pull a Lisa on us," Devon said, then left the room.

I knew what he meant. He meant don't do what Lisa did by going anorexic. All I could think to say was, "It's too late," but I didn't say anything. I didn't know what to say, but I didn't have to say anything more because the subject was dropped.

~ ~ ~ ~

Less than a week after I had started purging, my mom and grandmother arrived to Quebec from British Columbia for a two week visit. I took my car and went with Marie to pick them up from the airport. We had gotten to the city early so we could go shopping, but all the stores were closed except for the pharmacy. We spent our free time sitting in a parking lot until after dark.

My mom and grandma looked so good when I got to see them. My grandma was pushed over from the plane in a wheelchair by a stewardess because she had difficulty walking.

I got to hug them both. It felt so good to have people I loved dearly in my arms.

Mom was a bit taller than me and had very short blond hair. Her hair was the same blond as mine because the last time she visited, she used the rest of my bleach blond on an impulse. She said that she always wanted to dye her hair blond, but never did. So we were the same blond, and it suited mom very well. Mom already looked younger than her age, but with the new hair color, she looked even younger still.

My grandma was skinnier than the last time I had seen her. Since my grandpa died that year, she had been forgetting to eat and lost a lot of weight. I had to get used to the change in her appearance, but I was so glad to see her.

My mom actually complemented my leather wrist band. "That looks cool," she told me.

"Thanks." I smiled and wondered if she would still think it was cool when she knew what was hiding under it. I had made the decision that I was going to tell my mom about my self injury the night I went to get her. I didn't feel right about telling her over the phone, so I waited until I could see her in person.

I had already told Devon about it. All he said was, "Okay."

The hotel we stayed at was beautiful. I had never stayed in such a nice place. It was a new building right next to airport. The lobby was huge and had a bar. There were beautiful paintings and the service was impressive. Dogs were allowed in. They even provided little dog beds and bowls, so my mom's dog Mishou was treated very well.

We put all the luggage onto a trolley and pushed it to our room. It was on the ground floor because my grandma's legs were too weak to go upstairs.

The room was beautiful as well. There were two double beds and a large flat screen television. The decorations were pretty and even the bathroom was exquisite.

I was starving by the time we got to the hotel. I hadn't had a meal all day and it was nearly midnight. I was weak and I was shaking. I searched through my purse and pulled out a peach. I had bought several peaches and felt that they were a safe food to eat.

I took a bite out of my peach and leaned on the bathroom sink for support.

I was very nervous because I was determined to tell my mom about what I had been going through, but I didn't see anywhere in the room where we could talk in private. An opportunity arose when my mom said that she was going to take Mishou for a little walk.

"I'm coming with you," I called out to her, then whispered to Marie, "I'm going to tell her."

Marie shook her head to show she understood.

I was terrified as I followed my mom down the hall of the hotel and out the door. Fear had a grip on my heart and was squeezing it.

We stood on the lawn outside the hotel door and let Mishou sniff around.

I was still holding my peach, but was waiting before I finished it. All of my concentration was devoted to gathering enough courage to say what I had to.

I was so scared to say the words. I was screaming at myself inside my head, trying to convince myself to just tell her. Finally the words were coming out of my mouth and I wanted to turn back, but it was too late.

"Mom," I started. "I'm glad I have the opportunity to talk to you without grandma around. I have to tell you something."

"Okay."

I didn't say anything at first. The words were hard to find and to say. I looked across the road and drew in a shaky breath. I knew the silence had to be worrying my mom. Tears rolled down my cheeks.

"Mom," I whimpered. "I wasn't at the hospital just because of anxiety. Mom, I'm a self-injurer."

Moms face dropped and for a moment her eyes got wide.

I used the silence that followed to explain more precisely. "I'm a cutter. I bruise myself, I burn myself and I scratch myself. I'm a self-injurer."

Mom regained some of her composure. "Oh my daughter," she breathed and we hugged for a long while.

After that, I sat down in the grass and took another bite of my peach while Mishou sniffed the grass. I was weak and it was hard to stand.

"I've been doing this for a while now," I informed her. "I burn myself here," I pointed to my leather wristband. "And I cut my leg here." I indicated my lower leg. That's the reason why I drew a tattoo on my leg with a black marker last summer at the pool. I was using it to hide the scars."

"Oh!" mom cried out as she looked upwards with an expression of sudden comprehension. "Now I understand."

I got up and we let Mishou walk around the building.

"I wish I knew what to do to help you," mom told me.

"I have doctors and nurses and therapists for that," I told her. "All you have to do is be there." I paused. "Are you freaked out?"

"Well, I'm used to this kind of thing because of Hue and Hannah," mom referred to two of my cousins who had a history with cutting.

I didn't know what else to say, and it didn't seem like mom did either. We walked back into the hotel and didn't talk about it again.

"Did you tell her?" Marie asked in a whisper.

I nodded my head, yes.

It was late, so we got into bed. I shared the bed by the far wall with Marie. While getting comfortable, Marie accidentally rubbed her foot against mine. "Gross, your feet are rough and scaly," she complained.

I knew that my foot felt that way because of all the scratches I had made on it when I was at the hospital, but I said nothing about it. Marie and mom knew about my cutting, but my grandmother didn't and I wasn't about to say anything that would give it away.

Some of my families visit was spent at my home, and some was spent at my brothers home.

Over the course of my families visit, I tried hard to not let anyone notice how little I ate or how I went to the bathroom after every meal. There were so many people around, but at home it was just me. Being covert was only something I had to do when I was at Devon's house. I would turn up the sound of the television to make sure they wouldn't hear me heaving.

A real challenge for me was getting the courage to go swimming in the pool out back. I had bought some skin colored, water proof tape to wrap around my lower leg. I also had a tight arm band for my wrist that could go in the water.

LADY INJURY

Most of my family were aware of my problem. They wouldn't wonder why I was wearing tape on my leg, but I was still afraid to go out like that. I felt embarrassed and exposed.

I once stood in the bathroom at my brothers house in my bathing suit while wearing all the things I needed to hide my wounds and scars, but I couldn't work up the courage to to out the door. I could hear the others outside at the pool and I longed to go with them, but fear held me back. After a while I heard a small knock at the bathroom door.

"Melissa." It was mom. "It's okay if you come out. Grandma won't notice."

I knew she was referring to the fact that my grandma had Alzheimer's and was not always able to be very observant.

I couldn't go out of the room like that though. I put my clothes back on and took a nap on the couch instead.

There was an afternoon where I was downstairs alone. Some were sleeping while others were gone outside mowing the lawn. There was nobody to see me go from the bathroom to the pool. I took a deep breath for courage, wrapped my towel around me, and ran outside.

I hadn't been able to swim in so long. I had to make so many excuses as to why I could not or did not want to swim. I missed swimming. I missed it a lot.

I loved the feeling of finally being submerged in the water. I closed my eyes and swam slowly on my back. It was a difficult barrier to cross, but I crossed it, and I was proud. I felt that for all the courage it took to tell my family the truth, being able to swim was one of the prizes.

I regretted that I didn't get out of the pool in time though, because soon my sister in law, my sister, and my mother were getting in with me. I pretended like I wasn't phased by it, but I got out of the water and quickly hid in my towel. None of my scars or wounds were exposed, but it still felt like they were.

Some things were getting better, while other things were getting worse. I was losing weight. I was happy for the weight loss but ashamed of how I was achieving it. I was eating and eating and purging every day, even several times a day. I would throw up until I had no strength left to get up off the bathroom floor.

I met with my psychiatrist, Dr Silk. I was supposed to give her an update on my progress and how the new medication was doing. I admitted that I still felt really depressed and that I thought the anti-depressants were making it worse. I wasn't sure if she believed me; most doctors didn't.

Dr Silk looked at me reflectively. "It feels like there's a barrier between us. Is there something you aren't telling me?"

I was startled by her intuition and wondered how she could have known that.

"Yes," I admitted.

"And why do you feel you need to keep it a secret?" the doctor asked.

I hesitated, but answered honestly. "So that I can keep doing what I am doing."

Dr Silk wore an expression of realization. She knew I was doing something I shouldn't have, but didn't know exactly what.

I wanted to protect my secret despite my fear of it.

I was so scared of becoming what I called a skeleton, and yet I didn't know how to stop the purging and over-exercising. I had seen my friend Lisa fade away until there was nothing left of her but bones. I had hugged her small frame and cried. I didn't want to go there too. I didn't want to be nothing but bones, but I had to lose weight. I was too fat.

I reached my goal weight, but by then I was too worried that if I started eating again, I would get really fat. I decided to lose even more weight to keep me skinny for when I ate again.

I was trying to get back control. I was trying to make things right.

Sunday, July 20

I met up with Lisa after three weeks of binging, purging, and starving. It was a Sunday.

I gave my friend a short hug, but I was too full of emotion so I started to pull away. "I can't hug you for too long or I'll start to cry," I told her, but that only made her hug me harder.

"Do you want to go somewhere and talk?" Lisa asked.

"Yeah," I accepted.

We closed ourselves into a small room so we could be alone.

"What's going on with you?" Lisa asked when we sat down. "Have you been cutting again?"

I took a deep breath. "I managed to keep from cutting for a while after the hospital, but now I'm just as bad as I was before."

"Are you going to ask for help?" she worried.

"I don't know," I replied. "I don't even have the courage to admit to everything."

"What can't you admit?" Lisa wanted to know.

I looked for a long time at my friend and remembered how absolutely I had confided in her in the past and wanted so much to have that again.

"I've been starving myself," I confessed and watched Lisa's startled expression. "Some days I don't eat and others I eat too much and give it to the toilet."

"When did this start?" Lisa asked.

"Three weeks ago," I told her. "It was the saturday of the convention."

"Oh," Lisa's tone was of realization. "That's why you were so out of it."

"Yeah."

"Is this my fault?" Lisa asked with guilt lining her voice.

"Why would this be your fault?" I was confused.

"Did you think to do this because I do this?" Lisa asked.

"No," I reassured her. "I've known for years that you were starving and binging but it never gave me the desire to do it as well. I never used to care about my weight, but now that I'm on this new anti-depressant, I crave food too much. I gained weight, then I panicked and decided to lose it as soon as possible. At first it was only junk food that I wouldn't allow, then it was anything really fatty, and then it was anything at all. This isn't your fault. You didn't make me want to do this. It just happened that way."

"You have to stop this before it gets worse," Lisa warned. "I know how bad it can get."

"I know," I understood. "It's ridiculous that I could do this after seeing what it did to you."

"Did you eat anything today?"

"I had some sunflower seeds," I told her and pulled out a bag of sunflower seeds from my purse. "I eat just what I need so I can have some protein and keep from passing out."

"If I asked you to eat a pinch of those seeds, would you do it?" Lisa asked.

I opened the little bag and drew out a pinch of seeds then put them in my mouth. I hoped that eating them would reassure my friend.

"When are you going to see your doctor again?" Lisa asked.

"Monday," I informed her. "Tomorrow afternoon."

"Are you going to tell him about your trouble with food?" Lisa asked. I could tell that she was trying to guide me into doing the right thing.

"I don't know," I told her. "What if I have to go to the hospital again?"

"Then at least you will get some help," Lisa reasoned. "You need to go to the hospital.

I hesitated. "But my mom and my grandma aren't leaving until wednesday. I can't miss the end of their visit."

"This is more important," Lisa insisted. "Promise me that you will tell your doctor about your eating."

I saw the worry on Lisa's face and knew what I had to do. "I promise."

When I got home I gathered some things together in case I was admitted again. I wanted to be prepared. I worried about starting to eat again, but I worried more about losing control.

That afternoon my whole family went shopping. We went to an electronics store, but mom wouldn't say what we were going there to get. The fact that she wouldn't tell me let me know that she was planning on getting me something. I assumed it would be a camera. I had been talking about getting a digital one and mom knew how much I loved to take pictures.

I felt guilty though because I had been planning on asking mom to help me out a bit financially if I went to the hospital.

I was right. Mom led us to the camera section of the store.

"This will be a gift from grandma and I," mom told me.

"Are you sure about this mom?" I asked her. I couldn't ask for a camera as well as financial help.

"Yes," she said gladly. "I want you to pick the one you want."

"Wow, thank-you mom," I said appreciatively. I was really very touched by my mothers love and giving heart.

I didn't want to be a financial burden, so I picked out a small grey one for under 200 dollars.

"Oh no," mom said. "That's too cheap. I want you to pick one with all the zoom and options that you want. I want this camera to be with you for a long time."

We all looked at the descriptions for the camera's. Devon knew more about digital camera's, so he was a good help in finding what I wanted, but we didn't find the right one there.

"That's fine," mom said. "We'll go to another store, but first we'll look for Marie's gift."

We were led to the home electronics section. Mom was wanting to get Marie a small dish-washer that could fit on a counter top. I didn't even know dish-washers like that existed, but it seemed rather ingenious. Marie's apartment was small and couldn't fit anything big. A small dish-washer was truly the perfect gift because Marie had such trouble with getting motivated to do housework. This was a gift that would help Marie a lot, but there was no such thing at that store.

While the others were browsing and pushing grandma around in a wheelchair, I took the opportunity to talk to mom.

"Mom," I began nervously. "I don't feel right about taking a camera from you. I was already thinking about asking you for financial support if I get hospitalized again."

"Well, I can do both," mom assured me. "I can help you out too."

"I don't want to ask too much," I worried.

"It's okay," she reassured me. "You need a camera. It's like therapy for you to take pictures."

As I looked at my mother, I realized that buying me a camera was her way of helping me. In a situation where she felt helpless, at least she could give me a camera and whatever happiness that came with it.

"Okay mom," I accepted. "Thank-you. Thank-you so much."

When we were ahead of the others in the parking lot, mom quietly asked me a question. "Are you suicidal?"

"No," I reassured her. "I'm not."

I could hear her sigh of relief. "That's good."

We searched through four stores before finding the perfect camera. It had a large zoom and a large memory capacity. It could take up to an hour of video. My camera was so special, and I was so happy with it.

"Thanks mommy. Thanks grandma." I hugged them both.

I wished that I could give them something as amazing as what they got for me.

LADY INJURY

~ ~ ~ ~

That evening Mom and grandma were treating us all to supper at a buffet. There were eight of us there. There was mom and grandma; there was Marie and I, and there was Devon with his wife and two kids. We all gathered around a long rectangular table. Most of us went to pile our plates full of food. Grandma stayed behind and let mom chose her food for her.

I used the occasion to try out my new camera. I took pictures of the family and even managed to snap a close-up of a stranger across the restaurant. I was glad to be able to bother everyone by rudely pointing a camera at their faces while they were eating.

There weren't as many meal options for a vegetarian, but I managed to fill my plate with interesting new foods. Desert was my favorite part. I filled my plate full of cake and chocolate and even returned for seconds. I was out of control, like a bulimic at a buffet. No wait....I *was* a bulimic at a buffet. I loved being exposed to so many different kinds of foods without having to gain weight.

I liked eating, but I didn't like purging. I felt miserable when I'd get in the bathroom stall and give away the food. I wanted to cry. I wanted to escape myself and the life I was leading. I hated what I was doing, but I didn't know how to stop. It was much worse than anything I can convey. If you haven't been bulimic, then however bad you imagine it, I can tell you that it was worse.

I was trying to lose weight so I could be happy with myself, but I wasn't happy. I was growing more and more disappointed with myself and my life.

When I met with Dr Stone I told him about how my self injury was just as bad as it was before the hospital and that I had been starving myself. I said that I needed help and it was arranged that I would return to the hospital.

Monday, July 28

I refused to eat while I was in the emergency room, but when I was up on the eighth floor, there were consequences when I didn't. If I didn't touch my meal, I had to wear a hospital gown and was put into an isolation room. I also had to fill in a reflection form about why I didn't eat, what the consequences were, and what I could have done differently. Eventually I grew tired of being stored away in that room and filling out reports, so I started eating again. I ate, but the food didn't stay with me. Nothing and no one was stopping me from giving my meals to the toilet, so I did.

I know that sounds disgusting, but like I said, the experience is much worse than it sounds. It was a mess. I was a mess. It was sick to be reduced to putting my fingers in my mouth.

At breakfast, I managed to hide a plastic knife in the upper lining of my underwear. I twisted the plastic around until it snapped in half. I kept the sharp end and threw away the handle.

I also found a soda can and managed to pull off the little metal piece from the opening. I hid it safely at my waist along with the knife. I thought of hiding my new tools in my room, but it made me nervous to think of leaving them unattended.

I knew it was wrong. I knew that I shouldn't. My conscience troubled me, but my urge to damage myself was strong. I wondered what I should do. I had the tools. Once I had the tools it was too late to turn back. Or was it?

I remembered what the wards psychiatrist said when she learned that I had been hurting myself during my stay but didn't ask for help. "This is what you are here for," she told me.

I was there to get help. What I should do was ask for help. I was afraid though. How could I approach them? I was so shy and nervous, and it seemed that almost every day I was getting a new nurse; A new person to take care of me and who expected me to confide in them. I had to start over with too many different nurses and be expected to tell my story again and again. I didn't want to. I wanted to talk to the nurses I met on my first days at the hospital. I had already confided in them. The barriers had already been crossed.

What was I supposed to do? Walk up to some stranger and say, "Hey, look what I got"?

By supper time I was still struggling with the answers. I remember leaning against the wall in the hallway around the corner of the cafeteria while waiting to hand back my empty tray. I must have looked as upset as I felt because Saul, the orderly, asked me if I was okay.

Saul was a man who looked to be in his early fifties. He had short grey hair and a mustache to match. He had a kind face. I had seen Saul many times before. He had served me my meals and watched over me and the other patients on most evenings. He carried my bag down on the elevator on the day that I was released from my first stay.

We had exchanged small talk, but I had never stopped to really talk to him.

I admitted to Saul that I was troubled.

"You can talk to your nurse about it," Saul suggested once he stopped to talk. There was a break in his work as he waited for the next person to finish eating and bring their tray.

"I don't feel comfortable doing that," I admitted. "I've talked to nurses before, but I don't know these ones. There's new people all the time and I don't know how to talk to them."

"You know me, don't you?" Saul asked in a helpful tone that indicated an offer to listen.

"Yes." I knew Saul much better than any of the nurses on staff.

Saul waited patiently for me to say something. What could I say? Words were too big and I didn't know how to just jump in and say it.

Instead of words, I decided to show him part of what was troubling me. I pulled at the elastic lining of my underwear and took out my two tools. I showed Saul what I had been hiding on my open palm.

Saul nodded his head in realization, then held his hand out for me to pass the tools to him.

"Do I need to have you wear a hospital gown and go into the isolation room? That's what I'm supposed to do in this situation." Saul didn't ask his question in an intimidating way. His voice was calm and soft.

I shook my head, no. I didn't want that at all, though it was probably what I deserved.

"I'm going to put these away," Saul told me. "If you need to talk, you can come see me."

I was grateful for the offer and the kindness.

I was able to walk away with a clear conscience. I had done what I was supposed to do. Was this progress? Was my willingness to surrender a sign that things were going to get better?

Wednesday, July 30

Only days later, I found myself in the same situation. I had taken a knife at breakfast. I kept the knife hidden until I needed it and was alone. I crouched down in a corner of my isolation room where I couldn't be seen from the door. I lifted my sleeve and began to saw into my shoulder. I was disappointed at how dull the teeth of the blade were. I had to carve back and forth many times, but even then, the cut was red, but I drew no blood. I was disappointed. I had waited all day to use it and it wasn't working the way I had pictured.

I heard footsteps. They were light and I barely heard them on time to hide the knife by folding it in my fist with my fingers curled around it. It was Saul that appeared before me. He bent down at my side and asked me what was wrong.

I didn't answer his question, but from the expression on his face I could tell that he realized I had something in my hand.

"Give that to Saul. What do you have?" he coaxed.

I thought it was interesting how he referred to himself in the third person.

I hesitated, then showed him the knife.

"What were you going to do with that?" Saul asked me.

I looked at my sawed shoulder and his eyes followed the direction of my own.

"Poor little girl," he said with sadness when he saw what I had done.

I was puzzled by his sympathy. "This is my fault," I told him. I wasn't someone else's victim. I was my own. If it was my fault, then how could I possibly be a poor little girl?

Saul got me to sit on the bed where I could be seen by the door. He then left the room to get me a hospital gown and tell my nurse what I had done.

My nurse was a young woman with shoulder length black hair. She put disinfectant on my wound, then she told me to sit on a chair in my doorway where they could keep an eye on me. I stayed in that chair until it was time to take my medication and go to sleep.

Thursday, July 31

I got to see a familiar face the next day. Ashton was on staff, though he wasn't assigned to me.

I was leaning against my door frame when Ashton came to see how I was. Before he said anything, his eyes narrowed while looking at my left shoulder.

"You did that with a pen?" he guessed.

"No. With a plastic knife," I corrected.

Ashton nodded his head in disapproval, then he talked with me as we walked in the halls. I don't remember much of the conversation we had that day, but I remember him saying that he believed me when I said that cutting helped.

I spent most of that day on my chair in the doorway to my room. I thought that my nurse from the night before had had a good idea that had also worked for me in the past. If I was in the doorway, I was less likely to hurt myself. I felt safer in the doorway.

Sometimes I would just watch people go by and see the nurses writing in files at their desks.

Looking back, I wish I had spent much of that time filling out the pages of my journal so I could remember all that happened, but I had fallen out of the habit.

There was one opinionated nurse who thought it was dumb for me to be sitting in the doorway. She said I should be able to control myself without staying where I was always seen.

Some people pick at little things that don't need to be picked at. They didn't need to babysit me. Sitting there didn't change anything for them. So I didn't like being criticized, but I didn't move to please them either. I knew why I was in that chair. I had a hard time controlling my impulses. If I were alone, I would hurt myself, but I would never self injure in front of others. So when I was in the door, I was safe from myself.

Later that afternoon, I wasn't so determined to fight the urge to cut. I had found another metal piece from a soda can. I had it hidden in the upper lining of my underwear.

I had been searching desperately for a time when I could use my crude tool.

My nurse that day was a very heavy woman with short, brown hair. Her name was Bertha. She didn't seem cruel, but she didn't seem kind either. She wanted to talk to me, but I had no patience for it. I didn't want to talk to this woman. I didn't know her and I really felt the need to be doing something else at that time; something self destructive. I wanted Bertha to leave so I could be by myself with my piece of metal.

When Bertha finally left, I backed into my room where I wouldn't be seen and pulled my small tool out of hiding. I stood in the corner and started dragging the metal piece over the same place as I had done with the plastic knife. I had made several thin red lines by the time that Joseph had called into my room to ask what I was doing.

I was startled at the intrusion and felt a slight panic. "Nothing," I told him. "I'll be out soon."

That was when Joseph walked into the room and poked his head around the corner. He got wide-eyed. "Oh!" he cried. "Don't do that!"

"I'm fine," I replied. Joseph had already seen it and he was aware that I did that kind of thing. I wished he hadn't defied the rules by entering the room.

Joseph disappeared and I heard him calling for help and telling them what I was doing.

The heavy nurse I had come to know as Bertha came storming into the room.

She took my piece of metal, then grabbed my arm. She angrily guided me to the door where she wanted me to sit in the chair where I could once again be seen.

I remember my heart racing and wishing I could disappear.

Ashton came by and noticed the new cuts on my upper arm. He nodded in disapproval, but said nothing.

New nurses came out of the elevator and met with those who were at the end of their shift. Bertha was gone. I was glad that she wasn't there to look at me while knowing what I had done. If the new nurses knew what I did, they didn't say anything about it.

I don't remember much more about that visit, but I know that I stayed a week. I know that at the end, Dr Knoll asked me how I had dealt with eating all week.

I admitted that it didn't affect me because I had given all my food to the toilet.

Saturday, August 2

 I didn't do any better after that hospital stay. I was throwing up at least once a day. I would either not eat, or eat and toss it up. I ate a lot of boxes of dozen donuts. I ate chips, cookies, cinnamon buns and cake with ice cream, but none of it stayed inside me.
 The most I weighed was 122 pounds, but soon I was down to 105 pounds. I was beyond sick of throwing up. I had played in my throat until it bled and became painful. I would spit blood into the sink and rinse it away. I was exhausted and out of breath; choking on my own fingers. After purging my meals, I'd become so hungry again. I didn't have the energy to stand, so I laid on the bathroom floor until it would pass.
 Eating filled a hole, like I was swallowing and burying my emotions. Afterwards though, purging was discouraging and nearly brought me to tears.
 I was sick of it. I was so sick of it that I started dreaming of pouring oil on my arm and lighting it on fire. I wanted a pain so great that I wouldn't think of eating. I expressed this dream to my psychiatrist, Dr Silk. I told her that I couldn't do it anymore. That admission was the beginning of a third hospital stay that lasted four weeks.
 From that first time that I tossed up a bag of donuts to the day that I had walked into my psychiatrists office, and said that I had given up, I had lost 17 pounds.
 My face was thinner.

My pants didn't fit.

No one said anything though. I thought that maybe it didn't show and I was still fat. How could I have lost all that weight and still be fat? I kept setting goals for myself. First I decided I had to get down to 112 pounds, but once I lost that, I had to get down to 110 pounds for insurance purposes. When I started eating again, I would likely gain weight, so I was going to give myself 2 pounds of a head-start. When I reached 110 pounds, I still hadn't had enough. I had gotten it into my head that unless I was losing 1 pound every day, I was fat. If I gained weight, even a fraction of a pound, I was horrified and self-loathing. If I stayed at the same weight, I was disappointed, but if I lost weight, I was happy. I didn't stay happy for long though. Every day was a competition with the day before. Every day I had to lose a pound or I was fat.

This time I was even more determined that I would change, but change wouldn't come easy and my fear of gaining weight was my greatest obstacle. Even when I was at the hospital, I would eat very little of my meals. I would have to go to the isolation room every time I ate to make sure that I wouldn't throw up the few mouthfuls I had swallowed.

Even with what little I had in me, I felt I had to use every spare minute to walk around my room and burn calories. Walking meant that I was breaking the rules. I wasn't allowed to walk more than one and a half hours a day.

I had never even thought about calories before the day that a nice nurse named Annette was assigned to me. Annette used to be bulimic. She told me about what calories were in what foods and how many calories would be burned with a certain amount of walking.

I believe Annette was trying to inspire me to overcome my disorder and to show that she understood. I liked talking to her, because she did in fact help me feel understood.

I hadn't thought to put numbers to foods. Calories meant nothing. I wasn't prejudiced. I threw up anything that I ate, whether it was buttered or sweetened, or low in fat.

It was too late to turn back. The numbers were already in my head. There were 300 calories in a donut, 110 in one portion of Rice Krispies, and 60 in a slice of processed cheese. If I walked fast for one hour I could burn 200 calories.

That's when a change was made. I began walking to lose weight and not just because I liked it or it calmed me down. I began to walk at any chance I got.

I was functioning off of very little food, so even to date, I don't know where I got the energy.

For breakfast I would sprinkle a bit of Rice Krispies on the bottom of a styrofoam bowl and added some milk. My meals consisted of merely a few mouthfuls.

For lunch and supper I'd taste a bit of the main meal, then have jello or some fruit.

After a few days of eating next to nothing, my nurse and my doctor changed the rules. I had to eat everything on my plate. If I didn't I wouldn't be allowed to walk at all and I'd lose the right to having visitors for that day and the next day.

I was terrified every time I sat in front of a plateful of food. I viewed it as an insurmountable obstacle, but most of the time, I succeeded.

I would eat everything, but for lunch and supper, I was able to throw up most of what I ate, even after my mandatory two hours in the isolation room.

Along with the new rules came new rewards. I would be rewarded for every pound I gained. If I gained one pound, I would be allowed one hour a day on the outside.

The weight gain didn't come easily because I fought it in any way that I could. I knew that it was what had to happen, but getting heavier scared me. I didn't want it and couldn't face it.

I would get reprimanded every time I was caught walking around and around the bed in the isolation room. I could tell they were growing irritated with me, but there were no consequences to my actions.

The staff seemed surprised that I hadn't gained any weight, but I was certain not to tell them why that was.

I had brought a bag of dried fruit with me to snack on. I thought that if I ate healthier things then I would be more inclined to keep it down.

There was little over half a cup of dried fruit left in my bag and I ate it all. The presence in my stomach made me nervous enough that I vowed to get rid of it. I closed myself into my bathroom. It took a lot of effort for me to try and bring up the fruit. My body wouldn't give it back easily. I worked so hard to force it up that my eyes watered and tears dripped off my nose and into the water.

I grew panicked when I heard a knock at the door. Since my fingers were in my mouth I couldn't answer immediately, so Roger opened the door to find me bent over the tidy bowl with stomach acid dripping from my mouth and fingers.

"What are you doing?" Roger asked sternly. "Trying to make yourself throw up?"

I was humiliated. "Yes."

"You don't want to help yourself do you?" Rogers question was more of a statement. "Come on. You're going back to the 62."

I didn't say anything to him after that. I wiped the acid from my fingers with some toilet paper and rinsed out my mouth before following Roger back to the 62 that I had just gotten out of.

My nurse came to me a few hours later to confront me. "I heard that Roger surprised you in the bathroom. You're not using your time here to your advantage. You came for help, but you're not trying."

Her words made me mad. "Judge as you may, but it's not easy to come here and eat and keep my food. It's not easy to get caught in the bathroom with fingers in my mouth. I'm trying. I've been eating well. I can't get everything right."

It seemed that my nurse didn't expect me to talk back. She didn't say anything more.

~ ~ ~ ~

Marie came to visit me.

I wondered if she knew that I had an eating disorder, but that she was just staying quiet about it. I had been told that it showed a lot that I had lost weight. Surely she must have noticed.

"Are we going to talk about the elephant in the living room?" I nervously asked my sister.

"What?" Marie was confused.

"I recently lost 17 pounds," I told her. "I've been starving myself. Did you really not notice?"

"I noticed, but I thought you lost the weight gradually over time. I thought you were losing it normally," Marie guessed.

"Well, I didn't," I let her know. "I've been making myself throw up. I'm really sick."

"Did you throw up the chocolate peanut butter cups that I gave you?" she wondered.

I smiled at the question and where her worries laid. "No. For some reason, I can't throw up peanut butter. Maybe because it's sticky."

Marie accepted my answer.

My sister was supportive of me even if she couldn't understand what I was going through.

I was close to Marie and saw her to be as much of a friend as she was a sister, so I felt that I could tell her. I was still very embarrassed by my disorder though and didn't want to tell anyone else.

~ ~ ~ ~

I started dreaming of donuts; of so many donuts. I decided that as soon as I was permitted an hour on the outside, I would drive down to the donut shop and buy a dozen. I planned to either throw up my prized sweets at home or at the hospital when I returned. When I say that I dreamed of donuts, I don't mean to underrepresent. I thought about and lusted over the idea of donuts throughout my every day. My yearning for binging was so strong that it actually became painful.

When I finally gained a pound, I was told that I could go out in the afternoon of the same day.

LADY INJURY

I made the mistake of asking for some Quetiapine in order to calm down. I had been anxious and thinking of hurting myself. I admitted as much to the woman who was my nurse for the first time that day. She was a pretty young nurse with blond hair.

"I decided that you wont be taking your hour outside today because you are in danger of hurting yourself," the young nurse told me.

I tried to explain that they were only thoughts of self injury and that I wasn't going to act on them, but she still refused to let me go.

I was desperate and my donuts were in danger, so I wasn't about to give up. "Just ask Harvey. He knows that I wont hurt myself today," I suggested. I knew that Harvey could vouch for me because I had passed up some very serious tools that day.

I had been standing in my doorway, watching the patients with freedom on the outside of the isolation room. I watched two separate patients throw away their razor blades in the trash in front of the offices. Blades were supposed to be given to the staff and disposed of where the other patients couldn't get to them. I found it incredible that I witnessed this happen twice with only minutes from each other. Both times I had gotten Harvey's attention and pointed to the trash can for him to retrieve the blades. I was impressed with my ability to pass up a very intense and desired method of self injury. I told Harvey that it felt like I was being tested.

Even after I told this tale of two razor blades, my nurse still refused to let me go. She wanted to talk to my doctor first, but my doctor was in a meeting and I feared that It would be too late for me to leave by the time that we got to see her.

I complained and begged a lot. I was behaving quite unlike myself. I was almost crying over something that seemed as trivial as one hour on the outside. It was more than just an hour out to me. It was a chance to binge like I hadn't in weeks. Since I had begun my eating disorder, I found that over eating was more than just a desire, it felt like an aching need. Parts of me would tare into pieces over wanting food.

I was called in to a meeting with Mable and my nurse.

The psychologist started by saying that there had been a misunderstanding.

"No," I corrected. "There wasn't. I was taken for a liar. I said that I wasn't going to hurt myself and she didn't believe me."

"Marge made the right choice," The psychologist defended my nurse. "We had a meeting and all the doctors and nurses agreed with what Marge decided."

I got upset. I even cried. Crying was something that was difficult for me to achieve on other days, yet it came so easily to me then. I was behaving very much like a child and had no excuses.

"What's the point in working to gain weight to get an hour outside if it isn't going to be given to me?" I asked them. "I worked hard to gain weight, but now what's the point?"

"To get better," Mable told me.

I knew that she was right and I felt foolish. I was foolish, but my emotions kept bubbling up inside me and crawling out. "I'm not a liar. I said that I wasn't going to hurt myself and I won't. There's a difference between thinking of cutting and intending to go through with it. I'm not a liar."

Another meeting was called later that involved my doctor, but I was already embarrassed as it was and I didn't want to talk about it anymore. I was reassured though that I would still be able to go out the next day. It was just that one day that was lost.

~ ~ ~ ~

I didn't get my donuts that day, nor the next. I did get to go out for an hour though, but after leaving the hospital, I met up with Joseph who was walking to the hospital to see me. I hadn't expected to see him and I knew that any plans for binging were gone.

Before my re-admission, Joseph had finally been released from the hospital after a three month stay and was now living in an apartment down town. He wasn't alone because at his request, I gave him my kitten. Joseph came to visit me sometimes and we would take a walk or play ping-pong.

I was really enjoying my time with my friend. I had forgotten all about Dr Knoll's warning to be careful of Joseph. He earned his place as my friend by his own right.

Soon though, there was something about Joseph that slowly started to change. He would talk a lot about how the world would be saved if everyone grew a garden and gave the food away for free. This would bring an end to all forms of world suffering.

His interest in the bible seemed to grow. Although I admired his faith, there was something more extreme about the faith that Joseph possessed.

"I've been writing to the radio stations. Soon it will be the four hundredth letter that I send them. I tell them all about how we all need to grow a garden," Joseph spoke excitedly. "Sometimes if I listen really close, I can hear them answering me through the radio. You need to listen to the radio and you'll hear it."

"Okay."

Yeah, *okay* may not have been the thing to say, but I didn't know what the right thing was. I vowed to be supportive and look past his illness.

We found Devon crashing at my place, so I had a nice first outing with my friend and my brother. I thought that maybe some strange force was keeping me in line; keeping me from eating my way into my own destruction.

The same couldn't be said about the days that followed. Every day that I was allowed out, I would binge on donuts or chocolate bars. Also, on most evenings at the hospital, I would binge on little social tea cookies and orange juice. I had to smuggle the cookies into my room and I hid them in my drawer until I could eat them. I reminded myself of Lisa and the stories of cookie smuggling that she had told.

Every day I had my meals at the desks where I could be watched and have my nurse take note of what I did or did not eat. Most of the time, I forced myself to go ahead and eat it all, but once in a while, I refused to eat at all.

Gaining weight wasn't a pleasant or easy thing to do, so I found myself filling out a lot of forms explaining why I refused to eat and how it made me feel. I wrote things like that I was sorry and that I hated myself. I wrote that I was afraid and didn't understand what I was doing.

I hurt myself several times during that stay. The first cuts were made with a plastic knife and were minor, so my doctor decided to overlook it. She felt that I shouldn't be made to work on two problems at the same time. It was decided that we would be concentrating more on my eating disorders.

The next time I self injured was in the isolation room. I sat in the corner and used a safety pin to tug away at bits of skin. I managed to make a rather decent sized hole.

Carson was my nurse that night. When he came in to find me, he immediately took the safety pin away. "Who gave this to you?" he asked with agitation. "Where did you get this?"

"Nobody gave it to me," I answered nervously. "It was in my things."

Carson had me get out of the corner and onto my bed where I could be seen. He then asked to see what I had done to myself. "You had time to do all that?" he was surprised as he pointed to my exposed leg.

I realized he was referring to all the lines on my lower calf. "No, of course not. Most of these are scars, not scratches. I've gotten them over a long period of time."

Carson seemed mad and I didn't like seeing him that way. I wondered why someone would be mad over my hurting myself. I realized that what I was doing was wrong, but was it something to grow angry over? I noticed that several people reacted in anger. I found that puzzling.

Carson left the room to get me a gown to wear. I couldn't wear my own clothes after hurting myself; That was protocol.

I had a habit of needing to feel my wounds and my scars. I'm not sure where that need came from, but at the hospital they frowned on it because it could cause infection. Saul stopped by my room while doing the rounds. He caught me touching my leg. I quickly covered my wounds with my hands so he couldn't see what I had done.

"Show me what you did," Saul instructed. When I lifted my hands and let him see, his face grew sad. "Oh, what did you do?"

Saul left the room and I heard him telling Carson that I had hurt myself, but Carson already knew.

By the time Carson came back into the room, I was passing my fingers over my wounds to feel them.

"Am I going to have to tie you down?" Carson spoke sternly.

I pulled my fingers away from my leg with urgency. "No."

I had been threatened to be tied down to the bed once before that. It was a few weeks earlier. I had been peeling my band aids back several times to check on my burn wounds. I wasn't doing it to hurt myself. I just felt the need to know what kind of state the wounds were in. I would imagine that I wasn't supposed to play with the band aids in order to prevent infection. They seemed to worry a lot about infection at the hospital. The threat to tie me down if I didn't stop was efficient both times that it was used. The thought of being tied to a bed seemed intensely terrible. Would they really do that? The concept seemed barbaric. I felt that I had to do what was necessary in order to not meet that end.

Once Carson came back with the gown, he closed the door and told me to put it on. I realized that he intended to watch me undress. The idea of having someone stand there and watch me take my clothes off was offensive and embarrassing.

"There's no way I'm going to change in front of you," I told him immediately. I also crossed my arms and sat down on the bed to further indicate my defiance.

Carson hesitated, then called out the room to another nurse, "Could you come? She doesn't want to change in front of a man."

Carson left the room and another nurse that I had come to know as Ella came in. Ella was probably in her mid to late forties. She was slim with short blond hair. Ella was much more respectful than Carson. She took the gown and held it up as a wall in between us so I could change with greater privacy.

Saul came to see me afterwards and we talked. I can't remember now all that was said, but I know he was trying to understand my reasons for hurting myself.

I laid down to sleep and at about 8:00 pm Carson came in to give me what I called *my disgusting snack*. It was a nutritional supplement in the form of a drink. It came in three different flavors and each one of them was slightly more offensive than the next. I had already refused to take my supper so I wasn't going to get into any more trouble for refusing to drink that stuff either.

Carson insisted, "Go on." He nodded towards the drink so that I would take it.

I did take it, but only had a few sips before attempting to hand it back.

Carson nodded towards the drink once again, "Go on. Have some more."

I took a deep breath and then finished the drink.

At this point Carson was sitting next to me on the bed because it had taken a while for me to bring myself to finish drinking.

"I'm sorry for having made you mad earlier," I apologized and fell into tears. "I only wanted to hurt myself. I didn't mean to make you mad."

"It's okay," Carson consoled me.

"I don't know why I'm like this," I continued. "I didn't used to be like this. I didn't care about my weight and I ate whatever I wanted."

I don't really know that this man cared to listen, and even though he had been so angry shortly before, it was still a comfort to talk to him.

Carson generally wasn't of much help. If I said that I was starting to feel badly, all he told me was that it had to go well. "It has to go well." What was I supposed to do with that? What was the point in admitting that I needed help if that was all I was going to get?

That day ended calmly. I did nothing further to defy what they called rules.

Tuesday, August 19

I was quite worried about money since I wasn't able to work to pay my rent. In order to stay in treatment, I applied for welfare and was accepted. It was only the basic amount, and it was barely enough to pay my way, but it was money and I was grateful to have it.

As for my job at the old age home, there was one of the girls who wanted to have my shifts for the next three months. I realized that it may have been my boss who asked the girl to take my shift in order to give me time to recover.

Considering my situation I thought it was a good idea. I would have three months to try and get back up on my feet.

~ ~ ~ ~

Joseph called me regularly on the phone. He still called me his little sister. He came to visit me too.

My friend managed to quit smoking as he had promised. He was proud of his success.

He was also still very exited about saving us from world hunger by having everyone grow a garden and give the food away for free. He said that on that day there would be an end of this old world and the beginning of a new one.

"I stayed up for three days reading the bible," Joseph told me. "I'm finding so many messages that are addressed to me or about me. It's incredible! Isn't it incredible?"

I didn't see the point in going against his delusions. "Yeah. That would be amazing, but Joseph, don't you think that you should slow down? Get some sleep and read with a clear mind? You would be able to better absorb the information."

"I'm absorbing it. I sure am," Joseph said joyfully and with a spring in his step. "I can't wait to get home so I can read some more."

I didn't know what to do about my friend. He was clearly in trouble. He needed help. "Have you been taking your medication?"

"Yes, they bring it to my apartment every day and watch me take it," Joseph informed me.

"You know, your medication can't work right if you're taking speed at the same time," I worried. "It might be time for you to return to the hospital."

"What? No," Joseph declined. "I don't need help. I'm happy now."

"Maybe the next time that the social worker brings you your medication you can tell them that you need help," I suggested.

Joseph didn't reply, so I just let things go.

~ ~ ~ ~

There was a very interesting elderly woman who was admitted to the ward around the same time as I was. The first time I met her was after my second stay on the eighth when I had come to the hospital to visit Joseph. I had stepped out of the elevator to find several people gathered in front of the offices. I found Joseph and waited as he signed some papers permitting him to leave the hospital for an hour.

I was amused and enchanted when a woman that I would later come to know as Evangeline walked up to me and started talking. She was wearing a hospital gown and had thin grey hair that was about four inches long. She spoke to me at great length about something that she clearly found important and amusing, but I understood none of it. Her words were a series of mumbles. She would smile and even laugh when she felt she said something funny. I didn't know what was funny, but I couldn't help but smile at her intensely upbeat and amused mood.

Once in a while I could pick up on some of her sounds that resembled a word that I thought I recognized, but that was the most I could do.

I couldn't help but fall in love with the sight of that woman. There was something poetic about her scattered appearance.

When Joseph was ready, I bid her goodbye, but weeks later I got to know her much better when I was a patient alongside her.

Very often Evangeline was placed in a large chair that held her down so she couldn't get into trouble when no one was watching. She had to be on high surveillance. She wasn't always kind and smiling. Evangeline had a mean side to her where she would yell at everyone. She would spit at us and bang on the chair that held her down. It didn't matter how much she cursed in words I couldn't understand, because I always felt fondly towards her and often stopped to speak with her.

I knew how to approach her considering my years working with the elderly, but for Evangeline it was my experience with children that really helped me. Though she was elderly, her attitude was highly childlike.

Evangeline was always hungry and spoke a lot about wanting a ham sandwich. If she asked when lunch was going to be, and I said, "One hour," she would scream, "No!" at the top of her voice. I found her passion endearing.

~ ~ ~ ~

During that stay it was Dr Goodshaw that was in charge of my case. She was probably around 40 years old. She had shoulder length brown hair.

I had been worrying more and more about the healing burns on my wrist. My burns would soon be well enough that I wouldn't need bandages. If I didn't have bandages and I wasn't allowed arm warmers, my burns would be in the open for everyone to see. I brought this up with Dr Goodshaw.

"These bandages are the only things covering what I did to myself," I told the doctor.

"You can learn to deal with it," Dr Goodshaw suggested. "It's nobodies business anyways. I can't let you have the arm warmers."

This was when I felt that I had to be very honest and direct. "If I don't get to wear my arm warmers and this bandage comes off for good, I would be willing to burn my wrist just so that it would need another bandage and be covered again."

The doctor was surprised. "Oh, well, you won me right there," she told me. "You can have the arm warmers. You won me right there."

I was relieved and pleased to get my arm warmers back.

It was Dr Goodshaw who allowed me to have my rubber bands the way I wanted to. She felt that it was better for me to snap a rubber band than to cut myself.

I was so grateful, and I put that rubber band to good use. It helped me avoid hurting myself several times. It wasn't always enough, but it was worth if for the times that it was.

I wasn't to use the elastic when there were patients around, but the sound of it carried far.

Saul would tell me sometimes that he heard me using it. He said that it hurt him inside. It really struck me as significant when he said that. I hadn't considered that hurting myself was painful to others. I did think of it hurting my family, but I didn't stop to think of anyone else being affected by it. I should have though. I should have known, because in their place, it would have hurt me too.

~ ~ ~ ~

It was about two weeks into that particular stay that Dr Goodshaw came to me with an idea.

"I've been looking over all of your files and your history," Dr Goodshaw told me. "In my opinion, you have enough evidence against your offender to be able to take him to court."

"I don't think that I do have enough evidence," I told her. "It takes a lot to get someone convicted around here."

"You have enough," Dr Goodshaw reassured me. "You would have the hospitals backing on this. We could testify for you. You don't get sick like you are unless something causes it. Your state of mind is part of the evidence."

"It sounds scary," I admitted.

"It could be liberating for you," the Doctor told me. "If you do this it would be like you were standing up for yourself. You might be able to deal better with the past if you do this."

I wondered if there was truth to what she was saying. Would taking a man to court help me? It sounded awful. The most I had done to protect myself was to try to keep his hands away from me. I couldn't speak. I could only panic.

"I like the idea of standing up for myself," I told her. "When I was a kid I never wanted to do anything to defend myself in case it would offend someone else. I didn't tell him not to hurt me. I didn't make him stop. I was too scared and too loyal to my ideals," I paused. "If I do this, maybe it would be like telling him no."

"This could be really good for your healing," the doctor said to me.

"I don't know what to say," I told her. "I've always been afraid to hurt anyone in any way. If I did this it would hurt him."

"He hurt you," she pointed out.

"Yes, he did," I agreed. "I heard a case on the radio about a man who was convicted of rape and he was sentenced to one week working full time at a meat pie factory. That's all he got. It's not even worth it if he gets one week at a pie factory or if he doesn't get convicted at all."

"We need to think about the good this will do for you, for your progress," Dr Goodshaw worked to convince me.

I hadn't expected for anyone to come and tell me these things. I was taken by surprise and I didn't know how to react. It seemed unreal.

"I'm going to think about it," I told her.

Before moving forward with a plan like that, I needed to be sure that it wouldn't be hurting my family. I wanted to talk to my mom, my sister and my brothers. I was sure I would have most of their support.

I anxiously dialed the numbers to talk to Devon. I was surprised and relieved when he said that I had his backing. He said that I should do what I needed to do.

My whole family was behind me. It was just me that I wasn't so sure about. Could I do it? Would I break? Would it be too much? I didn't see myself as a strong person. I felt things too intensely. If I went through a trial, would I completely self destruct? Would my cutting and my eating disorders get worse?

It felt like I would be taking a really big chance that may not be worth it.

Saul wanted me to do it. A few of the nurses and the psychologist wanted me to do it as well. They all spoke of how healing it could be.

I had to let it run a lot in my mind. I kept reasoning with myself as to what would be right for me and right for the situation. It was a big decision.

Monday, August 25

I got to have another visit from Joseph. He was good company even if things weren't going so well for him.

We took a walk around the halls in between ping-pong games.

"Did you know that when certain people are a patients here, they aren't allowed to listen to a radio station or a TV?" Joseph quizzed me.

"I didn't know," I told him. "Why is that?"

"Because of those people who hear messages in the songs. They think that the radio is talking to them," he explained.

"Yeah?" I asked with a smile. "Like schizophrenics?"

"Yeah."

"Like you?" I asked pointedly in reference to his belief that the talk show hosts were talking to him.

"I'm Schizo affective," he corrected.

"The same thing applies," I reasoned.

"It's different for me."

"How is it different?"

"Those people hear the voices because they are sick, but I hear the voices through the holy spirit," Joseph explained. "I've been glorified by Jesus."

I worried about Joseph and what his state of mind meant for him. I knew he was slipping away but I didn't know how to stop it.

"Check this out," Joseph invited as he stopped walking and faced me. "If we try really hard, we should be able to see Jesus between us."

I watched Joseph in deep concentration.

"What does he look like?" I asked casually.

"Kind of shimmery, like water. It's hard to explain." Joseph gave up when Jesus didn't appear. "I don't know why I can't see him. He's at my apartment all the time."

~ ~ ~ ~

A few days later I found a bent up staple at the desks while I was there to eat my meal. I waited until no one was looking and I reached out and put it in my pocket. For several days before that I had been dreaming of poking a pin into my vein to do just enough damage so as to make a trickle of blood flow from halfway up my arm. I had gotten the idea when a nurse took a blood sample.

A band aid was placed over the hole in my vein, but even then the blood overflowed. I'd had blood tests taken many times before that, but I had never seen it make my blood run out of the hole. I liked the idea of being able to make a bit of a mess with my blood and yet only have a temporary little hole as evidence. I liked the idea a lot, so when I saw the staple, I didn't pass up the chance.

At the end of the day, after everyone had taken their night medication and had gone to bed, I closed myself into my bathroom and sat on the floor. I used both the staple and a safety pin to poke into my veins where blood tests were usually taken, but no blood came. I wasn't successful at drawing blood from my arm so I tried it from my wrist, but that didn't work either. I kept pocking holes and nothing would happen. I got sick to my stomach watching the needle wiggle around in my arm as I tried to draw blood. I heard myself screaming inside my head for me to stop. I could see that what I was doing to myself was sick, but a very controlling part of me didn't know how to stop.

I began using the safety pin to rip the skin away from around a vein on my wrist. I thought that I would be able to get better access to the vein that way, but it didn't work.

I gave up trying to puncture a vein and decided to start hurting my leg. I used the safety pin to rip away bits of skin until I had a hole into my leg. When I heard noise outside my bathroom door, I knew that it was Saul coming for the rounds. He came by every half hour.

I quickly hid the safety pin behind the toilet so I could pretend that I had done all that damage with the staple.

The door opened without them even knocking, and soon beyond the flashlight I saw Saul and Ella standing in the doorway.

I had pulled my pant-leg down so they couldn't see what I had done.

Saul put a pair of blue rubber gloves on and bent down to my level. "Show me," he directed before pulling my pant-leg back up. "Why didn't you come talk to me? You know that I'll always listen."

"I know, and I did talk to you," I answered.

"Did you see your psychologist today?" Saul asked.

"Yes."

"And did you tell her what you were thinking of doing?"

"Yes."

"And what did she say?"

"That we were there to talk about something else," I revealed as I stared blankly ahead of me. I was too embarrassed to be able to look at Saul for more than just a second. I could feel Ella's eyes on me too. She wasn't mad like Carson had been. She seemed more sympathetic.

"Did you hurt yourself anywhere else?" Saul asked.

I said nothing as I pointed to the holes over my veins.

"What did you use?" Saul wanted to know.

I held up the bent staple and he took it from between my bloody fingertips. I could see then why it was a good idea for him to be wearing gloves.

"Okay," Saul said. "Lets go."

Saul gave me his hand to help me up, I then followed him and Ella out of my room and into the isolation room. I was made to change into a gown and stay there for the night.

~ ~ ~ ~

I was forgetting to mention that there were more guys after me than I could handle during that particular stay on the eighth. My theory was that having men cooped up in a ward made them target whatever female was most available.

I often asked if I could go hide in isolation room 62 just to be alone and avoid getting pestered by the guys.

There was this young man named Emerson who flirted with me for my entire stay. He would call my name through the halls. He'd say, "Where's the pretty girl?" or "Did you see the pretty girl?" He would call me Princes or Hot chick.

It was actually embarrassing to hear him call for me that way when everyone could hear.

I felt that Emerson was getting too physical with me though. He would put his arms around me like I was his girlfriend. He would try to take my hand, but I rejected him every time. When he tapped my butt I told him that he had crossed a line and that he shouldn't do that again, and he didn't. At least not at first. The second time he tapped my butt, I tried to make light by saying, "Hey! I'm going to tell Carson on you." It wasn't a joke though and I was really bothered by it.

After that I went to fold laundry. It was a quiet task that I found calming. Once in a while I would stop and stare into space. I noticed that Carson was watching me space out from a distance.

Finally, I said to Carson, "I don't want him to touch me anymore."

"Well, you can't just let them have their way," Carson told me.

I had never been good at defending myself. I let people hurt me and walk all over me. "That's the problem. I don't stop him," I said to Carson. "But taps on my backside is going a little far."

LADY INJURY

Carson took what I said seriously and he had Saul talk to Emerson. He told Emerson that we were getting too close and it wasn't appropriate at the hospital.

Emerson didn't tap my butt again, but he would give me long hugs when no one was looking. I had told him that we weren't together and he shouldn't do that, but he did it anyways. I wished desperately that I was one of those girls who were confident and capable of sticking up for themselves. I wished I had that in me, but I didn't, so I let him hug me.

Emerson would talk about how he was falling in love with me. He was planning his future with me in it. He promised me diamonds and he promised me the world. The sad thing was that if he weren't such a jerk and have such violent issues, I may have liked him. Lots of guys flirted with me at the hospital, but with Emerson it was different because I liked who he was when he was calm. I liked his crude personality. He was interesting. He called cartoons, comic-toons. We watched Dora the explorer together.

There was another guy too. His name was David. He was 22 and he also kept telling me how pretty I was. He said he wanted to protect me, take care of me, and give me a daughter.

David and Emerson would argue over who got me. One would tell the other to stay away from me. They would make up stories to make each other back off, like that I had a boyfriend and was therefore unavailable.

Another time, Emerson got in a fight with an older gentleman who looked like he was in his early seventies. They fought over which one of them that I belonged to. I just rolled my eyes and walked away.

There was a middle aged man who took a liking to me, but he was more polite about it than the others. He liked talking to me and told me that he would take me out for a ride on his motorbike some day. I told him that considering my past, I wasn't ready for a relationship yet. I needed to trust men first. That's when he told me that I have to expect that when a man talks to me, it means that he likes me.

I wondered why men and women couldn't talk without it meaning something more.

~ ~ ~ ~

My elderly friend Evangeline had just undergone electroshock therapy. I found the idea disturbing, but the therapy truly did make a difference for her.

Evangeline was less aggressive and many of her words were more distinguishable. I could get a better idea of what she was talking about and respond accordingly.

Sometimes they would let Evangeline move around instead of restraining her and I was able to walk with her around the halls.

I very much liked spending time with her and making her feel more calm. It was a nice feeling to be useful after having been away from my work.

~ ~ ~ ~

I found myself arguing often with one of the orderlies so that I could have as many salt packets as I wanted. I always used an unholy amount of salt on my food. It was shocking to most people.

"That much salt is really bad for you," Harvey lectured after only allowing me to have two salt packets.

"But my food doesn't have flavor without it," I complained. "I need at least 6 packets."

"That's not going to happen."

"What about 5?" I asked. "Saul and Roger always let me have as many as I want. Why can't you do the same?"

"I'm not Saul and Roger."

Harvey wasn't going to budge, but then again, he never did. I knew that on the days that Harvey was watching us, my food would be bland.

Eventually I got the idea to start smuggling salt out of the cafeteria on the days that Saul or Roger were in charge. It was the only way I could get as much as I wanted. I hid my salt in my coat pocket. The taste of my food depended on it.

~ ~ ~ ~

Sometimes I felt unsafe in my room where I could have access to things to hurt myself, so I asked if I could sleep in isolation room 62. Unless someone was already in that room, the answer was usually yes.

There was one night where the nurse in charge of me didn't want me to stay in the 62. I tried to explain why it was important, but it didn't change her mind.

I was conflicted as to what to do. Eventually I just sat in the little hallway between the kitchen and the staff elevators where people didn't usually pass. I sat between two elevators that were only used by the staff and were kept under lock so patients couldn't escape.

When it was time for me to go to my room at lights out, I refused. I said that I wasn't safe there because there were always things I would think of to use against myself; even things that it didn't seem like could be used. I was very creative and could hurt myself with most anything.

Finally my nurse changed her mind and let me sleep in the 62 where there was nothing but a bed bolted to the floor.

The next day, my doctor congratulated me for taking a stand like that. She liked that I protected my own safety in a way that wasn't violent or inappropriate.

~ ~ ~ ~

I wasn't always in a state of mind where I did what I had to in order to keep myself safe. Some days I didn't even care to try. I'm not sure why my resolve couldn't stay with me all the time.

There was one day when I took a chance in order to acquire something with which to hurt myself. There was a rare moment during the shift change where all the staff were in the back room giving each other their reports. My purse was hanging from a hook in the center of the main office. I knew that I had several safety pins inside of it. I quietly rushed to my purse and pulled out the pins, then ran back into the hallway without anyone seeing me.

At the end of that day, I waited until everyone went to bed, then I sat on the bathroom floor. I took a large safety pin and pushed it through a chunk of the skin on my leg. It took a surprising amount of force and time to push the pin through me but I succeeded. I closed the pin, then picked up a smaller one and used it to rip my skin bit by bit until I had dug deeper than I ever had before. I must have ripped a hundred bits of skin. The safety pin became more and more misshapen as I pulled constantly in order to tare my skin with it. My stomach twisted as I watched myself pulling the blood from my leg and coating my hands. I wished I would just stop. I didn't understand why I didn't just stop and I actually found myself wishing that someone would come and make me stop; but no one came.

I dug too deep. The wound was too great for me to leave it like that. If I were at home I could have used my bandages and taken care of it, but I wasn't at home and I needed help. I didn't know how to stop the bleeding and I was worried because of how deep it was.

I wrapped a white hand towel around my lower leg, then pulled my pant-leg over it. I left my room and walked towards the offices.

Carson saw me walking towards where he stood and he said, "Good night." I could tell in his tone that he meant, "Go to your room." It was after 10:30 pm and no one was supposed to be up, but I wished he didn't dismiss me so quickly.

I didn't turn around the way that I was asked to. I kept walking towards the offices and Carson met up with me there.

I walked over to Sara. She was a nurse that I had grown to like, though we hadn't spoken much. Sara asked me what was wrong.

"I need bandages," I spoke with a shaky voice. I held out my blood stained and mangled safety pin so as to make her understand what was wrong without me having to say it. I didn't like to say what I had done.

Carson asked to see what I did, so I slid down the length of the wall to sit on the floor. I was so anxious that I was shaking. I unwound the towel from my leg and let them see.

Carson looked closely at the wound. "This is going to need stitches," Carson said to his colleagues.

"It will be hours before the doctors downstairs can see her though," Sara guessed.

"Maybe first we can have a nurse from the ER confirm for us that she needs stitches," Carson suggested.

I was made to go into the 62 and to wear a gown. Soon a nurse that I didn't recognize came into the room with Carson and Sara to look at my wound. She said that I definitely needed stitches.

They didn't know what to do with me because none of them had time to take me down to the ER.

There was a guard though that was keeping watch on a patient who was in isolation room 7. The man he was watching was talked about a lot on the ward because he constantly made loud barnyard noises. This mentally handicapped man was on constant supervision. The guard watching him said that he would stay past his shifts end at midnight in order to take me down to the minor surgery room.

I fell asleep, but was woken past three in the morning.

I was made to sit in a wheelchair so they could push me downstairs. Once I got to the ER with the guard, I waited for a long time on an examining table.

The guard sat on a chair next to me. He didn't say much, but then again, neither did I.

The doctor that came to see me was a balding man in his forties. He wasn't rude or angry with me at all. I had become apprehensive of people getting mad at me. I didn't like it and it worried me a lot.

Getting stitches was something new to me. I had never needed medical help for my self injury before that day. I had made deep cuts before, but I handled them myself. I had all the supplies I needed in order to disinfect and patch them up.

I was given injections to numb the area. After that I was given two stitches to close the wound, then I was permitted to go back upstairs.

I finished the night in the 62. When I got up before breakfast, I left the room the same way I had done on all the other mornings that I woke up there. The difference was that this time, someone stopped me.

"Where are you going?" The orderly who watched the ward from midnight to eight in the morning spoke to me me.

"I'm going to my room," I answered. "I only really have to stay in the 62 for two hours after I hurt myself."

"Not anymore," Gordon informed me. "You have to stay there for 24 hours."

I grew wide-eyed. 24 hours? How could I stay there for so long? Why did the rules change? I was hoping that it was just another misunderstanding, but it turned out to be right. I had to stay there. From then on I would have to stay in the 62 for 24 hours every time I hurt myself.

I was allowed to leave the room for half an hour in the morning in order to shower. My knee high socks had been taken away, so I grabbed a pillow case to hide my lower leg on my walk to the showers.

"What are you doing with that?" Bertha asked me in reference to the pillow case that I had wrapped around my calf.

"I need it to hide my leg," I explained.

"I don't agree with you doing that," Bertha told me. "You hurt yourself for attention so you should go out there and show everyone what you did."

Bertha took my pillow case away, so I sat on my bed in defiance.

"I didn't do it for attention," I stated sternly.

"I know you did it for attention, just like you did to me last month," Bertha told me.

I was confused. "What are you talking about?"

"We were talking at the end of my shift, but when it was time for me to leave the hospital, you hurt yourself to make me stay," she explained.

"What?" I grew even more confused. At that moment I remembered the day she was talking about. I had cut my shoulder with a piece of metal from a soda can. Bertha had come in and she roughly brought me to the doorway where I could be seen and then she left. I remembered talking to her too, but I wasn't hurting myself to make her stay. I'm not sure if this sounds mean, but I didn't care about her. I mean that in the sense that she wasn't on my mind. I wanted her to leave the room so I could be alone and hurt myself. Why would I hurt myself to keep her from leaving? I didn't even remember that Bertha was my nurse that day. I didn't care that she was leaving.

"I wasn't going to play into your game," Bertha continued. "So I slapped a band aid on your shoulder and left."

This woman must have thought a lot of herself in order to come to that conclusion. Did she think that I would break my skin in her honor? That was ridiculous.

"I didn't do it for attention," I repeated.

"I could tell you did this for attention when I got the report from last night. You came to the offices and said, *I need bandages.*" Bertha said the words, *I need bandages* condescendingly.

I tried to explain to her what self injury was really about, but I don't think she understood. It was like talking to a brick wall, so I gave up. "I'm not leaving this room unless my leg is covered," I told her.

I didn't know this nurse very well, but I knew that I didn't like her.

Cutting for attention? Certainly not hers. Though, in a way, I did want attention. I wasn't going to get something to stop the blood unless I got someones attention.

Bertha gave me back the pillow case. She then followed me to the showers because I had to be watched at all times. I showered with the door partly open so she could listen in.

~ ~ ~ ~

I made the mistake of not telling one of my friends that my eating disorder was a secret. When this friend met up with my brother, she assumed that he knew and she mentioned it to him. Devon was surprised and asked Marie if it was more than just cutting with me. Was there a problem with food too?

So Devon knew about my new problem at that point. I didn't like that he knew, but he knew.

Things like that would make my anxiety rise, but I was able to deal with it in time. My mood was easily manipulated. My emotions always seemed high. The doctors and psychiatrists didn't believe me when I told them that my medication was making me more depressed. They thought that my increasing depression had nothing to do with the medicine. I knew this was their area of expertise, so I willed myself to believe them. I tried to have faith when they rose my level of medication. I would wait and see how it affected me.

~ ~ ~ ~

There were a few days on the ward with these dumb, made up rules.

I had a friend bring me some mixed nuts, but the staff wouldn't let me have them. They thought that I wasn't allowed to eat anything that was from outside the hospital. In my treatment plan, I had to eat everything on my plate. I even had a list of things that had to be on the menu every day. The list was made so that I would have those foods as a minimum, but the staff thought it meant that those foods were the only things I could eat. It took a few days before that misunderstanding was cleared up.

Another stupid, made up rule that they had was days later. I had refused to eat my meal, so I had to spend two hours in the isolation room and fill out a reflection form. After my two hours were over and I went into the halls, I was invited to play ping-pong with one of the patients and I accepted.

There was a very adamant nurse who wouldn't allow me to play ping-pong though.

"Why?" I asked.

"It involves physical exertion," she explained.

"If I don't eat, I'm not allowed to walk around for the sake of walking around. The rules say nothing about ping-pong," I argued.

"You need to go back to the isolation room," the nurse ordered.

"I already spent my mandatory two hours in there," I reminded her.

"You need to go," she repeated as she pointed to the 62. I would tell you what this nurse looked like, but I don't remember. It's probably better that way. She should remain a nameless, faceless member of the past.

"Tell me why. I didn't do anything wrong," I insisted, but she wasn't telling me why.

"You are supposed to stay in there. You agreed to this," she stated.

"I don't remember agreeing to this," I told her.

"Go!"

"Why?" I continued to defy her wishes. I was surprised at myself. I wasn't usually so argumentative. I was something of a pushover.

"Because you didn't eat," she explained.

Annette signaled for me to go towards her. I liked Annette, so I complied. I followed her towards the isolation room door.

"Since you didn't eat lunch, you have to stay in your room until your next meal," Annette explained.

I wondered when the rules had changed like that and why I hadn't been informed.

I wanted to say, "Show me in my file that it says I have to stay here. I want to see." Out of respect for Annette, I decided to trust her words and stay in the 62.

I also refused my supper, so I had to spend the whole evening in the 62 as well.

The next day I brought up this issue during a meeting with my psychiatrist and my nurse Michelle. Neither of them had heard of a rule stating that I had to stay in the 62 until my next meal after refusing to eat. I was grateful when they said they would make a correction in my file. They would let the staff know that I didn't have to stay in the 62 for so long, and that I could eat foods that weren't on the list.

I had been at the hospital for three weeks when I stopped eating again. I had gained weight and I was trying to fight it. I could feel my body changing.

That was when my doctor told me that if I didn't make any effort, I would have to go home.

Going home scared me as much as food did. If I went home I didn't see any hope of getting better.

Monday, September 1

Nights were usually the worst. My anxiety would skyrocket; sometimes out of nowhere.

I heard someone call a code white on the speakers. Code white indicated a violent patient. When they call a code, available nurses, orderlies and guards from all levels of the hospital would come up and help detain the patient. They would usually bring the patient to the isolation room and very often tie them to the bed. My heart hurt for everyone who got tied down. I felt it as if it were happening to me.

They called a code white for a schizophrenic patient named Sabrina. Sabrina didn't want to take her medication. She said that it was mind control and that she was going to call the police. She put her thumb to her ear and her index finger to her mouth as though her hand was a receiver. Sabrina spoke to the police through her hand. It might have been funny if she had been joking, but Sabrina really believed that she was talking to the police.

Roger, the orderly managed to get the agitated Sabrina to take her medication, but soon after she lost control and they had to call for back up. Elevators full of people arrived on the ward to help control Sabrina. I watched the woman being dragged to the isolation room and I saw one of the nurses carrying their big yellow box into the room as well. The yellow box, was a plastic container that was shaped much like a tool box. It contained the straps needed to tie a patient down. I hated that box. It meant something deeper than sad.

I cringed as I heard the shuffling feet and then Sabrina began to cry out. "You're raping me! You're raping me!"

The pain inside me grew and blistered as I listened. They were screams that cut deeper than my blades ever could.

I turned up the volume on my MP3 player to tune out the sound of the screaming, but once in a while I would take out my earphones to listen and see if Sabrina was all right.

Tuesday, September 2

By morning I had already decided that I was going to hurt myself that day.

My anxiety was high after Sabrina threw another fit and she was dragged screaming once again to isolation room 7. She had broken the ping-pong table by throwing herself on it repeatedly.

By that time my heart was racing fast and I had trouble breathing.

I took some Lorazepam before leaving the hospital for an hour that morning. I asked for my purse that was full of chocolate and I went outside. The moment I left the hospital, I started unwrapping and eating the contents of my purse. I ate while walking to the pharmacy to get shampoo. I ate while waiting in line at the bank to pay my rent. I ate on my way to the general store so I could buy even more chocolate to fill my purse.

I started thinking that I shouldn't be allowed out of the hospital anymore, because every time I was out I had a bulimic episode. It was disgusting and discouraging and desperate.

When I returned to the hospital on an empty stomach, I had to face my lunch once again. Even with knowing that I was going to lose the right to walk and have visitors for yet another day, I still refused to eat the full contents of my tray. I ate some mandarins and two slices of processed cheese. Because of my refusal to eat I spent another two hours in the 62 and filled in yet another reflection form.

I met with the psychologist in the afternoon. We did another 45 minutes of EMDR. It was meant to help me deal better with my emotions related to traumatic memories. It was awful. I pictured a memory of being molested over and over while following Mabel's finger with my eyes. I had to describe my thoughts, emotions, beliefs and sensations.

After about half an hour I started to not be able to handle the process anymore. I kept thinking that I didn't want to be inside that memory. I should have told Mabel that I couldn't handle it, but instead I continued the exercise and kept picturing those awful moments of my life. The guilt, the fear, the darkness and the paralyzing stillness beneath an invasive presence was overwhelming.

The only part that I liked was when Mabel got me to imagine that I had defended myself when I was abused and to tell her all the violent things that I wished I had done to my offender.

After the appointment I was a mess. I tried to fold laundry to calm down, but once in a while I would whip a towel repeatedly in the air to vent my feelings. I liked the snapping sound it would make. It was a way for me to feel like I was hurting something without actually hurting something.

Marge was my nurse that day and I asked her for some Lorazepam to help with the anxiety.

"Why are you anxious?" Marge asked me.

"Because I had an EMDR session today with the psychologist," I explained.

"What's EMDR?" she inquired.

"It's when you follow a finger and picture an awful moment of your life."

"What's the point of that?"

"It's supposed to help put things in the right place in your head, like memories and emotions."

I grew increasingly uneasy with talking about the subject.

"Did it go well?"

I really wished she would stop asking me questions. "Not really," I admitted. "It was awful."

"Why was it awful?"

"Because I had to picture myself getting abused by some sick pervert." I had gotten really impatient at that point so my tone was irritated.

"You don't have to talk to me like I'm supposed to know that already," Marge told me.

"Sorry," I apologized. "I'm just really anxious and I really want that Lorazepam."

"You're going to get the Lorazepam. I just wanted to ask some questions first."

I apologized later for being rude, but Marge said that I hadn't been. She offered that we could talk so we sat in the rocking chairs at the end of the hall.

"Have you been thinking of hurting yourself today?" Marge asked.

"Yes," I admitted.

"Are you planning on going through with it?"

I didn't want her to know the answer to that, but I grudgingly said, "Yes."

"Should I send you to the 62 right now?" Marge wanted to know.

I paused. I didn't want to go. I wanted to be free to hurt myself. I wanted it a lot. "I don't want to go. I want to stay in my room."

"I can put you in there now, or I can put you in there after medication," Marge offered.

"I'll go after."

So I was going to the 62, but not right away. I was glad because it gave me time to hide some tools in my pajamas.

I had the perfect tool with which to hurt myself. That day at lunch I was sitting at the front desk in front of two drawers that contained the supplies for the patients showers. There were razors in one of the drawers. I waited until no one was looking and I pulled out a razor and tucked it in the side of my pants. Part of me wasn't sure that I would get away with it, but I was relieved that I did.

In the privacy of my room, I broke the razor apart and kept the two blades that were inside of it. I discreetly threw out the plastic in a garbage can by the smoke room. I didn't want any evidence in my own trash can. I had the perfect tool. I only had to wait until I needed it.

I started walking around to self-soothe. I met with Saul in the hallway. I admitted that I wasn't doing so well. I said that I wanted to hurt myself and that I didn't want to be stopped.

I later walked into the 62 just to watch the sunset from the window. Saul followed me into the room. He clearly wanted to help.

We got to talking again about my fears of taking my offender to court. I was still very hesitant.

"How would you feel if you had a daughter who was hurting herself?" Saul tried to reason with me.

"I would be really worried about her," I said the first thing that came to my mind. "And no, I wouldn't want her to do that."

"What would you do?"

"I could tell her about my experiences and get her help," I imagined.

"What if she was abused, would you want her to go to court?"

"That would be really hard for her and I don't know if I would put her through a trial," I told him.

Saul smiled. "You are turning this towards your favor."

I did turn it in my favor. I knew that it would be hard for me to go to court and I wanted to protect myself from it.

It wasn't long after 8:00 that evening that I closed myself into my bathroom and sat on the floor with one of the razor blades. I cut two lines into my leg and then traced over them to make them deeper. It was strange and unnatural to watch two sides of flesh split apart so suddenly. There was a lot of blood, but I felt that I could handle more, so I cut a third line and watched it split apart the way that the others had.

I'm not sure how long I sat there bleeding after making those cuts. It wasn't too long; maybe five minutes.

I heard lite footsteps outside the door and I knew that it was Saul coming to check on me. I covered my leg with the towel in time for Saul to open the door. He didn't knock first. It was a good thing that I wasn't sitting on the toilet. I wondered how he knew that I was hurting myself and not doing something normal in the washroom.

Saul paused to put his blue rubber gloves on, then he kneeled down and pulled the towel off my leg.

"Show me what you did," Saul instructed. "Show it to Saul."

I didn't look at him. I couldn't. I stared straight ahead at the pipes under the sink.

Saul looked at my leg, then he took my right hand, just to hold it; to comfort me. I closed my eyes and leaned my forehead down on both our hands. I just sat waiting like that for a few seconds.

"How do you feel?" Saul asked me.

"Bad," I answered. "Really bad."

"Why didn't you come talk to me?"

"We talked," I said. "But I wanted to do this."

"Why?"

"I wanted to make a mess of myself," I explained. "I succeeded." I realized that success could come without victory. I had succeeded, but I wasn't happy about it. I wasn't happy at all. I had wanted to cut so bad, but when I did, it only made things worse.

"Are you ready to go?" Saul asked.

I knew he meant for me to go to the 62. "No. I want to stay here. Please. I want to stay here. I'm okay."

"Well, no. Of course you can't stay," Saul said then rose up from his bent down position. "Come on. We're going to find a way to get there without having everyone see."

The 62 was on the other side of the ward. I may have had to walk in front of several people to get there.

I took the towel and wrapped it around my wounded leg.

"Oh," I said as I noticed blood on the floor and started to wipe it up with my towel.

"Leave it there," Saul told me.

"I can't." I was thinking of someone else coming into the washroom and finding the blood stain on the floor. I didn't want that.

"Leave it there."

I didn't leave it. I had to get rid of it.

Once the floor was clean and my leg was wrapped, I walked to the 62. Saul gave me a gown to wear, but I stained it badly with blood right away, so I had to change into another one.

Marge came in after that.

Once I was on the bed, Saul told me to lay back and he put my wounded leg on the bed, but I didn't lie down.

"Lay down. You can do it," Saul insisted.

I didn't lie down.

"I'm disappointed in you Melissa," Marge told me after she walked in and stood before me.

"I know."

"We had talked and we could have avoided this," Marge continued. "Next time I'm going to put you in the 62 right away."

They used lots of gauze to sap up the blood, but the blood soaked through really fast. Marge then layered much thicker gauze and told me to press down on it to stop the bleeding.

Marge was sure that I had cut myself for attention.

"Yeah, right," I scoffed. "Like I would do this for attention? This doesn't feel good at all. This is awful. Even if I did want attention, this wouldn't be the kind I'd want. There are much better forms of it out there than what I have to deal with here. It's embarrassing and people tend to be mean to me and highly judgmental about it."

"Then why do you do it?"

"To distract from anxiety or sadness. To look how I feel. To make a mess out of me. I succeeded," I told her. "I've been hurting myself since I was five years old and I didn't tell anybody. I did it in secret and not even my parents knew. If I was doing it for attention, I was doing a pretty bad job of it. Nobody knew. It wasn't for attention then, and it isn't for attention now."

Carson came in and looked at the cuts and so did a few of the others. There was a question as to whether I needed stitches, but they decided to use steri-strips to close the wounds instead. They put 2 long steri-strips along all three cuts, and then it was bandaged up.

Saul came in to see me afterwards. He asked me if it was possible that I hurt myself because I was afraid to get my leave from the hospital.

"No," I answered. "I actually wondered if this would make them angry and make me leave, but I did it anyways."

I was left alone in the room briefly, but then Saul came back in and kneeled in front of me. "You've always been honest with me and I need for you to be honest now. Are there any other blades?"

"Yes, there's another," I admitted.

"Where is it?"

"In my bedside table," I told him. "I taped it inside the roof of it."

"Okay." Saul left to find the other blade, but came back to see me minutes later. "I can't find it. You're going to have to show me."

"I can't go," I denied. "I'm only wearing a gown. People will see my leg."

"Bring your blanket," Saul instructed.

I wrapped my blanked around myself and followed Saul to my room. I kneeled down by my bedside table and reached my hand inside. I peeled off the blade from where I had hidden it and pulled it out.

Saul reached over and grabbed my wrist from the arm that was holding the blade, and with his other hand he took the blade from between my fingers.

I would imagine that he was holding my wrist to make sure that I didn't use the blade against myself or maybe even against him.

"Thank you for showing me this," Saul was grateful. "Where did you get this?"

"It was in the drawer in front of where I ate," I told him. "But the blades aren't there any more. This afternoon some of the nurses realized they were there and took them out in case one of the patients were to hurt themselves with it."

"So you proved them right," Saul noted.

"I guess so."

I slept in the 62 that night, and I had to stay there until 9:00 pm the next day. It was my second 24 hour stay in the isolation room.

Wednesday, September 3

The next day I got a visit from my doctors assistant. He had a message for me. He said that if I were to starve or cut myself again, I would get sent to the emergency room to get fixed up, then sent home with my things.

So I didn't cut myself again after that warning, but I did cary around a plastic knife and held the blade tightly against the inside of my hand when no one could see. It didn't cut me, but it would hurt a bit, and no one would have to know.

~ ~ ~ ~

Joseph came to visit me around supper time and he asked why I was in a gown.

"Because I did a monumentally stupid, stupid thing," I admitted with a discouraged tone.

I took a walk with Joseph around the halls.

As far as Joseph was concerned he said that he was doing well. He was taking care of the kitten that he got from me, so he had some company at home.

We usually played card games when we were together. Sometimes he would show me his magic tricks again. I had already seen them, but I didn't stop him because I knew that he liked to show them.

I spoke with Joseph too about going to court. I wanted to have as many opinions as I could. So far no one told me that they thought it was a bad idea. Everyone was really hoping that I would go through with it.

I spoke a lot about wanting the chance to stand up to that pervert. There was a part of me that hated myself and was so ashamed of the fact that I didn't fight back. I wanted to fight and to say no, but I just froze. I was so scared to the point of being paralyzed. Sometimes the guilt would make me feel sick and nauseous for days. I had hurt myself so many times for that reason.

On the day that I was to be released, I walked up to the desks and asked for the number to the police station. Soon I was nervously dialing the numbers and found myself talking to a policeman. I asked if someone could be sent directly to the hospital to meet with me. I wanted to be in a supportive environment when I was interviewed. The man suggested that it would be better if it was done at home with the support of family. So I arranged for Marie to come to my place on Saturday.

I felt a bit more free once I had decided what to do. The indecision had been difficult.

On the last few days at the hospital, I was allowed to eat in the cafeteria with the others. I liked having that freedom of being unsupervised. I was quite at peace with leaving. I had been there long enough.

Friday, September 5

On that hospital stay and the previous one, I had a mandatory snack in the afternoons and evenings. I had to have an energy drink. There were three flavors. The vanilla was disgusting and I wouldn't drink it. The chocolate was gross, but tolerable, and the strawberry was borderline okay.

I used to go up to Saul and ask, "Has my disgusting snack arrived yet?"

That was the first time that I was able to make Carson laugh.

I would complain often and at length about how bad the snack tasted, so Saul promised me that one day we would both sit down and drink one together. The problem was that we had a hard time getting two of the energy drinks upstairs at the same time in order to do it.

When I left the hospital at the end of my stay, I went to the pharmacy to pick up my prescription. While waiting for my order to be filled, I looked around and came across some energy drinks and I immediately thought of Saul. I chose the chocolate one because that one tasted weird. I wanted the drink to be gross enough to make it worth making Saul drink it.

I went back to the hospital that evening to bring back a book I had borrowed. While I was there, I pulled out the energy drink and told Saul that he had to fulfill his promise. I could tell by the look in his eyes and the smile on his face that he knew what I meant.

LADY INJURY

There were three nurses around the desks and we filled them in on the reason for the drink. They became very interested in seeing Saul fulfill his promise.

I got two small glasses and filled them both.

"Not too much," Saul told me. "You should have gotten the strawberry. I like strawberry."

"Oh no," I denied. "This has to be gross for the experience to be complete."

Saul and I both swigged the drinks down while the nurses watched, laughed, and cheered.

It was a worthwhile moment.

Saturday, September 6

On Saturday Marie rode the bus to come see me at my apartment. It was noon hour when I called the line to the police once again. This time a woman answered.

"Hello." My voice shook.

"Yes. This is the police department," the woman told me. "How can I help you?"

"I want to report a case of child sexual abuse," I informed her.

"Is it a recent case?"

"No, it's years old."

"Where are you?"

I gave her my address and phone number.

"An officer is being sent to meet with you,"

"Now?"

"Yes, you will see someone within the next few minutes," the woman told me.

I was surprised that they would come so fast.

"Thank you," I said and hung up.

I had cleaned my apartment impeccably. Everything was ready for a visitor. I had never received an officer in my home. The table was cleared. I sat down at it. I was restless and had nothing to do as I waited. I got back up and started pacing from the front window where I could see cars arrive and the kitchen where my sister was waiting.

LADY INJURY

There was a knock at the door. I waited a few seconds before answering to make it seem like I wasn't already right next to the door.

A young policewoman stood in my doorway.

I led the officer to the kitchen down the hallway so we could sit at the table. She pulled out some forms and a pen and asked some simple, and some difficult questions. First she wanted to know things like addresses and birthdays.

The other questions she asked were embarrassing. Some things I found hard to reach back and remember.

The process didn't seem surreal. It didn't feel like I was in a movie like where I had seen that kind of thing before. It was just me and a girl at the kitchen table, answering questions about things I preferred to forget.

We finished talking and the officer left. A police car pulled away from my parking lot. It was a good thing that I didn't know the neighbors well enough for them to ask me questions.

It took a week before I got a letter in the mail. I was so happy and relieved to see that my case was approved for the next level of questioning. The letter said that I had enough proof for there to be an investigation.

I was assigned an officer in charge of my file. We met at the police station days later. It felt strange to be there, like I didn't belong. I wasn't meant for that kind of thing, but then again, I don't think that anyone was. I knew I was doing the right thing though. I wasn't doubting at that point.

The next step was to wait to get an answer from the Crown Attorney to see if my case would be accepted to go to trial. I was told that it could take months to get an answer. All I could do then was wait.

~ ~ ~ ~

I was able to eat on most days at the hospital, and when I was released I was able to keep eating my three main meals a day. I was surprised and pleased at my progress. My self injury was still extreme though. I wasn't afraid to cut deeply like I was when I first started. There was little fear left in self injury. It was something I always desired and I even missed it if I couldn't do it. I didn't understand my own mind. Why was I like this? Did anyone else feel this way?

I saw Saul twice around the city after my release. Once outside the general store and once at the ice cream shop. I thought of Saul as one of my heros. He had helped me so much just by talking through the deeper parts of pain. I came across several other people from the hospital too. I saw patients, nurses and even doctors. It was like having two worlds collide.

My friends were worried about me spending time with Joseph. They said it would lead to trouble. I heard what they were saying and understood that they were worried. I remembered the doctor at the hospital warning me about him. I told everyone that we were just friends so I wasn't too deep into the situation.

Joseph came to see me sometimes and we took walks or went rollerblading. I had never been on rollerblades before and I was quite fearful. I fell and got scratched up, but I had a lot of fun. I had been quite isolated before going to the hospital. I liked being able to get outside and do things for the sake of relaxing and having fun with a guy that I adopted as a brother.

Joseph was truly kind and gentle. I had a hard time seeing him as a danger in any way.

It took a bit of time, but I began to really like spending time with Joseph. I wasn't just seeing him because he wanted it, but because I wanted it too. I cared about this new brother and felt he added something good to my life.

~ ~ ~ ~

My psychiatrist took me off of the anti-depressant I was on and put me on a new one. I was grateful for the change and soon I saw a difference in my depression. The doctors didn't believe me when I said that the old medication was making me depressed, but I had no doubt. I had less anxiety and depression on the new one and I noticed that I had less obsessive compulsive tendencies as well. The frequency of my self injury lowered too. I was quite pleased with the change.

The bad news was that my progress was short lived. Once I had reached 115 pounds, I started to freak out and crash diet again. The need to be thin had me at its mercy. My mind had been starved beyond the point of reason. I wanted to escape. I wanted something better, but wanting wasn't enough.

I kept nothing in my stomach. I would either purge my food or not eat at all.

I had a lot of support though. I had a support group in my borderline personality disorder program at the outpatient hospital. I had a meeting with a therapist every two weeks. I had my psychiatrist, Dr Silk every month to keep track of my medication. I also had Dr Stone who offered that I could go see him if I felt like cutting myself.

I bought lots of bandages and steri-strips so I could take care of my wounds without needing to go to the clinic. Even the nice nurse at the clinic offered that I could go see her whenever I needed, but I didn't want to bother her.

I only went one time to see Dr Stone for a last minute appointment. I was feeling panicked after talking on the phone to a lady asking difficult questions. It was about an application I made to a program that helps victims of sexual abuse. I was taken by surprise. I wasn't ready to answer those questions to a woman over the phone that I had never met. The woman on the phone said that yet another lady would be calling me with questions for some forms.

When I got to the clinic Dr Stone wanted to know why I was so shook up and I told him about the phone call. Dr Stone was upset that I had been bothered with that and said that it shouldn't be my responsibility to answer those questions. He said that my healthcare providers knew all that they needed to know and they should answer the questions for me. He said they shouldn't be upsetting his patient. So he arranged through Asia, the nice nurse, that someone else would take care of those questions for me.

My doctor wanted me to relax. He'd had me try massage therapy in the past, but it didn't work very well. I had only tried it the one time though.

In order to help me not want to cut so much that day, he asked me to punch his open hands. He held his hands out and readied himself for the blows, but I didn't want to hit him. I only wanted to hurt myself.

"I don't want to hurt you," I told him.

"You won't hurt me," he reassured me. "Hit my hands."

I knew he wanted to help me vent my emotions in a safer way, but I didn't want to hit anyone.

"Hit my hands," he repeated. "Come on."

I let myself slap his hands a few times. I felt really self-conscious so I laughed and loosened up a little bit.

After that Dr Stone had me do squats with him at his desk. We both held on to the side of the desk and bent our knees until we were close to the ground, then we came back up.

Dr Stone looked over at how I was doing the squats. "You aren't going low enough. You're cheating."

I was cheating at squatting? I laughed.

So I left feeling less anxious and I didn't cut that day.

~ ~ ~ ~

After having gone to the mall in Quebec city with my family, my brother Devon made mention of my frequent trips to the bathroom.

It sounded like he was asking if I was throwing up. I hoped strongly that he wasn't.

"I wasn't cutting," I told him.

"What about food?"

"What about food?" I echoed. I was hoping to play innocence. "I ate."

"Did you keep it?" Devon wanted to know.

I laughed nervously. I was horrified that he could poses that information and I was hoping to find a way to not answer.

"Did you?" he insisted.

"No. I did not." I answered simply. I felt very uncomfortable. "My psychiatrist tells me that I developed an eating disorder as a way to think less about my problems."

"And what do you think about it?" he asked.

"I think it makes a lot of sense."

~ ~ ~ ~

Each day was a win or a lose, but I never gave up trying. Things were going downhill despite my will to get better. I had lost 12 pounds in 3 weeks.

I was only keeping enough food and water inside me to keep from passing out. I came close to losing consciousness a few times. Everything went white but would come back into focus when I would calm myself and had a few mouthfuls of sun flower seeds.

When I was working in the meat shop at the grocery store, I was feeling so weak that I had to lie down on the dirty, meat and grime covered floor a few times just to keep from passing out. The room spun and I felt sick all through me. I wasn't sure I would be able to finish the job. I had hours of work left to do, but I did it. It was a miracle that I made it through.

I was more thirsty than I was hungry. The thirst was so intense that it was all I could think about. It felt like I was walking through a desert, dying of thirst, and then I would start to see a mirage…an oasis….water.

The difference was that it wasn't a desert and the water wasn't a mirage, it was real, and all I had to do was take it, but I didn't…. couldn't….wouldn't.

I had managed not to drink all day, but by the time it was night, I'd lose control and drink as much as I could. I guzzled down water, soda, chocolate milk and juice. After that I would throw it all up, and go to bed thirsty.

The thirst was powerful and I grew weaker every day. Walking was hard and climbing stairs was a challenge. Every day I got worse, and everyday I wondered how much longer I could make it.

Tuesday, November 11

The day I reached 100 pounds I was weighed at the outpatient hospital, just like I had been for many weeks before; Every Tuesday I would be weighed and the results were sent to the psychiatrist.

I had an appointment with Dr Stone later that day. My appointment was at 4:00 pm, but with delays in their schedule, I didn't get in to see him until 5:00 pm.

Dr Silk had me make a deal with her that if I ever got down to 100 pounds I had to go to the hospital. Dr Stone was made aware of this arrangement and I was willing to go to get help. I didn't know how much longer I would last on my own and I welcomed the intervention. I wondered though if they could really make a difference.

I stayed at the clinic with Dr Stone for an hour talking about all kinds of things. Well, mostly, he talked. We talked about my father and the impact he has had on me and my relationships with men. We talked about whether or not I was able to accept hugs from family and friends. I told him that I could. He asked if I could let myself hold their hands. I could do that too.

By 6:00 pm he brought me to the back of the clinic where the refrigerator was. With a certain amount of nudging and encouragement, the doctor convinced me to drink a small can of vegetable juice. I drank it slowly, trying to take in as little as possible, but I was so thirsty that I couldn't help but drink it all. I was offered a second drink, but I told him that I knew that if I drank it, I wouldn't keep it.

I found out that Dr Stone had started working on the psychiatric ward and that he could be my doctor if I was admitted. I liked the idea of not having to deal with new doctors all the time. I also had a good relationship with Dr Stone and trusted him to be able to help me.

I gathered my belongings and was admitted that same night. Our hope was that I could pass through the ER and be upstairs on the eighth by the next night.

I'm embarrassed and ashamed to say that I armed myself with as many tools as I could before admitting myself to the hospital. I didn't care about trying not to cut. What I wanted to do was get out of my eating disorder and I felt that cutting would help me do that. I wasn't seeing my cutting as such a problem anymore. Cutting didn't torment me the way that my bulimia did.

I had thought of ways to hide sharp objects in my things. I pinned about a dozen safety pins to the inside of my jacket sleeve. I taped some razor blades to the backs of some pictures that I would put on the wall, and hid others in the pages of my journal. I was also prepared to break and use the lightbulb in whatever room I was given. On other visits I had thought long and hard about using my lightbulb, but I ended up telling Saul to remove the bulb from my room before I'd have a chance to use it.

They set me up on a cot right outside the psychiatric section of the ER. I spent the night on that cot, right in front of the guard.

The next day I looked curiously through the cupboard right next to my cot. I found a drawer marked *razors*. It had become my nature to act on impulse. I grabbed a razor and placed it under my pillow. I was disappointed to find that the guard noticed and the nurse told me that it wasn't funny.

I didn't do it to be funny. It was their decision to put a cutter next to a bunch of razors.

So I was moved to another cot where there were no cupboards. I wasn't too disappointed. I hated cutting even though I wanted it so much.

I didn't eat while I was there, but I did drink a bit more.

There was an elderly patient who didn't know much about boundaries. He leaned in really close to talk to me, then he grabbed me by both arms and lifted me up to demonstrate something that he was saying. I can't tell you what he said because his words were indistinguishable.

The guard told the old man to stop, but then the man used both his hands to quickly pet my breasts. I grabbed his hands and held them still until the guard came and took him away. The elderly man was put in the isolation room until he was sent up to the eighth floor.

Apparently the same old man had molested one of the nurses only days before.

~ ~ ~ ~

I got to meet with a student psychiatrist and then the real psychiatrist. I was asked lots of questions about why I wanted to lose weight. He also asked how I saw myself both then and before I had eating disorders.

After seeing the doctors, I was taken as a priority case, so I would be the next to get a bed upstairs.

I was next, but it took longer than usual for a spot to free up. By the next night I was still on the same cot. I sat on the end of my cot while staring at the bathroom door. I noticed that the swiveling designs on the door started to grow. The shapes waved around then started to get more rectangular. I grew wide-eyed as a kind of black smoke rose from the top of the bathroom door. It was like a concentrated swarm of little black bugs.

I cocked my head to the side and stared in amazement.

"Hey," I mumbled to no one in particular. "I'm hallucinating. I think I'm hallucinating."

I stared longer at the wall. Mesmerized.

The guard came over and with one hand on each of my shoulders, he tried to guide me into laying down.

"Don't touch me," I warned as I pulled away. "Don't touch me."

I laid down on my own and the guard left, but I still kept staring at the wall. To the far right of the doors I began to see a large white mass grow out of the wall.

"What is that?" I asked as I pushed my blankets off of myself and walked over to the protruding white mass. I reached out my hand to try and touch it but I passed right through it. "What is this?"

"My shadow," the guard told me.

I knew that it wasn't his shadow, and I knew it wasn't real. It couldn't be real. It didn't make sense.

The guard put his hand on my shoulder and guided me back to my cot. I was so tired and confused that I didn't fight him off.

I got back in bed and repeated several times, "What kind of medication did they give me?"

The nurse came and reassured me that she had only given me my Quetiapine. I didn't know if I could believe her because I had a hard time remembering.

When I woke up the next morning this strange memory came back to me. I couldn't figure out if it was real or if I had dreamt it.

I went to talk to the patient who was sleeping next to me.

"I think I had the weirdest dream, but I can't figure out if it was real or not," I told him. "Was I hallucinating last night?"

The patient grew a goofy, exited grin. "Yeah," he confirmed, then he went on to describe the event just the way that I remembered it.

I was clear headed by then and realized that the visions could have been the result of severe dehydration. I thought hard about the importance of drinking, but only later learned that with dehydration, hallucinations are the step before losing consciousness and dying of it.

I had no idea that I was so close to death. Dying was not what I wanted. If I hadn't of gone to the hospital when I did, I probably would have passed out and died alone in my apartment.

Thursday, November 13

By Thursday morning a new patient was set up in the cot next to mine. He wore a baseball cap and looked around my age.

It's when I meet a guy like Anthony Wells that I realize that no matter how ugly a hospital gown I may be wearing, I can still be flirted with.

He was cute, and certainly a charmer.

I find it sad that I don't remember more of our conversation, but I know he made it clear that he wanted to be with me.

I told Anthony that I was seeing someone else. I thought it would be easier that way. I liked guys, and I was definitely tempted by them, but I wasn't going to be in a relationship at that point in my life. I had too much to work on. I could barely keep myself together.

"But if it wasn't for the other guy?" Anthony probed.

"I'd be interested," I told him. It was true. I was interested in him. I just couldn't handle anyone else in my life.

Anthony took my hand in his. He said that he liked to feel my warmth, so for a second, I put my hand on his, then we looked at each other, and it kind of felt like we were saying goodbye.

I was given my things and I followed a nurse up to the eighth floor. It was almost 3:00 in the afternoon.

I met a familiar face once I got to the ward. Ashton was my nurse and he took care of receiving me. I was shown to my room. It was number 856. I got the window side of the room and had a roommate that I recognized from a previous stay. She was a heavy set girl who looked to be around my age.

Ashton got me to sign the regular papers about agreeing not to exchange my medication with the other patients.

After that I had to be weighed. I didn't like that part so Ashton told me that we didn't have to look at the numbers. Clearly he was kidding.

So I was standing in a brown gown, on a scale that read of a girl disappearing.

At that point we went back to my room and Ashton explained about how things would work. My roommate came in and I told her that Ashton was one of my favorite nurses because he was good at talking when we need it.

I also had to sign the same protocol paper as the last times I was there. The protocol basically said that I had to eat all my meals or I go into the 62 for two hours and then fill out a reflection form saying why I didn't eat. I also had to stay in the 62 for two hours after every meal to make sure that I wouldn't toss my cookies. So basically, I was in the 62 for two hours whether I ate or not. It was a lose lose situation.

If I refused to eat, I would lose the privilege to take walks around the hospital, and I would lose the right to have visitors for the next day. If I ate, I could walk around for an hour and a half every day. I had half an hour at each meal to eat at the offices where I would be supervised. If I didn't eat, I would still have to sit there for half an hour. The idea was to see if maybe after a few minutes of being made to stare at my plate, I might be moved to take a few bites.

I agreed to all the rules and signed the paper. Minutes later I was having my first meal at the desks.

Thankfully I had asked if I could work into a full meal gradually. They agreed that I could start by eating smaller portions and work my way up to having everything on the tray.

I would have preferred to be dealing with Dr Stone, but he was on a three day vacation. Until then, it was another doctor making the rules.

LADY INJURY

One rule that Dr Stone made before leaving was that if I hurt myself, I didn't have to go into the 62 for 24 hours. I was simply supposed to show what I did and talk about it. I thought that was a good way for me to focus more on my eating problems, not that I liked admitting that I had any. I was deeply embarrassed about my eating issues.

I was allowed to have my arm warmers to cover my wrists.

I put up pictures of my loved ones all over the wall next to my bed. I had my childhood teddy bear sitting on my pillow, and I had my Jack O'Neill action figure keeping guard on my bedside table. I was trying to make it so I wouldn't feel so lonely.

It was only my first day back at the hospital and something had already happened to upset me.

My mother called and said, "I hear things aren't doing so good."

"Well, that's why I'm here," I answered.

"Devon tells me that you haven't been eating or drinking."

My heart sank. "Well, he wasn't supposed to tell you that."

"I don't want you to die," my mother told me as her voice broke up.

"I'm not going to die," I consoled her. "I'm getting help, but you weren't supposed to know about that. I wasn't ready for it and Devon didn't have my permission."

"I'm glad he told me."

"I'm not," I said simply. "This wasn't my decision. Who else knows about this?"

"Brian and Evelyn," she informed me.

"Make sure it doesn't go beyond that, okay?"

"Okay."

Dr Stone was allowing me an hour every two days on the outside. I decided to use that time to do chores at home and feed my animals. Regretfully, I wasn't able to use those hours without binging and purging.

My doctor said that if I was going to throw up, I should do it at the hospital. I didn't want to do that because I was afraid that I may not be permitted to do so while I was there.

I told Dr Stone about my binging on my outings. He told me not to put myself down for it. He was consoling me because I was pretty discouraged.

That's when my doctor made a plan with me. If I were to eat a bit of chocolate, I would also have to do a bit of exercise afterwards instead of purging.

"Try some pushups," Dr Stone requested.

"Right now?"

"Yes, right now."

"But I can't do pushups," I told him. "Whenever I try I can only do the first part. I can go down and meet the floor, but I can't come back up."

He had me do the pushups anyway and I met defeat as I predicted. I just flopped to the floor each time and laid there in failure.

Afterwards, Dr Stone spoke with Saul about rationing my chocolate into three pieces each time and about finding me some exercise equipment, like dumbbells.

It was Parker, my friend from previous hospital stays that offered me a piece of his brownie. I was with Dr Stone and Saul at the time. I told Parker that I shouldn't have any, but when he insisted, I said yes and took it.

Dr Stone then spoke to Parker in his charming French accent. "It's really nice of you to want to share with her, but it's better if you don't bother her with food."

"Okay," Parker agreed.

So I had to pay for that really good piece of brownie with about twenty minutes of exercise.

Saul found me two large cans of prune juice to use as weights. He coached me as to how to use them. Later he brought me two mustard bottles to use while in the 62. I complained that the bottles weren't heavy enough. I also complained that one bottle wasn't as full as the other.

"I'm going to exercise myself into a lopsided person," I joked.

I was uncomfortable about being the only one doing exercise while someone else watched. I begged Saul to do the exercise with me, but he would just smile and tell me what to do.

After 5 minutes, I wanted to stop. "But haven't I done enough exercise to have worked off the two bites of chocolate?"

"No."

Tuesday, November 18

I noticed that when I was doing better with my eating and I was throwing up less, I was thinking of self injury even more. I realized then that binging really was another way to hurt myself. I had to have at least one or the other in order to cope.

Emotionally I had been doing better with the new medication, but since arriving at the hospital, I had become more anxious. I think it must have been my second or third evening upstairs when I decided to pull a safety pin out of my jacket sleeve.

I sat on my bed and tore away at my skin bit by bit until it became a deep cut. When I was satisfied with the damage I had done, I wrapped the towel around my lower leg and pulled my pants over it.

When my nurse later checked my leg for new wounds and found some, she cleaned the area and placed three steri-strips over it to pull my skin back together.

"The Lorazepam I gave you wasn't enough?" my nurse Amanda asked me.

"No," I replied simply.

"Why did you do this?" Amanda inquired.

"It doesn't matter." I didn't care to say or think about my reasons.

Once I was bandaged up, I was left alone. That felt unusual because I would usually have been sent to the 62 for what I had done. I was glad that my doctor had prescribed against that. It was much less stressful that way. I felt better after cutting, and it felt like that was all that mattered.

Thursday, November 20

Parker taught me a new card game that I actually liked.

Parker usually liked playing with stakes on the game. He decided that if he won, he would get a kiss. I decided that if I won, he would have to kiss Roger.

Parker won, but got no kiss.

We ran into a problem when Joseph came to visit me. Joseph was upset with Parker because he was convinced that he had spit on his head from a three story building. Even though Parker said that it wasn't true, Joseph had decided to take him to court. I didn't know who to believe, but I was going to be a neutral party and be kind to them both.

Parker wanted to play cards with Joseph and I and a group of other friends, but Joseph turned him away. Parker got mad about being excluded and left while calling Joseph a few choice names.

One of the nurses came to speak to us about a concern the staff had. They weren't sure if Joseph was legally allowed to be near Parker considering that he was taking him to court. So Joseph and I went down to the cafeteria and each had a hot chocolate.

Joseph was starting to talk more and more about his ideas on saving the world. I found it something of a bother to keep hearing the same things over and over again, but I didn't let on.

Everyone had to grow a garden and give the food away for free. I thought it funny that Joseph himself didn't have a garden the way he expected everyone else to. I had a garden, and I did give some away, but the world was not saved.

"I haven't been able to check my emails," Joseph told me. "The library is closed. Do you mind if I check them on your computer?"

Should I give Joseph the key to my place? He had been there before and I didn't think he would steal anything from me.

"I'll make you a deal," I told him. "You can check your emails at my place if you feed the animals."

Joseph happily agreed.

We arranged that Joseph take my key and be back an hour later, but Joseph did not return an hour later. In fact, he didn't return that day at all.

~ ~ ~ ~

I learned from the past and asked if that time around I could have a glass of chocolate milk instead of the disgusting energy drink. The milk was an improvement to the energy drink, but I didn't find that they put enough chocolate in it.

There was one evening when I told Saul that the chocolate milk he gave me wasn't good enough and that he was giving me low-grade products.

"Is there any chocolate powder in the kitchen?" I asked hopefully. "We could add it to my milk."

Saul wasn't wanting to admit to possessing any chocolate powder, but eventually he did. "I don't want to give you any," he told me. "I'm not sure if you're supposed to have it."

"I cry foul!" I exclaimed jokingly. "I'm going to complain to Megan," I threatened.

Saul was unfazed. "Go ahead."

I walked from the cafeteria to the offices and Saul followed. Megan opened her window in front of her desk so I could talk to her.

"Can I help you?" she asked.

"Yes," I confirmed then pointed to Saul. "This man is withholding legal contraband. My chocolate milk is weak, and he admits to having what is necessary to fix it, yet he won't let me have it."

"It's weak?" she asked. "Let me see." I passed Megan my glass and she smelled it. "It seems fine to me," Megan surmised. "But I don't see why you can't have more in it."

"Ah ha!" I cried. "Now you must use your powers as a superior authority to command this man to put more chocolate in my drink!"

Everyone laughed, but I still didn't get my chocolate. I gave up and just drank it.

I did manage to win myself some chocolate though. The father of one of the patients brought me a chocolate bar when he came to see his son.

I thanked him very much.

He said, "I know you like chocolate."

"How do you know?" I was puzzled.

"I heard you ranting earlier about wanting more chocolate in your milk," he explained.

I laughed. Complaining was good. Complaining got me chocolate.

The son of the man who bought me a chocolate bar was a very sweet kid. He looked a few years younger than me. He was very quiet, but he had a beautiful smile. It was like he always knew of something funny, but didn't say what. It was very captivating.

I played cards with this young man a few times. We played a card game and he beat me every time by a long shot.

He also often came to talk to me when I was having my meals at the desks. He sometimes mistook me for an employee because usually patients weren't allowed to go where I was. He asked me a few times as to why I didn't eat meat. Another time he wanted to know my last name. He wanted to know some very random things, but he always had a question.

He gave me a card from a deck once. I was puzzled as to why that was. Maybe he just wanted to give me something and a playing card was all he could think of. I think he had a crush on me.

The last time we had played cards he asked, "Can I ask you a question?"

"Yes."

"Who gave you those rings?" The young man pointed at my right hand.

I realized he may have thought they were engagement and wedding rings. "I bought them for myself. They aren't engagement rings. If they were, they would be on my other hand."

~ ~ ~ ~

My brother Devon came and played ping-pong with me a few times. I liked that. I hadn't gotten much practice in since Joseph got his leave from the hospital. Also I was touched that Devon took the time to come and see me. I liked playing with my big brother.

Saturday, November 22

When Joseph came to bring me back the key to my apartment a day later, it wasn't even during visiting hours. He didn't seem to have a sense of time.

By then I was worried about him and what he was doing at my apartment.

Joseph started talking really fast. "I was at your place all night cleaning up and sending you emails. I didn't sleep at all."

I could tell he was on something.

"This is not visiting hours," Ella told Joseph. "You have to go. I'm also telling security not to let you up anymore outside of visiting hours."

Joseph left and came back less than two hours later, but this time he was allowed to be there.

Joseph started talking to me really fast and he wasn't making any sense.

"Melissa, I have to talk to you," he said as he showed up at the door to my room. "I went to a pool hall and someone sat beside me, but they weren't really there, and they had a different name."

I dug my hand into one of the front pockets of Joseph's winter coat, but found nothing.

"I gave them the keys," Joseph informed me.

That made sense because I had told the staff that I was worried about my keys considering Joseph's condition. They were kind enough to take them from him for me.

"What pool hall did you go to? The one in town?" I tried to make sense of what he had come in mumbling about.

"No. On the internet," he corrected. "And my heart was racing and the person that wasn't there left."

"Joseph." I spoke his name to make him stop. "Do you understand yourself? Do you know what you are saying?"

My friend looked confused. "Yes."

"Joseph." I spoke his name again. "When we met in June, you made a deal that if you didn't stop smoking then we couldn't be friends anymore, but that wasn't true because I still would have been your friend."

He didn't seem to understand me.

"Joseph. You're high."

"Yeah." He looked offended.

"You're not the same person I used to know." My words were sad.

"I'm with God," he said, then turned to leave, but I grabbed his coat sleeve.

"No," I told him. "You're with your drugs."

William the orderly was next to us and he made a face like he agreed with me.

"I have to go," Joseph told me as he pulled out of my grasp.

"I have to talk to you," I told Joseph as he walked away, but I had to stay behind on the ward.

Joseph waved goodbye and stepped onto the elevator.

I turned and went to my room where I started to cry. The tears were painful and I hated them.

I started to beat my wrist against the windowsill.

Ella walked in when I was calmer. "I understand how you feel about Joseph."

"He's my friend."

"I know, but he wasn't making sense," Ella told me. "He came up and told me that he met a girl at a bar that wasn't there."

"Yeah," I remembered. "He told me that too."

"Write him a letter," Ella suggested. "That way when he comes back to see you, you can give it to him. That way it won't matter if he doesn't listen."

"That's only if he comes back," I said. "He doesn't want to hear what I have to say."

"He's so high that he wont remember your conversation," Ella consoled me.

"He's the only friend I've got that uses. Well, my father was a drunk, but I don't care about him."

"I know."

"This hurts."

"I understand."

~ ~ ~ ~

That evening I asked my nurse Amanda for some Lorazepam. When she gave it to me, she inquired, "Are you okay? You know what happened last time you asked me for some Lorazepam."

I thought about that for a second and remembered opening my leg with a safety pin. "It's true that I'm asking for medication because I'm thinking of hurting myself."

By the end of that evening I knew that if I went to my room I would end up sitting in my own blood again, so I asked if I could sleep in the 62 just to be safe and away from my things.

Amanda said it was okay. She even let me sleep in my own night clothes instead of in a hospital gown.

"Promise me that you aren't hiding anything in your clothes," she requested.

"I didn't," I reassured her. "And I promise."

Sunday, November 23

I had a nightmare that night. It was one that I couldn't handle. I was laying in a bed in my room at my old house. There was a dark presence leaning over me. He said that he could find me anywhere and that he missed me and wished he could touch me like before. The dream didn't make sense because after that he said, "Don't worry. I won't pick you up this time."

I didn't know what that was supposed to mean. I knew that I was dreaming though and I tried to wake up. There were a few times when I thought I had woken up because I was sitting in bed and looking around the 62, but I soon realized that I was still in the dream. I tried to scream so that the staff at the hospital would hear me and come wake me up. No matter how much I screamed, no one came, because no one could hear the screams within a dream.

I was panicking, and every time I thought I had woken up, I would realize that it was a trick of my mind and I was still trapped. I was trapped within my mind with a dark man in a dark room.

By the time that I had woken up for real, I was so panicked that I couldn't breathe right.

I immediately went to the desks and asked one of the nurses for some Lorazepam to help me calm down. It was 1:30 in the morning.

While waiting for the nurse to get the medication I took a moment to walk over to the window to the smoke room.

Harvey was the orderly that night and he came over to ask me if I was okay.

"No, I'm not," I admitted. "Is it okay if I don't go back to sleep tonight?" I was afraid to sleep; afraid to dream.

"That's fine as long as you stay in your room," he told me.

"Okay," I accepted.

I took my Lorazepam and went into my room and stood in a corner with my eyes closed. My nightmare ran through my mind and soon I found myself banging my head against the wall behind me. Harvey was in my room moments later and he pointed his flashlight at me.

"You can't be knocking your head against the walls," he told me.

I heard one of the nurses ask what was going on.

"There's something going on with Melissa," Harvey said to her.

A middle aged nurse with dark hair and a soft voice came in and asked me what was wrong.

"I don't remember all that happened," I replied. I was mumbling mostly. "I have to force myself to stay awake enough so I don't slip back into that dream."

"You had a dream? What kind of dream?" she asked.

I paused and watched the nightmare run through the darkness of my mind. "It was of being molested. I....he was…abusing me. I couldn't make it stop. I screamed and I screamed for you to hear and come wake me, but you didn't hear. I was trapped."

"Did you say something to him?" she asked.

"Say something?" I repeated her words. I wasn't sure what she meant.

"Yes. To your abuser," she clarified. "To make him stop."

"No I didn't. I never did."

"You can start now," she suggested.

"No. It's too late," I told her.

"It's never too late," the nurse told me. "Do you want to come sit with us at the desks until your Lorazepam helps you calm down?"

I agreed and grabbed a blanket to take with me. It was cold.

I sat on a black office swivel chair and spun around a bit. After a few minutes I started snapping my rubber bands on my wrist. Eventually my skin turned red.

Harvey came and said that he wanted me to give him my rubber bands.

"I'm allowed to have these," I told him.

"But you're making your wrist red, so I need for you to give them to me," Harvey told me.

I hesitated to give up my means of coping, but I finally pulled off my rubber bands and handed them to Harvey.

After about half an hour my Lorazepam started to kick in, so I went back to my room to sleep again.

I woke up again at 7:30 in the morning. I had to get up and be ready for a CPR course that was mandatory for my return to work. I needed the course to serve me for when I was feeling better. The course was being held for free at the old age home. I received permission from Dr Stone to be able to attend. I had to be there for 9:00 in the morning.

I grabbed two towels and went to the desks for my shampoo and personal effects.

The nurse with the dark hair that helped me in the night told me to wait. She said that the other nurse had something that she needed to tell me.

"You had something to say?" I asked the blond nurse.

"Yes," the kind blond nurse said as she walked over to me. "I was beaten by my husband for ten years."

I was saddened by what she said, but I knew that she was likely telling me this because of my nightmares about my own past. "Did you have a lot of nightmares after?" I asked her.

"Yes," she confirmed.

I don't remember if anything was said after that because I suddenly got very dizzy and had to lean on the desk. I had to sit down. I knew that if I didn't I would lose consciousness.

By then the nurses were fussing over me and telling each other that this had to be because I hadn't been eating.

I thought they had to be wrong because I had been eating most of my meals, but I didn't tell them as much.

I tried to push myself forward on the swivel chair but I didn't have enough strength. "Could someone push me to my bed?" I asked.

They attempted to push me forward, but my feet were dragging on the ground and keeping the chair from rolling.

"Lift your feet up," Harvey directed.

I couldn't lift my feet, so Harvey turned the chair around and dragged it backwards so my feet weren't in the way. The chair stopped when I was next to my bed. My attempt to get into the bed was weak because I only managed to flop my top half onto the bed while the rest of me was still on the chair.

I hadn't expected it, but suddenly I was rising into the air when Harvey picked me up. My arms dangled and my upper body flopped somewhat sidewards.

"You can hang on to me," Harvey told me. The next thing I knew I was lying in my bed.

I needed to go to the bathroom and be helped to get there, but soon I was the only one in the room and I couldn't ask. It was just as well. I could never have made it to the bathroom in the state I was in. I barely had the strength to lay there.

Soon the nurses were bringing in the blood pressure monitor. They wrapped it around my arm and suddenly I was hearing the machine beep. I didn't ask them what the monitor said.

Next my finger was being pricked so they could take my glucose level.

I heard them say a few more times that this had to be because I wasn't eating. I had no energy to disagree.

They told me that I shouldn't go to my CPR course. I couldn't disagree to that either.

I fell back to sleep and an hour later I was awake and feeling fine. I had only half an hour until my CPR course started, so I hurried up and got ready. I had no time to shower, but I called the old age home and let them know that I would be a little late.

I walked over there as quickly as I could. Luckily Shy-Anne and her husband saw me on the road and picked me up to bring me the rest of the way.

I was in a bad mood for the whole course. The nightmare I had in the night really messed me up. I was glad to see all my loved ones at my job. I got to hug the elderly that I missed so much. I got to see my boss and my colleagues. It felt nice. They wanted very much for me to come back to work. My three months away from the job were almost over, but I wasn't ready yet. I couldn't handle it yet.

The course was over by early afternoon. I had wished that it would finish sooner, but at least, with a lot of practice, I learned how to kiss a dummy to save its life.

The course ended with a video. When it was over, my friend Gene who was the cook, gave me a ride back to the hospital, so I didn't have to walk.

I didn't feel like eating when I got back, but my nurse insisted that the kitchen send up a tray.

After two in the afternoon my sister Marie came to see me. She crawled into bed with me in the 62 like we had been doing by laying next to each other for our entire lives.

A nurse passed by and seemed to think it was strange that Marie was laying in the bed with me. Marie defended us by saying that we were sisters.

I still felt pretty badly at the time. I told Marie about the nightmare I had and how it was affecting me.

After Marie left, I got some mail from my friend Lisa. Lisa wasn't doing well with her eating disorders either. She was too sick to work and had to leave her job temporarily. She was finally prescribed some Lorazepam for her anxiety. I was glad for her because I knew she needed it. I worried about her, and I wished her well.

It was sad that she wasn't doing well either. I could understand her so much. All I felt like doing that day was to crumple up and cry.

That evening, Parker told me that he found someone to play cards with us.

LADY INJURY

I recognized the girl only because I had seen her get admitted hours earlier. Her name was Samantha, and from the first time I saw her, I could tell that there was something not quite right about her.

The three of us tried playing a card game called Janitor, but Samantha seemed confused and couldn't grasp the game. We ended that game and moved onto a simpler game of cards. Samantha still seemed confused and kept putting out cards that didn't match the game.

As I watched Samantha struggle to play the game, it finally dawned on me; the girl was skin and bone. The small size of her arms was shocking. Samantha caught me staring at her.

"Do you have an eating disorder?" I asked bluntly.

Samantha shook her head yes and tears began to form.

"Me too," I related. "You aren't alone. Hey, maybe we'll even get to eat together at the desks."

We had to stop the game because Samantha was crying too much and Parker got up and left.

I tried to console Samantha by describing how much I understood her.

"Are you anorexic, or bulimic?" I asked her.

"Im not anorexic," she affirmed with a surprised look. "I'm not crazy."

"I didn't say you were crazy," I told her. "I have an eating disorder and I'm not crazy. We're sick. Sick doesn't mean crazy."

I told Samantha about how eating disorders were generally dealt with on the ward. After a few more minutes, she stopped crying.

I invited Samantha to walk around the halls with me.

"I don't really have to sleep here, do I?" Samantha asked me with a dazed look after we got up to start walking.

"Yes, you do," I told her. "They gave you a room. Do you remember what room you were given?"

"Yes," she confirmed. "But I don't know who can come and get me."

I wasn't sure if I was the one who should have been answering her questions.

"Nobody is coming to get you right now," I informed her. "You're going to have to stay here, just like the rest of us. When you are well again, they will let you go home."

"I don't understand why I'm here," Samantha was confused. She looked around us as we walked as though everything she saw was new and puzzling. Just by looking into her eyes I could tell that her mind was searching.

I couldn't tell her why she was there. I could tell though that there was something wrong with her, but I was far from able to diagnose. I looked at this tall, thin girl. She wore big, fuzzy pink slippers, some pajama pants and a long pink robe.

"Are these the only clothes you have?" I asked her as I pointed to her robe.

"No. I have lots of clothes," she said politely but defensively.

"Oh," I said. "It's just that sometimes people are brought here against their will on an ambulance. Sometimes all the clothes they have are what they have on their backs at the time."

"I have lots of clothes," Samantha defended her wardrobe once again.

I didn't believe her. I was sure that her pink robe was the only thing she had to wear, but I wasn't going to contradict her. I had actually been thinking of lending her some of my own clothing, but I could see that at least for right then, her clothes were a sensitive subject and I let it go.

Samantha looked so sad. I really felt for her.

"You look like you need a hug about as much as I do," I told her. I wasn't offering her a hug. I didn't know her well enough for that, but I guess it was my way of telling her that things were bad for me too.

We continued to walk around the halls. I told her about my first time at the hospital and how nervous I was. I told her how I had a guard who followed me around for days. I talked about how I hadn't seen my face for days until I figured out that I could see my reflection in the electric socket. I just wanted her to know that I understood her and how freaked out she could be in the beginning. I made it all sound really funny and she laughed a lot.

Samantha eventually asked me how I got the scar on my shoulder.

"I did this on purpose with a plastic knife and a small piece of metal," I admitted.

"Oh!" Samantha was wide-eyed. "Don't do that!"

"It's too late," I told her.

"I used to do that too," she told me. "It's a terrible thing to get into."

"Did you make a habit of it?" I asked.

"No, but I know what it is to do it," she confessed. "I had carved words into my arm. When my mom saw what I had done, she freaked out and admitted me to the hospital. You have to stop doing that."

I appreciated that she cared, but simply having her say that I shouldn't do it wasn't going to change much. "I've been doing this for a long time. I've tried, but I haven't been able to just stop. Even tonight, I have a very strong urge to hurt myself."

When Samantha and I parted ways, she went to her room and I went to get two towels from the cart.

I laid one towel on the floor next to my bed, and in the other towel, I wrapped a freshly washed lightbulb. I used my shoe to smack the bulb, but it didn't break. I then put my shoe on and stood up to stomp on the bulb, but it squirmed around in the towel and remained unbroken. I then used one foot to steady the bulb in the towel and used the other to stomp down on it. The bulb broke in a silent smash under my foot.

Inside the towel I found several pieces of broken glass in a variety of different shapes and sizes.

I already had one cut on my leg that was healing in the shape of a half moon.

I picked up a piece of glass and started cutting some lines around the half moon. The glass wasn't as sharp as I had anticipated. I expected fast, clean, deep cuts, but instead I got superficial wounds. I would trace and retrace the cuts and watched the blood run down to the towel.

It was therapeutic in a twisted sort of way. It was a silent fascination as I felt the warm trickles on my leg. It was a burst of color and sensations. It was unpredictable. It didn't feel wrong. I felt it draw the badness from my mind.

Time went by and the blood continued to drip. I didn't know what to do with myself, so I just made more cuts; Another cut after another cut.

I was startled when my name was called on the intercom. I had a phone call waiting for me, but I wasn't in a position to answer.

My name was called a second time, but I still didn't get up.

After a few minutes my nurse came knocking at my door. My nurse was a middle aged man. I hadn't known him before that day.

My curtain was drawn for privacy, so the nurse couldn't see me.

"You have a phone call," he told me.

"I can't go," I told him.

"Do you need help Miss Water?"

I hesitated. What should I say?

When the nurse pushed my curtain aside and looked down at me he wore a shocked expression. "Miss Water, what have you done?"

The man seemed to panic and left the room immediately in search of help.

I didn't understand what the panic was about. It was only blood. I had actually found that the thick red designs looping around my leg were quite artistic.

I heard the man calling out to Ella in the halls, "Melissa mutilated her leg!"

Great. Clearly he was good with confidentiality when he was announcing it to all the patients as well as the staff. I wasn't happy about that.

Ella and the panicked nurse came to my room with medical supplies.

First the man wiped up some blood with cotton balls. I didn't see how cotton balls were a good means of sopping up great amounts of blood. It seemed like he was just spreading it around.

"Can I just put my leg in the sink and rinse it all off?" I asked

"No," he denied.

I should have expected that. They always told me I couldn't take care of my own wounds. I knew how to bandage myself up. I had been doing it for years. Rinsing my leg off in the sink was time tested and true.

I didn't like being fussed over. I only needed the bandages. I didn't need their help.

I was asked several times as to why I did it, but I always said that it didn't matter and that I was fine.

I remember looking at Ella's shoes and thinking how cute they were; small, brown shoes with high heals. They were both classy and casual.

The shoes of the male nurse weren't nearly as nice, but then again, he wasn't anything impressive to look at either.

I think I fixated on random things like that to keep from feeling so self conscious. I could go somewhere else in my mind.

"You're going to come and sleep in the isolation room," he told me.

I was surprised. "But I'm not supposed to go to the 62 for hurting myself."

"Yes, you do," he told me. "There's no way that we can just let you get away with this."

I didn't care if I slept in the 62. Either way I was sleeping in a hospital room.

"I can keep my pajama's though?" I asked in hopes of avoiding a brown gown, and because I knew what had been prescribed.

"No, you need to really think about what you did," he told me. "You definitely have to wear a gown."

I wasn't as accepting of losing my clothes. I didn't like this man's attitude either. It confused me when people reacted in a hostile manner.

I used some leg and arm warmers to hide my leg and wrist, but once in the 62 I had them taken away. They told me that they couldn't take the risk of leaving them with me. I wondered what was so dangerous about a leg warmer. It wasn't long enough for me to hang myself with it, but even then, there was nothing for me to hang myself from.

"Is this what my doctor wanted?" I asked them in the hopes that they would rethink things. "I'm not supposed to be put in a room plan."

Roger told me that they had to do it for my protection. They even had one of the female nurses come and take my underwear away.

I was upset at how they were reacting when it was prescribed for me to not have to go through all of that. I wasn't supposed to be striped of my things. It was written clearly in my file. Didn't they know how to read?

I even had to sleep with the light on so they could see me through the window of my closed isolation door. Since when did they close my door? I was often in an isolation room, but I was not isolated. The door was supposed to stay open, but this time I was in true isolation. They had isolated me under spotlights.

They told me that I would be in there for 24 hours.

I was mad, but I didn't react in anger. I took what they dealt and went to sleep in the 62.

Monday, November 24

When I got up in the morning, my nurse let me leave the room because she knew that isolation wasn't what Dr Stone had prescribed.

The nurse said that I could leave, but I laughed at the idea of leaving the room the way that I was. "They took my hiding places away," I told her.

The nurse seemed confused, so I showed her my bare and scarred wrist.

"Oh," she said.

"I need something for my arm and for my leg," I instructed.

"We can go get that," she accepted.

She left and came back with my arm and leg warmers and also had what she needed to change my bandages.

The nurse pulled off the bandages and tape, and when she looked at what I had done she said, "Oh Melissa!"

There were so many cuts. Blood seeped through the protective grids like streaming fireworks.

I was glad of what I had done. It made me feel better. It seemed to me that I looked more truthful that way. It looked terrible, and that was truth.

The nurse said that I had to stop doing that.

Well, they all say that. They would all say it but it would never make me any better.

Samantha, the new girl said that she wanted to walk around with me since she had a good time the night before.

We talked about a lot of things. We talked about the hell of eating disorders. We talked about our families. When we touched on the subject of self injury, she begged me to stop. I knew that wouldn't work because I had begged myself to stop many times before and it got me nowhere.

When we were playing cards with Parker, she asked why I always had rubber bands around my wrist. I told her it was so I could cause a bit of pain when I was too anxious.

Samantha wore a shocked look and got tears in her eyes. I didn't expect an emotional reaction. I didn't understand why people cared. It didn't matter when I hurt myself because it was only me. I wasn't hurting anyone else.

I watched as Samantha took the rubber band from around the deck of cards and put it around her wrist. She snapped it a few times. It surprised me, but I realized that she was trying to make a point. She snapped it a few more times while looking intently at me.

I wasn't sure what to say, so I just asked, "Does it help you?"

"No," she disagreed with rising emotion. "Does it help *you*?"

"Only when I do it to myself."

She was crying too much then and excused herself from the game.

Parker and I exchanged awkward looks and finished playing on our own.

Later when I was at the water fountain, Samantha came up to me and asked for my rubber bands. She was very upset.

"Why?" I asked.

"Because I like them," she answered. "I think they are pretty and you should give them to me."

"I'm not going to give them to you because I know you aren't going to give them back," I told her. "If you want some, you can ask for them at the desks."

"No," she refused. "I want those ones."

"It might be hard for you to understand, but I need these," I told her.

"Give them to me," she demanded.

"I'm allowed to have these," I informed her. "They're prescribed by my doctor."

"I don't believe you," Samantha stated.

"Don't believe what?"

"That a doctor would prescribe something that would hurt you," she clarified.

"It's to prevent me from hurting myself worse," I explained then turned to my nurse who was nearby. "These are prescribed, right?"

"I haven't heard of that," my nurse told me. "What are they for?"

"Oh," I realized. "Maybe it was just the doctor from the other times I was here that prescribed it."

Samantha and I kept walking. She was still very emotional.

"I don't understand why you need that," she told me.

I hesitated and thought about my answer for a moment. "I was abused as a kid and doing things like snapping a rubber band on my wrist helps me to forget or deal with that stuff."

Samantha was crying again by then. I put my hand on her shoulder.

"I was hurt too," she admitted. "I was the one who told on my uncle."

"I'm sorry that happened, but I guess we understand each other," I related.

"I still want you to give me the rubber bands," she told me.

"I'm going to try to explain," I began. "These rubber bands cause pain, but they leave marks that fade."

"That's why they're bad. You can't do yourself pain," she protested.

"I know, but if I don't do simple pain like with these rubber bands, I sometimes find myself doing much worse things that don't fade. Yesterday I broke a lightbulb and used the glass to cut about 40 lines into my leg."

"You what?"

"I have 40 new cuts, and it's because of these elastics that moments like that happen less often."

"I still don't like it," Samantha told me.

I thought about it for a moment. "What if I gave you just one of my rubber bands. Would you like that?"

"Yes," she accepted and I gave one to her. "Thank-you."

~ ~ ~ ~

That evening I saw something that I wished I could give back.

I was swirling around in an office chair at the desks where the staff could keep an eye on me. I was waiting for my medication to kick in so it would be safe for me to go to my room. On many evenings I asked and they accepted for me to stay for my safety.

Things were so calm. I was making jokes and trying to convince Saul to let me use the stapler that was on the desk. I didn't want to hurt myself with it, but Saul didn't want to take the risk. I just thought it would be fun to snap the little staple through some paper or cardboard. It took me several minutes before I convinced Saul to let me use it.

I cheered victoriously and claimed my prize. I picked up a piece of paper and fed it to the stapler. I made the stapler bite down, but nothing happened. Nothing clicked and the staple didn't go into the paper. I studied the device and discovered that Saul had removed the staples. I booed and laughed at being tricked.

My mood was good, and I would have been feeling well enough to go to bed without the risk of hurting myself.

I didn't hear her come, but a middle aged woman with short blond hair stepped onto an elevator that was just across from us. Usually this wouldn't call for attention if it was day and she had permission, but the woman on the elevator was a patient trying to escape.

Saul pressed the emergency button so that the elevator would lock. One of the nurses rushed to the intercom and called a *code white* right away.

I knew that *code white* meant violent patient, but this woman didn't look violent to me at all. She wasn't even yelling.

"I don't feel safe here," she told us. "I've seen things here; things that scare me and it's not okay. I want to go home. Bad things happen here. I don't feel safe."

I felt for this woman and wondered what things she had seen.

"I don't feel safe," she repeated as she stood in the far end of the elevator with her back against the wall. The only protection she found was from hiding in a corner.

Several men in various different types of security uniforms arrived through the second elevator minutes later. Once they had an understanding of the situation a few of the men walked towards the woman and took her by each arm. They started dragging her forward as she screamed desperately for help. My heart hurt for her as she was taken to isolation room 7. When the 62 was taken, they had to use the 7.

The sounds of shouting and shuffling feet were hard for me to hear. I felt a great swell of sympathy for this woman that I had never met, but had recognized from seeing her around the ward.

The staff had all left the office where I had been swirling around in my chair. They all went to tend to the woman whose screams came from a room so nearby.

I slowly approached the 7 and swallowed my fear as I looked in through the small window of the isolation room door.

My eyes grew wide in fear, sadness, empathy and horror. My stomach twisted in painful emotion. I looked through the window to see the woman sitting on the bed, topless and crying in wails like a child. Her clothing was being forcefully removed from her body. I felt sick as I watched her scream. Her bare breasts were exposed to the air where about 10 men surrounded her bed and held her down. They put a hospital gown on her and tied her limbs to the bed.

I knew then that I would never forget the look of terror, humiliation and hopelessness that I saw on her face that night.

I had seen that woman in the halls the next day. It was amazing to me that she was walking around. How did she find the strength to stand after what they did to her?

My eyes stayed wide with visions of that woman's struggle for days. I was so scared that the same could happen to me. What if I was next?

I was very watchful of anyone who came close to me. I planned what I would do if someone tried to hurt me like they did her. I was prepared to scream. In my mind I was already screaming. The fear was nearly paralyzing, and it suffocated me.

My memories of what happened to that woman followed me like a threat wherever I went.

I was so afraid that I would never get better, and I would be stuck in terrifying and threatening places for the rest of my sorry excuse of a life. When a nurse asked why I was so nervous and scared, I explained what I saw.

"What if that happens to me?" I asked her with painful fear. "I don't know how I'd survive if a gang of men undressed me."

"They would give you a chance to undress yourself before forcing you," she explained. "They would also take your past into consideration."

I felt a bit better, but I was also puzzled. If I didn't have post traumatic stress already, it would be okay for them to forcefully undress me? Would not having a traumatic past make it so I didn't care about having my body forcefully undressed and exposed? How could that exist in any legal way?

Tuesday, November 25

I didn't find Megan the most helpful nurse to talk to. We had spoken several times, but she was more blunt and insensitive. Maybe it was just her way of dealing with a difficult patient. I would understand if she had a problem dealing with someone like me.

I did talk to Megan about how I was feeling and I asked her for some Lorazepam.

I realize looking back that I asked very often for medicinal help. It may have been a crutch but I don't doubt that it helped to get me through.

I took a walk to clear my head and let the medicine start to help. There were times when the Lorazepam didn't do very much. I think over time it's effect had weakened on me. Even after an hours walk I was still wanting to hurt myself. After 8:00 pm I picked up one of the white towels from the cart and brought it to my room. I sat on the floor by my bed with a razor blade that I had brought with me in my things. I made over a dozen cuts in my leg.

The blood dripped down and made a puddle on the floor. I used my fingers to play in the puddle and break up the gobs of blood. My hand was entirely coated so I pulled out a sheet of loose leaf and made a hand print on it. I used my stained fingers to write the word *sorry* on the floor. I played in my blood for a long time. Another silent fascination where I didn't have to think about what was going on in my mind. It was peaceful. My heart rate slowed to a degree where I could breathe again. I breathed like I didn't know what breathing was before, and I felt a calm sense of happiness.

Eventually, Saul came to my room. He asked if he could come in because the curtain was closed and he may have thought I was changing.

I said it was okay. I trusted him.

I watched as he turned the corner and looked down at me. He didn't seem surprised. This was nothing he hadn't seen before. Saul put on his blue rubber gloves, then he came over and grabbed my right wrist. I wasn't holding the razor, so I imagine that he did that to keep me from playing in the blood. After that he picked up the razor from the floor without letting go of my wrist. I tried to pull away, but he kept his grip on me. I'm not completely sure as to what he was afraid I was going to do.

Carson arrived in the room and he took over and held my wrist while Saul went to get rid of the blade. He wasn't going to let go of me either, even if I tried to make him let go.

When Ella came she brought some wet rags to clean me up.

Saul used a wet face cloth to clean my bloody hand that was still being held tightly. I felt like a two year old getting her hands cleaned after sticking her fingers deep into a glazed chocolate cake.

When my hands were cleaned I was guided away from the mess on the floor. They had me sit on the bed so they could tend to the wounds.

Ella asked me how I was feeling.

"Bad," I answered. "Really bad." The attention they were giving me was ruining what I had gained by cutting. That was something I missed about cutting at home. At home I could take my time and I could take care of my own mess. I usually didn't have any intrusions that would take away from what I had done.

I wasn't sorry that I did it though, because I did feel better. I was more relaxed. It was a mess, but it was a mess that relieved my mind of what I felt I needed to do.

Carson cleaned my leg with a wet medical compress. I asked if I could take care of it myself. I could wash my own leg and bandage it.

He said no. All of them always said no. Was it unsanitary for me to do it myself?

I remember watching Saul clean up the puddle of blood on the floor and wishing that he could just leave it there. It might sound twisted, but I liked having my insides on the floor, growing cold. It was proof of pain. Proof of something ugly that lived inside me. It was proof that I was as ugly as that lumpy, clotted up pile on the floor.

"Why didn't you talk to me?" Saul asked.

"You weren't there," I answered.

Saul had been gone on his supper break. I probably would have done it anyways. I wanted it too much and I didn't have it in me to care about trying. I wanted to do it, so that's what I did.

Megan said that I had done everything I needed to do. I asked for some Lorazepam. I talked about what I was going through. I walked to burn off my emotions.

All that was left was cutting. The final thing that made things okay.

After I was bandaged up, Saul asked me to show him where I had hidden any other blades.

I refused to tell him, so he began going through my clothes to find them himself.

"This would be a lot easier if you just told me where they are," Saul prodded.

I stayed silent and Saul started looking through my underwear and arm warmers.

"I wouldn't have to look through your things if you just told me," he said. "Ah ha!" he exclaimed as he pulled a plastic knife and razor blade out of my underwear drawer.

"Are there any more?" Saul asked.

I didn't answer. I didn't want to lie, but I couldn't tell him where they were.

"Come on. You and I have a good relationship," Saul began, and by then we were the only ones in the room. "You've always been honest with me and I need you to be honest now. Where are the other blades?"

"I'm not being dishonest," I told him in almost a whisper. "I'm just choosing not to say. Not saying something is not lying."

"Come on," he insisted as he used his blue gloved hands to cover mine and pull me up from where I was sitting on the bed. "Where are they?"

"I can't say." I sat back down.

Saul dug his hand into my coat pocket that was laying on a shelf and pulled out a handful of salt packets. Saul looked confused. "Why salt?"

"Harvey won't let me have as much as I want so I keep some hidden for the days that he's in charge," I explained.

Saul understood and moved back to the subject at hand. "Come on, tell Saul where the blades are," he requested as he pulled me up again. "It's 10:30 pm and I have to put the stuff away."

"Great," I accepted. "Let's do that and come back to this later."

"No, you stay here and I'll be back soon," Saul told me as he picked up the bloody towels and left with them. Saul came back less than a minute later. "Tell Saul where they are. Come on."

Saul had me standing next to him. He squeezed my shoulder to encourage me to tell him what he needed to know.

We were facing my cupboard where he wanted me to pull my blades out of hiding. I knew there wasn't much there. I used my right foot to point towards the bottom of the dresser. Saul leaned down and pulled off the small scissor razor that I had taped to the underside of my dresser.

"Okay, is there anything else?" he asked.

I sat back down. "I don't want to say."

"You don't want to say," he echoed. "That means that there are more."

"It means that I'm not going to lie, but I'm not going to tell you where they are either," I explained.

"Come on. Help me," he begged. "I'm trying to keep you safe. You can't hurt yourself like that anymore."

"Why?"

"Because it's bad for you and it's my job to protect you."

"I need them."

"The blades?"

"Yes," I confirmed. "I need them to make me feel safe. I need them so that when things get bad, I'll have something to make it better."

Saul listened kindly. "You need to find something else to make it better."

"I have other things," I offered. "Like talking, walking, music, Lorazepam, but nothing works as well as cutting does."

"You can give them to Saul," he insisted. "Come on."

"What if I don't?" I asked.

Saul gave it some thought. "Well then you will have gotten hurt and I won't have done my job to protect you."

"You don't have to protect me from this. What will I do without them?" I asked feeling concerned and lost.

"Without your blades?"

"Yes."

"You'll find safer ways of dealing with your suffering."

"What if I can't?" I asked Saul. "What if I never find anything as good as this?"

"Come on. Stand up," Saul insisted once again. "Where are they?"

"No," I refused.

"You know you can give them to me," Saul tried to reassure me.

"I need them."

"For what?"

"To make things better when nothing else works," I explained, but it felt like we were going around in circles.

We were both quiet for a moment. I was tired. Saul was tired. And I wasn't sure if it was worth it to defend my blades when I could just get new ones.

I stepped over to the bedside table and picked up my second journal. I opened some loose papers and pulled off a piece of tape that had a razor stuck to it. I gave the blade to Saul.

That was the last razor and I promised him that it was. It was my last razor, but I still had safety pins....

I didn't have to sleep in the 62.

By 10:30 pm, I didn't feel like sleeping. I sat on the floor in my doorway with my back against the doorpost.

"Why are you sitting there?" Megan asked when she passed by.

"I like to see the people moving around," I answered.

Later Carson and Saul told me that I wasn't supposed to be there. It was bed time and I had to be in bed.

I told them that I didn't want to go. I didn't want to risk dreaming.

"It's okay, I'm going to protect you," Saul promised.

"You can't protect me from dreaming," I replied.

I did get up and went to my bed. They wanted me to lay down, but I didn't want to, so they just left. I sat for a long time on my bed, and when I felt ready, I laid down.

"Why did you do that?" my roommates voice found me in the darkness.

"Why did I avoid sleeping, or why did I hurt myself?" I asked for her to specify.

"Why did you cut yourself?" she asked.

"I have a lot of reasons, like needing a distraction and expressing my anger." I explained.

"I bet there a lots of reasons," she echoed sympathetically.

"Yes, there are," I agreed. "Sometimes I have to make myself bleed to feel like the person that I really am. There is a part of me that is so disgusting, and infected, and wrong, and ugly that sometimes I have to create that reality on my skin. That way I truly look like who I am."

"I've felt like that before," she related. "I used to make cuts all over my face. To this day you can still see the scars and dents that are left of it. I was convinced that nobody knew what I looked like and that was the only way to show it."

"I understand," I said softly.

"But that feeling of disgusting, that's from abuse from when you were young?" she asked.

"Yeah, that's a big part of it."

Wednesday, November 26

The next morning Dr Stone paid me a visit.

"You can't be bringing anymore dangerous razors in here anymore," he spoke very seriously. "If you still have some, you have to get rid of them now."

"I don't have anymore razors," I spoke truthfully. "Saul took them all last night."

"You can't have super dangerous things," he told me. "You can have a plastic knife though."

"Really?" I asked. I found that to be a surprising thing for him to say. "What about safety pins?"

"Do you have safety pins?"

I didn't want to answer that. "I just want to know if they are okay to have."

"I'll think about that, but if you have any more razors, I don't even want to know about them. Just send them home."

"Okay," I accepted. "But I don't have any more. I gave them to Saul."

I think I had been so willing to bring tools into the hospital because I had gotten used to having my self injury be such a known fact. They all knew that I cut. I had to show several of them what I did, over and over. I lost my fear of them. I lost my fear of having them know. I still had fear of my family seeing, but not when it came to the hospital. It didn't make much of a difference anymore.

Some felt that my willingness to hurt myself at the hospital was because I needed the attention. I thought a lot about that. I took a step back and asked myself if that could possibly be the case. I looked into the depths of myself to see what my motivations for cutting were.

My father used to say that if someone were attacking me I should scream *bloody murder*. I used to think that it meant that I should scream the words themselves; scream "Bloody Murder!". It wasn't until I had grown up that I realized that the expression actually meant to scream really loud. Its kind of funny; No one ever hears me scream because I never make a sound, but I'd been screaming inside of myself for years. Screaming *Bloody murder*. Screaming and screaming, and becoming so exhausted that I could barely come up for air.

For me, self injury was a basic need. It was a very wrong, basic need to make the screaming and the exhaustion go away. It was the deeper parts of sadness wrapped in desperation. It was making things better in the way that I knew how. It was something that I could want so badly that I was literally scratching at the walls. It was something that I grieved for if it couldn't be had. It was the grinding of my teeth in angered longing. It was so powerful and immense, yet it managed to fit inside me. Cutting was for all those things.

When I thought about it and made myself feel what I felt in those moments, I knew it wasn't for attention. It was an act done for myself and not for anyone else.

It wasn't for attention, though in a way it twisted in that direction. I did like when someone showed that they cared or took a moment to help me. I liked feeling like I was seen and that I mattered. I liked the attention I got when it was positive, but the act in itself, was not done to attain it. It was more like a by-product. I could definitely appreciate attention.

Every action brings a reaction. Whether it was in a good or bad form, attention was something that most would give.

I thought a lot about it. I wondered though as to why it was so insulting to be told that I cut for attention. If someone was so desperate to get attention that they would be willing to cut themselves to achieve it, then didn't they need it? Shouldn't it be given to them?

LADY INJURY

Attention could be achieved in so many different ways; cutting was simply one of the more unfortunate ones.

~ ~ ~ ~

I started to learn a lot about Sabrina. Sabrina was the first person I had spoken about who got strapped to the bed while yelling that she was being raped.

I had started talking to her more and it felt good to see that she liked the attention I gave her.

She said and did strange things, but I never made her feel that I didn't believe the things she said.

I learned a lot about another reality that lived inside of Sabrina.

She told me about how she worked for the police by contracts. She could communicate with her fellow officers by talking into her hand. She had a boyfriend who was a criminal. She said that this was a complicated relationship because he was a criminal and she was the law.

"I'm the Boston Sheriff," Sabrina would tell me. "You need to be careful," she warned. "Saul has been going around the ward making all the women pregnant."

"Oh," I pretended to accept. "Thanks for the warning."

I didn't tell her that I didn't believe her. I wouldn't have made anything better by attacking her reality.

I found it fascinating that there could be so many realities. There was the truth, which was the world we lived. There was also the worlds we would create for ourselves in our minds. In truth, there are countless universes and realities hiding within all of mankind.

~ ~ ~ ~

The girls on the ward had been fighting.

Samantha said that her roommate Cindy had been calling her fat. Samantha was very underweight and it's understandable that a girl with an eating disorder would be extremely sensitive to that kind of talk.

Samantha was giving Cindy a hard time; even following her around the halls and making menacing movements towards her.

Samantha and my roommate were talking about how Cindy must have been stealing their things, like lipstick.

I asked if someone actually saw Cindy take the lipstick, but apparently their theory was completely based on a hunch and the fact that Cindy was the kind of girl to do that.

I felt bad for Cindy. She had to go to the nurses and file a complaint about the harassment.

Maybe she stole the stuff; maybe she didn't. It really didn't concern me. I was trying to be as nice to Cindy as possible. She had been walking around in huge beach sandals because she was taken away from home by ambulance and just grabbed whatever clothing was near the door. Because of that she had to always wear her boyfriends big sandals and always wore a hospital gown because she had no shirt.

I scrounged through my closet and found a shirt that was close to Cindy's size. I lent it to her along with a pair of socks. It fit her well and she was grateful.

I liked peace. I didn't see why girls had to fight so much. It would be nice if we could all just understand each other for the stupid things we do, because we all make mistakes.

~ ~ ~ ~

My mothers cousin called me and said something that I keep close to my heart. "You are a baptized servant of God, and everything that belongs to God has value."

~ ~ ~ ~

My mom called and we got to dream together about a trip that we were planning. It was going to be a beautiful gift from my mother.

She wanted to pay for her way, and both mine and my sisters way to go to Cancun, Mexico, for two weeks in the month of February. It was an epic gesture because my mother didn't have it easy in terms of money. I was glad that she was going to go on a trip like that. My mom deserved it. I don't just mean because she kept having to fight off cancer, but she was an all around generous and admirable woman. I was proud to love her and come from her.

We dreamed of beaches, and dolphins and horse back rides in the ocean. We dreamed of underwater diving and dressing fancy for evening meals. We were truly looking forward to it.

My sister and I had to take care of other details on our end. We both needed passports and I had to be out of the hospital so we could go get them.

Thursday, November 27

I started taking Lorazepam regularly instead of just as needed to keep my mood more level.

An intern came and took my blood pressure and asked me if I was anxious.

"Yes, I am," I answered.

"How would you say your anxiety is on 10?"

I hated that question. I knew the staff were supposed to ask that question, but I had very little patience for it.

"Ah," I moaned. "I don't feel like putting my anxiety into a number. It's already bad enough that I have to feel it. Can't I just feel it without labeling it?"

"Okay," she accepted. "So without a number, how do you feel?"

I hesitated and sighed, then said, "I feel depressed; deeply so. I feel anxious. I feel like crying and I feel like hurting myself because I hurt this way."

I should have asked her what number that would have been....

~ ~ ~ ~

I met someone just like me. When I first saw him, I asked him his name. He said it was Terrance. He looked to be in his early twenties. Somehow I could see on his face that years had been hard for him. I could see the difficulties he had endured.

I asked Terrance if he wanted to play cards with Parker and I and he accepted.

We started playing a game of Janitor and soon I noticed some unique cuts and scars on Terrance's arms.

"Those are self inflicted," I stated while pointing at his arms. Terrance didn't seem to react, so I asked, "You can tell me that it's none of my business, but are you here for self injury?"

"No. Not this time," he answered.

"I self injure too," I confessed. "I'm not here for that this time either, but I get to hide mine." I raised my arms so he could see that I was referring to my arm warmers.

"Yeah, I don't get to hide mine," he told me. "I don't know why."

"They want to make sure they can see when or if you make new cuts," I explained.

Later that evening I was sitting on the floor in the small hallway, between the staff elevators. Terrance came and sat with me even though the nurses said that we weren't supposed to be there. We both agreed that it was a really good place to sit.

Terrance showed me his wrist. It was red.

"Did you burn it with the water tap?" I asked him. I felt guilty for having told him about the water tap when he asked me how I had managed to burn myself.

"Yeah, but it only made it red," he said.

"Really?" I was surprised. "When I did it, the skin came off."

"You must have really soft skin," he said. "Mine is tough."

"Yeah, I got caught tonight using a soda pop top," I admitted.

"A what?"

"It's the little piece of metal in the mouth of the soda can," I explained.

"Let me see," Terrance requested.

I checked to see if there were any onlookers, but we were the only ones in the hall, so I showed him my leg. I pulled the large bandage off to reveal the dozens and dozens of cuts I had made. I didn't point out which one was made by the soda can though.

Terrance looked at it a bit surprised and then put the bandages back over my cuts. "Yeah, you're like me," he concluded.

~ ~ ~ ~

I was allowed out once every two days and I used that time to feed my ferrets. I also had to go shopping because my clothes were too big and my pants wouldn't hold up anymore.

~ ~ ~ ~

Dr Stone said that I may be released on December 5th. I had gained some weight and was eating much better, but I still didn't feel ready to go. I was hoping to stay a little longer to make sure I was okay.

"What would you do if you were tied down to the bed?" Dr Stone asked as he sat next to me in the 62.

The question struck me. I hadn't expected that to come up between us.

"I would freak out and hurt myself after," I guessed.

"You can't hurt yourself," he corrected. "You are tied to the bed."

"Are you suggesting that I should be tied down?" The subject worried me.

"I'm seeing how you feel about it," Dr Stone specified.

I didn't want to get tied down, but if it was going to happen, I had to at least think of all I needed in order to protect myself.

"If I were tied to the bed, I would want to keep my clothes and not be made to undress into a gown," I told him as I thought back to the horrible cases I had seen.

"Okay," he accepted and wrote it down.

"I also wouldn't want anyone to call a *code white* and have twelve guys come to force me to the bed," I told him. "I'm not a violent person."

The doctor wrote that down as well.

We began talking about many things. We spoke of how our attitude towards a situation can change things. If we were outgoing rather than reserved things would be different.

Dr Stone was saying how pain is only bad if we think it's bad. He said it was a matter of perspective. If we embrace our negative emotions they can become good.

I disagreed. "Pain isn't good. Pain hurts. I hurt inside and that's not good."

In the end we respectfully disagreed and changed subjects.

Thirty minutes into our conversation, I stopped to say, "My stomach hurts."

"Would you like to lie down?" Dr Stone asked.

I moved sideways to lie down, but I ended up falling backwards off the side of the bed. I tried to fall slowly, but my head hit the floor. The next thing I knew, Dr Stone had scooped me up and placed me lengthwise on the bed. I was laying on my back and the doctor sat down and placed my feet on his shoulder so that my legs could be raised.

I waited quietly like that for a minute. I was trying to breathe better and was covering my eyes because the light was bright. I was also quite embarrassed, so covering my face was my only hiding place.

"Why did that happen?" I asked. "I've been eating. That shouldn't happen."

"Heightened emotion can sometimes cause this," he explained.

I sat back up and soon the doctor left.

~ ~ ~ ~

Samantha was put in the 62, but for her it was true isolation because the door was closed and locked. She was being punished for her bad attitude with her roommate Cindy who had supposedly stolen her lipstick.

Samantha was having trouble listening to the staffs directives to stay calm. She was very upset at having to stay in that room.

I would often pass by while I was walking around the halls and saw Samantha's sad face peeking out of the small window in her door.

When Samantha was calmer, she was permitted to have the door open, but she still had to stay in the room.

By the beginning of the evening, Samantha had left the room and began walking in the halls.

"You are allowed out?" I asked Samantha as our paces met.

I took my friends silence to mean no.

I walked with her anyways, but soon Saul saw her and ordered that she go back to the 62, but she refused.

Saul stood near the door to the 62. "Walk over here with Melissa," he said to Samantha.

I tried to encourage her to go, but she wouldn't.

We did a full tour of the hallway and that brought us back to the 62, but Samantha wasn't going in.

Saul was blocking the path so she couldn't continue passed the room and down the hall.

"Come on," I coached. "The more trouble you give them the longer you're going to have to stay in there. If you go now, you get out sooner."

"Yeah, right," Samantha's tone was of sarcasm. "They want to keep me in there forever."

Saul spoke, "Samantha, you just have to go back into the room and stay there."

"No way," she scoffed.

"Please Samantha," I begged. "If you don't go, they are going to call a code white, and a bunch of guys are going to come up to force you into that room. They may even tie you to the bed. I couldn't bare it if that happened. I care about you."

"Just let them try," Samantha's tone was of defiance.

Did she really think that her small frame was any match for a dozen men and women?

"Samantha, you can't win against that," I reasoned. "Please go in on your own accord and not because you were forced. Please don't make me see that. I don't want to see that."

Finally Samantha went back into the room.

I was deeply relieved, but soon my friend was behind her locked isolation room door while banging and yelling. It was hard for me to hear, so I went into my room and put my MP3 player to my ears.

~ ~ ~ ~

Saul had me doing all kinds of work to keep me busy and keep my mind off of wanting to hurt myself. I took a moment to try and calm down during times when my anxiety was more crippling. I had to stop somewhere that I could be alone, then try to slow my breathing that had become erratic.

Later that evening I was sitting in the small hallway between the elevators again. Terrance found me and sat down with me.

He showed me bandages from having burned himself again, but this time on the shower head. My guilt came back to me once again because I knew he got the idea of how to do it from me. I wondered how I could have been so foolish as to tell him how I had burned myself. I tried to tell myself it wasn't my fault because he had asked me how I had done it, but the responsibility still stayed with me.

After Terrance left, I started banging my head against the wall. Saul came to take me away from there and to where I could be supervised. He had me sit on a chair outside of the smoke room. I didn't like the chair though and I hopped up on the white cupboard that the games were kept in.

"You stay here and do guard duty," Saul directed.

A guard for the smoke room? Not interested. I decided to be a guard for the water fountain instead and monitor the people who drank from it. I made it my duty to ration the water provisions so there would be enough to sustain us all.

I told one man who drank from it that I was going to cry for the small children who wouldn't get any water because he'd had too much. "So many will go thirsty," I dramatized.

It was almost 10:30 in the evening. I heard a patient named Mark complain that the cigarette lighter in the smoke room didn't work.

"We always cut the power to the lighter at 10:20 pm," Saul informed Mark.

Saul went back to his work and I turned to talk to Mark who was standing next to me. "I have a lighter in my purse, but I doubt Saul would pass me my bag so that I could get that kind of thing out."

I decided to make up a bunch of bull and I called out to Saul who was working at the desks. "I need my glasses from my purse," I said as I walked towards him.

"You don't wear glasses," Saul replied knowingly.

I changed my tactic, "There's a very small person inside my bag and I have to let him out for air."

I got no response.

I tried again. "I wrote down the solution to world hunger on a piece of paper in my bag. I need to get it to pass on the information before the phones shut down."

"Why don't you just say the truth?" Mark interrupted.

"I need my lighter," I admitted finally. The truth wasn't nearly as fun.

Saul smiled and shook his head no.

I turned to Mark. "You can't say that I didn't try."

After that I went back to my post by the smoke room and water fountain, but was soon told that it was bed time.

For dramatic effect, I laid back across the white cupboard that I had been sitting on and said that I couldn't leave because I was protesting. "Trees!" I yelled. "The forests are disappearing and I can't leave this spot until all the woodland branches have grown back to their rightful places."

"Come on," Carson ushered as he took my arm and guided me to bed.

Friday, November 28

When Marie came to visit me while I was in the 62, I was feeling discouraged and reflective.

"How does my self injury make you feel?" I asked my sister when we got into conversation.

She thought about it for a moment. "At first the cutting part freaked me out, but now, as your big sister it hurts me more to know that you hurt so much. I wish that I could take away your pain and I pray many times a day for God to help you."

Marie had started crying and then so did I. Out of a sisters love she wiped the tears from my eyes.

A nurse passed by and told us that we shouldn't be two to a bed, so Marie got on her knees beside me and we rested our heads next to each other.

I felt bad for being the cause of her pain. I wished that I had kept my problems to myself so my family could have been spared.

Marie and I played cards and had some chocolate cake that she brought along. We had a truly nice visit, even with the crying and hard discussions.

When Marie left I was alone with my thoughts and my guilt over the effect my cutting had on my family.

~ ~ ~ ~

Later that afternoon while I was folding laundry at the towel cart again, Terrance came up to me and asked for some tips. He wanted to know what I used to make all the cuts on my leg.

I was foolish enough to answer. "I broke a light bulb."

Then Terrance said, "Shh," as though we were doing undercover work.

~ ~ ~ ~

I hurt myself again that evening. I wanted to have done more damage than I had achieved, but my nurse came in to see how I was doing.

The nurse cleaned what little wound I managed to create and said that my doctor had prescribed for me to be tied down.

Was that my reality? Was I the one being tied down? My heart squeezed tightly in my chest.

I was taken to the 62 and was made to put on a gown.

I protested about the gown because Dr Stone was supposed to prescribe that I keep my clothes. I was afraid of the gown riding up while I was being tied dow and showing parts of me that I would have rather kept private.

"We can't tie you down with your clothes on," I was informed. "Your doctor is new and he didn't know the rules. Everyone wears a gown when they are tied down. We have to see your hands and feet to make sure the restraints aren't too tight."

I was upset about this event and wondered what kind of clothes they thought I had that could have hidden my hands and feet when I wasn't wearing socks.

Roger and Carson came in with the straps and set them up around the bed.

"Lie down in the bed," Roger directed.

I obeyed and tried to stay calm.

"Can I have some Lorazepam?" I asked my nurse.

"You just got one," she told me.

Once my feet and hands were in the straps, they covered me with a blanket and left.

There was only a crack of window left open on the closed door. Once in a while I could see someone peeking through.

Being restrained was difficult for my mind to bare. It made me panic. Eventually I started pulling at my straps. With a lot of work I managed to pull my hands out, and after that it was easy to undo the straps on my legs.

I got up to go to the bathroom, but it was locked.

Outside my door, I heard my nurse tell the others that I had gotten free.

Shortly afterwards Roger and Carson came in with leather straps that were much stronger than the ones that I had escaped from.

That time around, Roger got the bad idea to put large padded mittens on my hands to keep me from scratching my cuts. I didn't see the purpose to it as being tied down had already taken care of that issue.

When the men left, then closed and locked the door, the mittens were the first things that I took off. I knew that they were aware that I had removed them because I noticed someone staring in at me through the little window.

When I was no longer being watched, I worked hard to get my left hand free but it was a challenge. I succeeded, but didn't use my free hand to undo the other straps. I allowed myself to fall asleep, which was a much easier thing to do with at least one arm free.

I woke up with nurses from the midnight shift putting my hand back into the restraint. It was made tighter that time and I wasn't able to get out. I wasn't able to fall back to sleep like that; it was too uncomfortable. I started singing a few songs in a low voice in order to pass the time.

After a certain time had passed, I started clanking the metal on my wrist against the metal on the bed. When a nurse came, I expressed my anxiety and was given some Lorazepam.

About ten minutes later I clanked and clanked against the bed once again. I had to make noise for a much longer time before someone came in to see me.

"I need the bathroom," I told the nurse when she came in. I was hoping that my need to pee would be reason enough for them to let me go free.

To my silent horror she brought a bed pan that I was supposed to stick my butt over. I was too embarrassed to be able to go in a pan on my bed, so she took it away.

"How much longer do I have to stay like this?" I asked her.

It was 1:30 in the morning and I had been tied down for two hours.

"It's up to the team to decide Beauty," the nurse informed me.

She called me Beauty. I wondered, was I Beauty? Or was I the Beast? Maybe I was both.

About twenty minutes later I was released and allowed to fall back to sleep.

I felt like crying and like I needed a hug, but I wasn't going to be asking the nurse for one. I was so sad that I felt sick to my stomach. I fell asleep that way, but by morning those restraints were dreams away.

Saturday, November 29

During the day my nurse was Sylvia. She was in her forties and had long red hair. I liked Sylvia. She was giving of her time and let me talk to her when I needed.

I was allowed outside the hospital for an hour, and when I came back, Sylvia asked me if I had brought any tools to hurt myself.

"I didn't bring any blades," I side-stepped her question but with a tone that gave myself away. I hated to lie, and if I was asked a question, I felt I had to answer truthfully. In this case, I didn't tell the truth, but I didn't lie either.

Sylvia called Dr Stone and he asked to talk to me.

I took the receiver.

"Is it safety pins that you have?" he asked.

"Yes," I answered honestly.

"You can keep them for today, but you can't use them," he compromised. "I'm going to talk to you about them when I come see you later."

I passed the phone back to Sylvia and Dr Stone informed her about what he had told me. After she hung up she begged me to give her the safety pins. "This worries me too much," she told me. "My job may be on the line since I know that you have them."

I told her no many times. "I need them and Dr Stone said it was okay," I argued.

Sylvia pleaded with me enough that I felt bad for her. She was truly scared about her job.

To make her feel better I went to get 4 or 5 safety pins and gave them to her. I didn't say that those were all of them, but she just assumed.

"I'm really proud of you for giving me this," she told me with a smile. She even bought me a chocolate bar to thank me. I felt guilty for taking it because I didn't deserve it, but I didn't want to tell her that.

~ ~ ~ ~

By the end of the day I had taken a lot of anti-anxiety medication because my prescription had been raised.

Ashton was my nurse that evening and I was grateful to have someone that I knew I could talk to. He took my blood pressure to be sure that it was okay to give me another Lorazepam. I was okay, so I got to have one.

When I wanted more, Ashton told me that he would rather we talked instead.

I accepted and we went to my room. He sat in a chair while I sat on the bed.

"Do you think I'm going to get my safety pins back after?" I asked Ashton.

"I wouldn't give you those pins even if I had a gun to my head because I know that you would use them to hurt yourself," he told me, then corrected himself. "Even without the gun, as a nurse and human being I wouldn't give you the pins. Do you understand my point of view?"

I wouldn't want for someone else to hurt themselves either; So I understood. "Yes," I acknowledged. "Can I sleep in the 62? I'm pretty sure that if I stay here I'm going to hurt myself."

Ashton talked to his team about it and they agreed that I could sleep there.

I took my medication for the night, then got under the covers of my bed in the 62. I laid there quietly for a long while, but as my mind tried to stay away from harder things, I started to think more and more about my leg and the damage I could do.

I sat up and started digging my fingernails into my leg. I made several red lines and the pain made me wince.

Ashton walked in and I pulled my hand away, but I realized that he had still seen me doing it. I wished I had an advance warning.

"You couldn't just lay there, huh?" he asked in a patient manner.

"I'm sorry. I tried," I said and wondered if I had truly tried enough. Clearly I had given in too quickly. "I didn't want to do it so I came here, but."

"It was stronger than you?" he asked.

"Yeah," I admitted.

Ashton covered my leg with my blanket.

"I'm sorry," I apologized again. "I don't know why I'm like this. It doesn't make any sense that I'm like this. Normal people aren't. I get into this place in my head where cutting is the only thing I can think about. I want it so bad that it's painful not to do it. Why am I like this? I wish I wasn't like this."

Ashton left and came back with a salve to put on my wounds. I was embarrassed for him to see them. "You must think I'm disgusting when you see that," I guessed.

"No, when I see this," he said. "I see suffering."

"That's strange," I thought aloud. "Because when I see this, I see what more I can do."

"And that comes from pain from your past," he reasoned. "I know what happened to you. It's in your file. I can't imagine going through that, but you don't deserve to keep putting yourself through pain. You've suffered enough. It's time to find a new way to feel better."

I looked at my leg. It was a battleground. Many lines of deep color that time hadn't taken away. Deep purple lines would always serve as a reminder that no matter what smile I wore, there would always be some part of me that would not be okay.

I started breathing deeply; Too deeply. I couldn't catch my breath and I knew that I had started to panic. My mind was all jumbled up. I couldn't cry and I couldn't breathe right. I couldn't keep from hurting.

I held my hands over my chest and tried to breathe more steadily.

"You can't breathe?" Ashton asked.

I shook my head no as I tried to breathe in deeply.

"Try to breathe more slowly, okay?" he instructed.

I shook my head yes.

"Breathe with me," he offered.

I tried the best I could to follow the rhythm of Ashton's breathing. Eventually he calmed me down enough to be able to go and get me some Lorazepam.

I took the medication. He left, and I went to sleep.

Sunday, November 30

By the next morning I saw Sylvia again and she was still assigned as my nurse.

"I don't understand you anymore," Sylvia told me. "I don't understand how you can have a nice visit with your sister and then hurt yourself barely a moment after she was gone."

I explained to Sylvia about the conversation that Marie and I had and how it had made us cry. "I was already in a bad mood before her visit, but the emotions made things worse."

"I understand," Sylvia told me and then she got an idea. "You should try venting your anger and emotion on something else. Maybe you could get a doll and do to her the things that you want to do to yourself."

I thought about it. "I think I like that idea."

I liked the idea of taking out my feelings on a doll, but I didn't want to cut her. I thought maybe I could draw blood on her with a red marker.

I found a doll that I really liked at the general store. I didn't want to pick a doll that was of a baby because I would have felt bad about drawing blood on her, so I chose a Strawberry Patch Girl. She was old enough to suit my needs.

I bought some black and some red markers. I drew dark, black make-up around her eyes. Then I drew blood dripping as tears on her face. I drew cuts with stitches on her cheeks and blood running from her forehead. She had blood on her right hand because it got messy while she was hurting herself. I drew burns on her left wrist and cuts on her right leg. I even put a rubber band around her wrist so she could snap it.

Others may have found her sadistic, but I loved her.

I named her Assilem. It was my name backwards and sounded like the word asylum; which was fitting for a doll whose first home was an asylum.

We were both in an asylum. She and I; together.

Monday, December 1

I was moved into a new room because of the night before. I had used my roommates lightbulb to cut into my arm and leg. So I was back in the first room I had ever been in at that hospital. I was in room 861. It was a room with only one bed that had no roommates and no light bulbs to be dismantled.

I was being watched more closely. My bathroom door was locked at all times and I wasn't allowed to go to the parts of the hallways where there were bedrooms. I could only go where there were the desks, or the cafeteria, so my walking grounds were cut in half.

I had several visitors that day, but I was really tired. My friend noticed and told everyone that they should go.

I was alone then and I tried to sleep, but couldn't manage.

Dr Stone arrived around supper time. I was glad to be able to talk to him because my nurses wouldn't leave my bathroom or closet unlocked unless it was prescribed.

"For as long as things go well, they can be unlocked," he permitted.

"And what about the rule that I can't walk in the halls where there are bedrooms?" I asked. "That's ridiculous."

"You know why they made that rule?" he asked.

"Yeah," I admitted. "It's so I don't take the other light bulbs, but come on! It's not like I'm going to skulk into someone else's room and take their lightbulb! I used a lightbulb to hurt myself but it was from in my room. I'm not going to take other people's breakables."

I got up and demonstrated what it would look like if I were hunched over and covertly crossing into a strangers room. "See?!" I cried. "It's ridiculous." I threw my hands in the air to emphasize my point.

Dr Stone consulted with my nurse. It was decided that when I was feeling well I could walk where I wanted, but if I wanted to hurt myself, I had to tell my nurse and my privileges would be restrained.

I agreed.

I spoke with the nurse I had that evening and found we had some things in common. She said that she had an abusive father as well and that she was also anorexic. I liked that she had confided in me and made me less alone.

I decided to go to bed early because I preferred to be sleeping and unconscious than awake and wishing I could hurt myself.

Tuesday, December 2

I went with Marie to get our passport pictures taken at the pharmacy. It felt strange posing for them because we weren't supposed to smile.

After that we went to the general store to get a few things. I was able to get some light bulbs to give to the hospital and replace the ones I broke.

I paid my rent and checked my emails.

I returned to the ward, but not for long because I had my borderline personality disorder group that afternoon. I went there by taxi with another girl who was also in my group.

I was so nervous during group that all I could think about doing was leave, but I endured and stayed to the end.

I let my nurse know how badly I was feeling when I got back. I didn't tell her though about the small pair of manicure scissors that I was smuggling in.

That evening I made it clear to my nurse Amanda and to Saul that I was planning on hurting myself. That was a deal I had made with my doctor. I had to say when I wanted to cut.

The nurses on staff that night were Amanda, Ella and Carson.

Saul didn't want to leave me alone so he had me sit in a chair by the desks where he could see me.

I was so tired that all I wanted to do was cut and go to bed. I could hardly sit up straight in the chair. It felt like the world was in a haze. I got up to go to my room, but Saul and the nurses stopped me. I was in bad shape because I could barely walk. They had to help me get back into the chair and I barely made it.

Amanda took my blood glucose levels; they were fine.

I later dug into my wounds with my fingernails and reopened them. That was a strange and uncharacteristic thing for me to do when I wasn't in private.

Amanda had to disinfect the damage, so I clumsily turned around to let her pour the liquid over my leg.

When she was done, I got up again to go to my room, but this time they didn't stop me.

Amanda asked if I was all wobbly and confused because I had taken drugs, but I swore that I didn't. The only thing that was different was that my Lorazepam and Quetiapine doses were higher.

They noticed that I was confused and had a hard time understanding them, so I walked to my bed.

Saul told me, "Good. Go to sleep."

I didn't sleep though. I continued to open my wounds. I was in a strange state of mind and I wasn't stopping no mater who tried to make me.

"I hate tying people to the bed," Saul told me. "It's the last thing I want to do, but you have to stop hurting yourself."

I was nearly in tears when they brought in the straps.

I didn't understand my own mind or my own reality.

After I was in the straps and my blankets were put over me, Saul took my hand for a moment, then left the room with Amanda.

I tugged at the restraints a few times, but I didn't feel panicked. I trusted Saul.

Every once in a while, someone would look in through the little window to see if I was okay. After about fifteen minutes, Saul came in and checked all four restraints. He had to make sure they weren't too tight and weren't hurting me.

"Is it finished?" I asked him and noticed that my voice sounded as weak as I felt.

"No, not yet my dear," Saul answered.

LADY INJURY

Every fifteen minutes Saul would come in to check my restraints and every fifteen minutes I would ask him if it was over; every time but the last time, he said that it was not.

Finally I was let out of the restraints, but I was too tired to do anything but sleep.

Wednesday, December 3

I remember getting up and stumbling out of bed at around three in the morning. I must have had a nightmare or something because I was really freaking out. I wobbled clumsily over to the desks and asked if I could have some Lorazepam.

Charlotte was the nurse on staff, and she said that I was already in too much of a mess from all the Lorazepam that I had taken and that I should just go to sleep; so I did.

Even by 7:30 in the morning I was still wobbly on my feet while on my way to the scale to get weighed.

My nurse said, "It's a good thing I didn't give you the Lorazepam. Just look at you."

~ ~ ~ ~

One of the patients was an elderly lady that I liked very much. We called her Annabelle. She was almost my height and had short curly hair that she dyed brown. She walked slowly, but she got around well.

She had expressed to me how much she liked all my arm warmers, so I offered that she could have a pair. I told her that she could have one of any color. I had extra material to remake more at home anyways.

Annabelle chose to have a black one, so I went to my room and picked a black one with silver flowers. When Annabelle put the arm warmers on, it was clear that she felt very pretty. She stroked the material over her arms with a childlike smile. She told me that she felt really fancy.

Once I had gotten to know her, I had vowed to take care of her.

I watched Annabelle go up to the desk that morning and she asked for the injection.

The nurse was confused. "What injection?"

"The one to die," Annabelle answered.

Of course she wasn't going to get the injection, but I went to her and gave her a hug as her eyes brimmed with tears. She looked like she needed affection.

During my hour on the outside later that day I met up with Joseph and he came to the flower shop with me. I bought a red flower for Annabelle. The lady from the shop made the flower look fancy by adding leaves that complemented it well, then she covered it in paper to protect it.

I wrote Annabelle a card saying that someone thought she was special and that she was a real treasure.

When I gave Annabelle the flowers, I also gave her a hug and told her that she had value and should never forget it.

After my conversation with Annabelle I had a meeting with a dermatologist. My nurse Amanda had arranged the encounter so we could know what to do about all the healing cuts on my leg. She wanted to know if there was any kind of cream that should be applied to help it heal better.

A man with partly greying hair came to see me in my room and Amanda accompanied him. When he requested to see what we were talking about I sat on my bed and pulled up my pant-leg. I got an immediate reaction.

The mans eyes got wide and his expression and tone of voice was of repulsion. "That's really ugly," he told me while looking from my leg to my eyes. "You've made yourself really ugly. Look at that. It's terrible. How could you do that? It's so ugly."

I was surprised at the reaction he gave me and I covered my leg as he continued to go on about how ugly it was.

"Did you know that those scars will never go away?" he asked me with continued disdain.

"Yes, I know that," I told him. "I've been doing this for a long time."

"Well, you're a pretty young girl and you're making yourself ugly," he carried on. "When I look at that, I can't believe my eyes. It's repulsive. It's really terrible. There's nothing I can do to make it less visible."

Yes, I understood him. I was ugly. Did he have to say it and be so mean about it?

"I wasn't expecting you to make them less visible," I clarified. "I know that the cuts are deep and that it's been days."

Amanda tried to turn the conversation back to what she originally intended. "Should we put any kind of cream or bandages on it?" she asked him.

"There's really nothing you can do. Don't bother bandaging it and just leave it to the air." The man never ceased to speak in a demeaning tone.

"What about the itching?" Amanda asked because I had been scratching incessantly at my healing wounds.

"You can apply moisturizers, but don't scratch it," the man directed. "If you do it will just increase the risk of infection. I don't see any infection, but if you keep going on like this you could lose your leg. How would you like it if we told you that we had to cut your leg off tomorrow?"

"I wouldn't like it at all," I tried to reply calmly to the mans hostile manners. "I would be very upset with myself."

"You need to take this seriously because that is honestly very repulsive," he spoke adamantly.

At that point, and maybe a while before that point, I felt like telling the guy to shut up. I couldn't wait for the conversation to end. I knew that it was stupid and hideous. I knew that there was never a chance of it not being hideous. I knew that I messed things up, but he needed to shut up about it because he wasn't helping anything by being so arrogant and cruel.

When the meeting was finally over and the dermatologist left, Amanda apologized for how the consultation had turned.

"I'm sorry," she said. "I tried to steer the conversation a different way, but he kept going on and on. I feel really bad about this."

"It's not your fault. It's not you who needs to feel badly," I consoled her. "Thank you for trying. I feel really badly too. How could he be so mean?"

Amanda sympathized. "I know. I thought so too."

Amanda went back to working and I tried to think about something else, but what happened really bothered me.

A friend was what I needed so it was good that Joseph showed up. I gave him a hug and told him how badly I felt. He consoled me and suggested a change in scenery.

We went downstairs to the vending machines and this time it was Joseph's turn to treat me to a hot chocolate. We sat in the basement cafeteria and I got to go on about all the things that were bothering me.

Joseph made for a good brother, but it wasn't easy caring for someone with problems like Joseph. He was still trapped in his messiah complex. I tried to guide the conversation away from that stuff as much as possible.

We played ping-pong when we went back upstairs and then had a few games of cards until he left at 6:30 pm.

I walked around the halls after with my music playing in my ears.

I was honest and admitted to thinking about cutting. My nurse was Carson that night, but he was never useful with that kind of thing. All he had to say was that it had to go well. That was all he ever had to say. "It has to go well." I was tired of hearing it and frustrated that asking for help did nothing. I was supposed to ask for help but the help didn't know how to help me.

I had been dreaming all day about using the manicure scissors to stab my leg. I couldn't tell him that things were going to go well because that wasn't what I felt like would happen.

Saul was watching out to keep me from hurting myself.

I had gone into the washroom to pull out the scissors I had hidden and tucked them into the side of my pants. I almost had them tucked in when I heard Saul coming.

I barely heard him knock and less than a second later he was opening the door. I wouldn't have had the time to say I was on the toilet bowl by the time he was already seeing me on it. I was glad he never found me like that.

I spoke bitterly, "I do go to the bathroom for real sometimes. I'm not always cutting."

"I did knock," he defended himself.

Saul was satisfied that I hadn't hurt myself, but he went to talk to Carson. He told him that he had caught me trying to use nail clippers.

They weren't nail clippers, but I knew that if I didn't use them right then, I would never get the chance. I pulled the scissors out and stabbed my leg, but the scissors didn't sink as well as I had hoped. I didn't even draw blood.

I went to stab myself a second time, but when Carson came in the room, he saw, then ran over and grabbed my arm. He took the scissors before I got the chance to stab a second time.

"I got here just in time," Carson said between breaths.

"I would have liked it if you had taken longer," I told him.

Carson sat down and asked me why I had done that.

My answer always seemed to be the same. "I had to. I needed it. I've been wanting it all day. Please give me my scissors back."

"Of course!" Carson said with a wide sarcastic smile. "I'll just pass them to you and let you do what you want with them."

"Sounds good," I told him and outstretched my hand to receive them.

He then smiled again and shook his head no. "Of course not," he told me.

"I'm supposed to say when I'm going to hurt myself," I said to Carson. "I said I was going to hurt myself."

My actions had consequences. I knew what that consequence was when the yellow box of straps was brought in. Part of me knew it would happen and another part was always surprised to see that box.

I was allowed to pull out my pajama pants and a shirt to wear while being tied down. I had complained to Dr Stone that they had taken my clothes away the other times and he took care of it for me.

I got changed in the bathroom, but when I came out, the men left so that Megan could check my underwear for tools. She wanted me to pull my underwear down so she could see if I had hidden anything in my backside. I refused to pull my underwear down no mater how she insisted. What she wanted was degrading and humiliating. As a human being I knew it was my right to refuse.

Megan finally stopped pushing me to search where she had no right and she let the men back in.

I sat on the mattress as the straps were being wrapped around the bed. When the lower straps were ready, Saul took one foot at a time and placed them in the brace.

After that the arm straps were ready but I didn't want to lie down. I closed my eyes and felt Saul's hands on each of my shoulders as he guided me down. I found it hard watching someone I cared for wrap my wrists into restraints.

When I was all strapped and covered, everyone left.

The straps on my arms were barely long enough for me to scratch my face when it was itchy.

I remembered half agreeing to being tied down, but to say that I hated it would be an understatement. It was dehumanizing. It was long and desperate. I feared it very much. The part I feared most was when they were putting me in the straps. It felt aggressive and cruel. Once I was tied down and left there, the worst thing was a great discomfort and helplessness.

I wondered why the fear of being tied down wasn't enough to keep me from hurting myself. Self injury was a completely different life form than fear of consequence though. They didn't mix enough in me.

I twisted around a bit in the bed until I was in a position to clamp my teeth down on my arm. I bit hard into my skin a few times before Carson peeked in the small window and I was caught.

Carson disappeared from the window and a minute later he came into the room with some black straps. Seeing them made me nervous. What was he going to do with them?

He attached the black straps to the ones that were already on my wrists and pulled on them until the cords were shorter. I had much less freedom to move my arms.

I resisted and said that I didn't want them to be shorter. I pulled on the cord as hard as I could, then Carson pulled back in his direction.

"I need my arms to be able to scratch my face when it's itchy," I insisted.

"It's the fact that you're scratching that's making me put these on here in the first place," he told me.

I knew he was right, but I didn't give up my end of the fight.

I can't say that either one of us won the battle. Carson left and came back with Saul. Carson explained to him that I was bitting my arm.

I struggled and pleaded as much as I could, but Carson used both his hands to hold my arms down one limb at a time while Saul tightened the restraints.

"We're doing this to help you," Saul said to me. "We can't let you hurt yourself. You can't control yourself, so we are here to control you."

I felt so helpless from being pinned down that way. I felt like crying but didn't allow it. With the straps shortened, I could barely move my arms anymore.

I was alone again. I was trapped. It felt violent. It felt terrible. It hurt me inside my chest.

Someone came in to check on me every fifteen minutes. Either Saul or Carson would come. They would stick their fingers between the straps and my skin to make sure they weren't too tight.

After a time, I managed to twist myself into an impressive position that I actually found comfortable. I thought that I may actually be able to sleep like that. I had twisted my upper body and hips sideways. I slumped down and my head was next to my hand on the side of the bed. It was good. I liked it.

Saul didn't like it though. He wanted me to lay straight, so he pulled me up.

Saul had to come in with Carson again later and they pulled me up when they found me slouched down again.

"Why do I have to lay straight?" I asked

"That's the way it's supposed to be," Saul told me, but I didn't think his explanation was any better than a parent saying, "Because I said so."

"To keep you from getting ouchies," Carson would say.

In my mind, I silently made fun of his use of the word *ouchies*.

"But I'm more comfortable down there," I insisted.

I felt more comforted lower in the bed where I was sort of curled up in a near fetal position, so I continued to sink down.

As a compromise Saul put my blanket over my arm and under my head so that I wouldn't bite myself.

I was left alone again.

The blankets were easy to remove with the use of my teeth, but by then I didn't feel like hurting myself as much anymore.

I had too many blankets on me and I was getting much too hot. I tried for a while to take them off with my teeth, but I was only able to make them move a little.

I started clanking on the metal bars that my hands were attached to. Soon Carson came to the window and I yelled to him through the door that I was too hot.

Both Carson and Saul came in and took some layers off.

"It's true that you were hot," Carson admitted.

"Do you still want to hurt yourself?" Saul asked me.

My urge wasn't nearly as strong, but I was still thinking about it a little, so I said that I was.

As the men were leaving I called out Saul's name.

"Yes?" Saul turned around.

"Can this be over? Can you untie me?" I asked pleadingly.

"No," he denied. "You admitted that you still want to hurt yourself."

I regretted my admittance. I didn't think it would work if I said that I only wanted to hurt myself a little.

"Please?" I asked again.

"You'll be let out when you fall asleep," Saul told me. "The people from the next shift change will do it. I'm gone in fifteen minutes."

I said it was okay, and they left. I changed my mind quickly though when I started thinking about being tied to a bed with people surrounding me that I didn't know. I trusted Saul to be around me, but I didn't know the people who were around when everyone was sleeping. I didn't know the nightshift very well. I began to panic. I started clanking on the metal bars again, but that time it took much longer before someone came to answer.

Finally, Saul entered. The key turned in the lock and he walked in to stand at the end of my bed.

"What's going on?" he asked calmly.

I was relieved to have him come. "You can't leave me tied up with people I don't know. Please, untie me before the shift change. You can't leave me tied down with them," I pleaded.

"You know Tina don't you?" he asked as he pointed out the door to a nurse checking into her shift at the desks. .

I only knew Tina from when I asked for my shampoo in the morning, but I had met her. "Yes."

"And you know Gordon?" he asked.

I only knew him as well as I knew Tina. "Yes."

My heart was racing fast.

"Does that reassure you?" Saul wanted to know.

I thought about it. I wasn't exactly reassured. I knew though that those people had never hurt me, so I said, "Yes."

"Okay," he said. "I'm going to tell them that Tina is going to come in here and untie you. You won't be alone with Gordon when you fall asleep. They will let you out. I would have liked to let you out but you didn't fall asleep."

I was untied like he said, but it was hours later. Soon after my release I was able to sleep.

Thursday, December 4

Dr Stone had a theory that I was the reason that I wasn't hurt more than I was as a child. He thinks that I saved my whole family from a worse fate because of the uncontrollable love I had for my father. Seeing the look of fear and love in my eyes would have made him take a step back and think about what he was doing. In some ways I was my fathers favorite child. I had a deep impact on him because of the depth at which I loved him.

"You don't have to feel guilty for not defending yourself," Dr Stone told me. "It was your inaction that made him think about what he was doing."

It was an interesting idea and it sounded like a nice thing to be true. I liked listening to Dr Stones thoughts, but my father still didn't love me enough to put his selfish needs aside in order to protect me.

My doctor planned on taking me into the city on the weekend. He thought that getting out and seeing things would be good for me. I didn't know where he would take me, but I knew that I would be dropped off at Marie's when we were done and she would take me to the hospital.

~ ~ ~ ~

After my shower and breakfast I took my hour on the outside. I went to the store and got some chocolate and looked for some drawing pencils because I was thinking of picking up the art of portraits again. I had put a few of the portraits I drew on my wall at the hospital and since then I had been getting requests for more. I had to find more pencils because I had lost the ones I had, but there weren't any in the store I searched. I thought maybe that could be one of the things that I could do with Dr Stone when we went into the city. We could get some drawing pencils.

I didn't bring any new tools into the hospital when I returned. Dr Stone had asked me to stop bringing them in because I was freaking out the staff. The nice blond nurse from the night shift was afraid of having me hurt myself during her shift because in that time she was responsible for me. Other nurses felt the same. It was up to them to keep me safe, but I was chopping myself up.

I had been hoping that I could at least use my blades in a bathroom when I was downstairs at the vending machines, but it was specified that I couldn't do it there either. I wasn't to use them anywhere in the hospital.

~ ~ ~ ~

I was confused when I looked through my things and didn't find my hairbrush. I looked several times through all the same things, but it didn't come up.

I was surprised, amused, and increasingly confused when one of the nurses found my brush in Mr Borders room. The nurse had found it earlier and wondered what it was doing in his things.

Mr Border was the elderly pervert from in the ER who grabbed by breasts. The man hadn't touched me since, but he had a strange fascination with me.

Mr Border said that he had taken my brush in order to clean it. He said that he was a professional hairbrush cleaner and that only he should do it.

It was funny, but it was also very creepy.

~ ~ ~ ~

Lisa's mom came over and I taught her to play a game of cards. She liked the game and got really into it. We laughed a lot. It was a nice change in mood because I had been feeling badly all day.

I talked to my nurse later about how anxious, depressed, and near tears I had been feeling.

Saul and the nurses had a theory that it was my Lorazepam making me depressed, so Dr Stone removed it from my prescriptions and gave me a regular dose of Quetiapine instead.

The possibility of haloperidol as a prescription was brought up, but we were going to try the Quetiapine first.

Roger spoke to me that night and told me that I needed to be making more of an effort to get better.

"I have been making an effort," I told him defensively. "I have been eating and keeping all my food down. As for my self injury I've been doing all the things that I was asked to do. I tell my nurse when I want to hurt myself and I talk about it. I distract myself with music and walking and I ask for medication to calm down. I'm still messing up, but I am making an effort. I'm here because I'm making an effort. I'm letting them tie me to the bed because I'm making an effort."

"You are right about those things," Roger agreed.

I was glad he agreed because as hard as I had been trying to hurt myself, I had also been trying not to.

~ ~ ~ ~

In the evening when I admitted to wanting to self injure, I was tied down as a precautionary measure. I didn't fight them on the idea. They did what they felt they had to do and I tried not to care.

I pulled at the restraints a bit, but I must have fallen asleep in less than fifteen minutes because I didn't remember anyone coming in to untie me.

Friday, December 5

I got up at about 8:30 in the morning. Roger woke me and said that it was time for breakfast, then he opened my blinds.

I spent that whole day dreaming of hurting myself. I thought about where I would cut and how much I would cut. I pictured the color of it.

I was noticing again that when I was eating well, I was hurting myself more. Also if I was eating badly, I was hurting myself less. It made me think more about how an eating disorder really was a form of self injury.

Everyone had the impression that I was fine because I had been keeping myself busy. I had been walking a lot and playing cards with Samantha. After lunch I took a nap, then walked more. I had a hot chocolate that Parker gave me in exchange for having given him my malted chocolates the night before.

I spent the whole day pretending to be fine so that I could be sure that no one would stop me from taking my hour on the outside. I spent the whole day planning what I would do when I got out. I planned to buy deodorant and chocolate. I planned to go home, check my emails, feed my animals, and then mutilate the life out of my leg.

I was thinking about it a lot. I hadn't gotten a decent injury all week.

I felt guilty about keeping up a charade. I was supposed to say that I planned on hurting myself but I wasn't. I didn't want to do anything that would make them stop me.

I was having trouble too with the memory of one of the times that I was tied down. It was after I was biting my arm and they shortened the straps, then pinned my arms down to do it. Carson had used both his hands to hold my arm down. Being pinned down like that….it made me feel so haunted. I hated it. I hated the memory. It gave me this returning fear. When I would think about it, there was this pain that would shoot through me like a needle passing through my heart and into my gut.

~ ~ ~ ~

By the beginning of the evening, I was able to laugh for real and not feel the sadness I had been carrying with me. I was having fun talking to Saul and some of the patients. I was playing around and making jokes.

I heard Megan's voice from across the room. She was sitting at her desk. "Speak like a grown up," she said to me with irritation. "Stop acting immature and childish."

Her attitude and words really struck me. I even got mad. Why did she feel she needed to criticize something innocent and harmless when I was in a good mood? I wasn't hurting or bothering anybody. Why did she say that in a cruel and insulting manner?

"What you just said was really mean," I told her in a serious tone.

"Talk like a grown up," she replied.

I couldn't believe her attitude. "I'm going to talk however I see fit."

"Talk like a grown up," she repeated rudely.

"The way I talk isn't for you to control," I told her angrily. "What you said isn't okay. I was just having fun. What is wrong with messing around? This was the first time today that I was in a good enough mood to play around."

Shortly after it was time for me to take my hour on the outside. It was Megan that brought the papers I had to sign for the records to say I was leaving. What she had said was still bothering me.

"Why did you feel that you had to ruin a good mood and be mean?" I asked with clear hurt feelings. "I was just having fun."

"Well, that's not how a lady should act," she told me. "You're old enough to know better than to talk like you're drunk."

"I don't see what the problem was," I told her. "I was just making jokes. I was playing around."

"Well then you should have said that you were playing around," she criticized. "Sometimes I act goofy and say, *Aren't I silly?* so that people know that I'm messing around and not being serious."

"I didn't have to specify that I was messing around. The idea was clear," I told her. "Everyone was laughing and having fun."

Megan didn't look or act apologetic, so I remained mad at her. If she had cared that she had been mean and rude, I would have let it go.

"You need to learn to accept criticism," she told me.

While I was waiting for the elevator Megan told me that it was cold out so I should dress warm.

I didn't answer.

"Melissa," she spoke my name to make me pay attention, but I wouldn't turn around to look at her or acknowledge her. "Melissa," she repeated.

I said nothing and got on the elevator.

~ ~ ~ ~

Nobody stopped me, so I did get my hour outside. I did all the work I had planned on getting done. I even got to shave my legs because they never let me do that at the hospital.

When I had accomplished everything on my *to do* list, I grabbed my self injury kit and headed to the bathroom. I couldn't cut in the living room like I usually did because the light bulb had burned out, and I couldn't see well enough.

I sat down on the floor with my back against the tub and I pulled out a clean double edge razor. Those had become my favorite. I had considered using a precision knife to stab myself, but the blades were all dirty.

I didn't count the amount of cuts I made into my leg, but one by one I made a new line and watched the blood dribble down into a pill container. Catching the blood in a container was something new for me. It had never occurred to me before, but I also never did it again.

I filled the pill container. Then with my leg dripping down to my foot and onto the floor, I went to the kitchen to find something bigger to catch the blood. I quickly chose a tupperware glass and ran back to the bathroom to fill that as well.

My hour was running out and I had to clean up as quickly as I could. I didn't want to risk leaving the mess and having my brother or someone else walk into my place to find it there. I used a wet rag and sopped it all up.

I put my leg in the sink and rinsed it off. When it was dry I put the bandage that I already had from at the hospital back on my leg.

I zipped my bleeding leg into a beige winter boot. When I was all dressed up for the cold and snowy evening, I walked to the hospital.

When I checked in, Carson searched all my things for tools. He even searched my coat and boots, but there was nothing to be found. I had honored my doctors wishes and I didn't bring any in.

"How did your hour go?" Carson asked me.

"Not well."

"Let me see under your arm and leg warmers," he instructed when I had gotten to my room. "Did you bring anything in?"

"No," I answered. "I brought nothing."

"Okay."

I wondered why I was being searched so thoroughly. A search to this degree was out of the ordinary.

I wasn't feeling strong, so it took effort to remove my layers of winter clothing. I showed Carson that I hadn't cut my wrist, then I had to show my leg.

"Let me see," he requested, and when he saw the blood soaked bandages, he said, "You played in your wounds again."

"No," I corrected. "I made new cuts when I went home."

"What did you use?"

"A razor."

"Okay, stay here," he instructed and left me sitting on the chair in my room.

I got up and laid down on my bed in a sort of curled up position.

Saul came in my room and asked how my hour went.

"Not well." I gave him the same answer that I had given Carson.

When Saul saw my hand laying on my leg, he asked what happened. He didn't see any blood, but he knew something happened.

"Show me," he requested.

I pulled up my pant-leg, unwrapped the gauze and pulled off the bandages.

Saul looked at the mess of my creation. "I'm going to go inform Carson."

"He already knows," I told him.

Saul left and I sat waiting in silence.

I looked across the room at the sink by the door. I thought about the heat within it. I had used a water tap to burn myself before. I knew it would work.

I walked over and turned on the hot water. I waited for the water to grow as hot as possible and let it heat the metal of the tap. When it was ready I laid my wrist down against it. At first I winced and pulled my arm back, but then I called upon my courage to leave my wrist against it so it could burn properly. The pain was intense. I remember screaming three times before anyone arrived to stop me. Saul took my wrist from the tap and Carson turned the water off.

"We're going to take care of this right now," Carson said. "We're tying her down."

I knew too well what that meant. Powerlessness, struggle and sadness.

It was my fault though. I was to blame.

They brought the straps in and I was tied down.

LADY INJURY

As Saul was leaving I said, "Tell Megan that I didn't do it because of her." I was worried that Megan might think it was her fault because of our confrontation before I left.

I was mad at Megan, but she wasn't the reason that I cut. She certainly didn't help, but I would have done it anyways.

When I was first alone in the room, my body rocked as if by sobs, but no tears came. Every part of me needed to cry, but I wouldn't. And why not? Because it would make me weak? Because I was better than that? Because there wasn't that much that I had left other than staying strong enough not to cry?

Megan looked through the little window in my door a few times, so I had seen her, but we hadn't spoken. I hoped we would be okay because she was a nice lady in general.

Samantha tried to come into my room while I was tied down, but Carson told her that she had to leave and had no business being there.

I didn't have access to a clock, but I was able to guess how late it was by the amount of times that someone came in the room

I would sing when I was alone, but when I heard a key in the lock I would be quiet and wait for them to check my restraints and leave.

I usually didn't say anything, but once in a while I would ask Saul how much time there was left for me to be tied down.

"The time that it takes," he would answer.

Eventually I was asked if I still felt like hurting myself. I did, so I had to stay longer.

Once, Saul asked, "Do you want to stay tied up all night?"

"No."

"Then go to sleep and I will untie you," he told me.

"Were you the one who untied me last night?" I asked him.

"Yes."

"I don't remember," I told Saul. "It didn't wake me up." I thought that was unique because that would usually wake me.

"That's because I'm real gentle," Saul concluded.

I couldn't dispute that.

Afterwards, Saul told me that he and the rest of the staff were 99% sure that I was going to cut myself when I was out.

"How did you know?" I was curious.

"It was in your eyes," he replied.

I realized then why they had searched me the way they did when I'd gotten back. They saw the desire within me.

"Do you have a few minutes to talk to me?" I asked him.

"Sure," he accepted.

"Do you think that I'm childish?" I wanted to know.

"On the contrary, I think you are very intelligent," he said to me.

I wasn't sure if I had asked my question right. "I mean that sometimes I act kind of strangely. Megan said that I was childish."

"Sometimes we take things with a grain of salt, but sometimes when we are depressed like you are, it's easy to take things too seriously; like a mountain.

"Yeah," I agreed. "Maybe."

Saul changed the subject. "I'm trying to understand you," he started. "When you hurt yourself, you're looking for a strong sensation to distract yourself; I get that much. It's when you used your blood to write the word sorry on the floor that I don't understand. It's playing in your blood that I don't understand."

I wasn't sure what to say. How could I explain an obsession with my own fluids? "I was just sitting there watching the puddle of blood grow and I did what came to mind. I wrote *sorry* because a part of me was sorry for having done it. Sorry for not being strong enough to resist the temptation to hurt myself."

"Yeah." Saul didn't sound like he understood, but he didn't say anything else. He left the room quickly after that.

I felt like a freak show for having written in my blood and I was embarrassed that it was something that stuck in his mind.

I couldn't stand being tied down anymore, but I wasn't falling asleep. I needed to sleep to be let go, so I made sure to keep my eyes closed and not say anything when Saul came in to check on me.

My plan worked. After pretending just once to be asleep, I was untied fifteen minutes later.

LADY INJURY

I fell asleep with my stitched up doll Assilem next to me. I had asked Saul to put her by my pillow. I'd said that we were both being tied down together.

Saturday, December 6

Someone came in to wake me when it was time for breakfast. I got weighed and had my Rice Krispies with no sugar like I did every morning.

I felt depressed, really sad and anxious. I was like a mess basically; more so than usual.

I had been taken off of the Lorazepam because they thought that it was making me depressed, but I hadn't had any in days and I was still depressed. I didn't know what the answer was.

~ ~ ~ ~

The hospital was full of symbolisms.
Self injury was the Exit doors.
I was the stained and leaky roof about to fall.
I was the music in my ears saying, "I don't want to be me."

~ ~ ~ ~

Dr Stone called to confirm that I would go with him to the city and that Marie would be able to bring me back. I said yes.

"How are you doing?" he asked.

I said, "That's it," as a way of answering, but not answering his question.

He laughed and said, "That's it."

Dr Stone said that he would pick me up before 2:00 pm. By then I was taking a nap, so he woke me up and said it was time to go.

I got all dressed up for the winter day and followed my doctor down to his grey jeep in the parking lot. Asia was waiting for us in the car. She was the nurse from the medical clinic that I liked very much. She was also the one who told me that I could go to her for help with my injuries at any time. She would be coming with us to the show.

Asia had her hair loose. It was the first time I had seen her that way. I thought that it suited her and that she looked pretty.

Dr Stone drove us to city hall. We were going to see a local show put on by some Russian people that apparently lived in trailers.

They were Gipsies.

"It's supposed to be a quality show," he told me.

The point of the outing was to evaluate my levels of stress throughout the afternoon so that he could better identify a way of helping me.

The front door to the building was locked, so we passed through the library and went up some stairs. When we walked into the room, the show was already started. There were about four rows of children sitting on the floor in front of the stage. Behind them were rows of parents sitting on chairs. Asia found us a seat at the back and we joined her.

"It only just started," Asia told us as we took our seats.

The show consisted of three people who played music and sang to tell a story about a Babushka. They interacted with the children. They playfully pretended to not know what the children were.

"Are they elves?" They asked as they looked down at the kids. "No. Not elves. They have no pointy ears. Are they trolls? No. Not Trolls. They don't stink. Are they aliens? No. They are human children!"

The little ones laughed.

At the end of the show the characters went around and put fairy dust in everyones hands so that they could all make a wish. After that they passed around paper ribbons that we were supposed to swirl in the air.

I was really anxious most of the time. Going into a crowded room was intense and stressful for me. The loud yelling really made my heart race.

There were a few times though that I felt better, like when I looked over at Asia and she was laughing. It was infectious to watch her enjoy the children's show so much. She held my hand for a few minutes. I liked that. Also Dr Stone looked like he really enjoyed the fairy dust. We all had fairy dust spread around our hands. They were gold sparkles.

After the show, we drove into Three-Rivers. We didn't talk about anything medical. Dr Stone told me about how he cured himself of being anxious of having people stare at him. "I took a dance class where there were only women. After that there was nothing that could embarrass me."

When it was asked if there was somewhere that I wanted to go, I told him about the art store where I could get some drawing pencils. I was able to get some that I really liked.

After the art store, he took me to Marie's place and dropped me off. We had to get directions because I had only been there once before, but we found it okay.

Marie couldn't take me to the hospital right away because she was waiting for a friend to come and help her install a ceiling fan. While we waited, I helped her change a light bulb on the deck, but the new bulb didn't work either.

We waited for nearly an hour for her friend to come, only to find out that he had forgotten. He came soon after though and so did his wife. It took a long time to change the fan and I was impatient. My anxiety and depression were weighing down on me heavily. I couldn't wait to go to the hospital and crawl into bed. It hurt to be awake and experience life. I felt the emotional energy being drawn out of my entire body. I felt like I was dying.

We finally got onto the road home. Marie had to have picked up on my bad mood because she offered me her hand to hold, but I didn't take it. I didn't mean to be rude; I just couldn't handle the emotion.

All I wanted to do was sleep and not know about anything.

"You don't have to feel obligated to come up to the eighth," I told Marie when we approached the hospital.

"I never feel obligated," Marie told me. After thinking about my words for a few minutes she asked, "Did you tell me that because you want to be alone?"

I did want to be alone. I wanted to sleep. I wanted to stop feeling so badly. I considered though that it was a long enough drive from Three-Rivers and that it would be a shame for her to not get out of the car.

"You should come up for at least a little while," I told her.

We got to the hospital at 5:30 that evening and I ate the supper that was saved for me while Marie waited in my room.

After supper I sat on my bed and Marie sat in the chair. We just talked for a while.

I was thinking a lot about my own mind and my way of suffering and I wondered if others felt the same.

"Do you ever feel like you're dying or like you don't exist?" I asked my sister. "Do you ever feel that you are talking, but no one can actually hear you because you aren't really real?"

Marie's expression was of surprise. "I have thought that. I didn't think anyone else felt that way. I've also thought that every person speaks in a different language and the words that people hear aren't the words that we mean to convey."

It was my turn to be surprised. "I've thought that too." I laughed. "We are definitely related."

After Marie left, my nurse sat and talked to me for a little while.

We talked about how I was feeling. I was worried that I would never get better.

My nurse Adel changed my bandages and put lots of salve on my leg. I knew that she wasn't supposed to put that salve on my wounds. The cream she was using was meant for scars, and not open wounds, but I was too tired and out of it to say anything. I just wanted her to be done.

It was early, but I went to sleep. I was woken up three hours later so that I could take my night medication.

Samantha came into my room after that.

"You weren't here today," she said. "I missed you."

Samantha told me about the night she was taken to the hospital. She said that she was very combative and they had to put her in the ER's isolation room. They had to tie her down and gave her sedative three times in the thighs. It was after that happened that she was sent upstairs and we met. All that sedative explained why she was so confused during that first card game. It explained why she was so emotional. She was much more clear headed the next day.

Samantha left my room at 10:30 that evening and I went back to sleep.

Sunday, December 7

I was weighed before breakfast and my nurse, Sandy was was surprised at my weight. "Is this possible?" Sandy asked as she looked at the numbers on the scale. "You weigh 108, but to look at you I was sure that you were more like 99 pounds."

I had come to understand by then that most people thought that I weighed about ten pounds less than I actually did. This fact made me look anorexic years before I actually was.

After my shower I needed new bandages. When Sandy looked at my leg, she found that it was infected. She was surprised that the wrong Salve was put on my leg. She said it must have happened because Adel was inexperienced. I didn't find that hard to believe because Adel was young.

The doctor that was in charge of all the patients for the weekend prescribed some cream for the infection.

~ ~ ~ ~

I saw Lily that morning. Lily was a small framed woman. She was unique in her character. Whether she loved you or she hated you, she came on strongly.

There was something different about Lily that day. There was a long strip of hair missing from the top of her head. Apparently, she had been pulling her own hair out strand by strand.

"If I shaved it off it would have grown back," I heard Lily tell the nurses. "But now that I pulled it out it will be gone forever."

Lily was then assured that she was wrong and that her hair would still grow back.

Lily was very open about her feelings on her hair. "My hair is ugly. I had to get rid of it. I'm ugly and I was always ugly."

I disagreed. I didn't think she was ugly at all.

She was also telling the nurses and several other people on the ward that she wished that she was two feet tall. I thought that was a curious thing to say, but she didn't explain herself.

I later saw Lily while she was on the couch at the end of the hall. She was pulling her hair out of her head again, so I informed her nurse. At that point the nurses put large padded mittens on her hands. I recognized those mittens as the ones that Roger made me wear about a week earlier. When I was made to wear them, I had taken them off right away, but I was surprised to see that Lily kept them on. She kept them on all day. She sat where she was told in a rocking chair beside my room where she could be seen from the desks.

A few times I saw Lily making a kind of measurement with her hand from the floor to half way to her knee. She had done so several times that day.

I stood in my doorway next to Lily and she would talk to me. "I wish that I were this high," she told me as she was bent over and had her hand placed half way up to her knee. I looked at the hight she was showing me. I gathered that she didn't know how high two feet was because the measurement she was showing me was half that.

"Why do you want to be that high?" I asked her.

"So that no one could see me," she confessed.

I found her answer sad. "So that you can hide better?"

"Yes, and I want hair all over," Lily told me as she motioned over her body with her hands.

"Like an animal?" I asked.

"Yes," she confirmed. "And I want to work in the fields like the mexicans."

LADY INJURY

I found her story to be getting increasingly interesting. "That sounds like honest work."

"It is," she agreed. "But those mexicans don't get paid much."

~ ~ ~ ~

I got my paper and pencils and I chose a picture of my mother to draw. I brought my things to the cafeteria where I planned to work. I got as far as setting the dimensions to moms head before I couldn't continue. I just started staring into space instead of drawing.

I gave up on the portrait and put my things away.

I did a lot of walking, and that helped. I still had to ask for some Quetiapine several times throughout the day though.

I was laying down in the evening for a nap when I heard a loud crash and smash. It sounded like breaking glass. The next sound I heard was on the intercom when a *code white* was called.

I got out of bed right away because curiosity hadn't killed me yet. I stood in my doorway and saw that the Christmas tree was laying on the floor. The tree had been high and reached the ceiling, so when it was fallen it laid far across the floor.

I watched Annabelle, my sweet elderly lady being taken to the 62. A guard had his hand on Annabelle's shoulder to guide her, and his other hand was holding the back of her gown closed. Her teeth were chattering. She looked sad and like she was really freaked out.

I could tell that Annabelle was being put under true isolation because they closed the door. Annabelle started banging on the door the moment that it was closed.

I wondered what had happened because I had never seen her like that. She had always been so quiet and sullen.

Afterwards I heard stories of how Annabelle had been walking around the halls naked, which was probably why she was wearing a hospital gown. After being put into a gown she was in the smoke room. She had knocked over a whole row of chairs before leaving the room and throwing herself onto the Christmas tree.

I found it hard to listen to my lady banging on the door because I heard the staff decide that they would have to tie her down.

I watched them pull out the yellow box with the straps and bring it into the 62. I had come to see those straps as instruments of emotional terror. Watching the group of guards and nurses that came up in response to the code white made me think of a mob of terrorists. I looked at the straps and wondered if I would be the next to wear them.

One of the patients put the tree back up, then a few others helped to put the ornaments back on.

I walked up to them and asked if anything was broken.

"Not really, but Santa Clause is very unhappy," a young woman answered as Santa was being placed back onto the top of the tree.

The whole scene added a lot of anxiety onto what I was already carrying.

I asked for some Quetiapine, but I had to wait a while because the nurses were busy cleaning up after Annabelle. Ella gave me the Quetiapine and I asked her if it would be possible for me to get some Lorazepam because the other medication didn't work very well.

"I don't want to give you any Lorazepam. It makes you all woozy and strange," Ella told me, and she made a kind of melted face to demonstrate what I looked like on too much Lorazepam.

"But I'm depressed with or without the Lorazepam," I told her. "Maybe that's not what's making me depressed."

"No," Ella disagreed. "I had never seen you like that before. That stuff has a bad effect on you."

"Not in smaller doses. That only happened because I was given too much," I theorized. "Please?"

"It's not on your prescription list anymore," Ella denied my wishes.

At 7:00 pm I went down to the basement cafeteria with Parker to get a hot chocolate. I really needed it because I was freezing. I melted a chocolate bar into my hot chocolate. It was very good. Parker thought that it was funny, but I said that I was making it better.

I complained that evening to my nurse Adel that the medication wasn't working and that I still wanted to hurt myself. Adel came to talk to me for about ten minutes.

"I'm so messed up and I don't know why," I confided. "I know how I'm feeling and I know that if I'm left alone for long enough I'm going to hurt myself."

I got distracted during our conversation by how scaly the bottom of my feet were. Dry skin was sticking out all over my heel and getting snagged on my blankets. It was so scaly that when I brushed my heel against my leg it could make me bleed.

Adel allowed me to sit on my sink and soak my feet in water. I was going to let my foot get soggy enough for me to scrape the dead skin off with a pumas stone.

We continued our conversation while my feet were in the sink.

"We're going to give the medication thirty minutes to work," Adel told me. "If you're still thinking of hurting yourself by then, we're going to tie you to the bed."

"I'm not a fan of that plan," I complained.

"It's in your file that we can tie you down as a preventative measure," Adel informed me. "Let me know if we have to do that."

"I'm not going to tell you to tie me to the bed," I expressed my distaste for the idea. "Have you ever been tied to the bed?"

"No," she answered. "But I've tied people to the bed."

"It's not the same."

"No, it's not."

~ ~ ~ ~

Parker came to talk to me while my feet were soaking.

"Do you want to play cards?" Parker asked.

"Yup," I answered. "Give me a minute to finish up here."

Parker went off to set up the game while I dried off my feet and found a place to hide the tool I found in the kitchen trash. It was another metal piece from a soda can. I hid it under the cushion on my chair.

When I got to the cafeteria Parker was playing cards with a new lady. I sat down to play in the next game, but I didn't stay siting long because I was too anxious to keep still and concentrate.

I went back to my room and stood in a corner and started banging my wrist against the metal bar on the back of my chair.

The new lady from the game of cards came by my room to tell me that they were ready to play, but I declined.

Roger came to my room less than a minute later. "I heard banging," he said as he entered.

I hadn't realized the sound would carry so far. I didn't think it was that loud.

"It must have been my music," I said as I pointed to my MP3 player.

"No, it didn't sound like that," he concluded.

"That could be because the song changed as you came in the room," I explained with a reassuring smile.

"Yeah, right," he said disbelievingly. Roger then left the room, but less than a minute later he came in with the yellow box.

"Oh my goodness," I breathed.

All I did was bang my wrist and that earned me the yellow box?

I tried to slyly leave the room but Ella stopped me by reaching her arm out and putting her hand on the doorframe.

"I have to put my MP3 away," I told her in the hopes of leaving the room.

"I'll do it," she told me in order for me to stay.

"I need it to be hooked up on the charger," I specified. "Do you know how?"

Ella looked confused and said that I could go with her. I hooked my MP3 player to the charger and Ella guided me back to my room.

Roger told me to lay on the bed, but he had only just started to put the straps on, so I said, "No, not now." I wanted to spend the least amount of time possible on that bed. I backed up to the wall and sat on the floor with my arms hugging my knees.

"Get on the bed," Roger insisted.

"I'll get on when the straps are on," I compromised. "Do the straps and I'll wait here."

"We're just going to tie you down until you calm down," Adel reassured me, then she went to the yellow box with Roger to get more straps.

I got up and went to leave the room. "I'll go find someone for you to tie down," I told them with dark humor.

"No," Ella stopped me. "You stay here."

So I sat back down.

I had to delay getting in the bed for as long as I could. I couldn't stand the idea of laying there with a bunch of people around me while they made me defenseless.

When they were ready, I sat on the bed cross legged.

"The straps are too high up on the bed for my feet," I informed them. "I'm not that short."

I sat there while they fixed it.

Roger set my right wrist in a strap while Adel did the left one. The left one had to be re-done though because Adel was too inexperienced and didn't really know how.

When all was done they put my blankets over me. Roger asked if I wanted my doll.

"Yes," I answered.

That was when the obnoxious man shoved Assilem in my face and told the doll that I was the reason that it had to be in the bed. He put Assilem down on my chest so that she was still right in my face even when he wasn't holding her.

Adel was nice enough to move Assilem for me. She put her next to my pillow.

Roger left, and before Adel did, she asked me if I wanted the door to be left open.

I was horrified at the idea of the door being open and having everyone be able to look in and see me tied to the bed. That would have been humiliating.

"No, I don't," I answered. I assumed that she asked because she didn't know procedure. "They usually shut the door and lock it."

And that's what she did. The door was shut and locked.

I was very uncomfortable and itchy. It seemed that I was most itchy when I didn't have the option to scratch. I twisted and squirmed around in the bed to relieve each passing itch. I squirmed a bit too much though because Assilem slowly slid off of the bed. I tried to catch her but that only made her fall more.

Ella was the first to come in and check on me.

"Would you mind putting my doll back up on the bed?" I requested. "It was a tragedy. I saw her falling and I couldn't do anything about it.

Ella put Assilem next to my pillow.

"Thank you," I was grateful. "The whole experience was like that movie where the guy was stranded on an island and his only friend was a volley boll that got lost at sea."

Ella laughed at my dramatization.

Adel was the next to check on me.

"I'm healed," I told her. "I heard the voice of the Lord say that he had removed my wrongful thoughts."

Adel laughed and asked, "Really? Did he give you the power to part water as well?"

"I don't know," I thought about it. "If there were water in the room I could find out."

The next time Adel came in she asked me if I still wanted to hurt myself.

I admitted that I did. I couldn't bring myself to lie about it. It felt wrong and my conscience bothered me just for thinking of lying. I knew I still wanted to hurt myself because I was thinking about that piece of soda can that I tucked under the seat cushion. I was thinking of using it to tare all the flesh away from the vein on my wrist.

At first I regretted having to tell the truth, but later I realized that it was the right thing to do.

After a few more times of being checked in on, Adel asked me again if I wanted to hurt myself.

"No," I replied with a crazy grin that let her know I was lying.

"Yeah, right," Adel said. "Like I'm going to believe you with a smile like that."

LADY INJURY

In order to get untied without directly lying, I pretended to be asleep. The next time the door was opened it was to let me out of my restraints.

Monday, December 8

In the morning I asked Dr Stone how much longer I would be staying on the ward. He said that he would come back in the afternoon and that in the meanwhile I could think about how long I needed to stay.

I spent much of my day with my sister.

We went shopping and I got myself two of my favorite kind of chocolate bars in the form of a bat. They were good, but nothing compared to the original.

We got kitty litter and picture frames and when we were done we went back to the hospital.

Marie stayed and talked until she realized that she had parked where she could only stay for thirty minutes.

I moved on to playing cards with Samantha until Mr Border came by. He was the old man who grabbed my chest and stole my hairbrush. He had been hovering around me a lot. It was bothering Samantha more than it was bothering me.

Mr Border started talking to me in an agitated manner.

"You're going to lose all your hair if you aren't careful," the old man told me as he studied the top of my head. "You're going to lose all your hair. All of it. It'll all be gone."

"That's fine," I told him. "I won't have to brush it anymore."

Mr Border got increasingly agitated. It worried me because it seemed like he could get violent.

LADY INJURY

Samantha had a temper and she was really mad at the old man.

"Scat!" Samantha yelled as she partially charged towards him to scare him off. "Go away!" she cried out and charged again.

I was somewhat amused by the whole scene.

Mr Border continued to tell me that I would lose my hair.

Samantha went to get the orderly and he made Mr Border leave.

The next time that Mr Border came around, two women who were sitting nearby came and stood at mine and Samantha's table to keep him from stopping to talk to me.

They say that he's obsessed with me because of how I look. I wouldn't know. I never asked the man.

~ ~ ~ ~

When Dr Stone came, he didn't ask me how much longer I felt I needed to stay.

I told him about how I was the most anxious in the evenings and that I was anxious right then. "The little Quetiapine pills I've been taking are useless now. They are like eating candy."

My dose of Quetiapine was doubled.

"Are you more anxious because you sense that I have something important to tell you?" the doctor asked.

Oh no. That didn't sound good. I hadn't sensed anything, but his question made me nervous.

"No," I answered.

Dr Stone played around with his papers for a while, then he said that he was changing my treatment plan.

"We had a period of complete tolerance for your self injury, and I think that allowed you a way of personal growth," he told me.

I hadn't thought about it that way. I wondered if I was the better for it.

"Now things are going to be at zero tolerance," he informed me. "There will be strict supervision. If you feel you want to hurt yourself, you will be restricted to your room. If you still feel like hurting yourself half an hour after you take your medication, you will be tied down. If you hurt yourself you will be tied down."

My eyes grew wide and I felt my heart pounding in my chest.

"You won't be allowed to leave the hospital anymore. Your belongings will be searched for things that you can use to hurt yourself whenever a need is seen for it," he continued. "You won't be doing yourself any favors by hiding it when you want to hurt yourself. You need to admit it to your nurse. The point of this is to make the consequences of self injury so unbearable to you that you won't want to do it anymore."

I grew more and more nervous as he continued.

"Can we make sure there are no strip searches?" I requested. "Last week a nurse tried to make me pull down my underwear and look at my body."

"I'll make sure that doesn't happen," he reassured me. "They wont have to search your underwear unless you start hiding things in them."

Oops. I felt guilty for hiding things in my clothes. I still had some safety pins in my bra. I saw a difference though between searching my clothes and searching my body.

I thought of something that I wanted to ask. "I'd like to request that my bathroom door not be locked anymore."

"You don't need it locked anymore?" he asked.

"No, I don't," I told him. "I don't feel the need to throw up anymore. I stopped wanting to. I don't need for it to be locked."

I was proud of my progress and part of me was surprised that I had made it that far. I was also allowed to have the restriction on my walking removed. I was then allowed to walk as much as I wanted to.

Dr Stone had a question for me. "When you hurt yourself, do you feel out of control? Does it feel like someone else is doing it?"

"No," I told him. "I know it's me."

I had no excuses and yet I did it anyways. I was my own monster.

"Okay," Dr Stone accepted. "What do you think of the new plan?"

I didn't have to think long about how I felt. "I think it sounds awful," I told him. "I also think that I'm out of control. I tell myself not to hurt myself, but then I do it anyways. Every day I want it so

LADY INJURY

badly. It's all I can think about. I think that the plan sounds awful, but maybe it's what I need."

"Okay," he said and offered me his hand to shake.

"Okay," I thought. "This doesn't feel okay."

~ ~ ~ ~

I walked really fast through the halls for about half an hour. I tried to be too exhausted to hurt myself. As I got more out of breath, my anxiety lessened, but when I stopped….it always came back.

I thought a lot about Dr Stone's question. Maybe I was wrong.

Was I out of control? It certainly felt like it.

Maybe I just needed a way to not be responsible; to not be the guilty party.

Could I have helped it? Was there no other choice?

The desire to hurt myself was so strong; like I was being guided by some greater force. It felt like I had to; like there was no other choice. The desire wrapped its hands around my neck and squeezed until my knees buckled.

I took one of the three safety pins that I had hidden in my bra. I pulled my arm warmer down so I could see my wrist, then I pushed the pin through the back of my wrist.

It looks like it should be easy to push a pin through flesh, but it's not.

I was more protective of my doll than I was of myself. I looked at the blood that I drew on her and I could see this broken part of me. I got Assilem so that I would hurt her and not me, but it would hurt me to hurt her.

I closed the safety pin over my arm. It felt like I had done what I was supposed to do; like things were made right.

Adel came into my room and found me sitting in my chair in the corner. I covered my wrist with my right hand.

"Are you busy hurting yourself?" she asked

"Why would I do that?" I feigned innocence.

"Show me your arm."

I put on a big grin to distract her. "Hi. How are you?" I asked in the hopes of changing the subject.

"Let me see," she insisted.

"See what?" I asked but I knew I was on the losing end.

"Come on."

I finally pulled my hand away from my wrist and held it out for her to see.

The nurse looked stunned. "How did you do that?" she asked and then leaned in to get a closer look. "Oh," she paused. "I have no choice but to have you tied down."

I didn't say anything at first. I just looked away. It's hard to describe the kind of sadness that comes with realizing that you're about to be completely powerless.

It took a lot of effort to say, "Okay."

Then Adel left the room.

I tried not to care.

I tried not to remember what it was like the other times.

I heard Roger's voice at the desks outside my door. "What did she do this time?" he asked. He had a tone that made it obvious that he had been down that road before.

And then, there it was again. That famous yellow box. The symbol of something coming that couldn't be controlled.

Or it was controlled then, wasn't it? It was my fault; my bringing. I did what I felt I had to do, and then they did what they had to do. I knew there would be a consequence and yet I did it.

After I was tied down and before closing the door to my room, Adel said that she would be back to check on me in fifteen minutes.

Fifteen minutes is a long time when you're tied down, but time passed by the way that I pleaded that it would.

Adel was usually the one to come in to check on me. The first time she came back in, she asked, "How are you doing?"

I laughed like she made a joke. "You have to be kidding me."

"Okay. How are you considering the circumstances?"

"All right, I guess."

"Good. I'll be back in fifteen minutes"

And she was; but it seemed like too many fifteen minutes were passing by.

"What does it do to you?" I asked when she returned. She didn't grasp what I meant, so I clarified. "When you tie someone to the bed, what does it do to you?"

She hesitated, "Well, none of us like tying people to the bed. It's in your plan that we have to do this."

"I know," I agreed, "I know why you did this. It's to create a consequence great enough for me to stop cutting."

"Yes."

"When there's a code white, and I see someone get dragged off to get tied down in an isolation room, it hurts me inside. I feel so bad for them that it feels like I'm breaking." I explained.

"Really?"

I was done thinking about it. It was too much for me. "I'll be fine," I said, and then waited another fifteen minutes for someone to come in. The only thing that made staying there mildly bearable was watching someone come in and check my straps. Other than that I had nothing but the ceiling to look upon.

Time was dragging on and I was wondering how much longer I had to endure.

"What has to happen for this to end?" I asked. "Do I have to fall asleep?"

"You have to have no more thoughts about hurting yourself."

"None?!" I asked in wide-eyed discouragement.

"Don't pretend to sleep so you can get out of this," Adel warned.

I smiled, but I didn't let her know that I had done just that on the nights before. I thought about it for a second and spoke. "I have more thoughts of wanting to sleep than I have of wanting to cut." I told her in an effort to negotiate. We were both quiet for a moment. "I won't do it," I stated. "If you let me out, I won't hurt myself. All I want to do is sleep."

"I'll think about it," she said as she walked to the door and condemned me to fifteen more minutes.

Carson came in once. I saw his curly black hair in the window before he opened the door. I didn't pretend to sleep, but I didn't look at him either. I only saw his movements from the corner of my eye. I let him check my straps and leave.

Adel came in five minutes later.

"Carson was just here. It's already been checked." I informed her.

"He was? I'm going to have to get after him for that."

"Why?"

"Because you weren't due yet. We make a note of the time when you're checked and your fifteen minutes weren't done yet," she explained.

"Oh"

Before Adel left, she gave me some bad news. "I'm going to leave you here for just a little while longer."

"How long is that?" I asked feeling discouraged.

"We'll see."

And she was gone again.

The next time Adel came in, I pretended to sleep. Too many fifteen minutes passed as I pretended to sleep. Every time she came in, checked my straps, and left without untying me, I got just a little more desperate for my plight to end.

I considered that I had brought my own downfall. I shouldn't have asked Adel if I had to sleep for things to end. I made her suspicious and consider that I may not really be sleeping. Maybe pretending to sleep wasn't going to work for me anymore.

I never knew for sure who had checked my straps until they walked towards the door and I allowed myself the risk of opening my eyes. I came to recognize the way that each nurse would check on me. I memorized the sound and speed of their walk or the way they touched me as they passed.

Once, the person who checked my straps brushed their fingers over my hand, like they were petting it. It was like they felt sorry for me and treated me like something delicate.

I was very curious as to who had been so tender with both my hands, but the person who checked on me turned out to be a stranger.

She was a new orderly that I had seen for the first time that evening and would never see again, but I was grateful for her passing compassion after so many hours had come and gone.

The shift changed and so did the nurses.

I knew that it had to be passed midnight, and I knew that more than fifteen minutes had passed before someone came back.

I began to feel hopeless, like I would never be freed and I would never get to sleep.

The challenge was to stay straight faced when pretending to sleep because the dishonesty humored me. I lost all capacity for pretending though when I realized that I was about to be untied. I couldn't keep my eyes closed because I had to know who my saviour was.

I saw a girl kneeling at my side as she pulled at the cords that held my straps to the bed. I stared at the top of her head and at her dark pony-tail. It wasn't until she raised her head to face me that I realized that it was Sara. I had always found her fascinating to look at. Mostly it was because of her crystal blue eyes. The rare and intense color was captivating, but I was never as happy to see those eyes as I was then.

"I think we woke you a little roughly," Sara remarked when she saw my eyes were open.

"You didn't wake me." I regretted admitting to my failure to sleep as soon as I said it.

Sara wasn't the only one to come in. Gordon was tugging at the cords to the left of me. "How are you feeling?" he asked as I turned to look at him.

"Tired of this." I answered.

"Tired of being tied down?" Sara asked for me to specify.

"Yes," I admitted as I stared at the ceiling and they began to untie my wrists.

Gordon let go of my straps, but left my wrist tied. "Okay now," he began. "You're going to tell us if you have any more safety pins."

I said nothing.

"You're going to tell me or I'm going to leave you tied down," he threatened.

He'd gotten my attention. That was not an idea that I liked; but still, I said nothing.

Gordon continued, "You're going to tell us. We're not messing around anymore. I'm not talking as an orderly; I'm talking as a family man. Do you have any more safety pins?"

"Yes," I admitted with difficulty.

"Okay," he said. "Where are they?"

I said nothing.

"Do you want me to leave you here?"

I didn't say anything, but I reached in through the top of my shirt with my one free hand and unpinned one of my remaining tools.

"Okay. Thank-you," Gordon said. "Are there any more?"

No answer.

"Okay," he began. "Either you put on a hospital jacket and we look through your clothes, or you get undressed in front of Sara. Now you're going to to show Sara what you have in your clothes, right down to your underwear."

"No," I replied sternly.

"No?"

"You're not allowed to do a strip search." I told him.

"A what?"

"It's against the doctors prescription," I explained. "You can't make me undress in front of you."

"It's true," Sara confirmed. "It's the doctors prescription. We can't."

Gordon was surprised. "But there won't be any contact. It's just looking."

"Yes," I said. "But you can't do it." I was so glad that I had thought to ask my doctor to prescribe against that. I would have been devastated to have to undress in front of someone.

"It's prescribed by the doctor," Sara admitted once again.

"We can't?" Gordon's question was more like a complaint.

"No," Sara replied.

"Okay," Gordon turned back to me. "I'm going to stay here all night if I have to. Are there any more safety pins?"

I grudgingly reached in and pulled out the other pin.

"Okay," Gordon said as he held both pins in front of his face; One small one and one big one. "We have the baby and the daddy. Is there a mom?"

"No. I pushed mom through my wrist a few hours ago." I told him.

"So there aren't any more?" he asked for confirmation.

No more? Well, there were no more safety pins, I thought as I remembered the soda piece under the chair cushion.

"No," I said. "There are no more."

"Okay," Gordon accepted my words, untied me and left the room.

Sara was kind enough to offer me my Quetiapine before she left the room and I graciously accepted.

I followed Sara out of the room, took my medication and got to look at the clock for the first time since I had been tied down.

1:00 am.

"Eww," I mumbled as I thought about the late hour and the few that I had left in the night to sleep.

I had a hard time calming down; even with my medication. It took me until nearly 2:00 am to fall asleep. All the while I was thinking that my safety pin in my wrist wasn't worth the nearly four hours of psychological torture.

Tuesday, December 9

Sara woke me at 7:45 am to weigh me. She said that she had waited as long as possible before coming in to wake me.

I was glad, but I was still really tired and trying to rub the sleep out of my eyes.

I weighed a bit more that morning, but I didn't go to the washroom before hand either, so I didn't discourage myself with the number.

I was glad to see Ashton as part of the staff, although he wasn't my nurse; Sylvia was. I wasn't disappointed because I liked Sylvia. She had a whimsical side to her that I found quite amusing. Though, when she came to my room with the change of bandages and the heart rate monitor, she wasn't in a playful mood.

"Girl, do we have a lot to talk about," Sylvia declared as she parked the heart rate monitor in front of me. "What happened last night?"

"Oh yeah. They left me tied up until 1:00 am."

"I'm not talking about that," she corrected me. "What did your doctor talk about last night? There have been some changes made to your plan."

"Oh yeah." The memories of that heart racing conversation came back to me.

"So what is your game plan?" she asked.

"Huh?" I didn't grasp her meaning.

"How are we going to make this work?" Sylvia wanted to know. "How are we going to arrange things so this day goes well and that you get through it safely?"

"Um, I don't know," I stammered and wondered for a moment what the correct answer to that question could possibly be. If I had known how to get through a day safely, I would have done it already.

"Listen, you're an adult who is acting like a child. You're intelligent. You're smarter than me. You know better than what you're doing to yourself. You're playing this game with us. You're hurting yourself everyday and bringing in new things. When are you going to stop bringing in new things?" Sylvia demanded to know.

"It's not every day," I told her while avoiding her question. "I think about hurting myself every day, but I don't do it every day."

"You're making excuses," Sylvia reproached me. "And that's another thing. I find it baffling that someone who is under as much medication as you are manages to still think about hurting themselves as much as you do."

I didn't know what to say to that. Was I under that much medication? Was I failing to achieve a level of sanity that was expected of me? If so, why wasn't I any better?

"I don't know why," I was at a loss for answers.

"You're getting worse," Sylvia told me. "Every week your leg gets uglier and uglier."

"I know," I admitted. "It seems that the better I eat, the more I hurt myself. I'm trading one major problem for another."

"That's because you keep bringing stuff in," she pointed out. "It's contradictory to come here for help and then bring things in all the time so you can hurt yourself. You're like an alcoholic who says she wants to quit and then stocks up her cupboards with bottles. When are you going to stop bringing things in?"

"I can't bring things in," I told her. "I'm not allowed out anymore."

"That's not the answer I'm looking for. You should say that I'm right and that you shouldn't do that."

"You are right," I admitted. "I know that I shouldn't do it, but I'm afraid to be without these things when I need them."

"You came here asking for help and you make sure to provide yourself with what you need in order to fail. You may as well ask your doctor for your release." Sylvia spoke with more conviction and seriousness than I usually saw in her.

"I didn't come here for help with my self injury. I came here for help with my eating disorder," I pointed out in my defense.

"But Melissa," she spoke my name with a lot of heart and pointed to my leg. "This is worse than an eating disorder. You're hurting yourself worse and worse. It's good that your doctor changed the rules because you need a *stop plan*. This has to *stop*."

"I know," I confessed solemnly. "This has to stop, but there are these two parts of me that are at war; one wants to get better while the other is afraid to live without mutilating myself."

"Look," she spoke pointedly. "I've been trying really hard to help you. I want to keep trying to help you, but even if I give three hundred percent, if you give less than a hundred then my efforts are for nothing. I really want to help."

"I know," I acknowledged again and reflected on how much Sylvia had put into listening to me and encouraging me in the past. "I'm really grateful for what you've done for me."

Sylvia looked at me for a moment, then said, "I want to be able to meet you on the street one day and have you tell me that it's really hard, but you're making it through. You'll be walking with your head high instead of staring at the sidewalk."

I wondered for a moment as to how she knew that I walked while staring at the side walk. "I want that too," I spoke sadly, knowing how dumb I was for getting myself into so much trouble. I stared at the wall for a bit. I looked at the electrical sockets and noticed that they looked like two surprised faces. I didn't know what to say in my defense, so all I could do was stare at a wall. I felt stupid for ever starting this problem. It was my fault that I was messed up. It was all my fault.

"I sense that you are sad and disappointed," Sylvia commented as she studied my face. "You're disappointed that I told you these things."

"No," I corrected. "These are pretty much all things that I thought of before. You're right about all of it."

"So what are we going to do to change it?"

I was at a loss. I didn't know how to answer questions like that. "I don't know. What am I supposed to do?"

"You ask for some meds if you feel anxious and like hurting yourself. If you can't get it under control, then I put you in the 62. You come and talk to me. Don't hurt yourself. Come to me and tell me when you need help."

"Okay."

Sylvia looked around. "Are you hiding anything else on you or in this room?"

"They took my safety pins last night. I have none left."

"What about other things? Do you have anything?"

I stayed silent; not wanting to give up the only thing I had left.

Sylvia took my silence as an answer. "So that means you do. Are you going to give it to me? If you keep things to hurt yourself then we may as well give up now."

I considered giving it to her, but I didn't want for her to see where I had it stored in case I needed a hiding place in the future.

"But even if I had no tools, I would still have my fingernails to scratch myself and my wrist to whack," I pointed out.

"Stop keeping exit doors with you," she requested bluntly.

"Can I think about it?" I asked.

"Okay. You think about it," she accepted and left me to rest.

I stared at the ceiling for a long time. It was the same ceiling that seemed so depressing for so many hours the night before. The ceiling didn't look as sad that morning even though I was laying in the same place.

Sylvia was right about everything. I think I needed her to say what I was thinking. My behavior was terrible and immature. What was I thinking when I was bringing all those tools into the hospital? I hadn't really stopped to think about it at the time. I didn't think about consequences. It was like nothing sunk in with me. I saw what I wanted and I would take it. Did it matter how much I wanted it? Was that worth the taking?

If they were mad at me, they had a right to be.

The more I thought about it, the more I figured that I should give the soda piece to Sylvia. If I was going to do this, I'd better do it right.

Sylvia was right. This had to stop.

No more exit doors.

~ ~ ~ ~

When I went to ask for my Quetiapine that morning, Sylvia was on her break, so Ashton gave it to me. Bertha offered to come and talk to me until Sylvia came back. I didn't want to talk to Bertha, but I knew that having someone in my room with me was a good preventative measure, so I accepted.

Bertha sat down on the chair by my bed and asked me if I had any tools in my room.

I tried to keep from smiling because the woman was pretty much sitting on the answer.

"Sylvia already asked me that," I informed her. I didn't want to give what I had to Bertha. It was Sylvia that had made the difference for me. She was the one that really made me think. I wanted to give it to Sylvia so she could know that I really heard her.

When we were done talking, Bertha left the room, and I went to get my soda piece out from under the chair cushion. I checked inside the trash can for any possible tools. I found a wooden stick that Sylvia used to spread the salve on my wounds. I remembered that the last time I had stayed in the hospital, I had used a stick just like it. I had broken it up and hid it in my socks.

I thought about what Shy-Anne said that day. "When you hurt yourself, you hurt me."

I remembered that Saul said something similar. "When I hear you do that, it hurts me inside." The expression of pain on his face had really made me think.

I wasn't just hurting myself when I did those things.

This had to stop.

I thought of all this as I walked to the desks just outside my room. I looked at Sylvia who was sitting at her desk, then held out two tools that could have hurt me, but that I didn't give the chance.

It was hard to hand it over, but I was glad that I did. Ashton and Bertha were also there. Bertha took the tools from my hands. Sylvia wasn't the one to take them from me, but I think she knew that I had understood her heartfelt words.

"Do I just throw these away?" Bertha asked her piers.

I pointed to the stick and said to Sylvia. "You shouldn't put those in my trash anymore."

Sylvia nodded her head in understanding.

I felt self conscious as the three nurses stared at me. I had done what I set out to do, so I turned around to leave.

"Wait." Sylvia got up and walked over to me. "So what's the plan?" she asked with motivation.

"The plan is to walk," I answered, then put my earphones on. I walked for an hour and a half. I had a lot of anxiety to push through.

I felt sick to my stomach and like I was going to throw up. At first I thought it was due to my anxiety because it had made me feel that way in the past. Soon I started to wonder if I had caught the flu that was going around on the seventh floor.

I found Sylvia in the computer room in the back end of the hospital. It was a small room connected to where I would go to get weighed. "I might have the flu from the seventh," I told her.

"What?" Sylvia's eye's grew wide and she took a step back from my possibly contaminated body. "Do you have the runs?"

"No, but I feel sick to my stomach and I think I might throw up," I explained. "But then again, it could just be my anxiety. Anxiety makes me feel like this too."

"Well, you know yourself better than we do. If it turns out to be the flu, let me know. We're supposed to isolate patients for 48 hours when they catch that."

48 hours?!

At that point I really crossed my fingers that I wasn't sick.

As time went by and I kept walking, it seemed more likely that I was sick. I felt dizzy and the hallways kept going in and out of focus. I was relieved as the lunch hour approached because by then I was feeling much better. I breathed a sigh of relief that I wouldn't have to go into isolation.

"So are you feeling better?" Sylvia asked as I sat at the desks with my lunch tray.

"Yes, I am."

Her smile grew wide. "Good!"

"I have a migraine though. Can I have my pain killers?"

"Yes," she answered and then disappeared to get the medicine.

The pain was strong and slow to subside. I still wasn't much better by the time the obligatory nap was over and I was called to an appointment with the psychologist. I watched her through squinted eyes as she spoke, but despite how badly I was feeling, Mabel gave me a lot to think about. She said that the childish, wrong things that I did to myself weren't my fault and that they were imposed on me by my father and by the man who sexually abused me, but I didn't have to continue down that road. I could change things. The part of me that I insulted and hated, the part of me that cuts, and the part of me that was hurt so young will always be there, but I can let my grown up part, my more rational, adult part, take over.

My darker half had too big of a place in my life. If I gave a bigger place to the good half, there would be less place for the darker half.

So that's what I learned in therapy, but I wondered if saying that my behavior wasn't my fault was the same thing as my father saying that alcoholism was a disease and that it wasn't his fault. That was his fault. Nobody forced that stuff down his face with a funnel. Nobody made me pick up that first blade either. Shouldn't my problem be my fault as well?

The lights in Mabel's office seemed brighter than usual and they made my migraine worse. I was glad when the appointment was over so I could hide somewhere darker.

LADY INJURY

"When can I take more meds for my migraine?" I asked Sylvia when I approached the desks.

Sylvia looked through my charts. "You only took them an hour and a half ago. Your next dose is at 7:00 pm."

It was 2:30 pm. "Oh no!" I complained about the pain. "I'm going to freak out."

"Go lie down," Sylvia told me and I gladly obeyed. But even with rest and an ice pack my migraine didn't go away.

By the time Dr Stone got there that evening, I was sitting on my chair in the doorway, writing in my journal. I was glad to have the chance to ask for a prescription.

"Is 800 Ibuprofen the most I can take? I took the meds earlier today and it's still really bad," I explained my request as I laid a cool hand over my forehead.

"No," he replied. "That's not the most you can take. I can prescribe 2 Acetaminophen in addition to that."

I was beyond grateful.

After Dr Stone wrote my prescription in my file, he asked how my day was. I told him everything that came to my mind, including the events of the night before.

"You didn't ask your nurse for help?" he asked when he learned of my encounter with a safety pin.

"No. I asked," I corrected. "But afterwards I got stupid. They tied me to the bed for 4 hours. I couldn't fall asleep until 2:00 am. Can there be a limit on how long I'm tied to the bed?"

"They can leave you tied down for as long as there is a danger of you hurting yourself."

"But there wasn't a danger," I complained. "After an hour, all I wanted to do was sleep, but she didn't believe me."

"She?"

"Adel. I told her that I didn't want to self injure anymore, but she didn't believe me."

"Maybe if you didn't hurt yourself for a few days they would have a reason to trust you. I'm going to leave it in the hands of your nurses to decide when to let you go. They know what they are doing," the doctor told me.

Wasn't anybody going to save me from reliving that? Would I find no compassion? Or was leaving me to struggle the compassionate thing? Was this how I was going to get better?

Dr Stone looked tired and I pointed it out.

"I had a long day," he explained.

"Did you get tied to a bed?"

"No, I behaved myself."

My mouth dropped at his humorous honesty. "But I got tied down and all I did was use a pin! There wasn't even any blood. I got 4 hours for it!"

"Well then you shouldn't have done it," he said blatantly.

There was that honesty again. Too true. I should not have done that.

At 7:00 pm, after the doctor left, I still had my migraine, so I went to get my medication at the desks.

Saul sat in the centre of the office as he filled out his report. "Where do you hurt?" he asked after he heard me ask for my pain killers.

The lights were strong and I used my hand to put shade over my eyes. "I have a migraine, and there's these spotlights and these pills that don't work enough," I complained.

"Well then, you probably won't feel like talking," Saul observed.

I liked talking to Saul, so I didn't want to let an opportunity get away. "Well, it's not as bad as it was this afternoon," I manipulated. "I can talk."

I told Saul all about the new plan that the doctor had made for me and the reasons for it.

"But when you go home, you wont have us to stop you," he pointed out.

"I know. I'm worried about that," I admitted.

By then Saul had gotten up and walked over to me so that only a desk would separate us. I leaned on the plastic boxes in front of me as he said, "You have a lot of help surrounding you. A lot of people are willing to help."

"I know. I don't know what I did to deserve that."

"We see a potential in you."

"I think I need more sleep to reach it," I said in reference to my short nights sleep. "It would help if I could get some hot coco, but I'm not allowed downstairs anymore. That's a problem because the hot chocolate machine is downstairs, and I'm upstairs. Do you think we could get a hot chocolate machine up here?" I asked knowing that the answer would be no.

"We could always ask," Saul humored me.

"Good," I spoke dreamily. "Because there's the yumminess of a hot chocolate combined with a melted chocolate bar inside of it, creating a chocolaty wonderfulness."

My nurse Amanda laughed from behind her office window.

"Hmm," I pondered. "Do you think that I could melt a chocolate bar into the chocolate milk you give me tonight?"

"We don't have a microwave," Saul answered.

"No microwave?!" I was disappointed and didn't hide it. "Well, can I just have a chocolate bar then?"

"Nope."

"No? Why not?"

"You're already going to get some chocolate in your milk later," Saul explained and I could tell that he was purposefully being difficult.

"But there's not much chocolate in that and I have snacks prescribed as needed."

"That's what the chocolate milk is for."

The man wasn't going to budge so I had to get more creative. "But it says on my new treatment plan that I can have chocolate. I swear it's got the word chocolate in there somewhere. I've got a copy of it in my room."

"Show me."

I went to get my paper and returned as I studied the words scribbled onto it. Amanda stood next to me and looked at my doctors chicken scratch writing. She found the word *chocolate*.

"Ah ha!" I yelled and held the paper victoriously in the air. Saul smiled, and so did I. I couldn't help it. I was enjoying the debate. "Can I have my chocolate from my bag?"

"Nope."

I grew wide eyed and my jaw dropped as I recognized my failure.

I thought about it for a moment and then slowly crept behind the desks towards my bag that was hanging on the wall. Saul rolled his chair over and blocked me.

"I don't think this is going anywhere," I admitted. "We are both just as stubborn."

Saul laughed and I grudgingly accepted my failure to acquire my goods.

I sat on my bed and wrote in my journal under the limited light I had over me. I looked up when I saw Parker walk up to my door holding a cup of hot chocolate.

"Oh wow!" I cooed as I jumped off my bed and took the treasured liquid from his hand. "You're saving my life! I'm going to repay you for this."

"Buy me a soda some time."

"Deal," I agreed and he left.

I immediately brought the hot chocolate to show Saul. With a smile spread generously across my face I held out my prize. "I got my hot chocolate. Now I need my bar to melt into it."

Saul hesitantly got up and brought me my bag so I could pick my chocolate from it. I wanted to melt the whole thing, but he only let me use half. I made sure to complain bitterly, but I was still glad to come out on the mostly winning side.

My victory came with a price though. Saul said that I had to do fifty push ups for it.

"I can do twenty push ups," I informed him. "Um, no, ten, I can do ten. But it's the girl push ups. You know, when you do them on your knees. I can only do half of one when I use my feet."

I never did the push ups. I played cards and never got around to doing them.

LADY INJURY

I made it to 9:00 pm without making negative waves. I wanted to be able to tell Sylvia that it went well. I didn't know why I deserved it, but she was putting a lot of heart into me.

I decided to escape into sleep so I could be sure to behave myself.

Wednesday, December 10

I got up at quarter to eight and Sylvia was already there.

"So how did it go," she asked and then winced. "No, wait. Don't tell me. It's negative."

"No it's not," I smiled. "I made it."

"Yeah?!" Sylvia's face changed from afraid to exited.

"I went to bed early so I couldn't do anything stupid," I explained.

"That's great!" Sylvia told me. "And today is going to be good too."

"I hope so."

"Tell yourself that it will. You have to be positive."

The only thing I was positive about was that I made it through one night. Each day would be its own challenge.

I walked a lot that morning. It felt like my heart would pound out of my chest.

A few times Sylvia passed me in the halls and gave me a loving tap on the back of the head. I wasn't feeling well, so getting my head knocked around wasn't helping no matter how chipper and happy she was to tease me. I just took a deep breath and concentrated on making it through every next moment.

I thought of something that I needed to do that would also be a good distraction; shaving my legs. I had people looking at my legs every day to change the bandages or see if I added anything new to my collection of wounds and scars, so having hair all over was particularly embarrassing.

Sylvia was gone on her break, so I talked to the nurse that was at the desks.

"Am I allowed to shave my legs if someone is watching?" I asked Annette.

"Yes," Annette answered. "But I have so much to do already. It would take five of me to accomplish all that I have on my list today. Maybe this afternoon I'll be able to help."

"Okay, that's fine," I accepted.

"I could help. I have nothing to do right now." I looked to my left to see one of the interns standing next to her teacher. She looked to be in her late twenties, with blond hair brushed back in a pony tail.

"Really?" I asked. "Because that would be really great."

"No problem," she smiled. "I'm Hydie."

"Melissa," I introduced myself. "I'll need a razor."

It felt strange to acquire a razor in a legal fashion. I didn't have to sneak it in or steal it.

"I don't have any hot water in my sink," I informed her. "I'm not allowed."

"That's okay, we can use the tub. I'll be there so it will be okay."

I followed Hydie down the hall to the bathroom next to the shower. I was glad to be heading towards some warm water. Cold water wasn't so bad for washing my hands, but it would have been pretty uncomfortable to soak my legs in it.

I turned the hot water on as Hydie took a seat in the corner. I rolled up my pant-legs and put my feet in the tub. I was embarrassed to have Hydie see my leg. I hadn't even warned her that it was mutilated. I wondered what she thought as she sat there watching me shave.

"Can I ask you a question?" Hydie asked.

"Okay," I answered, feeling unsure of what I was getting into.

"Why do you do that?" Hydie nodded towards my right leg.

I thought about it for a minute. I wasn't sure how to answer when she knew nothing about me. "I do it to distract myself from memories of abuse. I do it do calm down when I'm anxious. I do it if I need to tare myself apart or when I'm really sad. I do it out of anger towards myself. Basically, I run away from my emotions."

Hydie didn't say anything to my explanation. I wasn't sure if I sounded completely insane.

When I was done shaving, I let the water out and dried off my legs. Red streaks ran down my mutilated flesh. "Oh, I guess I wasn't careful enough," I observed.

"Next time go slower," Hydie advised before we left the bathroom.

At first I just let my leg bleed in the hopes that it would dry up, but it stained my pants, so I went to the desks to get some medical gauze.

Time passed and my leg was fine, but I was still very anxious, so I asked for my Quetiapine.

Sylvia's face fell. "But I thought it was going well."

"No, it's not."

Sylvia was the picture of positivity. A real force of nature. But I think that she was putting so much energy into trying to be fun and encouraging that she was blind to how much I was struggling. I wasn't okay. I couldn't even pretend to be.

"Are you using your Quetiapine as an exit door?" Sylvia asked. "Are you running away from what you're feeling?"

I thought about it for a moment. "Isn't that what Quetiapine is for?"

"You need to let yourself feel."

I needed to feel? I had already done plenty of that. I had too much of that. What I needed was help getting through the day. If my medication was what was keeping me away from sharp things, then so be it.

"I really need them," I told Sylvia with an expression that could only convey desperation.

"Okay, I'll give them to you," she accepted. "But after that, what's the plan?"

"Walking."

"That's what helps you?"

"Yes."

LADY INJURY

So I walked for a few hours. I took a break only once to play cards with the young nurse that was nice enough to watch me shave my legs. We had met up in the hallway.

"You're walking an awful lot," Hydie observed.

"I like walking," I replied.

"Would you like to play cards? I have nothing to do. My patient is really calm and easy," she explained.

The interns only got one or two patients each.

"Okay, we can play cards," I answered. "But I'm warning you; I cheat."

"You don't really?"

"Of course."

"Well you won't while I'm watching you."

And she didn't let me. I tried. Believe me, I tried, but she stuck to the rules.

I won the game and Hydie admitted to being a sore loser.

After playing cards, there was still time before lunch, so I started walking again. I met up with Sally in the hall. Whenever she asked how I was doing, I always said that I was fine, no matter how I was feeling.

A new woman walked up to us. I remembered her from the beginning of my Borderline group. She had only attended once, but I hadn't forgotten her face. She was hard to look at. Her name was Cindy.

We stood outside Cindy's room as Sally picked up some of my hair and let it fall from her fingers strand by strand.

"She's pretty. Isn't she?" Sally asked as she turned to Cindy.

"Yes, she is," Cindy answered and then directed her words towards me. "Look at you. You're beautiful, you're thin; What problems could you possibly have?"

Cindy's words made me mad, but I didn't let it show. "The way a person looks has nothing to do with their problems. We all live in the same world," I said.

"That's true," Sally agreed. "That's true."

I tend to get upset at the assumption that I should be problem free just because I'm easy to look at. It seemed that I couldn't be taken seriously because of my appearance.

I had forgotten her words fast though. I was having trouble keeping my head above water. I was trying so hard to make it through that day, so when I found something that I could use to hurt myself, I was tempted nearly beyond my strength. It was a sheet of glass on the hallway wall that covered a *no smoking* sign. The corners of the glass were sharp enough that I could have used them to break the skin on my wrist. It was in the short piece of hallway that I often used to sit on the floor between the elevators and be alone. I could have used the glass and have no one notice.

I pulled down my arm warmer and raised my wrist to the lower left corner of the glass. All I had to do was press down. I was so tempted, but I remembered my nurse and all the people that wanted me to succeed.

I didn't do it. Instead I walked away and found Sylvia at her desk.

"I'm not doing well," I told her. "I just found something over there and I almost used it." I pointed down the hall towards the staff elevators.

"Okay, let's go to your room," Sylvia directed and I obeyed.

Sylvia sat on the chair in the corner. I laid down on my back with my head at the foot of the bed and I stared at the ceiling.

"What did you find that could hurt you?" Sylvia asked right away.

I studied the rectangles on the ceiling above me. I didn't need a light on because there was enough coming in from the window.

"It's nothing that I could take to my room," I tried to avoid answering as my eyes followed the contours of the ceiling grids.

"What is it?"

I didn't want to say. What if I said it and the glass got taken off the wall? I didn't want to risk losing even more control.

"I can only use it when I'm in the halls," I tried to keep dancing around her question.

"What is it?" she asked again.

I knew there was no way that she was going to give up, so I finally gave in and told her. "It's on the wall. I could use the corners to scratch myself."

"The corners are really sharp enough?"

"Yes."

"Show me."

We left the room and Sylvia followed me to the sheet of glass. She put her finger tip against the lower left corner of the glass.

"You're right," she said. "It is sharp. I'm proud of you for showing me this instead of using it."

I was told to go back to my room until I felt well enough to walk around again. I wondered if I would be trusted with the sheet when I went out to walk again. Was the fact that I had confessed to its whereabouts enough to be allowed un-denied access to the halls?

To my disappointment, when I walked by that hallway thirty minutes later, the sheet and the sign had been taken off the wall. Only the holes from the screws were left behind. I stood there and stared at it for a minute, until I accepted the loss of a potential tool. Chances were that I would have gone back and used it. Maybe it was for the best.

~ ~ ~ ~

Lily was crying a lot that morning. I found her on a chair with her arms and her face buried over the ping-pong table.

"Is there something I can do for you?" I asked Lily with worry.

"I never have visitors," Lily cried. "No one ever comes to see me." Lily spoke through her tears and then got up to go. She continued to cry as she walked through the halls.

~ ~ ~ ~

Every year in Quebec on the first of July, a great number of people move from one apartment to another. That way there are a high number of apartments to chose from when it's time to move.

It was the tenth of December, but it felt like the first of July on the ward. Everybody was moving.

Mr Border had to be put in my room because he was often found wandering around at night. He needed to be put where he would be seen as he left the room. The problem was that I had to be in a room alone because I was on higher watch, so several patients had to change rooms for it to work.

I moved from the 861 to the 808. I went from private room to private room. The difference was that my room was less in the view of the nurses from their offices. The new room also had a light in the ceiling so I could see at night. It had a bigger sink, but no counter top.

I was hoping that it would be forgotten, but Sylvia had someone come up and cut off my hot water.

The sad thing was that the corners of the radiator grid in the room were about as sharp as the sheet of glass, so I kept staring at it like it was calling to me.

The other rooms had the same radiator grid, I just hadn't noticed its hidden possibilities before.

Now that I knew, could I resist using it?

Could I hurt myself and hide it?

Could I take a few steps away from the bed and give in to my desire?

It was crazy, but I felt like I needed it.

I wondered what would happen if I refused to get in the bed when they would come to tie me down.

No. I told myself not to go down that road.

All I had to do was not hurt myself. It seemed like it shouldn't be so hard. I had already taken my Quetiapine at super, so maybe I'd be feeling better soon. Then I thought that maybe I should go tell on myself. Could I handle the consequence?

I stared longingly at the radiator corners, then I decided that I should tell and get help, but under no circumstance would I give up the identity of my new-found tool.

It was evening and Saul was keeping watch at the desks.

"Do you have time to talk?" I asked as I leaned on the outer desk.

"Okay," Saul had been at the centre desk, but he moved over to the one across from where I was leaning.

"It's like there's this voice whispering to me, saying, *do it*," I said as I looked down at the papers that Saul was writing on. "Just do it."

Saul looked up at me. "Who is saying this?"

"The voice in my head. It's like the cartoons where there's an angel and a devil on someone's shoulder, but the devil is whispering louder," I explained.

"And what about me?" he asked. "What do I say to you? Can I be another voice that whispers?"

"You are," I said matter of factually.

"Then listen to my voice instead."

"Okay." Then I thought of a question. "What about bruises?"

"Bruises?"

"Yeah. Do I get tied to the bed for just bruises?"

"It's zero tolerance."

I paused, then said with a hopeful smile, "But you can't tie someone down for something you don't know that they did, right?"

Saul looked at me with searching eyes. I could see him thinking, but he didn't answer.

Megan walked by me as she came back from her lunch break and I asked her for my Quetiapine.

"You're feeling anxious?" she asked.

"Yes."

Megan motioned for me to follow her and we took a few steps away from the office and from some patients who could have overheard. "Are you having thoughts of hurting yourself? Because if you are we have to act in consequence," she said seriously.

"I'd have to stay in my room."

"No, we'd have to tie you down," Megan said discreetly, so only I could hear.

"What?!" I asked in horror as my eyes grew wide. My voice was louder than I intended. "But the consequence to wanting to hurt myself is a room plan. I have to stay in my room."

"Yes," Megan said. "A room plan while being tied down."

"No," I corrected her in my defense. "That's not what my plan says. I have a copy of it in my room."

"Melissa," she said with so much seriousness that it made me even more nervous. "Do you want to hurt yourself?"

I didn't answer. I couldn't answer when the price of my words was too high. I knew that she was wrong. That wasn't what my plan said.

Megan became agitated at my silence. "I'm not willing to play this game of cat and mouse with you. Are you thinking of hurting yourself?"

I wasn't willing to resign myself to the barracks. I looked her directly in the eyes and spoke dryly. "Look at my plan and get back to me."

"Okay," she accepted and went to find the information on her computer. I watched for a moment as Megan consulted with Carson, then I decided to walk off my anxiety.

I found Saul with his arms crossed in the hallway near the rocking chairs. He was watching Parker as he shaved his beard in the doorway to his room.

I was relieved to find a friend to complain to.

"They want to tie me down for my thoughts!" I cried to Saul as I walked up to him. "Just for thinking it! This is a form of terrorism!"

"The idea is to show you that there are better ways of dealing with your anxiety," Saul told me. "That's also why we took away your hot water."

"But being tied to the bed is thirteen thousand times worse than having no hot water! They want to do it to me just because I think it. You wont let them do that to me, will you?" I asked as I nudged my shoulder against his arm and laid my head against his shoulder. "Not for my thoughts!"

Saul looked at me as I stood next to him but he didn't answer, so I sighed and started to walk away.

"You stay here with me," Saul said as he gestured for me to come.

"Melissa!" I heard Megan call for me through the halls. I was being called in two directions, but I decided it would be more wise to go see Megan. I met her near the door to my room. "You were right," she admitted. "You have to stay in your room."

I didn't mind laying on the bed as long as I wasn't strapped to it, so I laid there for quite a while. I had curled up under my pile of blankets and soon something unusual began to happen. As I laid there I began to feel different parts of my body twitching; Small but constant involuntary movements from my feet to my face. I wondered of the cause and hoped that it would stop soon, but it didn't. As long as I was laying down, I was twitching.

The only distractions I had from these movements were my wildly itchy leg and the times that Saul came in to check on me. "What are you doing to your leg?" Saul asked as he walked in and caught me scratching my wounds.

"Nothing," I answered. "It's itchy. I had to scratch it. I didn't hurt myself. I promise."

I continued to scratch my unending itch, so Saul picked my hand up and covered my leg with my blanket.

"I didn't hurt myself," I insisted.

"I believe you."

Every time Saul came in, he would ask if I had done something stupid.

"No," I'd say.

"Okay. I believe you."

I took my night time medication early and tried to fall asleep, but I was too anxious.

For a while Megan and her threats of strapping me to the bed had scared the desire to hurt myself right out of me. I was so scared of not being able to stop wanting to hurt myself. If I couldn't stop thinking about it, Megan said she would tie me down.

When I realized that I had made it to 9:00 pm without hurting myself, I was so relieved that my fear left me. The downside was that when I stopped being afraid, I started thinking of hurting myself again.

At 11:00 pm I got out of bed and asked Megan for more Quetiapine in the hopes that it could help me sleep.

"Are you feeling any better?" Megan asked as I appeared in her office window.

"Yeah," I lied. I always said I was fine.

"Are you thinking of hurting yourself?"

I didn't want to answer that.

"Do we need to tie you down?" Megan's question reached me as a threat and my heart ached.

"No," I replied immediately.

Megan consulted with Carson, and I was relieved that they didn't decide to have me condemned yet again.

I took my Quetiapine and went back to my room. I thought I would wait for my medication to work before I got into bed, so I went straight to my window and began looking outside. The more I looked out the window, the more I thought about the radiator grid right in front of me. Soon I was reaching down to the radiator grid like I was answering a calling. I rolled down my arm warmer so that my wrist was exposed and I began pressing it against the grid. After a long series of up and down movements against the corner of the grid, I went to look at my wrist under the bathroom light.

I had scratched my wrist enough that I had removed a thin layer of skin. Little bits of flesh stood up on my reddened wrist. I was disappointed that I hadn't caused more damage from all that effort, but at the same time, I was afraid of what would happen if my actions were discovered.

I pulled my arm warmer up again and went back to the window.

My conscience had begun to bother me. My doctor had told me not to hide it when I hurt myself. He said that if the plan was going to work, I had to be honest, but I was afraid of being honest. Which was better? A bad conscience, or a terrible consequence?

"What are you doing?" Saul asked when he walked in.

"Nothing," I replied from behind the curtain.

"Are you fighting your medication?"

"No. I just figured that I'd wait for my pills to kick in before I got into bed, otherwise I just end up staring at the ceiling," I explained.

"Ah," Saul voiced his understanding. "I can tell that you're troubled about something. Is there something on your mind?"

I didn't know what to answer, so I didn't say anything. It seemed that I did that a lot. Despite my efforts to with-hold the truth, my silence would answer questions for me.

I was grateful that Saul didn't press me for an answer, he just stood next to me while looking out the same window. He didn't ask me if I had hurt myself and I didn't volunteer the information. I wasn't sure if I should be relieved, or disappointed. My conscience was strong and my own honesty was my enemy. It was late though and I was too tired to deal with any consequences.

The next time Saul came to check on me, I was laying in bed with the covers over me. I had a question that took a lot of courage to ask. "If I hurt myself tonight, can the consequence be tomorrow?"

"You want to hurt yourself tonight?"

"Not anymore," I admitted.

"You already did it?" he asked in disappointment. "What did you do?"

I stayed quiet, so Saul directed his flashlight at my wrist and touched where I had scratched myself.

"What did you do?" he asked again.

"Not much. It's almost nothing. It barely counts. I only scratched it."

"Do you want for there to be a consequence?"

"No. Why? You wont tell them that I did it?"

"You don't want me to tell?"

"No."

"Okay. Close your eyes and go to sleep."

"Yay!" I exclaimed as Saul turned around and left my room.

I felt better for having told the truth, and I was so glad that Saul wasn't going to tell that I calmed down enough to be able to sleep.

Thursday, December 11

My nurse woke me at 7:15 am so that she could weigh me. I crawled back into bed afterwards and tried to fall asleep, but every time I started to get drowsy, some part of my body would twitch. Sometimes my leg would twitch and fifteen seconds later, my hand would twitch. Other times some random part of me would twitch every second for about a minute. These movements were coursing through the whole length of my body. There was no way for me to lie still.

My nurse was an intern that day. It was Hydie; the nurse that watched me shave my legs the day before.

When Hydie was changing my bandages, my leg twitched. Her face was near my leg when it happened, so it made her jump.

"Oh. You startled me."

"Yeah, that's been happening a lot. I've been twitching all over. I think it might be a side effect of my Quetiapine."

"I've never heard of spasms as a side effect to Quetiapine, but I can look it up," Hydie offered.

"I'd like that."

~ ~ ~ ~

Evangeline was back on the ward. The last time I had met her, I knew her as an elderly woman whose erratic and seemingly random noises were meant to be words. Her wild grey hair was just long enough to put into a pony tail. She would lean forward in her chair and scream and hit and spit on anyone who came too close. With some electro shock therapy, her noises became more comprehensible, and she became more calm.

When she returned to the hospital, she was still relatively calm, though she would often speak even if there was no one there to listen.

I spent a lot of time with Evangeline the day after she came back. She still carried a strong energy that drew me to her. We looked at magazines together while I described the images on every page. Evangeline would nod and say what she thought of the images, but I didn't understand most of it.

I pulled out some paper and crayons and we drew pictures. When Evangeline was tired of drawing, she was let out of the large grey chair that held her down. She was then allowed to take a walk with me in the halls.

Sylvia was very grateful that I was taking care of Evangeline and keeping her occupied. There were a lot of patients to tend to and Evangeline was a handful. She constantly needed attention and to be watched.

When Sylvia told me how much she appreciated my help, it made me think about how much I appreciated her as well.

I told Sylvia, "If I've never told you how much I appreciate you, I should lay it on thick. I'd have you as my nurse day and night."

"Why is that?" she asked.

So I told her about the night before and how well it went. I knew that I was doing better because of Sylvia.

"You can be very proud," Sylvia told me. "You've made it to three days without hurting yourself."

"Well, not exactly."

"Even though it's not until tonight, you can still call it three days," she reassured me.

"No, I can't."

Sylvia's face dropped. "What did you do?"

"Not a lot."

Sylvia reached out from where she sat on her chair and she smacked my leg.

"It's only this," I said as I showed her my wrist.

"Well, that's nothing compared to what you usually do."

"I know. I didn't have the tools to do anything worse."

I was doing better that day. I wasn't as anxious and I had less thoughts of hurting myself. Although, at lunch time I was very tempted to take my knife when the opportunity arose. It took a lot of strength, but I left it there. I went back to my room with nothing on me that I could use against myself. It was a strange and insecure feeling.

After lunch was nap time. I was tired, but I couldn't fall asleep.

The twitching was getting worse. There was no way that I could lie still long enough to get drowsy, much less to fall to asleep. So I sighed and rose from my bed to go complain to Sylvia.

"I'm sure that it's a side-effect of my Quetiapine. I've been on a high dose of it and that's the only thing that makes sense," I told her

Sylvia seemed concerned and she immediately got up to go inform Dr Stone who was working in the back office. I was told to go wait in my room and he would come and see me.

I sat in my doorframe, with my back leaning on one side and my feet up against the other. When my doctor appeared beside me, I began to get up to go inside my room.

"No, it's okay. You don't have to move," The doctor said as he held out his hand to signal for me to stay.

I didn't twitch much when he was there, but he took my words seriously. I was prescribed something whose name I can't remember, nor pronounce. It was supposed to reverse the side-effects of my other medication so that I could keep taking my Quetiapine.

I took the new drug, but even hours later, I was still twitching.

I was right though, it was confirmed to me that muscle spasms were one of the side-effects of Quetiapine.

~ ~ ~ ~

After a few tours around the halls that afternoon, I walked back into my room and noticed that my toothpaste was missing. I usually left my brush and paste by the sink. I searched through my make-up case and on the floor beside the sink to see if I misplaced it or it fell.

I couldn't find it anywhere. I even double and triple checked thoroughly.

I gave up searching and decided to act on a hunch that I had.

I spoke to Sylvia from in front of the desks. "I think that Mr Border stole my toothpaste. I had my own paste from home and it's missing. I remember that he took my hair brush once and he was in my room this morning pulling pictures off my wall. I didn't think to look at his hands to see if he had taken anything, but I think it might be in his room."

Sylvia sighed, "Oh, no."

She immediately went to Mr Border's room and opened the top drawer in his bedside table. The moment she opened the drawer, she found and grabbed my Sensodine tooth paste.

"Thank you," I said as it was placed into my hand.

"Don't leave it by the sink anymore," she told me.

~ ~ ~ ~

By the time the evening came, I was scribbling in my journal again.

I stared at the next empty lines of my journal and wondered what I should do next.

I had decided to admit to being in a bad place in my head, but not that I had already done something. I was caught though before I could confess to opening wounds.

I wasn't touching my leg, but Saul walked in and instinctively checked under my blanket. "What did you do?"

It always made me curious as to how he had developed a sort of sixth sense when it came to knowing if I had done something to myself.

I was grateful that Saul decided not to tell on me. He said that if he told, they would tie me down, and he didn't want that.

I had to ask for some advice from Saul because my conscience had been troubling me. "Do you think it's wrong of me to hurt myself and not tell? My doctor told me not to hurt myself and hide it. Do you think it's wrong if I do?"

My question wasn't answered.

"Draw a picture," Saul suggested as he pointed to the drawings that I had taped to my wall.

"Other than the drawing of my niece, I haven't drawn in years."

"Well then, draw her again."

"But I already drew her."

"Well, I haven't seen it," Saul tried to encourage me into action.

"I'm too anxious to draw. I tried to draw my mom the other day, but all I could do was stare into the space in front of me."

Saul paused, then said, "You know what I'm trying to do? I'm trying to keep you busy."

"Maybe I'll try later."

I didn't try later. I stayed in my room and tried to stay calm. It was hard to relax though because my leg was incredibly itchy.

Megan came in and caught me scratching my leg. "What are you doing?" she asked.

"Scratching," I said. "It's itchy."

"Show me," Megan requested as she walked around the bed to face me where I was sitting.

I lifted my pant-leg.

"Did it bleed?" she asked.

"A little, but that was earlier."

"Did the cream I gave you help?"

"It burned my leg."

Megan changed the subject. "Are you having thoughts of hurting yourself?"

As tradition would have it, I didn't answer.

"You need to let me know so that we can help you," Megan pushed for a confession.

"I know what brand of help you offer," I replied bitterly.

"Yes, but that's what your plan is."

"But I've only been in my room for ten minutes. I'm supposed to have time to change my thoughts before you jump to the next level in my plan."

"You took your Quetiapine half an hour ago; Did it help you? Are you still having thoughts?"

I didn't want to lie, but I couldn't tell the truth. "The price is too high," I told her.

"What do you mean?"

"Tying me to the bed is too high of a price," I explained.

"But that's your plan. You need to tell me if you're still having thoughts of hurting yourself."

I looked away from her and turned back to writing in my journal. "You decide," I told her in avoidance. Megan wasn't going to get a confession out of me; only attitude.

"I'll come back and see how you're doing," Megan informed me before she left.

"Okay, see you later then," I said blankly.

I didn't understand how someone could lack so much compassion and empathy. How could she so readily want to throw me to the lions?

I wondered if I could be tied down without a confession. If I didn't say it, were they allowed?

I thought back to a conversation I had with Hydie that afternoon. I told her that if they were going to tie me down for my thoughts, I was going to get violent.

"Well, maybe not violent," I added. "I don't have it in me to be violent, but I wont be so compliant. I wont make it easy for them."

"I can understand that," Hydie related as she looked over at me from the chair next to my bed. "I'd be the same. I wouldn't let them tie me down without a fight."

"I used to be terrified that they would tie me down. I would see other people go through it and it made me so sad and sick to my stomach with anxiety and fear."

Hydie paused as she seemed to think about my words. "I tied someone down once; I cried after."

~ ~ ~ ~

When Megan came in to check on me, I had a question for her. "How do you feel when you tie someone down?"

"I really don't like it," Megan answered seriously with her arms crossed. "But that's what's in your plan."

I had actually expected some kind of half hearted response that I would have no respect for.

"You have to understand our point of view," she continued. "We aren't used to having cases like yours."

"Really?" I was surprised. "I thought this was a common problem."

"But we aren't used to that here. We're only human. It's not easy for us to see someone hurt themselves, and it was almost every night."

I was glad to have asked her that question, because now I understood better as to how she saw things. I tried to think of my actions from the point of view of the staff. Even I would find it hard to see someone do that.

I thought about that guy named Terrance that was there not long before. I had looked at his arms full of cuts and burns, and just thought, "Hey, he does it too."

But what if I had never hurt myself? How would I have reacted to seeing something like that? Would I have understood? Would I have been freaked out? I know that I didn't want him to hurt himself, and yet I did the same thing.

By 9:00 pm, Megan was congratulating me for making it through the evening. She said that I looked calmer.

I was grateful that she hadn't asked me if I was still having bad thoughts; She just assumed that I wasn't.

That was the last time that night that Megan came to check on me. It was still before bedtime, but I decided to go to sleep right away. Despite my best efforts, sleep was kept from me. As I laid under my

LADY INJURY

covers trying to make the night bring me into the next day, my spasms got much, much worse. Instead of a finger, a foot, or a leg having a spasm, my entire body was rocked simultaneously by involuntary movement after involuntary movement. The spasms were so bad and so frequent that it must have looked like I was having a seizure.

I gave up on sleep and got up to ask Megan for more medication to help my spasms. She said that it was still too early to give me something because she had just given some to me at 8:00 pm. We made an agreement that if I was awake and not any better by 11:30 pm, then she would give me more.

I knew before I got back into bed that sleep would not come because the spasms were simply too severe. I was like a fish out of water.

Since the spasms were worse when I was laying down, I decided to sit up in bed and wait for 11:30 pm to get my medication.

I sat there, waiting for time to pass and once again I studied the veins on my wrist. I studied the spaces between them, then I looked at the wounds beside them and over them. I passed my finger over my burned skin and felt the roughness of it. The moment I touched it I knew it was too late. My thoughts had focused on that wound and I had to tare it off. I was doing it before I had to the chance to tell myself not to. The scab was thick, and blood had risen from underneath it the moment I had taken it off. My head was screaming, "don't!" but my hand acted with its own mind. I got a tissue and sopped up the blood. Once I was cleaned up, I placed the tissue into my sleeve and covered my wrist with my hand so that the blood would stop. "Oh no. I went and did a stupid," I thought to myself and fell into regret.

I hadn't even done it to hurt myself. For my whole life I found it hard not to pull scabs off. I would think obsessively about peeling them off and the thoughts wouldn't calm down until I did it. For once I honestly wasn't trying to hurt myself, but I did like that it was bleeding.

When Saul and Carson came into my room during their rounds, I was still sitting with my hand over my wrist. My shirt sleeve was covering my wound and the tissue. There was no evidence showing of what I had done.

Saul walked over to the left side of my bed and Carson was to my right.

"What are you doing?" Saul asked.

"Not much."

Saul tried to move my hand away to see my wrist, but I pulled out of his grasp, and I put my hand back where it was.

How could he have known that I had done something?

"Show me," Saul ordered as he took my hand for a second time.

My hand had been moved, but my sleeve was still covering the blood stained tissue.

"There's blood on your blanket," Saul observed as he pointed to the evidence that would condemn me.

"Show me your wrist," Carson ordered.

I knew that I wouldn't have a choice, so I removed the tissue and pushed up my shirt sleeve.

"It's not fresh," I told them as Carson shined his flashlight on my wrist.

"It's not new?" Carson repeated my words in the form of a question.

"No, it's the burn from last week. I only opened it," I said in my defense.

Carson gave me another order, "Show me your leg."

A flashlight was shone over the cuts on my leg, but they noticed nothing.

"You know what this means don't you?" Saul asked, but I didn't answer. "We're going to have to tie you down."

"No. It's not a new wound," I argued. I was willing to beg my way into continued freedom, but they had no reason to believe me. My record was against me. "I have to wait for 11:30."

"What is at 11:30 that can't be at 11:00?" Carson asked.

"My medication."

"Oh," Carson said.

"It's for my spasms," I explained.

"Spasms?" Carson asked for confirmation.

"Yeah. I keep moving," I told them. I had several spasms in front of them, but they didn't seem to grasp what was going on. "I can't fall asleep when I'm being jerked around. Is there something that can be done for my spasms?"

"Okay. I'll go inform myself about what can be done," Carson told me.

Both men left, but shortly afterwards, Saul came back and sat beside me on my bed. "So what are we going to do about this? Huh? What do we do?"

"Nothing; Preferably."

"We can't do nothing."

"I don't want to get tied to the bed," I said to Saul in a pleading way.

Saul left the room without answering.

I waited on my bed and l could hear the clicks of the latches on that yellow box. I heard the clanking of the straps as they were pulled out. It was the noise of the coming of doom.

When Saul, Carson and a nurse that I didn't recognize came into my room, I got up from my bed to throw my tissue into the trash can.

Saul stretched his arm out to block me from leaving.

"I just want to throw this out," I explained as I held out my hand to show my stained tissue.

I was allowed to pass and throw it out, but Saul put himself closer to the door in case I would try to leave.

I walked away from Saul, then leaned up against the wall and then slid myself down the length of it so I was sitting on the floor.

"No," Carson said. "You lie down on the bed."

"No. Put the straps on first," I requested.

Carson silently agreed and they set the straps at the end of the bed.

"Come on," Saul said as he pulled my hand to help me up.

I pulled my hand away and spoke sternly. "No."

"I don't want to force you," Saul told me.

He tried to take my hand a second time, but I pulled away once again.

To my disappointment, Carson came over and both men grabbed me by the arms and forced me onto the bed.

I was so anxious and afraid that I covered my face with my hands. I couldn't look at what was being done to me.

Carson had to force me to lie down because lying down was the worst part, and I wasn't brave enough to do it on my own.

"You've shown that you can't control yourself," Saul told me. "So we are going to do it for you. It's called a stop plan."

My spasms were getting worse and more frequent, and as the group of men left the room, Saul witnessed a heavy series of them.

Saul looked concerned as he paused in the doorway. "Are you okay princess?"

I didn't answer. I was so busy worrying about my state of being that I couldn't reply.

Every time someone would come in and check on me, they would find me having spasms so great that my left shoulder would lift off the bed and my head would jerk around on my pillow. If It weren't for the fact that my legs were tied down, they would have jolted into the air.

Someone I didn't recognize came into my room to check the straps. He looked young; I guessed that he was around twenty years old. He had black hair and was of medium build.

I was embarrassed from being tied down and for my constant state of movement.

He could see that I was awake, and at first we didn't say anything, then I asked him for the time.

"12:15 am," he answered.

After the young nurse left, I found myself waiting for an unbearably long time. It became painfully obvious that too much time had passed by.

I was discouraged each time the nurse and Gordon passed by my room and all they did was shine a flashlight through my window to make sure I was still there. They didn't come in to check my straps and I was beginning to fear that I had been abandoned and forgotten. Would they ever come in and let me go?

I was relieved when Gordon and the new nurse finally came into my room.

"So how are you doing?" Gordon asked.

"Oh. I'm great. I love it here," I spoke sarcastically, then I complained about my spasms, so the new nurse went to see what could be done.

I was alone with Gordon. "What time is it?" I asked.

"1:15 am."

"What?! I was left here for an hour without anyone to check on me?"

Gordon's expression turned to anger. "We came in here to see if you could be let out and you're complaining?!"

I was surprised at his reaction. "They are supposed to come in the room and check my straps every 15 minutes."

"We we're trying to be nice and let you sleep."

"I didn't sleep."

Gordon continued to express his agitation. "We were trying to come here to see if we could let you out, but if you're just going to complain, I can leave you here for the rest of the night."

The man was fuming and making me increasingly nervous. "No. Why are you talking like this?" I asked with rising anxiety. It felt like I was under attack. "Why are you acting like this?"

"If all you want is to complain, then I may as well just leave you here," Gordon threatened once again.

I was never good with confrontations, and rarely said what I needed to defend myself.

"Stop!" I yelled and was surprised at my courage. I took a deep breath. "I was afraid that I had been abandoned. I was afraid that I had been forgotten. I didn't complain just to complain. I did it because it really scared me and I was afraid that it might happen again."

Gordon was finally speechless. He left and soon came back to untie me.

"You were right. It was supposed to be every fifteen minutes. That nurse isn't used to it here yet and he forgot."

"I wont do it again," I told Gordon.

"You mean that you wont hurt yourself if I let you out?" Gordon asked.

"No. I wont."

Cindy came in as Gordon was untying the strap to my right leg. "We didn't forget you," Cindy told me as she untied the strap to my right hand. "We looked in and thought you were sleeping."

"I wasn't. I can't fall to sleep when I'm having so many spasms."

Cindy asked me the same thing that Gordon did. "If we let you out, will you hurt yourself?"

"No," I answered truthfully.

"Okay," Cindy accepted and they let me go free.

Before they left, I had a request. "Can I have something more for my spasms?"

"I'll make sure that you'll get something," Gordon told me.

"Well, at least it's not as bad as it was an hour ago."

Gordon looked surprised. "You mean it was worse than this?" he asked as he nodded towards my spontaneously rising body.

"Yes. It was worse," I answered.

After the new nurse gave me my medication I had the difficult task of falling asleep to the jolting spasms that wouldn't let me rest.

Friday, December 12

I was in a bad mood the next morning. I had been weighed and the numbers didn't agree with me. Every day that I ate normally, I gained weight.

My nurse Hydie came to my room to talk to me when she saw I wasn't feeling well.

We sat in our usual places; me on the bed and her on the chair. My body was constantly being jolted forward and I had to put my hands on the bed in front of me to keep from toppling over. I was self conscious, but throughout the entire conversation, she never reacted to my spasms.

I was surprised at what Hydie had to tell me. "I used to be anorexic when I was a teenager."

My eyes grew wide. "What was the least you came to weigh?"

"78 pounds," she answered. "It wasn't pretty. I didn't care about myself or the consequences of what I was doing. It took me a long time to figure out that what I was doing was hurting the people I loved. It hurts your family too."

"Yeah. I had realized that. That's why I didn't tell them I was sick until only recently."

"Your family needed to know," Hydie told me.

"Even if it hurt them?"

"Yes," she confirmed. "Do you know what helped me realize the weight of what I was doing? I was sixteen and at the hospital. There was a girl there who was about thirteen years old and had an incurable cancer. She was going to die. One day, she asked me why I was there. I told her that it was because I thought I was fat. That's when she told me, and I'm never going to forget this; she told me, *You're playing a game with your life. You might die. But me? I'm going to die. I'd do anything to have the chance you have at living. Don't waste it.* That was a real big reason why I stopped. She really made me think," Hydie paused. "You know, I didn't want you as a patient."

Wow, that didn't make me feel so special, but I suddenly realized what she meant. "Because I remind you of yourself."

"Yes. My teacher told me that I should do it, but I told her that I had been down the same road as you. It took me two days to decide that I was going to take your case."

"You had a choice?"

"Yes, but then I realized that you needed help, and that I could be the one who brings it to you."

~ ~ ~ ~

When I had been walking through the halls later that day, I noticed that the glass sheet had been put back on the wall with the no smoking sign under it. At first I was pretty exited at my discovery, but when I looked close enough, I saw that the corners of the sheet had been sanded down. The corners were round instead of pointy.

"Crap," I thought. "And I was so hopeful."

I decided to drown my disappointment in a game of cards. I sat alone at a round table in the cafeteria and had all my cards in front of me.

Samantha walked by my table and I could tell right away that she was mad at me, but I failed to understand why.

"You've been misleading everyone with your lies," Samantha accused me.

I was taken aback by the confrontation. The last time I had spoken with Samantha, we were on good terms.

"What are you talking about?" I asked.

"You know what?" Samantha asked. "I don't want to talk to you anymore. Lose my number, okay?"

I willed myself to stay calm because I didn't want to lose a friend. I got up from my chair to cross the cafeteria and entered the hallway so that I could follow Samantha as she walked away. "I'd like to know what you're talking about so that I can apologize," I tried to persuade her.

Samantha stopped walking and turned around to face me. "You made me walk for too long with you while you were wearing those rubber bands."

I finally began to gain some understanding. "These ones?" I asked and pointed to the bands around my wrists.

"You make lies for everyone," Samantha's anger hadn't faded and her expression of disgust was still just as strong. "You lied when you said that your doctor prescribed that you could have those."

I didn't raise my tone, but my anxiety was strong under her accusations. "I didn't lie. That's what happened."

We met up with Saul in the hallway so I took the opportunity to ask him a question with Samantha in earshot. "Saul, is it true that the last time I was here my doctor prescribed me my rubber bands?"

"Yes," Saul confirmed.

Samantha's eyes grew wide like she couldn't believe what she had heard.

"See," I looked Samantha in the eyes. "I don't lie, and I haven't lied to you."

Samantha said nothing and walked away, but we met up in the halls just about a minute later.

"Your doctor is an idiot," Samantha scowled as she walked passed me. I didn't have time to answer her, but I could tell that she'd had some time to think.

When we met up for super in the cafeteria, Samantha apologized honestly. "Do you forgive me?" she asked.

"Of course I do," I replied.

"I wrote a note in your journal because I wanted to apologize right away."

I smiled and said, "I can't wait to read it."

We ate super together. Samantha told me that she was leaving that night. I said that I was happy for her, and she told me that I could call her anytime.

~ ~ ~ ~

I had to change rooms again.

They had to put Evangeline where I was because the confused old lady kept putting her room mates night clothes on. She needed to be in a room by herself.

So Evangeline moved into the 808 and I moved into the 810. My room mates name was Cindy. She was a scary looking woman. The bright make-up caked thick on her face reminded me of a clown.

One great thing about staying in the 10 was that I got the side of the room with the radiator grid. I could also have the hot water from the sink.

There were so many wonderfully dangerous things at my disposal, including the knife from supper that I broke in half and tucked the sharp end into my pants.

I pulled that knife out two times that evening and sawed a total of four lines into my leg.

I succumbed to temptation, but I regretted it. I knew that the nurses checked my wounds every day. I knew I was going to be discovered, so I had to decide if I was going to admit what I had done, or hide it in the hopes of avoiding the consequences.

I could think of no plausible way to hide my actions, so I went to the offices to make my confession. I didn't really know the nurse that was assigned to me that evening, so I decided to talk to Saul. He was filling out his report at the front desk.

Saul looked up at me when I placed the piece of knife beside the files in front of him. There was still blood on the blade.

LADY INJURY

"Did you use this?" Saul asked as he picked up my tool.

Silence.

"Show me what you did," he directed.

I searched around me to make sure that no one else could see, then I pulled up my pant leg to let him look.

"Can the consequence be just going into the 62 for a while?" I asked.

"If you hurt yourself you're supposed to get tied down," Saul told me.

"But I don't want that. Have you ever been tied down?"

"No, but I'm sure I wouldn't like it," Saul answered. "But as hard as it is for the person being tied down, it's worse for those who tie them down."

I didn't understand how that could possibly be worse. "How is that?" I asked with skepticism.

"We have to make the decision to do it or not, and then we question ourselves as to whether we did the right thing. Could I have avoided this? Could there have been any other way?"

"You feel guilty," I said as half a statement and half a question.

"Yes, but we do it for you. We aren't the one's who will be gaining anything from this. It's you we want to help."

"I know that."

"I'm going to give you a chance. I'm going to put you in the 62. If you hurt yourself then I'll have to tie you down."

"Okay," I breathed with relief.

I didn't mind being sent to the 62. I had been there too many times to think of it as frightening.

I sat on the end of the bed and looked around at the familiar gratify on the walls. So many patients had been there before me. It was interesting to see the words and symbols created by all the angry people who came and went through the life of the 62.

I was angry too, but mostly at myself. I wasn't sure what it was that possessed me to hurt myself with whatever was at my disposal. I wasn't sure why it was so hard to stop something that should have been easy.

Just stop? No. That wasn't enough.

I pulled up my right pant leg and looked at the mess I had made of myself. I drove my fingernails through my fresh wounds and my older one's as well. I made them all bleed and the proof stained my fingers and the palms of my hands.

I was so disappointed in myself. So discouraged and so mad. Even to this day, what I feel about it is shame. My resolve should have stuck with me. I should have tried harder. Why wasn't it enough to want things to be better?

Saul came in and saw me quickly pulling down my pant leg. I wished I had more of a warning when someone came in.

"What did you do?" Saul asked as he came over to my bedside. He pulled my pant leg up to reveal the open wounds underneath.

"I made them bleed," I confessed while staring at the wall instead of at the man who would judge what the consequence would be. "I couldn't help it," I told him.

"Well you know what we have to do now."

I didn't answer. I wanted to pretend it wasn't true. Fade away. Disappear.

Saul left and came back with my skeleton print pajama pants and my green sweater.

"This is where we're at," Saul stated as he passed me the clothes I was to wear to my sentencing.

My eyes closed and I swallowed a feeling of dread as I heard the clanking of the yellow box. It made my stomach sick to know what was about to happen.

I considered the fact that Carson wasn't there that night and Saul was the only man on staff. Could I avoid being tied down If I refused? Or could he still make me?

I wished that I was a violent person so I could fight my way out of my situation. I felt trapped knowing that I was the kind of person who couldn't stand to hurt anyone else in any way.

With my passive aggressive and semi-hopeless personality, all I could do was stand outside my doorway and pray that I really wouldn't have to get in that bed.

Saul walked over to me and put his hand on my back to guide me into the room, but I pulled away from him.

Saul's hand was still on my back when he said, "Go in by your own will. Don't make me force you."

I was guided in a few steps and then I tried to back away. Saul caught me and pushed me over to the bed. I sat down on the bed side and then laid down.

I hid my face in my hands and tried to imagine that I was somewhere else; anywhere else.

The nurse that was helping Saul was Ashley. She was heavy set and looked to be around 20 years old. She had dark hair that she kept tied back. She seemed kind, but I hadn't known her long enough to know if that was true.

When Saul took my hand to put it in the strap, I pulled back as much as I could.

"No," I said in determination.

"You're trying to make things difficult for Saul," he stated. It didn't matter how many times I heard Saul refer to himself in the third person, it always sounded funny to me, but also strangely reassuring.

Saul strapped down my left wrist while Ashley did the right one.

I hated being so restrained, but I didn't have enough fight in me to stop them.

Saul tapped the restraint on my wrist to draw my attention to it. "If you get out of this, Saul is going to have to put something over you that keeps you from moving around. You'll be pinned down instead of just tied. Would you like that?"

"No, but I don't intend to take them off."

"Okay, we'll be back to check on you," Saul told me before he left the room with Ashley.

I laid there staring at the ceiling and imagining all the things I could do to myself once I was freed. My desire to tear myself apart wasn't fading. For a moment, I was almost grateful that I was tied down. At least that way I was safe from myself; safe from the beast within me.

After what seemed like an hour, Saul and Ashley came to see if they could trust me not to hurt myself.

"I'm going to trust that you'll behave," Ashley told me as she kneeled down and reached for the restraint on my right wrist.

I knew that they couldn't trust me. I knew what I would do if I had the chance and I was only too familiar with the consequence. The part where they put me in the straps was the hardest part, and I didn't want to go through that again.

They said they were going to trust me? Why would they do that? I couldn't even do that.

"You shouldn't," I admitted, knowing very well that I would have to stay longer.

"Ah," Saul stopped undoing my restraint. "That's what we needed to know."

So they left me there, powerless and discouraged. I was told that I would be untied when I fell asleep.

It was always hard to fall asleep while my body jolted with spasms. If you combine spasms with being restrained, sleep was an unattainable goal.

Saul came to untie me before his shift ended. "Can I trust you now?"

"Yes," I told him as I grew more tired.

So I was finally freed and I spent the rest of the night in the 62.

Saturday, December 12

The next morning I was writing in my journal when Sylvia flopped herself onto my bed and rolled over onto me. We both laughed as she got up.

Sylvia caught her breath. "I'm the only nurse that is this fun, right?"

I thought about it. Amanda had a good sense of humor, but she didn't have the same childlike insanity.

"Yes, you're the only one," I confirmed.

"I knew it," my playful nurse smiled.

Sylvia left and came back with the supplies to change the bandages on my leg.

"You've got to be ready for this, okay?" she warned me with a serious expression. I struggled to understand what she was referring to. "I'm going to pour this bottle of liquid all over your wounds. It's going to burn, okay?"

I wasn't afraid of pain. "Okay," I accepted.

Sylvia wasn't done preparing me for her actions. "You've really gotta be ready. When I pour this over your leg, all the skin is going to rise up and fall off."

I raised my eyebrows. "What's the purpose of that?"

"It's so that everything gets cleansed out," she explained. "Are you ready?" Sylvia asked as she brought the bottle close enough to pour over my leg. "Now, this is really going to burn, okay?"

Those stern words of warning didn't even make me blink. I was actually very interested in seeing my skin rise up and fall off. "Okay," I answered.

Sylvia drew back and laughed suddenly. "Wouldn't it be terrible if it were true?! And can you imagine doing that without any painkillers?!"

I certainly could.

I realized then that I had been gullible and that she was playing with me. I was a bit embarrassed. "I wouldn't have minded," I told her.

I was disappointed that it had been a joke. I really wanted to see that happen.

~ ~ ~ ~

Everyday I was reminded as to how little self control I truly had.

All it took was a moment. One moment long enough for me to secure a good enough tool to satisfy my yearning for pain and release. I had stolen a plastic knife from the lunch area and tucked it in the top of my pants before anyone was the wiser.

I couldn't help it. Something would pass through me and it was like I was guided. I would tell myself not to do it, but then I did it anyway. I told myself to stop, but I didn't. The end was always the same; More blood, more mess.

I remembered what had happened the night before. Images of blood and restraints passed through my mind. I didn't want that to happen again, and yet a small plastic knife was still with me wherever I went.

Pretty soon that knife was all I could think about. What would this knife bring to my future? I had to decide if I was going to use it, or give it up. Another thought occurred to me. I could use the knife, and then give it up. There were going to be consequences no matter what I did. If I was going to get tied to the bed, I'd better have done something to deserve it first.

I had noticed lately that I was becoming more and more moody and non compliant.

I didn't want to get tied down. It haunted me when I remembered what had happened the other times. I didn't want to feel like that lady who went into the elevator saying that she didn't want to stay, and then got tied down. She wanted to leave the hospital. She didn't scream or get violent.

She just said that she wanted to go.

I was grateful that I had an amazing doctor who arranged for me to be able to keep my clothes and never have a code white called on me.

I wanted to hurt myself.

How was I going to keep from doing it?

I was losing my mind while trying not to fix things the way that I wanted. Fixing things was to make the hurt go away fast. Although, I couldn't hurt myself as badly as I wanted to because I didn't have the tools to do it right.

I decided to tell my nurse that I was sending myself into a room plan, that way she would know that I was talking about self injury without me having to say it.

I stayed in my room and broke the knife in half, that way I would only be keeping the sharp end. The knife was then small enough to fit into the folded end of my coat sleeve that I kept on a shelf.

I wouldn't have the knife on me, but I would know where it was if I needed it.

After all my work of securing a suitable enough tool, I didn't even pull out my knife that night. Instead I used my fingernails to reopen the wounds on my leg and made them bleed. Although the idea of using the knife and the damage it could cause had called to me, I only used my hands. I had bloody fingertips and a determined force within me that made all possible wounds bleed.

Saul caught me with my hands moving under my blanket right where my leg was.

I swore inside my mind for getting caught.

It was hard to get away with things with Saul around.

"Let me see your leg," Saul asked and I pulled up my pant-leg so I could show him.

"What are we going to do about this?" he asked me calmly as he looked in my eyes.

"Nothing, I hope."

"You know that we can't do nothing. Yesterday I gave you the chance to only go into the 62, but you hurt yourself again."

"I know," I admitted. "I didn't manage to stop myself. I was very wrong to do that."

"Well, Saul is here to help you stop, okay?"

Saul left while I got into my pajama's and waited for doom to come.

With fear in every step, I walked over to the 62 where I was supposed to be trapped. Courage left me because when I got to the door, I didn't go in. In fact, I backed up a few steps.

That's when Carson came over and took my arm to force me into the room. "I don't want to force you," he said as he guided me.

The fear held me strongly and it cut through my stomach like knives.

"My stomach hurts," I complained to let him know what this threat was doing to me.

"You should have thought of that before," he spoke coldly.

When I was in the room, Carson left and it was Saul who had to force me into the bed.

I was so scared, and I couldn't hide it.

Saul had me sit down on the edge of the bed, then he put my legs up on the mattress. Once that was done, he had me lie down, because I still didn't have the courage to do it myself.

I felt like a puppet; like a puppet being made to lie down in its own coffin.

Saul had a soothing voice. "When you can't protect yourself, then we are here to do it for you."

When I was left alone, I squirmed around a lot and I pulled at the restraints to see if I could get free of them the way that I had the week before.

I couldn't do it. The straps were too tight and the restraints weren't the same one's that I sneaked out of.

LADY INJURY

I waited for hours to be rescued, but I wasn't sleeping the way that Saul had said that I had to be in order to be set free.

I was only drowsy, but they still considered liberating me.

"Can we trust you?" Saul asked as he loosened the strap on my wrist.

"Yes," I answered as my voice grew more groggy.

When I was finally let out, I curled up and fell asleep.

Sunday, December 13

Morning arrived for me at 7:15 when Cindy came to weigh me. I didn't like the numbers that came up on the scale, but then again, I never did. Every day I considered starving away the pounds I had gained, and every day I fought the urge.

It was an ordinary day. I walked through the halls a lot. Any time I would say something negative to Sylvia like that I didn't think I could make it, she would smack me. I'd get a slap on the back of the head if I was standing and a slap on the legs if I was sitting.

Like most days, I wanted to hurt myself. It felt like there was something inside me eating everything but my emotions away.

I was hard on myself because I messed things up so often and I prayed the doctors plan would work.

As much as I wanted to get better, another part of me was desperate to stick to my old ways. I had managed to collect two plastic knives and a metal piece from a soda can. I kept them all with me by slipping them into the top of my pants.

I wanted for things to get better, but at the same time, I didn't. Maybe there was a part of me that wouldn't know what my identity was if I wasn't a cutter. Maybe cutting had become a necessary thing that I couldn't go without. I knew there had to be something about it though. There was something that kept me coming back to do it again and again.

Doing what was wrong came to me much more naturally than doing what was right. Sitting in my own blood may have seemed sick, but to me, it felt like a necessary evil.

~ ~ ~ ~

I worked on the drawing of my niece, but it seemed like there was something off about the way I drew her face. I shrugged it off and decided to leave fixing it to the next day.

My spasms hadn't stopped yet, and they were growing stronger. When I'd lie down, I looked like a fish out of water. I was twitching and literally rising from the bed because of full body spasm after full body spasm. Thankfully it wasn't painful; Only annoying and embarrassing. Luckily, I only had to deal with it when I was in a resting position.

Joseph came to visit me that day. I was disappointed in my friend when I realized that he was still using. He even pulled a white pill from a paper bag and slipped it in his mouth.

I grabbed his bag and looked inside.

"Are these drugs? How high do you have to be before it's enough? I never cut myself in front of you, so don't think that you can use drugs in front of me."

I had to be straight with him because I never wanted to see that trash ever again.

"Did you already use today?" I asked outright.

"No, but I did yesterday," he confessed.

"Yesterday, but not today," I reviewed. "Other than what you just took. Okay. I don't want to see you high anymore. Do you understand that?"

"Yes."

"Okay."

"I have good news," Joseph began with a chipper mood as we started walking in the halls. "Jesus is coming this summer in physical form."

"Jesus is coming?" I asked in surprised disbelief.

"Yeah, I've been reading and reading, and I've learned that he's coming this summer."

"Joseph, it doesn't say that in the bible," I countered.

"Yes it does. I found it," he defended his finding.

"Joseph!" I yelled.

"What?" he asked and backed up a few inches.

"You're using!"

"Yeah."

"You have to stop that," I pleaded.

"I'm with God. I'm going to marry the five virgins."

"Joseph!" I yelled again and grabbed the front of his winter coat in both my hands. "You're crazy."

"What?"

"You're using drugs so now your meds don't work and you're crazy," I told him. "I can't understand what you're saying. You make no sense."

"Well then, let me explain," Joseph offered.

"Okay," I agreed as I let go of his coat and we continued to walk.

"If I stay single, I can serve God differently than if I get married," he began.

"Okay."

"I thought that I wasn't supposed to marry, but now I understand about the five virgins. Betty is going to be the first virgin. I asked her to marry me and she said yes. I used to be sure that you were one of the virgins and that we were supposed to be together."

"You're my friend Joseph. It's not like that with us," I told him.

"I'm getting married this summer."

I wondered if he ever actually asked Betty to marry him. Was Betty real? I sighed and looked at my friend who was growing further and further away from the man I used to know. "Joseph!" I yelled as I slapped the fluffy sleeves of his coat. "You're crazy."

There was an announcement on the speakers that there was a phone call for me.

"Wait right here," I told Joseph and ran to the phone. It was Marie. "I can't talk right now," I told her. "I'm busy yelling at a friend and I really need to keep yelling."

"Okay."

I hung up the phone and ran back to Joseph.

"Joseph!" I yelled again, almost like I hoped that yelling his name would wake him up. "You're crazy. I'm only telling you this because you're my friend. If I didn't care about you, I wouldn't say anything. I care about you and it hurts me to see you like this. Do you know what I did when you left the other day? I beat my wrist against the windowsill."

Joseph bowed his head. "I thought you might do that."

"It hurts me to see you like this," I confided.

"I can feel your pain," Joseph told me. "I can feel the whole worlds pain. It's going to be better when Jesus gets here. I'm closer to God. Do you feel God the way that I feel him?"

I was pretty sure that I didn't feel God like Joseph did.

We had stopped in the small hallway where I used to sit on the floor by the elevators. I closed my eyes and a tear rolled down my cheek. I looked at this man, but it seemed that the friend I knew had left his mind. His hair was everywhere. The drugs were ruining his face, making him look older and he still had a rash around his mouth from using. His very presence was painful to bare. I put my hands against the chest of his thick coat and looked in his eyes to find the man I used to know, but his presence barely flickered behind his expression.

I wrapped my arms around him and buried my face in his blue coat as I cried. "Why is this happening?"

"I don't know," Joseph said as he held me tightly.

I pulled away. "Joseph, I love you. You're my friend and you always will be. I've never given up on anyone and I wont give up on you. I want you to remember that you're my friend and that I will always be here, but you have to take care of yourself first. I can't be around you when you're like this. Tell the social worker that you need help. The once a week program you are in now is not enough. You need full time detox."

"It's like you're telling me that you don't want to see me anymore," Joseph was sullen.

"No," I corrected. "I'm saying goodbye for now, and I'll be here when you are well." I walked Joseph to the elevators. "Joseph, don't come back until you are okay."

"I am okay."

"No, you're not," I told him. "You're nuts. You're using. You're not okay. You have to stop that."

"I don't need help."

I swallowed my defeat. I knew that unless he recognized his problem, there was nothing I could do to change him.

"Good bye," I said solemnly as I turned away from him and went back to my room.

When Joseph left I walked again. I walked a lot. I walked into the evening. I was trying to calm myself down through exhaustion, but my thoughts were too strong. I needed the pain release so much.

I didn't trust myself. I couldn't. I knew what I would do if I was alone long enough

I decided to tell my nurse that I was sending myself into a room plan. The nurse was new and still a stranger to me. She said it was okay and that she would check up on me.

So there I was.

In my room.

Alone.

Able to do whatever my sickness would allow.

I fought the urge, but instinct took over and soon I had sat down on my bed and used my fingernails to make my wounds bleed. By the time Saul got to the Isolation room, I had started using the soda piece.

I hadn't heard him coming until it was too late. When he saw me pull my pant leg down, he asked what I was doing, though I was sure he knew the answer.

"Not much," I told him with an evasive smile.

"Let me see your hands," Saul ordered.

I showed him my hands and stained fingertip.

"Yeah, that's what I thought. So what are we going to do about this?"

"I don't know," I answered with a sinking feeling inside. "Nothing? I could deal with that."

"You know that's not what your plan says. You know we have to tie you down," Saul spoke seriously.

"Please. I don't want to," I begged.

"I know you don't like it."

"It's true, I don't, but maybe this will be what turns things around for me," I voiced the thoughts that I didn't even want to admit to myself.

I repeated those thoughts to myself as I watched Saul carry in that famous yellow box. Maybe this was what would turn things around.

It didn't matter what I told myself would be good for me, because soon instinct had taken over and I had gone to sit in the corner furthest away from Saul and the bed. My nurse had accompanied him in and was pulling things from the box.

They put the straps on the bed, and then they needed for me to lie down in it.

Helpless again.

I fought it though.

Saul had to push me towards the bed and my socks slid on the floor like skates on ice.

I didn't want to go. Not again. Not there.

Before we reached the bed, I sort of dropped to my knees so that he couldn't put me on.

"We might have to get Carson to help us," Saul suggested as he looked down at me on the floor.

"No," I said. "Please. Please."

I didn't know what was supposed to follow the word please. Please stop? Please don't do this? Please, I can't handle this? Please, see my fear and don't put me through this?

There were so many possible things to say, but all I could manage was, "Please."

Saul picked me up and put me on the bed. I then curled up by hugging my knees. I think I was protecting the parts of me that would soon be strapped down.

They tried to take my legs, but I pulled back, so they took them again, but held on tighter. After they strapped my ankles down, Saul took my hand that was covering my face. I didn't want to see. I didn't want to know.

I pulled back when I felt the strap on my wrist, so Saul had to take my hand a little more forcefully.

"You're really gonna make this hard on Saul, aren't you?"

"Hell yeah," I thought. I had finally found a part of me that could fight back and not simply succumb to other peoples wishes.

In the end, for all my fighting, I still ended up strapped to the bed of the 62; Helpless, afraid, and panicking. Trying to relax enough to be able to breathe.

When all was done, Saul and the new nurse left the room and locked it.

A few minutes later, I heard a girl crying. Her cries had no problem reaching my room, but it was the depth of the pain in her tone that made me hurt for her.

I was fairly certain that the cries belonged to my nurse. I imagined that maybe the experience of tying a girl down who was combative and afraid was too much for her.

I had hurt her because I wasn't co-operating like I used to.

Or maybe it had nothing to do with me, although the timing would have been very coincidental.

I fell asleep in the 62, but by morning I hadn't woken up in it because someone else needed the room.

Momday, December 14

My mood wasn't terrible by the next day, and I couldn't get my nurses cries off my mind. Had that been my fault?

No matter what else was going on, hurting myself was always on my mind. I thought about the things that I could do and about how much blood I could get out of every method. I thought about the color and the relief. I thought about blood dripping from the ceiling and falling on my face. I saw blood leaking out from where the wall met the ceiling.

That dark and stupid girl in my head was calling me and making all those offers sound appealing.

~ ~ ~ ~

Parker had been asking me if I had a room for rent at my place. I told him, "No."

He asked, "Will you come and see me after you get out?"

"You're still gonna be here?" I asked with wide eyes.

"Yeah, they say that I have to stay longer; Until after the holidays."

"Why is that?" I asked and then I paused. "Oh, is it because you drank?"

"How did you know I drank?" Parker was surprised.

"You told me," I reminded him. "But how did they know? Did you fail a urine test?"

"Yeah, and they said I smelled like alcohol. Maybe they heard me tell you."

"That's possible," I agreed. "We weren't too far from the desks when you told me."

"Oh no. That could be," Parker agreed.

"Are you still allowed to go down to the canteen?" I asked with selfish concern because Parker was my only hot chocolate provider.

"No," he said. "No outside and no canteen."

So both Parker and I had to find new suppliers. Claudine went for us once. Another time it was my room mates husband who went to get my hot chocolate fix at the same time as their order. I had offered to pay for it, but it came free of charge.

They were a nice couple.

Cindy was complaining that she didn't have a teddy to sleep with. "I've been asking for one for two weeks." she said.

"I have two stuffies. Would you like one?" I offered.

"Yes."

So I passed her Fred.

"This is a good bear. He's been with me since I was a baby."

~ ~ ~ ~

Sylvia had serious things to say to me when she came into my room the next morning. "I think you like being tied down."

"What?!" I asked in confusion and surprise.

"You're getting yourself tied down quite a lot lately. It's been almost every day," she pointed out.

"Yeah," I agreed. "I find it harder in the evening. That's when I'm more anxious and depressed, but I'm not sure why."

"Then write it down as soon as it happens. Write down all the things you think that triggers an episode."

I agreed with her suggestion, but I wasn't sure if she was serious about the part where she said that I liked being tied down. Sylvia joked with me a lot, so she was hard to read. If she was being serious,

I would find the idea both confusing and insulting. I was hurting myself just as often as before the times I was getting tied down. Did she think that I would hurt myself to get tied down? Did she think I liked being so disturbed from the experience and therefore have even more reason to hurt myself?

I thought that Sylvia should read my journal, then she would know what I truly felt.

I managed to gut my wounds again that day. I couldn't help it. The desire was there and I reached out for it without any real thought. I didn't get caught and I decided not to tell anyone that I did that, so I was free to go to the cafeteria and eat some vegetables and eggs. The eggs were a welcome difference from the sandwich food that I had suffered loudly through for the last month. Nearly every meal was a cheese sandwich. Very often I would get a cheese sandwich twice a day. It wasn't even a good sandwich. I had to add things to it to make it at least somewhat edible.

I said that I finally knew what it was like to be a cat; eating the same thing for every meal; the same dry bread and bad cheese.

It was a true test of human endurance.

I managed to make enough noise that the nurses complained to the kitchen and had a meeting with the dietitian. They told me that I was supposed to receive more quality meals at a greater variety.

I began to wonder when I was supposed to bust that joint. I knew that I couldn't stay forever. My eating disorders were in better control than I ever thought they could be, but my cutting was still very bad. I thought about cutting all the time. I was still looking for tools I could use and hiding them in my room until I needed them. I still wanted to cut just as badly.

If I left the hospital right then, I wasn't sure that I would ever win. I could ask to stay a bit longer instead of going to the day hospital again, but would that even help me at all? I wasn't getting better so far. Nothing was working so far.

I didn't want to go to the day hospital. I had hated it the summer before. I felt like it was just a waste of time.

~ ~ ~ ~

My thoughts were taken off of my own plight when my dear Annabelle handed back the arm warmers that I gave her.

"Here," she said as she placed them in my hands and her eyes filled with tears. "I'm never going to wear these. There's nothing to wear it with, and there's no event to wear them to."

"Are you sure?" I asked as I laid my arm over her shoulder.

"Yes," she confirmed and placed something small in my hand. "This is so you will remember me."

I looked at the small object that sat on the palm of my hand. It was a green, plastic Care-bear.

"Annabelle," I spoke her name as I gave her a hug. "I don't need things to remember you. I'll never forget you."

I leaned my head against hers and thanked her for the care-bear.

"They don't want me to die," Annabelle whimpered as tears streamed down her cheeks. "I'll be better off in heaven."

With my arm still over her shoulder, I told her, "It's not time for heaven yet. Let us have our turn first. We need you here. You're cared about here."

Annabelle smiled through her tears and nodded her head.

I really cared about Annabelle and so many of the other people I had met at the hospital. I wanted so much to make things better for them even if it was just for a little while.

Knowing that I could make a difference for someone else was one of the only things that made me feel good about my day. I guess it was kind of like a therapy for me.

~ ~ ~ ~

I got to speak with Evangeline a bit that day as well. She was a real sweetheart for me.

I met her in the hall when she was strapped down in her chair and talking to the air.

LADY INJURY

I said hello to her and asked her how she was doing. I didn't get to say much more before Carson reprimanded me.

"I want you to leave her alone," he said as he walked towards me with mild hostility. "You're only going to make her agitated."

I was taken aback by his statement. I hadn't expected it at all and it confused me as much as it made me defensive.

"No I won't. I talk to Evangeline every day and she has always been fine."

"I'd still like for you to leave her alone." Carson was unfeeling in his tone and he stared at me like he was waiting for me to leave.

I was mad. During the day, Sylvia was always grateful when I kept Evangeline occupied. She even encouraged me to do things with the elderly lady, so I did. I didn't spend time with Evangeline because I felt obligated to. I did it because I wanted to.

I had spent 7 years working with the elderly and I knew how to take care of them.

When I would talk to Evangeline, Sylvia would call me an angel straight from heaven, but Carson would shoo me away. The contrast made me angry, but I swallowed my pride and walked away as I was told.

I kept walking in the halls, but I said nothing to my elderly friend as I passed her by.

My anxiety would rise and fall, but I made sure to keep my pace and stay in the halls to make sure that I would behave.

I stopped dead in my tracks when I saw Annabelle standing in the door of the number 7 isolation room wearing nothing but a blanket. It struck me how she managed to find herself in such a different situation only an hour after I had talked to her in the halls.

"What happened to your clothes?" I asked her.

"They're dirty," she answered with an even sadder expression than she usually wore.

"Would you like for me to get you a couple of gowns? One for the front and one for the back?" I offered.

"Yes," she confirmed.

I had become used to encountering strange situations at the hospital and often found it interesting how calm and non-judgmental I was.

I brought Annabelle the gowns and she was able to dress herself. All I had to do to help her was snap the buttons in the back.

When I was satisfied that Annabelle was okay and that the situation had been resolved, I stepped away and began walking again.

About 10 minutes later, I heard a familiar crashing sound. Before I even got within sight of the Christmas tree, I knew that it had fallen.

That was the third time that Annabelle had pulled down the large and heavily decorated tree within the same week.

It always impressed me that a woman as old and small as her, still had the strength to bring down something at least 6 times bigger than she was.

~ ~ ~ ~

By about 7:00 in the evening I told my nurse Natalie that I was sending myself into a room plan because I was thinking a lot about cutting.

Parker came and asked if I would come and play cards, but I had completely forgotten that I wasn't supposed to leave my room, so I said yes.

Parker returned to my door frame when I didn't show up.

"I forgot that I have to stay in my room," I told him.

"Why? I thought you didn't have to do that anymore."

"It's not because I did or didn't eat. I'm here because I'm thinking some things that aren't okay. I have to stay here until my thoughts are better or I'll have to get tied down."

Parker thought it was a joke, but I wasn't laughing, so he understood that they really would do that to me.

"Seriously?" Parker asked with wide eyes.

"Yeah, but hey, we could play in my room; on the bed."

"Okay," Parker agreed.

LADY INJURY

"Do you mind Cindy?" I took my room mates feelings under concern.

"No, I don't mind, but you'd better pull the curtain so they don't see you. Boys can't go into girls rooms and girls can't go into boys rooms.

After a few games of Uno, Natalie poked her head around the curtain. "I don't think you are supposed to have visitors during your room plan."

"Why not?" I asked. "I'm way less likely to hurt myself with him here rather than being alone and doing what I want."

"That's true," Natalie admitted. "Well, you can go to the cafeteria and play if you like."

"I can decide when I get to leave?" I liked that idea.

"When you feel better you can go, otherwise, he goes and you stay," Natalie explained.

"Oh," I said. "Then I guess I have to stay here."

"You're not feeling better?" she asked.

"No," I replied simply.

"Okay, then I'll be back to check on you."

~ ~ ~ ~

There was a woman that walked by my room a few times that I was surprised to find was very familiar. She looked just like a girl who was a grade under me in high school. I remembered her name was Emma.

She seemed to be visiting one of the patients. When she saw me in my room, she paused, then shyly entered.

"Do you recognize me?" the girl asked as she walked towards my bed.

"Emma," I spoke her name in recognition.

"Yes."

"I thought that was you, but I wasn't sure," I told her.

Emma was even slimmer than she was in high school and she wore a woman's face, but I could still see that it was her. She was a reminder of how much time had passed and how much we had grown.

"What are you doing here?" Emma wanted to know.

I tried to avoid her question. "Oh, you know, writing, walking around my bed. There's not much else to do in this room."

"Why are you here?" she specified.

I hesitated to answer. I didn't know how the truth would sound to her. There were three people on the outside of my door who were listening in. I recognized one of them from when I was last in the ER.

"Self injury," I answered in embarrassment.

Emma looked surprised. "Why would you do that? You were so good in high school."

It was my turn to be surprised. Was that how I was seen in school?

"In high school I wasn't good at much else than writing," I admitted.

"You have your whole future ahead of you. Your whole life to live." Emma told me.

"I still do."

"Why do you hurt yourself?" Emma was curious, but her expression was solemn.

I looked down at my blankets and my bandaged wrists. "I have my reasons."

I didn't want to go into details of my personal life with a girl I hadn't seen in ten years, especially considering the audience outside my door.

Instead of talking about the gory details of my mental health, I decided to get her caught up to how my siblings had been since high school. "Brian has a two month old daughter. He works as a cook."

"Wow, that's really grown up," she said with a smile.

It was about then that Emma was warned that she wasn't supposed to be in my room.

As Emma left, I heard her ask her friends why I wasn't allowed visitors.

"Because she does things that aren't okay," her friend informed her.

"That's sad," Emma reflected, and those were the last words I heard her say before she disappeared.

I would have liked to have heard how she and her older brother were doing since high school.

That wasn't who I thought I would turn out to be; the girl with the bandaged wrist; the girl who made people turn away and say, "That's sad."

~ ~ ~ ~

Apparently I was scaring the nurses. They were all afraid that they might find me with open wounds and blood all over.

I could understand that. I wouldn't want to find anyone the way they would find me.

Most of the time, I could see why it would matter why someone else was hurt, but I failed to understand why it would matter when it was me.

For that day, Natalie would get to be my judge, jury, and executioner.

Would it be bed 10, or 62?

Would it be straps, or a peaceful nights sleep?

I needed for things to go well. I couldn't allow myself to do something dumb, so I went to the desks to ask for some Quetiapine.

Natalie was on her break, so I asked Anna for the medication.

I got a glass of water while the young nurse went to put 2 small orange pills into a paper cup.

When Anna returned there was only a desk separating us and I leaned against it. Anna had the medication in her hand but she didn't hold it out to me right away.

"How are you feeling?" she asked.

"Great. I've never been better," I replied with sarcasm in my tone.

"So, it's not good?"

"No," I replied.

"So why do you want them?"

"Because I need them," I answered simply.

"Well I don't pass these things out for the fun of it."

"That's okay. I'm not laughing, and I don't ask for medication unless I have a reason."

"So what's the reason?"

I looked at her pretty young face and dark hair. She was a nice girl, but I didn't really know her. I was tired of sharing highly personal details with whoever was randomly assigned to me, or who just happened to be at the desks when I needed something.

I could have said that my mind was racing and that I couldn't stand being in my own skin, but all I wanted to tell her was that it was none of her business.

"What's the reason?" Anna asked again.

I sighed, then looked longingly at the pills in the little cup that could have saved me. Instead of giving in and revealing the darkness in my mind, I just pushed my water glass aside and walked away.

When Natalie came back from her break, we sat in my room and talked. I let her know what I was feeling and told her how much I needed the Quetiapine. I explained that I hadn't wanted to tell Anna what was bothering me.

"It's none of her business," I spoke with frustration.

"She thought that you were messing with her," Natalie explained. "You said that you were feeling great. She couldn't give you the meds if you didn't need it."

"I was being sarcastic," I clarified while thinking that it should have been obvious. "I'm not doing well. I'm falling apart. All I can think about is what I could do, where I could do it, and how much blood each tool would draw."

"Well, I'm going to give you the Quetiapine and in 30 minutes I'll check up on you, but you have to promise me something."

"What?"

"That you won't hurt yourself in the next half hour. Okay? And then I'll check on you."

I thought about her offer. My thoughts weren't any better yet and the Quetiapine could take 45 minutes before it would work.

"I'm not sure that I could make it to 30 minutes," I told her.

"How about 15 minutes?"

I paused to think. That did seem more reasonable. "Okay."

"Do you promise?"

"I promise."

Natalie came back to see me just as she said she would.

"Can I trust you for another 15 minutes?" she asked.

"I don't think you can. I want it too much. It calls to me. I feel like I need it," I dreamed.

"Then what can I do to help you?" Natalie asked.

"I don't know what you can do about it, but I know what I want to do," I admitted.

"Then what do you suggest?" she wanted to know.

I thought about it for a minute. "Can I sleep in the 62?"

"I'll go ask the others and we'll see," she told me before she left.

A few minutes later, Carson came to get me in my room. "We've agreed to put you in the 62." Carson informed me, and then I followed him out of my room, through the halls, and into the isolation room.

When I started folding towels in the cart next to the door of the 62, Carson told me that I had to go back into the room. I complied to his orders and went back in, but I was still bitter against him for shooing me away from Evangeline earlier that day. I hated being treated like a nuisance.

I stayed calm and sat in bed writing in my journal.

Natalie continued to visit me every 15 minutes until I had taken my night medication and went to sleep.

Tuesday, December 15

I was greeted by a much more positive attitude the next morning. Apparently the nurses were all really happy that I had made it through the previous day without cutting. They said that they saw a lot of improvement in me. I would go to talk to them when I needed it, and I made an effort to distract myself by other means than cutting.

My nurse was Hydie that day. She said that her teacher had offered that she could take an easier case than me, but Hydie declined. Hydie felt that she could really make a difference with me because she's been where I am.

I was actually glad to hear that she was still my nurse because she wanted to and not because she felt pressured to. Before that I had felt badly that she had to take two days to decide if she could handle my case. I wondered if I was really that bad, but I still understood that it had more to do with her past than it had to do with me.

I got to meet with Dr Stone that morning. As usual I sat cross legged on the bed and he sat in the chair.

When he pressured me to go to the day hospital following my release, I still gave him a categorical no. I hated that day hospital. It was a waste of time to go there and I had responsibilities that I had to return to.

I asked if I could just stay in treatment at the hospital for a little longer instead of going to that program. Dr Stone said that he had a meeting coming up with his colleagues and that he would discuss it with them, and then with me. He said that he wouldn't make any decisions without me.

I liked that the staff were seeing progress in me and I didn't want to disappoint them, but unfortunately, I was still the Beauty that came with the Beast.

I had hidden in my room and used one of my plastic knives to cut my wrist and my leg.

I didn't get caught, so I just pulled my sleeve and pant leg over my cuts and turned to writing in my journal.

"*I did a stupid.*

I'm hoping to stay quiet about it at least until after super. Maybe I'll get a chance to cut again.

So here I am.

Writing again.

Taking breaks to bleed again.

I would pray to God, but he won't forgive me for what I've done. I could never even ask."

I was so dramatic, it was ridiculous.

Sometimes getting away with cutting bothered my conscience, but not that day.

I was able to go to supper, which was supposed to be a sandwich until I complained bitterly about it and they sent me rice and vegetables instead.

This I accepted.

After supper I told Annette that I was having a hard time and that I was sending myself to my room. I didn't admit what I had done that day, nor did I plan to. If I had told them about that they might have left me tied to the bed all evening and I couldn't deal with that.

Annette agreed with my decision to go to my room and said that she would check on me an hour later when she was back from her break.

So I went to my room where once again, I used a plastic knife on my leg.

I didn't admit my second self injury of the day either, so I was still free to negotiate a trade agreement with one of the new guys. I lent him my MP3 player and he went and got me a hot chocolate. It was rare that I failed to get my 7:00 pm double chocolate dose.

Annette passed by my room as I was breaking my mirage bar into my hot chocolate.

"Do you feel any better?" she asked.

"No, not really."

"So you're going to stay in your room plan?"

"Yes, for as long as I'm not supposed to go somewhere else," I agreed.

"Are you still thinking of hurting yourself?"

I was almost always thinking of hurting myself.

"Yes."

"So what can we do to keep you from hurting yourself tonight?"

"It's too late," I admitted.

"You already did it?"

"Yes."

"Give me what you used."

I went to my cupboard and pulled my plastic knife from one of my slippers and then gave it to her.

"Are there any more of these?"

"No," I mumbled a lie.

I was surprised at myself. It was rare that I allowed myself to make an outright lie and I regretted it immediately.

Annette accepted my answer and said that she would be back to check on me, but I didn't see her again until 9:00 pm when she brought me my medication.

I was able to go to sleep right after that.

Wednesday, December 16

I recognized the nurse that was assigned to me the next evening, but I didn't really know him. He was the young man who forgot to check on me for an hour when I was tied down. Lucky for him I wasn't prone to holding grudges.

His name was Cody and he said that he recognized me from the summer before. At the time he had the task of being a one on one guard for me.

When I asked for Quetiapine, Cody asked me why, but I refused to answer.

"Do you want to talk?" he asked.

I didn't really know the guy, so, "No."

I went to my room and he followed me, but I didn't know what to say to him.

When Cody asked me outright, I admitted that I wanted to hurt myself. I said that I was anxious but that I didn't know why.

"In the notes in your file, I saw that when your nurse checked on you regularly you managed not to hurt yourself. Can we do that?" Cody asked. "You promise not to hurt yourself for 30 minutes and I'll be back to check on you."

"Okay," I accepted.

During the 30 minutes that I promised to stay safe, I asked Saul if we could talk.

"I'm thinking about it a lot," I told him.

"Have you made plans?" he asked in reference to my means of self injury.

"Yes."

"Did you manage not to do it yesterday?" Saul questioned.

"No. I did it yesterday."

"So they tied you down," he assumed.

"No they didn't," I told him. "I think my nurse didn't have the guts to do it. I'm glad. I wouldn't have had the guts either."

"What about Roger?"

"He didn't know that I did it. I only told Annette. So I managed to hurt myself without consequence."

"If you had told Roger, there would have been."

"I know," I agreed. "I was glad at first, but then I felt guilty for getting away with it. I know that I'm not supposed to get away with it."

"I'm a little harder on you than Annette is," Saul observed.

"Yes," I agreed. "But I understand the reason. I have to learn to deal differently, but that doesn't mean I have to like the way we're fixing it."

"You don't like to not be able to hurt yourself."

"No, that's not it," I disagreed. "I don't like to be lying down with people around my bed. I don't like being incapable of defending myself. It feels like an attack."

"Saul never does it violently," he said. "I'm always soft natured."

"I know," I agreed. "And I'm grateful," I paused when I wasn't sure what else to say. I hadn't meant to suggest that he was cruel or threatening. "I guess I did my part then."

"And what is that?" Saul asked.

"I asked for my Quetiapine and I admitted that I want to hurt myself. That's what I'm supposed to do," I explained.

"That's not all of your part," Saul corrected me. "You have to keep from hurting yourself until your meds kick in."

"Okay. I'll keep myself busy until then."

"What will you do?"

"Write."

LADY INJURY

And I did write. I wrote until Cody came back to check on me.

"Did your medication help?" Cody asked.

"No."

"Okay, so can we try for another 30 minutes?" he asked. "Can you make it until then?"

"I don't know," I replied. "But I can try."

"Okay. I'll be back in 30 minutes."

Unfortunately Cody had to come back 30 minutes later to find me on the floor next to the radiator grid.

"Are you okay?" Cody asked.

I smiled and nodded my head yes like it was a joke. At least that way I could lie and know that he was aware that I was lying.

We were silent for a moment. It was quite awkward. Finally Cody asked, "Did you hurt yourself?"

I didn't look at him. I was too embarrassed. I kept my eyes fixed on the grid in front of me.

"I opened my wounds," I revealed, but I didn't mention the part where I scratched myself on the radiator grid.

"Okay," Cody said. "So I'm going to put you in a room plan in the 7."

"A room plan?" I asked feeling hopeful that I was going to get off easy once again.

"Isn't that what they do when you hurt yourself?"

"No," I said. "They usually tie me to the bed."

I washed my hands and followed Cody to the 7. I was relieved that I had free roam of the room.

There wasn't much to do in an isolation room, so I just crawled into bed and fell asleep.

I was still laying under my covers when Saul came back from his break. I opened my eyes to see him standing next to me.

"Hello," I greeted Saul when I registered who was there. Seconds later my heart sank and I breathed the words, "Oh no," when I saw the straps in his hand.

As per usual, I got out of bed and sat on the floor with my back against the wall.

"What are you doing?" Saul asked.

"I'm not here," I told him as I buried my face in my arms and knees. I looked up once in a while to see him setting the straps, then buried my face again.

"It's only going to be me," Saul told me. "I'm not going to force you. We can do this together."

I felt like I was being handed a gift. Saul was kind enough to arrange that there not be several people around the bed.

I thought to myself, "I really should take this deal." That's when I remembered the promise I had made to myself. I promised to never go without defending myself. Whether I fought or not, it felt like I was losing either way.

"Come on over," Saul invited as he reached an arm out to help me.

"No," I answered feeling guilty. How could I say no? Was accepting this offer really against my better judgement? Maybe I had no better judgement.

"I don't want to force you."

"I can't do it," I told him as I nodded my head no. "I can't make myself get into that bed."

"If you don't come then I'll have to get some help to make you get in. I don't want to have to do that."

"I know," I acknowledged, letting him know that I understood. I would feel sick to my stomach if I ever had to tie someone to a bed.

Cody came in and I asked him for a bandage to put on my wrist so that the straps wouldn't rub against my wounds. When Cody didn't go to get any, I got up to leave the room.

Saul walked over to the door to block me from leaving.

"I'm going to ask Megan for some bandages," I explained as I faced him.

"You're not going anywhere," he stated. "Cody will go get that for you. Get on the bed on your own," Saul ordered for one last time.

"No," I answered. The consequence to my defiance was having two men each grab one of my arms and forcing me towards the bed. I tried to keep from moving forward, but when that didn't work, I made myself limp, like dead weight.

I ended up in the bed anyway, but that didn't keep me from fighting.

"You're trying my patience," Saul told me. "I'm going to write in my report that tomorrow they have to have four people tie you down."

I didn't respond, but I really regretted not taking the chance that Saul had offered me before.

Saul moved to the opposite side of the bed, kneeled down and held my free left hand in his while Cody went to get the bandages.

I tried to pull away, but Saul asked me, "Why are you fighting like this?"

"I don't want to be helpless," I told him in a defeated tone.

"Saul would never hurt you," he spoke softly.

"I know that," I agreed. "You wouldn't."

After I got my wounds covered and all fours were strapped down, the end result was the same as if I hadn't defended myself; I was strapped to the bed.

The results made me think of the man who abused me. I couldn't seem to forgive myself for not fighting back or saying, no, when he wanted to touch me. I realized that whether I had fought him or not, the end result would have been the same. I would have fought, but he still would have hurt me. Could I have even fought him if I had tried?

I thought a lot about it, and I decided that if I were ever to get tied down again, I wouldn't fight it. I would let Saul strap me down without a fight. I would take my blows because I had earned them. If this had to be my consequence, it was mine to endure.

I was so tired after I was tied down that every time someone came into the room to check on me, I felt a little drowsier.

I was only tied down for a little more than an hour when Saul and Cody came in to free me.

I had paid my price, then fell asleep in the 7.

Thursday, December 17

Dr Stone came to see me early the next morning. He arrived to my room with Hydie. They wanted to talk to me together about going to the day hospital again. They put a lot of pressure on me to go there. Everyone else seemed to think it was a good idea. Both Dr Bell and Hydie thought that I should go too.

I whined and complained and slumped over on my side to display my emotional exhaustion.

"But going there makes me really anxious and I hurt myself more," I defended my point of view.

"If it made you hurt yourself more, that's a sign that they got things moving in your head," Dr Stone pointed out. "You have to let that emotion out, but in a healthier way."

I had no intention of getting in touch with my emotions. My emotions had already hurt me enough.

When we were done talking about the day hospital Dr Stone asked Hydie if my spasms were any better. She said that they were. I would still spasm a lot, but compared to a few days before, they were much less severe and frequent. I still had them wherever I was resting though.

People didn't usually react when I would twitch and jolt. As long as they knew what was going on, they would continue our conversation like nothing happened. They didn't even blink. I wondered if I could have done the same in their position.

Before Dr Stone left, he said that he would be back to talk more the next day. I wasn't looking forward to another conversation about some program that made me miserable.

When it was just Hydie and I in the room, I asked her, "Can't I just write my story instead? I've filled so many journals that I can transform them into a book. I write my experiences and how I feel. Can't that be considered as a way to get my emotions out?"

"If you think that would be helpful, but you need to work on the anxiety you get when you're in a group."

"I don't need to talk to them. I already have people to talk to."

It seemed like I was on the losing end, but I was too stubborn to give in and say that I'd give this program another chance.

Hydie had left, but it wasn't long before I went to find her in the small office in the back of the hospital. She was working there with the other student nurses.

"I need Quetiapine," I told her as my anxiety and my need to make it stop grew.

"Nope," she disagreed. "We're going to talk and play cards."

"Why can't we talk and play cards after my Quetiapine?" I asked.

"Because of your spasms. We need to give you as little of it as possible."

"Fine, but if I'm still anxious after, I want my Quetiapine," I argued. "I'll take the spasms over the anxiety any day. At least the spasms don't hurt."

We played a game of speed for about half an hour. We laughed a lot. Sometimes she won. Sometimes I won.

At lunch that day, they sent me a sandwich again. I had told myself that one more sandwich would make me violent.

I refused to eat the overly familiar packaged meal and I took it off my tray. I had a soup, a date square, and some orange juice left. That was okay because I wasn't very hungry anyway.

I met Hydie in the halls afterwards.

"Guess what they sent me for lunch?!"

"Not a sandwich?!"

"A cheese sandwich!"

When they later sent me another cheese sandwich for supper, once again, I refused to eat it. I took my sandwich and my pudding off my tray and put them on the lunch trolley.

"I'm not eating this," I said to Saul.

"You have to eat," he told me pointedly.

"Not this, I don't."

"Then I'm going to have to write in my report that you didn't eat," Saul warned.

"That's fine, as long as I don't have to eat that," I pointed with disdain to the sandwich on the trolley. "I have my soup and my juice. I'll be fine with that," I said as I walked away with my tray.

Annette was my nurse that night.

After she gave me my Lorazepam, Annette was direct with me before she walked away.

"Give me all the tools that you're hiding," Annette ordered.

"What makes you say that I have any?"

"You had a plastic knife the other day. If you have anything now, you need to give it to me."

Annette followed me to my room, but I didn't want to give her the two plastic knives I had hidden. I had one in my coat sleeve and one in my playing cards box.

"So where are they?" Annette asked.

I thought about it for a moment. How could I avoid giving up my tools without lying? I decided to protect my knives by confessing my least effective tool.

"You know what I do?" I asked her. "I scratch myself with that," I pointed to the radiator grid beside me.

Annette passed her hand over the front of the grid to see if it was sharp, but it wasn't. "How do you do that?"

"Not there," I corrected her and showed her the part of the grid that I would scratch myself on. "At the corners. It's a bit sharp."

Annette felt the corner of the grid, then shook her head. "Only you would be desperate enough to figure that out."

"Maybe."

LADY INJURY

"Okay, this is how it's going to work. I'm going on break for one hour. If you need anything, you can go ask at the desk. I'm going to have Carson and Megan check on you. If you hurt yourself, you get tied down. I'm only giving you one chance," she explained.

"Okay," I agreed, then added, "But tell them not to just ask if I'm okay, because I'll always say that I'm fine. Have them ask for specifics, like, asking if I hurt myself, because then I'll tell the truth."

"Okay. Have you hurt yourself today?"

"No."

Annette accepted my response and left me alone.

I had been without Quetiapine all day because of my spasms, so I didn't even have the desire to try to fight the urge to self harm.

I reached over to my bedside table and took a knife from my cards box. There was only so much I could do with a plastic tool, so the damage was minor compared to what I would have liked.

When Carson came in to check on me, I quickly sat on my knife and hid my wounded wrist.

"Are you okay?" he asked.

Of course, I said I was fine. I hadn't been asked the question that I requested, so he didn't get a confession. Carson turned around and left as quickly as he came.

Saul walked in soon afterwards, and as soon as he saw me lying in the bed, he knew that I had done something. I don't know how he knew. Both the knife and my wrist were hidden and I hadn't made any sudden moves.

"What did you do?" Saul asked as he signaled for me to raise my pant leg.

"I didn't do anything to my leg," I told him, but he wanted to see anyway.

Saul found no new wounds on my leg, and didn't think to check my wrist, but he decided to send me to the 7 just to be safe.

I passed a few hours in the 7 were I spent a lot of time biting my wrist, then I fell asleep right after taking my night medication.

Saul woke me around 10:00 that night because they needed the 7 for someone else.

"Are you okay enough to go to your room?" Saul asked.

"Yes."

Saul lifted my pant leg to see if I had done anything, but when he saw that I hadn't, he held both of my hands in his and said that he was proud of me.

"Keep on fighting," he said.

So I slept in my own room for the first night in days.

Friday, December 18

I weighed 50.4 kilos on the scale the next morning, but I didn't know what that meant in pounds, so I wasn't sure If that was bad or not.

A few people told me that they noticed I had gained weight and they said that it suited me because I had been too skinny. Apparently I had the body of a 14 year old. That certainly wasn't the look I was going for.

That day was a victory for Dr Stone because he finally convinced me to go to the day hospital. I declared my right to quit whenever I wanted, but I had to promise to at least make an effort to make it work.

I asked Dr Stone when I would get my leave from the hospital.

He said that he was thinking it would be the coming Monday or Tuesday.

"Do you think that you could go to your first morning at the day hospital and then go home?" the doctor asked.

"That sounds okay," I accepted. "I'm glad that I still have a few days because I don't quite feel ready yet."

"We can make it Tuesday then."

I liked that better. "Okay."

Hydie told me afterwards that if I didn't feel ready by Tuesday, I should say so.

I had art-therapy that morning. I chose to paint a mask with dark outlined eyes that cried blood. I worked hard to make her skin tone match my own.

It was both creepy and morbid. I loved it.

I was supposed to meet with Hydie after my art-therapy, so I slipped my mask over my face and poked my head into the back room where the student nurses were.

Hydie looked up at me and screamed, then her teacher looked up at me and screamed as well. The teachers scream was followed by another scream by a student who had been surprised by the 2 first screams.

"Never do that again!" Hydie was breathless.

The teacher told me that she was old and couldn't handle that.

Personally, I couldn't stop laughing because I hadn't expected a reaction nearly so loud and dramatic. I hadn't expected them to jump at all.

"You think this is funny?" Hydie asked as we walked to my room.

"Yes, I do," I said as I stepped into my room.

The two of us played cards for a while. The best part was that Hydie was a sore loser, so she complained a lot at my victories.

At noon hour that day, Hydie finished her nurses training at that hospital. I was sad that I wasn't going to see her again.

Hydie said that all the interns got to chose who their patient would be. She said that she had chosen me so that she could beat me at cards.

Hydie wished me success and gave me a hug. I could tell that she had put a lot of thought into how she would help me. I don't think that I'll ever get to thank her enough.

A lot of people had left the hospital, making it seem empty and lonely.

My roommate was gone, so I had the room to myself. Parker left after lunch, and Peter left the day before, and three other friends I had made were gone too. Samantha was still there though. She didn't get her release the way she thought she did.

So it was a lot calmer there at the old nut house. There had only been one *code white* in the previous two weeks. It was a fight that broke out in the smoke room. A couple of guys were punching each other, then got sent to their rooms.

I made an old mistake that day. After lunch I ate a few chocolate bars, but then I started feeling too badly for gaining weight and eating that much. That was when I did a bad thing. I threw up the chocolate and part of my lunch. It was the first time in a whole month since I had made a mistake like that. I was proud that I had made it that long, but sorry that I had broken my record. I felt guilty. Very guilty.

That was when I decided to hide in my room and I pulled out a plastic knife that I had stolen at breakfast that day.

When I used the knife, I sawed 3 cuts into the back of my wrist. After that, I went to the sink and let the hot water run long enough for it to be able to melt my skin. I laid my wrist on the steaming metal tap. At first the pain was almost more than I could take, but when I left my wrist there for a long enough time, the pain faded and all that was left was a feeling of warmth.

After I turned the hot water off, I pulled up my sleeves and decided to forget about the wounds I had just made; at least for a while.

I went to the cafeteria and played cards with Samantha. We made a deal that I would lend her my MP3 player for the evening.

After not too much time had passed, I had to roll up my sleeve because it was rubbing against my wound and the burn was leaking into my shirt sleeve.

"Wow, you really didn't miss your mark, did you?" Samantha said with wide eyes when she saw my wrist.

"I know. Im going to get in trouble for this tonight. I'll tell my nurse about this later. I don't feel like going right now. Besides, I trust Saul the most, so I want to wait until he's back from his break."

"Oh, I really hate things like this," Samantha moaned uncomfortably.

Richard was my nurse that night. I had seen him before, but he had never been assigned to me. When Richard walked into the room a few times, I was thankful to have been quick enough to hide my wrist. If it had been Saul that had walked into the room, he would have noticed for sure. Saul knows that if he walks in and I make a sudden move, it means I did something wrong.

It was too much for Samantha to know that I had hurt myself and that the wounds hadn't been taken care of.

I had met up with Samantha in the halls about twenty minutes later and she pointed at Carson. "I was looking for you so you could talk to him."

"I'm going to tell them. Don't worry about it," I consoled her.

"I already told them," Samantha's confession came out as almost a whimper. "I told him to go take care of you. Now I feel too guilty. I'm so sorry."

"It's okay Samantha. I was going to tell them anyway and I shouldn't have put you in that position," I told her. I was disappointed that she had told before I was ready, but I certainly wasn't mad.

We both walked down the hall and to the desk where my nurse was working.

"This has been bothering Samantha's conscience," I told Richard as I pulled the knife from my pants and tossed it on the desk.

Richard picked it up. "Where did you use this?"

"On my wrist," I said as I pulled up my sleeve to show him. "And I burned the other side."

"I feel too guilty," Samantha said again. "I'm giving you back your MP3 player."

"You don't have to," I told her. "I said that you could have it for the evening."

"I don't want you do be mad at me," Samantha pleaded.

"I'm not mad at you. It's okay," I tried to console her but my words meant nothing.

Richard added his own opinion to the conversation. "It wasn't an easy choice, but I would have done the same thing."

"You can take the music," I told Samantha and hoped that she would take it. She was feeling so bad that it was making me feel bad too.

"Okay, but I have to go to my room. I feel too badly about this," Samantha said as she walked down the hall.

Saul returned from his break as Richard was setting my bandages.

"Why did you do this?" Richard asked, but I didn't answer. I felt like I had no excuse. "You couldn't help it?" he suggested.

"No, I couldn't," I agreed as I remembered the strong pull that lured me towards that sink.

"This is a pretty extreme way of dealing with your problems."

"Yeah,"

"Im going to have you tied down in the 62 until your medicine kicks in and you calm down," Richard told me after giving me some Quetiapine. Then he turned away from me and directed his words to Saul. "We have to tie her down."

I went into the 62, but with Richard's consent, I left right away to get a pillow from my room. I passed Saul on my way. "Be careful Saul, I'm running away!" I mocked because I knew that he would try to stop me.

"She's just going to get a pillow," Richard explained to Saul.

I put the pillow on the bed and then I backed up a few steps so I could sit on the floor and lean against the wall. I had a familiar sick feeling inside my stomach as I watched them set the straps.

"Get on," Saul ordered when the straps were ready.

"But it's too far," I complained ridiculously as I sat less than two feet from the bed.

I didn't want to be forced into the straps again, so I got up willingly and sat on the bed.

First, my feet were put in the straps, then Saul told me to give him my hand, and I did.

"Lie down," Saul said before wrapping the strap around my wrist.

I didn't want to, so Richard tried to push me down, but I forced my way back up.

"I'll do it after," I said. "I don't like laying down with people around me."

Saul tightened the strap around my wrist and I cried out in pain.

"I shouldn't have put that burn on my wrist," I admitted.

Once the straps were set, I laid down and they set the blankets over me.

Saul dimmed the lights so they weren't as strong, and then he locked the door behind him.

I was surprised when Saul came back in only five minutes later. He kneeled down beside me and held my hand. "Why didn't you wait for me?" he asked in sadness. "We could have done like yesterday. Get by the evening bit by bit."

"I don't know," I answered sheepishly. "I got stupid."

"I didn't get to see what you did to yourself tonight. Was is only scratches?" he asked.

"A few scratches," I told him. "And I burned it too."

"Do I have to turn your hot water off?"

"You shouldn't have to," I said. "I should be able to control myself."

"That's true."

Since I was laying down, my body jerked repeatedly from the spasms.

"What's with those spasms?" Saul asked as he backed away slightly and pointed to my rising and falling shoulder.

I remembered telling him what my spasms were about a few times before, but I reminded him again anyway. "It's from my Quetiapine. It's a side-effect," I explained as my body jerked again.

"Okay," he said. "I'm going to count on you to tell me when your thoughts of self injuring are gone."

"Okay," I agreed, and he let go of my hand and left the room.

When Saul came back about ten minutes later, he knelt beside me once again and took my hand. I found him comforting when things were so hard.

"I'm sorry," I apologized. "The other day when you offered to be the only one to tie me down, I saw it as a gift, but I didn't take it. I was too stubborn and decided to keep a useless promise that I'd made to myself. Maybe tomorrow I can do it better."

"I wont be here tomorrow, nor the day after. I wont be here Monday either," Saul informed me.

"You're only coming back on Tuesday?"

"Yes."

I felt a sadness come over me. "Then I won't see you again."

"What?!" Saul said with an expression of disappointment and sadness. "Why?"

"I'm leaving Tuesday."

"And how do you feel about that?"

"I'm torn," I admitted. "I can not and do not want to stay here forever, but I'm afraid of falling when I get out. I'm afraid of not being ready."

"You will have people who will help you."

"I know. I don't know how I got so lucky."

"We see a potential in you."

I wasn't sure as to what kind of potential he was referring to, but I didn't ask either.

When Saul came back to check my straps, he felt my hands and feet and said that they were cold, so he covered them up more with my blankets.

I asked if I could be let go, but Saul didn't seem to understand the question, and I didn't ask again.

Before opening the door to leave, Saul asked, "On a scale of one to ten, how much do you want to hurt yourself?"

"Zero," I told him.

"Okay," and he left the room.

Richard was the next to come in. "Do you still want to hurt yourself?" he asked.

"No," I said simply. "Not now anyway."

"I need to be sure that you're being honest with me," he said.

"I'm very honest. Just ask Saul. He'll tell you that I'm honest."

"Okay, but if you start thinking of hurting yourself again, I want you to come find me right away. I don't want to play games."

"I'll tell you," I promised, though I wasn't sure as to what games he was referring to.

"Okay," he said. "I'll go get the key."

I was relieved that I didn't have to spend the whole evening strapped down like that.

When I got out of the 62, I went to my room and started to write.

Saul came by and pulled back the curtain that separated the room. "You don't have a room mate anymore, so you don't need this."

I slid the curtain back to where it was. "I like the privacy."

Saul closed the curtain again. "But I like to be able to see your blond head when I walk by in the hall."

I opened the curtain again. "But if the curtain is closed, you wont have to come in the room, and I like it when you come in to talk. That way, you get to see my blond head up close."

I smiled and leaned against the head of the bed.

Saul studied me with a strange grin, like he was wondering of my intentions.

"What?" I asked.

"What are you planning?"

"Nothing," I answered truthfully and felt sad that this was one of the last conversations I would have with my grey headed friend.

"I'm going to have to figure out what kind of stunt to pull on you since this is our last night."

"Okay," I agreed. "Make it a good one. I'll be waiting."

I wished that I had told him what a good friend he had been for me instead of going along with some jokes. I wished that getting better and leaving the hospital didn't have to feel so sad.

"At 10:30 tonight I want to see you in this bed," Saul said as he poked my mattress.

"Why?" I asked. "Because if I'm in here then I'm not in isolation?"

"Yes."

"Well then, I'll try hard to make it through okay."

"If you think of using your hot water to burn yourself, I want you to come and tell me," Saul insisted.

"Okay."

Saul passed by a few minutes later when I was washing my hands. He poked his head around the corner.

"I'm just washing my hands," I told him. "I'm not burning them."

Saul looked like he found something suspicious despite what I had told him. Saul put his fingers under the water to test the temperature.

"Ouch!" I cried out as if the water had burned him.

Saul quickly drew back, then he smiled and shook his head. "Oh boy, but you are so detestable."

I laughed.

I still had my hot water when Saul left and I went to get my medicine for the night. Richard wasn't there to give me my medicine because there were supposed to be fireworks across the water from the hospital. I decided to forget about my pills and I set my glass of water in my room. I joined the others that had gathered at the end of the hallway to watch the colorful show.

"Wow!" Samantha called out. "Fireworks in the winter!"

Samantha had always been full of expression and wonder. I wondered why I wasn't as exited over something so pretty.

I leaned down to get a better view out of the window and Saul moved me to the other side of him.

"You'll see better here," he told me.

Then Saul started goofing around by covering my eyes a few times with his hands.

I smiled and let him have his fun, but I couldn't help but feel sad that this was my last night with my goofy old friend.

Later that night, I got my medicine and went to my room where Saul came in to wish me goodnight. He said "Good bye."

I never liked final words.

Saturday, December 20

The next day I got to go out for an hour. First I had to see the doctor that was on call so he could check my burn and then Sandy bandaged it.

I brought a bag of stuff home with me so that I wouldn't have as much to take with me when I was discharged from the hospital for good.

I didn't want to ask for any anti-anxiety medication before I left for my hour out, because If they had known that I wasn't feeling well, they never would have let me out.

I had wanted to check my e-mails, but my lap top was missing from home. I wasn't worried. I knew that my brother had to have had it.

I had received mail. I curiously opened the envelope when I saw that it had come from the city. I knew it had to be about the legal complaint I had taken. I eagerly read the letter, but was disappointed when I realized that my case was denied with no mention of reason.

I tried to call the police station, but they didn't know the reason that it was denied either. I was incredibly disappointed, but at the same time, I was truly relieved. The anxiety of dragging subjects of a sexual nature through court could have been overwhelming.

When I returned and Sandy had given me my Lorazepam, she was too nervous about leaving me alone in my room. She was afraid that I might do something, so she put me in the 62.

I had to eat my supper at the desks that day because I was under surveillance. Stupid sandwich again. I ate it, but I was loud about my disapproval.

My nurse was Richard again that evening. He didn't want to let me go anywhere alone, so when I needed to go somewhere, he followed me. He even asked that I sleep in the 62 that night, so I agreed.

I wanted to keep my orange juice cup in my room, but Richard said he didn't want me to because I was too creative with ways to hurt myself.

Later, when I asked to have my orange juice and chocolate bar, he came to my room to watch me eat it.

Not a comfortable thing.

What was I supposed to do? Forcibly choke on the bar wrapper?

There was a new admission that night. I heard her ask what room she was in. They told her it was the 10.

Uh oh.

My heart sank.

I had a creepy new room mate. She was smelly too. She made the whole room smell like arm pits.

It was a good thing that I wasn't sleeping in the 10 that night.

Sunday, December 21

As I looked around the hospital the next day, I found that I didn't recognize many of the faces that were there. There was still Samantha, Alma and Lily, but all the rest were strangers.

I did that stupid thing again that day. I ate a bunch of chocolate bars and threw them all up.

Throwing up was coming much easier to me then. The food came up more quickly. Maybe it was because I hadn't done it in a while.

I wasn't out of isolation for a long time. Sandy gets nervous when I ask for Quetiapine.

"I'm afraid that you might hurt yourself," she would say.

In the evening Natalie was my nurse. She made short contracts with me to keep me from cutting. She checked on me every 30 minutes until I fell asleep.

Monday, December 22

I got up early the next morning so that I could attend the day hospital, but it turned out that I was in the afternoon group. The last time I went there, I was told that the afternoon group was for people who were less capable and independent. I was disappointed that I had fallen into that category. Had I changed that much?

So I had time to walk around listening to my music.

The afternoon group started at 1:15 pm, and soon after I was called in to see Dr Silk. The psychiatrist came to get me during group, but it was a medical student who was in his final year of studying to be a family doctor who did the interview.

Dr Silk sat in the corner and asked me questions once in a while, but most of the time it was the student who spoke.

"I've been told a little bit about you," the student said to begin with. "But could you give me a short description of why you are at the hospital?"

I made my answer to the point. "I stopped eating and drinking. I started getting dizzy and hallucinating."

"Do you feel that you've been helped?"

"Yeah, my eating is better, but my self injury is worse."

"You started hurting yourself at the hospital?"

"No, I started hurting myself years ago. I was in the hospital for that in June. This time I'm there for my eating disorders, but lately I've been working on my cutting."

"And how are you doing that?"

"Well, there used to be no consequence. I could cut as much or as bad as I wanted, but they couldn't punish me for it. Now the plan has turned to zero tolerance. I get sent to isolation or strapped to the bed."

"And how do you feel about being strapped to the bed?"

"I hate it. I used to be so scared that it would happen to me, and now it has," I said with a smile because of how ridiculous it sounded to me in my head.

"Why are you smiling? Do you find it funny?"

"Not exactly. I have a habit of telling things like it's a joke."

"And how do you feel about the day hospital?"

"I hate it."

"Why?"

"Because it makes me really anxious. I don't like talking in groups or laying down in a dark room full of people."

"Then why did you come?" the student was curious.

"Because my doctor doesn't understand the meaning of the word no. I protested greatly, but here I am anyway. The idea is that I'll be more surrounded with people after I'm released from the hospital."

"You don't think it will be helpful?"

"No," I answered. "It didn't help last time."

Dr Silk spoke up. "If you come here thinking that you will fail, then you will fail and you'll have proven yourself right. You don't have to talk only about your self injury and your eating disorders, or else that's all people will know about you, and that's all you will be. You can talk about the good things in your life."

"You mean, think positively?" I asked. "I could do that."

I jolted from my spasms several times when I was sitting there, so I asked Dr Silk, "How long until the spasms stop?"

"I'm going to talk to Dr Stone about that," Dr Silk said.

"Okay."

After my therapy group was over that day, I took a taxi back to the hospital. I got back in time for supper. Another lousy sandwich.

"They don't learn, do they?" Roger asked as he pulled out a tray holding my offensive cheese sandwich.

"No, they really don't."

After supper I went to the 62. Megan was my nurse that night, so I wouldn't have been surprised if she condemned me for my thoughts.

I had one or two nights left at the hospital.

I was afraid of going home and doing it all wrong.

I was afraid to fall and afraid that I wouldn't be able to get back up.

I couldn't live like that anymore.

It was too toxic.

Although, one good thing was that by that night, I had made it though three self injury free days.

One day ended and another began. Would this one be successful?

Tuesday, December 23

It was Christmas in looney town.

The cafeteria tables were moved around so that there were more places for people to sit, and every one of them were covered in red table cloths.

Terrance had returned to the hospital a few days before. I remembered him well, because he was the one who would hurt himself.

Later that day I met Terrance in his isolation room doorway.

"Did you succeed?" I asked him.

"At what?" he asked in reply.

"Last time you were here, you swore that you would never hurt yourself again. Did you manage?"

"Yeah," he said. "But that's not why I'm here."

I gave Terrance candy a few times and he was grateful because he had nothing else to do. He was getting tired of being cooped up in the 7. He would walk from the window to the doorway and to the window again. Pacing back and forth, angry and cursing under his breath. He reminded me of a lion pacing in it's cage.

When Terrance saw me tugging at my arm warmer, he reached out and took my arm. He knew what it meant when a cutter would pull at her sleeve. It meant she had something to hide.

"What did you do?" he asked in a sad and concerned tone.

"This is from a few days ago," I told him. "It's a burn."

LADY INJURY

Terrance let go of my arm. "Take care of yourself, okay?"
"Yeah, you too."
I walked around until Dr Stone arrived and we talked in my room before Christmas dinner.
We confirmed that I would leave Wednesday, and after that, he asked me the strangest question.
"Do you ever hug yourself?"
My eyes narrowed at where he was going with that.
"No."
"You should try it," he suggested as he put both of his hands on opposite shoulders like he was hugging himself.
"I don't think so," I replied. "That reminds me of my father. He used to have me do that. Not in a bad way. It just reminds me of him."
"How did he do that?"
"He stood behind me, then took both of my hands and guided them to my shoulders. Then he would sing a song about how I loved myself." I explained.
The doctor got up and sat behind me in the bed. He took my hands the way I had described. He held my hands like that for quite a while. He even started to rock me back and forth. It was strange and uncomfortable, but I didn't feel unsafe.
"It's good for you to feel your body," he said. "See how smooth it is. How broad your shoulders are."
I wasn't comfortable with compliments. "Those are lies." I replied.
"You think I'm lying?"
"No, I mean that the way I look is a lie."
"How are you supposed to look?"
"The way that I feel I look in my head. Ugly, dirty and disgusting."
The doctor got off my bed and sat back in his chair. "What makes you feel like that?"
"I don't know. That's what I see when I look in the mirror."
"What do you see?" he asked smoothly.
"The Stupid Girl."
"And who is she?"

"She's the one who was hurt. She was part of something wrong. She cuts and starves herself. She does stupid things. Stupid baby things. That's what they say my self injury is; stupid immature baby things."

"It's not stupid," Dr Stone corrected. "It's how you survived. Now you just have to learn new ways."

~ ~ ~ ~

There was a buffet set up in the cafeteria, so I got to pick out whatever didn't have meat. Luckily, sandwiches weren't my only option.

I found a seat with Terrance and a friend of his. Dr Stone sat down with us after Terrance left.

"Do you always use that much salt?" Dr Stone asked as I poured sachet after sachet of salt on my food.

"Yup. It gives it flavor."

"What about spices?"

"Those are good too."

"They have a lot of spicy foods in Cancun."

"Really? That's good," I said between mouthfuls of salty macaroni.

"Maybe I should prescribe you something to protect your stomach," my doctor offered.

I found it amusing that everyone freaked out about my salt intake.

Wednesday, December 24

By Wednesday morning I had all my stuff ready to go.

I gave Sylvia a card to thank her for helping me as much as she did. I wrote that it was hard, but I was going to make it.

Sylvia was exited and read the card right away.

Then I gave her another card that I wanted her to pass on to Saul that evening. I told him that I was grateful that he let me find a friend in him. I said that he had helped me more than he would ever know.

I asked Amanda that if Joseph was high and came by the hospital to see me, she should tell him that I didn't want to see him.

I was still nervous about leaving the hospital, but I gathered my things and left with my sister when she came to pick me up.

I wanted to go to a restaurant like Pizza Hut and get a stuffed crust pizza. I thought that would be a great way to celebrate freedom after 44 days in the nut house. My plans were crushed because it was Christmas Eve and almost everything was closed. Finally, we ate at some cheap place, but at least it was restaurant food, and that made it a celebration.

I drove home that evening and slept in my own bed for the first time in six weeks. I set Assilem next to my head on the pillow and I fell asleep holding her hand. She was a part of myself that I needed to protect.

I thought that maybe she could protect me too. Maybe I could recognize and protect the same broken part of me that I saw in her. Maybe she could save me from me.

~ ~ ~ ~

There was a knock at my door in the afternoon. I opened it to find Joseph standing there. He was happy to see me. I could also tell that he was high.

"I went to the hospital, but they said you were gone home," Joseph told me.

"Did you talk to Amanda?"

"Yes."

"Didn't she tell you that you weren't supposed to come and see me?" I wanted to know.

"Yes, but I'm so exited Melissa," he began. "I finally got a response from the radio station. They said that they want me to stop sending them mail, but I know this means they have heard me."

"Joseph, you know you weren't supposed to come until you were okay," I brought us back on subject.

"I know, but I missed you so much," He told me. "I hate being all alone. I'm supposed to marry the five virgins and help bring about the end of suffering in the world. I would marry you instead Melissa. You are worth more than the five virgins. I would take you instead."

"Things aren't like that Joseph," I told him. "I'm sorry that your feelings are hurt, but this isn't a romance we have. You're my friend."

"You could be with me when Jesus comes," Joseph told me.

"What would you say if Jesus didn't come this summer?" I asked.

"The pope says the end of the world is in 2012, but I'm sure it's this summer," he told me.

"And what if he doesn't come?"

"I'll wait longer. I've promised myself to God. I will not get married and I will stay chaste until Jesus comes," Joseph explained.

I didn't know what to say. There was no point in a debate and there was no point in going along with what he was saying. Most of what he talked about was of growing gardens and giving the food away so we can save the world. He was on a mission. He was dedicated. He was sick.

It took too much from me to keep worrying about him.

"Joseph. You need to go," I informed him. "I'm really sorry, but I don't want you to come back until you've stopped using."

I closed the door to the sad and hurt expressions twisted on his face.

I knew that wasn't the end of our friendship. I would see Joseph again. Time would come with better days for Joseph; I was too stubborn to believe otherwise.

Thursday, January 1

I was right to have been afraid of leaving the hospital. I tried to at least keep my main meals down, but in between it was a vomit fest. It had become so easy to throw up that I allowed myself to eat more things.

By Thursday, the week after I left the hospital, I was invited to a small party where I got to see my dear friend Lisa. It was good to meet with a friend who knew what I was going through. Two movies were rented for that night, but we all ended up talking so much that we didn't even finish the first one.

After a few social games, Lisa and I left together. We picked up two dozen doughnuts and brought them to my place. Our poor judgement led us to have a doughnut eating bulimic episode together.

That girl was amazing when it came to binging. She downed a large can of pears, some cereal, all twelve doughnuts and then a packaged cake! I was in awe. How could she fit that much down without busting open? I wondered how long it would take before my eating disorder would make my stomach stretch as much as hers.

I ate a little can of oranges, and then I made it though nine and a half doughnuts before I couldn't fit anything else down. I had to empty my stomach before I could finish my dozen.

It turned out that bulimia was way more fun by two than it ever was when I was discouraged and alone.

Lisa slept over that night.

I woke up the next morning to my friend coming into my bed and cuddling next to me.

It was sweet.

I had been thinking a lot about getting drunk. I had never been drunk before and I wished that I had someone to do it with me. Who could I ask? Lisa? No. Or maybe yes. Who did I know that wouldn't think it was a terrible idea?

I wanted to get so miserably drunk that I would finally understand what was so great about it. I would finally understand what my father was willing to trade me for; to trade his whole family for.

I would look at the rows of alcohol at the grocery stores and wondered which one's I should take. How much would I have to drink to get wasted? What complications would drinking have on my medications? How much would put me in a coma?

I didn't know anything about those things, but I had other things to think about.

Every day I would throw up.

Every day I would fail.

I made it to eleven days without cutting, but then I couldn't handle the pressure anymore. I decided to call the suicide hotline. I think it was the same guy that had talked to me the time before. He wasn't helpful. I played with my precision knife as I spoke to him. When we hung up, I cut my wrist, then cleaned up the mess.

After breaking my eleven day of no cutting record, I allowed myself to cut two more times. I didn't even know what my excuse was. I didn't know why I was feeling so bad. People would ask me what was getting me so down, and I didn't have an answer. It made me feel so stupid; like a moron. Shouldn't I know why I did the things I did?

Wednesday, January 7

I started planning things.

Planning no good plans.

I wanted to cut my upper arm with a double edged blade. I wanted to cut deep. There would be blood, and there may even be stitches.

I needed it, but I didn't know why.

And yet I kept planning.

I planned until planning turned into doing.

There was no choice but for it to become real. It was all I could think about, and when something was all I could think about, it didn't take long before I would make it come true.

And so it was that I messed up in extreme fashion on the Wednesday two weeks after I left the hospital.

The moment that I returned home from the day hospital, I grabbed a towel and sat down on my living room floor. I laid the towel over my lap and partly on the floor beside me. That's when I pulled out my self injury kit and took out the last unused double edged blade.

I cut a line in my shoulder that was only two inches long, but I cut deep; very deep. It felt like I was going to lose the blade inside my arm.

The cut was wide open and the blood ran down my arm, to my hand, and onto the towel. There were strange little pale pink balls throughout the inside of the cut but I couldn't figure out what they were. The uncertainty made me uneasy and concerned.

I knew that I had cut too deep to deal with it on my own, so I called a local health line so I could ask some questions.

After I described my wound, I was told to go directly to the hospital. So I stuffed a few necessary things into my bag, then I wrapped the bloody towel around my arm and tried to fit it into my coat sleeve. It didn't fit, so I slipped my good arm into one sleeve and just laid the other half of the coat over my shoulder.

It was a cold and windy walk to the hospital. The weather was three hours into a bad storm, so the snow was high and hard to trudge through. I tried to turn my face away from the wind, but the snow still whipped into my eyes and I had to try hard to see where I was going.

After I made it into the welcome warmth of the hospital, I didn't have a long time to stay in the waiting room. I think they pulled me in sooner because I looked really messed up with my spasms. A blond nurse took my hospital cards and entered my information into the computer.

I had to have her help me take my coat off because the towel made it very tight.

When the towel was peeled off to reveal streaks of dried blood down my arm and a very deep cut at my shoulder, the nurses eyes grew wide and she took a deep breath.

"Well, you certainly didn't miss your mark."

"I didn't intend to miss."

"So you want to be admitted to the eighth?" she asked.

"No, I just want stitches."

"That's a bad cut, but I'm a little more worried about your mental well being. I'm going to put you on a cot so the doctor will see you sooner."

I knew what that meant. I was going to the psychiatric section of the emergency room.

After getting my arm cleaned up and bandaged, I followed the nurse to the cot she had chosen for me. It was a section of the hospital that I knew very well.

There were only two cots in the room this time, so it seemed very empty. One cot was filled and the other was for me.

I knew the usual ER routine by then. Nobody had to tell me what to do. I got changed into their ugly green hospital gown and provided them with a urine sample.

Soon two different doctors had come to see my cut. Both of them said, "Well, you certainly didn't miss."

"Why does everybody say that?"

When I was left alone with only the other patient and the guard, I began scratching my right wrist with my fingernails. My healing wounds were itchy.

"Am I going to have to hold your hand?" the guard asked.

"No, that's quite fine."

"Then don't scratch yourself."

I tried to satisfy my itchy wrist by rubbing it against the blanket instead.

I asked for some Lorazepam so I could calm down. It helped a little, but not enough.

I had arrived at the hospital at 4:30 in the afternoon, but I didn't see the doctor until around 11:00 that night. By that time the blood had soaked through the layers of medical pads and tape. My gown and bed sheets were stained.

The guard threatened to tie me down if I didn't stop scratching at my burn wounds, but he didn't really do it.

I wondered why my healing wounds would always itch so much.

After that a young blond doctor had come to look at my cut, I was led to a room meant for minor surgery. I waited there on a table while a nurse and doctor got everything ready.

I had to lie down and she stuck a needle into several places along my cut. I was told that the needle was meant to freeze the area, like at the dentist.

"What's that stuff in there?" I asked her as I pointed to the lumpy shiny pink balls inside my cut that had worried me earlier.

"That's fat."

"Huh. Interesting."

LADY INJURY

I was disappointed that I didn't get to watch her sow it up. The cut was at an angle where I couldn't look without getting my face in her work.

My once open wound was now a slim red line with five little bows across it.

They asked If I would be safe going home.

I said that if I were to hurt myself again that day, it wouldn't be nearly as bad as what I had just done to my shoulder. So I would be okay.

They decided to keep me overnight so that I could be re-evaluated in the morning.

~ ~ ~ ~

The doctor that I saw in the morning decided that I needed to see the psychiatrist and therefore had to wait longer.

I figured that there was no way that they would send me upstairs. I had just been there two weeks earlier and they had been aware that I was leaving with this problem.

Time passed slowly as I waited.

I hid behind the curtains and scratched my right wrist against the windowsill. I was scratching in part because it was itchy, and in part because I wanted to hurt myself.

I was startled when the guard moved the curtain so I could be seen.

"I can tell that you're not doing well," he said.

I pulled the curtain back over me.

"No," he said and then noticed my freshly wounded wrist.

I tried to explain that I needed to scratch it but he didn't seem to believe me.

The guard left suddenly then returned with a group of people. He said that I was going to go to the small isolation room until the psychiatrist could see me. By the number of people around me, I knew that I wasn't going to have a choice in the matter, so I followed them to a small room with just a bed.

"No pillow?" I asked as I surveilled the room.

"No, you could use it to suffocate yourself."

"Not likely," I thought.

I was asked to change gown in case I was hiding any tools in my previous one.

Everyone left the room and I sat down in a corner but the guard complained that he couldn't see me there. There was a large window in the door. The window took up half the door, but still he couldn't see me.

They made me sit on the bed, so I did, and they left. I started scratching at my wrist, but I was surprised and caught. That's when the guard pulled out a red box. I knew instinctively what that box was. The yellow box upstairs was shaped just like it.

I got out of the bed and sat back in the corner.

They wanted me to lie down, but I refused. Soon, I was forced to the bed where several people held me down as they set the straps. I winced in pain as they tightened the straps on my wounded wrists. I asked that they put a bandage on my right wrist, but they didn't, so every movement was painful.

It was hard to get comfortable in that bed once they had left me alone.

Time passed slowly. I wasn't even let out so I could have lunch, and I was hungry.

I twisted around in the bed a lot. Eventually the strap for my right wrist came right off of the bed.

That was much more comfortable.

I took the strap off my wrist and hid it under the blanket that I was using as a pillow. Then I put my arm back to where it was supposed to be so that I wouldn't evoke any suspicion.

About ten minutes later I managed to release my right foot.

"Score!" I thought triumphantly.

The next trick became to free my other foot before anyone came to look in the window and see that I was sitting. Finally, I straightened my left foot and used the freed one to push at the leather strap and something clicked loose. My second foot was released.

The only limb that I failed to free was my left wrist.

My nurse hadn't come to check on me in a long time. I had time to sing *99 bottles of beer on the wall*, in it's entirety.

When my nurse came back to see me it was 3:00 in the afternoon. I had been there three and a half hours.

The nurse was far from happy when she saw that my straps were undone and she gave me a speech about how I should do what I was told.

A male nurse of large stature came by and she told him that I had freed myself from my straps.

"Hey Houdini," he greeted in an amused sort of way.

After that I was allowed to go back to my cot and I was served a late lunch. I was so hungry that I didn't care that it was a sandwich.

I got to see the psychiatrist around supper time. My guard followed me to the office. He was a one on one guard. He was there to watch only me.

"How special," I thought sarcastically.

So my guard waited on a chair in the hall while I went into the office of doom.

"So what brings you here?" Dr Fillips asked.

"I needed stitches."

"And you want to go upstairs?" he asked.

"Definitely not. I just wanted the stitches. I didn't think that it was going to be this complicated."

"Why did you cut yourself?"

"I had a bad few days. I've been very anxious. I just got this idea in my head and finally I just did it. Now I'm making other plans. They kind of scare me, but I want them."

"What other plans? What would you do?"

"I thought about making lots of deep cuts all over myself. I would be like a blood fountain. I wouldn't be doing it to die, but just to bleed a lot. Then I can look as disgusting as I feel," I explained and recognized how crazy my words were as I said them. I wondered why I wanted crazy things and didn't realize they were crazy until I said them.

"You think you are disgusting?" the doctor asked with an analytical expression.

"Yes," I confirmed. "But people don't seem to see me like I see me."

Dr Fillips rested his hand on his chin and rubbed it. It was like I could see him thinking. "It would be good for you to discuss this with your doctor too. They can decide what plan to use with you."

"What do you mean by my doctor? I'm not going upstairs, am I? I just wanted stitches." I was getting worried and felt a bit trapped.

"You don't think that you should go?"

"No. What good would it do?"

"It's for your protection. We can't let you go home knowing you are in danger," Dr Fillips explained.

My heart sank. "But I was just there two weeks ago! How long will I have to stay this time?"

"That depends on how things go."

I was beyond disappointed. Another hospital stay was not what I wanted. I thought that maybe the next time I should just stitch myself up on my own.

I was led upstairs with my guard and my things around 7:00 that evening. I was immediately put in the 7. My guard was set up just outside the room with a chair and a table on wheels.

I wasn't the only one being watched. There was another guard set up for the boy in the room next to mine.

"Saul! Look where they sent me!" I cried when I saw my friend.

"You've only been gone two weeks," Saul said.

"I know!" I agreed. "I didn't think they were gonna send me here."

"Why did you come?" Saul asked.

"I needed stitches," I explained. "They give me five stitches and they think that they should send me upstairs." I pretended like I didn't agree with the reasoning. I knew that if some psycho girl cuts herself up she clearly needs help. I just thought that I was beyond help and that they had given up on me.

LADY INJURY

I wandered around the 7, then I laid down on the bed for a while. When I scratched a bit, the guard told me to stop and I went to look out the window.

"What are you doing Princess?" Saul asked as he came in the room.

"Enjoying the view," I replied.

"You know that Saul can get real tough when he has to," my friend warned.

I looked at his semi-grinning face. "You don't look the part," I told him.

"You know what we have to do if you continue."

"No, I don't know," I said. "What is in my plan this time?"

"The doctor hasn't made one yet. We would have to tie you down."

"No, that's okay. I don't need that."

"Make sure that you don't," Saul warned and started to leave.

"Stay and talk to me," I asked and he turned around.

"Why can't you talk to your guard?" he asked.

"Well, he's kinda far away. Can he come in?"

"Yes," Saul accepted and my guard rolled his chair over to my bed.

We started by talking about the weather and our families. He was only 18 years old, but he looked much older. He had been working there for three months.

After talking, we played three games of cards. My young guard won best 2 out of 3.

Then it was time for medication and sleep.

Thursday, January 8

The next day I walked around with my new guard that started his shift at 8:00 in the morning.

I met Samantha in the hall and gave her a hug. I was glad to see her but sorry that she was still at the hospital.

I also got to relive all the embarrassing parts of having a one on one guard. I had to take a shower with the door partly open, but at least I was clean and avoided the flies.

Sadly Dr Stone was on vacation so he couldn't take my case, but I remembered the doctor who was assigned to me. She was Dr Goodshaw. She was the Dr who treated me for self injury and eating disorders for about a months time around three months before.

"I see you have a vacation coming up," the doctor noticed as she looked over my file.

That was a subject that I was interested in. "Yeah, I'm going to Cancun with my mom and my sister."

"We're going to have to see how things go, but you may not be able to go on that trip," Dr Goodshaw told me.

I grew wide-eyed and panicked. "But it's already paid for. This is something that I've been looking forward to. Can't I go to Cancun and then come back to the hospital?"

"I don't have loose rules like Dr Stone. I don't want you going to Cancun if you're in danger."

"My mom and my sister will be there. I would never cut myself this badly if they were around," I tried to negotiate. "I couldn't risk doing that to them. I might do smaller stuff, but nothing that they would know about."

"How do you think you could make a trip like that work in your condition?" the doctor asked.

I was getting desperate. "We could make a plan on how to deal with things."

"I don't know," Dr Goodshaw shook her head. "Ideas like human blood fountains scare me. We need to keep you safe."

Suddenly the idea of confiding my crazy thoughts seemed like a really bad plan. I regretted saying anything and felt like I was grasping at straws. "But all I needed was stitches."

"You didn't think that you would be sent up here?"

"No."

"Why?"

"Because I still had this problem two weeks ago and I was still let go. I figured that my problem have been given up on."

"We let you go the other times to give you a chance to prove that you could do it. By now, with everything we have on file about you, we could contact the courts to force you here for at least 21 days, and they would grant it. I was also thinking of sending you to a longer term facility afterwards, like Ste-Marguerite's just nearby, or like Douglas in Montreal, where they deal specifically with your problems."

"Self injury too?"

"Yes."

"Can't I go after Cancun?" I knew that I must have sounded like a broken record, but I didn't want to give up.

"We can't let you go while knowing that you're in danger."

"But I plan on behaving as much as I can while I'm there. No human fountain," I told her in the hopes that I could win her over.

"If you can show us now that you can control yourself then we will let you go."

I felt a sigh of relief, but I was still worried. "What if I cut only once?"

"Then you can't go."

"Please, I can't be expected to get everything right."

"It's for your safety."

I didn't care about safety. I felt like my heart had fallen into my stomach. I was devastated and terrified that I would mess things up. I was certain that I was incapable of not hurting myself.

My guard was sent home and Dr Goodshaw's assistant came to tell me what the plan for me was.

I was to stay in the 7 continually. I was only allowed out to shower in the morning, and I had a break for 15 minutes in the afternoon and evening.

I was not to hurt myself in any way, or I would have to stay longer and miss Cancun.

If I ever got to a point where I wanted to hurt myself, I would have to wear the giant gloves.

"Can I sign a refusal of treatment?" I asked him.

"Yes, but the judge would side with us."

I stared blankly at the wall.

"Are you okay?" he asked.

"No, but that's okay," I lied. It wasn't okay. How could it be okay?

"Okay," he accepted my answer and left.

I felt sick to my stomach and I laid down in bed. My mind was spinning and I felt like I could have cried.

I was soon moved to the 62 so that they could keep a better eye on me.

I filled out the reflection forms for the self injury I did in the ER.

When I finally got to talk to my doctor I had forgotten all the questions that I wanted to ask her. She used the silence to go over all the rules in my plan.

"But with the gloves," I began. "They wouldn't keep me from hurting myself. I could still scratch my arm on things and make bruises. There's not much of a point in them." I brought it up because I was afraid of messing up and losing out on Cancun.

"We aren't going to tie you to the bed. You like being tied down." Dr Goodshaw told me.

My face fell. I what? I figured that she should read my journals or see me fight my way out of being put in the straps. Someone actually had to sit on me the day before.

I was offended by this woman's judgement, but I didn't say so.

"I wouldn't keep the gloves on even if you put them on me," I told her. "Last time they tried, I took them off."

"Not with the way that I tie it on," the doctor informed me, but I was silently sure that I could get out of it.

"Are you thinking of hurting yourself now?" Dr Goodshaw asked.

"I have some thoughts of it."

The doctor left to get the gloves and came back with one of the nurses and Roger.

I refused.

There was no way that I was letting them put those gloves on me. I said that I would sleep instead.

I had to make saving my mom's Cancun vacation my motivation to succeed.

It was already hard, and I felt cutting calling me, but I wanted a life and not a line of recurring hospital stays. I wanted to be free, outside taking walks, playing with my ferrets, being with my family, and going to Cancun.

I chose living.

I chose no giving up.

No cutting.

I chose Cancun.

I was aching to talk to my mom, but I wasn't allowed out of the 62 for my break until 8:15 that evening. It was only 7:00 pm, so I had time to wait.

I wanted to tell her that I was sorry and that I may have messed things up. I felt sick to my stomach about it.

I was laying in bed looking at my stitches when Saul walked in. I quickly covered my stitches with my sleeve, but Saul looked to see what I was doing anyway. He sat on the bed next to where I lay.

"Why were you playing with that?" he asked.

"I wanted to know what it looked like. It used to be covered in bandages," I explained.

"Thank you for the card you gave me," Saul said in reference to the words of thanks I had left him two weeks earlier.

"You're welcome. It was honest."

"I'm sure it was," he agreed. "So what is going on now?"

"Now they put me in here. I didn't think I was going to have to come here, but I did. I really messed things up. If I make just one mistake, I can't go to Cancun."

"That's right."

"I feel like I'm letting them down. My mom is giving me this incredible gift and I don't want to hurt her by not being able to go. I never meant to hurt anyone. That's why I hadn't told them about my cutting to begin with. I wanted to protect them, not hurt them," I told Saul as I looked up at the ceiling and tears rolled down both my cheeks.

"This is the first time that I've seen you cry," Saul remarked.

"Well, I haven't done it in a while."

"We all cry," Saul told me. "I cry. You cry. It's okay."

"If I make one little mistake; just one scratch, it's all over."

"Yeah, but we have to do something more for you."

"Like what?" I was curious.

"I don't know, but something needs to be done."

I was hoping for a little more information because I really did want for something more to be done. I was tired of living that way. "They want to send me to St-Margaret's or Douglas." I told him.

"At Douglas they know how to handle these things."

"I don't want to go," I cried as Saul wiped tears from my cheek.

"I know you don't," Saul understood. "But something more needs to be done for you."

I thought sadly about the things they wanted to do. "They want to put those big gloves on my hands."

"Yes," Saul agreed. "They are trying something new because the other things didn't help."

"I don't want the gloves. I don't want this. I don't want to hurt my mom," I cried.

"You have to think about you too."

"It will be my fault. They are going to be hurt and it's all my fault," I told Saul as I was feeling really down on myself.

"It's still in your hands," Saul told me.

"I know," I agreed. "But I already find it so hard. I don't know if I can do this. It's calling me. I hear all these voices and they want me to hurt and to pay for being so disgusting. It's hard to think over all those voices and it's hard to know how to defy them."

"You can come talk to me," Saul offered. "Whenever you need it."

"Thank-you."

We heard new sounds and people at the post.

"It's a new admission," Saul recognized the noise and he left to take care of it.

~ ~ ~ ~

I had a surprising conversation with Roger that evening.

Roger asked me how I was doing.

"Not good, but there's nothing that can be done about that."

"Nothing can be done?" Roger was confused.

"Im stuck here and I didn't want to come. All I wanted was to get my cut patched up and they sent me back here."

"Oh, I hadn't heard the story about that."

"And now I've put my vacation at risk. I don't think that I'm strong enough to succeed."

"You are strong enough," Roger told me. "If you are strong and brave enough to cut yourself, then you are strong enough not to."

"I'm not so sure." I felt defeated already.

"But I'm sure," Roger said. "Just put the same energy you have been putting into doing what is wrong, into what is right. When there is a will, there is a way."

I smiled. "When there's a will there's a way. My grandma used to say that."

"And do you love your grandma?"

"Yes."

"Then that is something that you can tell yourself. When there's a will, there's a way."

"Thank-you."

I had mom call me as soon as I was on break because I only had a 15 minute window of opportunity.

As soon as I picked up the phone, I started apologizing.

"Oh, mom. I messed things up so bad. I'm back at the hospital and I didn't mean to be," I told her as I cried. "I came here for stitches and they decided to keep me. I didn't think that they would do that. If I hurt myself just one more time, even if it's only minor, I can't go to Cancun. They're going to have a court order to keep me for 21 days and then they will send me to Douglas."

My mother's logic was just like mine. "Can't you go on the trip and then go back to the hospital?"

"I did ask, but they said that they can't let me leave if I'm a risk to myself. Do you think that someone else can use my ticket?"

My mothers response was quick. "I don't even want to think about that."

"It's not too late though. If I manage to not hurt myself, they will let me go. Mom, I love you and I'm going to try really hard to make this okay. I'm going to try so hard. I'm so sorry for the hurt I caused you and the others. I'm so sorry."

"It's okay. I still love you."

"I know mommy."

"I love you," my mother said again. "I have grandma next to me. Would you like for me to say a prayer?"

"Yes, I would."

"Okay, we're holding hands," mom informed me.

"Tell grandma that I'm holding her hand too."

Mom said a prayer, and we hung up.

LADY INJURY

I decided to go to bed early, because I wanted to be safe and make sure that I didn't do anything stupid.
And I didn't.

Friday, January 9

The next day was long and I slept through most of it.

My funny family was trying to contact my doctor to see if they could convince her to let me go to Cancun.

They also wanted to see if they could take me away from the hospital for a day so that we could go get our passports.

I didn't think they were going to have much luck in their persuasions. It was all on me.

It was my success in not hurting myself that was going to make the trip happen, and nothing else would do.

I sat in the corner of my room where they couldn't see me from the door.

I just had to be somewhere that wasn't in the isolation bed. I just wanted to hide and pretend that my pain could disappear with me.

Saul walked in.

"What did you do?" he asked as he kneeled before me and picked up my hands to look for blood stains.

"Nothing," I told him. "I didn't do anything."

"I believe you," Saul said as he let go of my hands.

Saul stood up and he looked down at me in the corner. "Something is wrong," he noticed. "I know you. When you feel bad you hide in corners or in hallways beside elevators."

"That's true," I agreed. "I'm not feeling well."

"What's wrong?"

"Im afraid of hurting my mom. I'm afraid that I can't do this." I expressed my worries.

"You can do this. It's been a few days and you have been doing this. I'm proud of you for it even if you don't see it."

"Thank-you," I was grateful for any kind words. "But what if in the end, I really don't make it? The urge can be so strong."

"Listen to yourself. You're very pessimistic. You say that you can't make it, or wonder if you will fail," Saul noted. "Why don't you say that you can do it. Say that you will not fail."

"But I don't even know if that's true."

"No. You are setting yourself up to fail. You can do it. You will not fail," Saul said with determination.

"I can do it," I repeated his words with a smile. "I will not fail."

"That's better."

"I can do it," I grinned and finally felt some of my worries fade.

"I like talking to you," Saul told me.

"I like talking to you too."

"I'll be back in 10 minutes," Saul informed me.

"My mom is calling me in 10 minutes, so I'll see you later," I told him.

I sat comfortably in the phone booth. Sitting on the stool, I leaned back against one wall and put my feet up on the opposing wall.

"You sound better today," my mom observed.

I thought about that. "Yeah well, I didn't just get some really bad news, so I'm better than yesterday."

"That's good."

I took a deep breath. "I didn't hurt myself mom. I haven't lost my chance to go on the trip with you."

I wanted to tell my mother every day about how I hadn't given up and that I was still fighting.

I took a long nap the next afternoon. It was surprising to wake up to those walls. I didn't feel like I was where I was supposed to be. I kept forgetting that I was at the hospital, and a few moments after I would blink my sleep away, I would remember.

The walls of the 62 were not what they used to be. The holes had been filled and all the graffiti was covered over in white paint. The parts of the walls that hadn't had any graffiti remained a sickly green, so it looked very patchy.

All the proof of those who passed before in the life of the 62 were gone. Even the words, "I was here", that I scratched into the wall with my fingernails were gone.

I hadn't minded all the graffiti because it made me feel less alone. It had been like some part of the people who struggled through their story in that room was still there.

When Lily saw that I was back at the hospital, she called me her angel. I thought that it was cute, but I figured that if I had wings, they had to be broken.

Lily's hair hadn't started growing back yet and she wasn't wearing the mittens anymore.

Lily asked Annette, who was sitting next to me on my bed as to why her angel had to stay in that room. "She is really nice and sweet, and wouldn't hurt anyone," Lily told Annette.

"That's true," Annette said from where she sat on my bed.

Neither of us told Lily why I was there.

When people don't know how I'm broken, I get to be an angel.

I liked Lily. I thought she was beautiful in ways that she would never see. She thought she was fat? She thought she was ugly? She was so skinny!

Her world was so dark, but it didn't have to be. It reminded me of myself. When I looked in the mirror, I saw fat while everyone else saw a malnourished pre-teens body. I wanted to be better all of a sudden just for realizing that my logic was faulty. I was not fat. Why should I have been afraid of food?

Why should I hurt myself when I would never hurt someone else in the same, or any other way?

It didn't matter what logic told me, my mind would twist things around into lies that I would lust after. I was chasing desires that I never needed until I let my guard down and I was overpowered.

What would I have needed to avoid this? What did I need to fend it off now that it had me at the foot of its will?

Before the shift change, Roger came to see me in my room. I was surprised at what he had to say.

"Just in case no one else has told you this; I'm really proud of you," Roger told me.

"Thank-you. You're very encouraging."

"You deserve it," Roger praised. "You've been trying really hard. It's not easy what you're going through. Some of us have it easy, but sometimes I put myself in other people's shoes, and it's not easy for you."

I had never heard Roger be so sincerely encouraging to me. This was a side of him that I liked.

"Thanks for understanding," I told him.

"You've made it to three days. Keep your eyes on the prize; Cancun and spending time with your family."

I smiled. "Yeah. That's my motivation."

"Just think about how you would feel if you let that slip away." Roger made me think.

"I would never forgive myself."

Saul walked in.

Roger directed his next words to Saul. "I was just telling Melissa how proud I am of her. She made it to three days."

"That's what I was telling her yesterday," Saul replied.

I grinned widely. "Yup," I said. "I ain't done nothing stupid."

"You've got to be optimistic," Saul told me in reference to our last conversation.

"I am," I said. "I can do it."

~ ~ ~ ~

I was trying to stay positive, but as the day progressed into evening, my thoughts were getting darker. I wanted to hurt myself, but I also had my eye on that prize.

For that hospital stay, I didn't have any Quetiapine prescribed to me, so I had to find another way to calm down.

I called out to Carson from my doorway. "When Saul gets here, could you tell him to come see me?"

"Why?" he asked.

"To talk."

"You can't talk. You're in a room plan," Carson told me.

I didn't like how rigid he was with his rules.

"But then, how am I supposed to make it?" I asked him.

"Make it to what?"

"To the end of the evening."

"You know what will happen if you do that," Carson warned when he picked up on what I meant.

By *do that*, he meant *hurt myself*. Sure I knew, but what I needed was help to keep from doing it.

Carson left and came back just a few minutes later.

"It has to go well," he told me.

I had to blink away how irritating his sentence was. "Saying that it has to go well doesn't make it go well," I spoke to Carson and he left again. Clearly the man had no conversation skills.

Carson came back when I was sitting in my corner.

"Are you okay?" he asked.

"I guess so," I answered, feeling like the answer didn't matter anyway. I wondered how many times he would leave and come back without regard for anything I said.

"You know what will happen if you do something," Carson warned.

I couldn't believe he had just said that….again. Why would he just come in to deliver threats of doom and say nothing more to make things okay?

I knew exactly what would happen. I knew it, but this curly headed little man was trying my patience, so I decided to try his.

"What will happen?" I asked defiantly.

"We would have to put the gloves on you."

"I won't let you, and if you get them on me then I'll take them off," I rebelled.

"We can also tie you to the bed. We will act in consequence to your actions," Carson warned.

"Listen to yourself!" I huffed angrily. "All you do is tell me that there will be consequences. I'm human. I'm having a hard time. You can't just spout off consequences and expect for that to work. Tell me how to help myself before I do something wrong. Don't just wait for me to crack before you act. Right now I am saying that I have a very strong urge to hurt myself. I can see in my mind what I want to do."

"You know what will happen if you do," Carson warned again.

"Stop that!" It was unbelievably difficult to stay calm, but I managed to just sound stern and not loud. "That doesn't help. Help me make it so that I don't hurt myself in the first place. Don't throw me in the water before I know how to swim. I'm told that there is all these different things that I can do instead of hurting myself, and then I'm tossed in a room where I can't do any of those. All I have is what I already know, and that's to hurt myself."

"You're putting the responsibility on us," Carson said as he leaned against the wall.

"No, I'm not," I told him. "This is my fault. I made that first cut because I couldn't stand myself. I did that and it was nobody else. I'm here now because I made bad choices and I need help, so help me, please, before it's too late. There must be something in my plan that says how to keep me from hurting myself."

"We can tie you down."

How could he have such an unfeeling one-track mind?

"My doctor says that I won't be tied down because I like it," the words tasted strange in my mouth. "I never said that I liked it. I've never heard of something so ridiculous. But you can't tie me down."

"Well, what happens is up to you," Carson told me.

"No," I corrected. "It's up to you. I already told you what I want to do and it's up to you to make sure that I don't. If I could control myself better I wouldn't be at the hospital. I have to do my part, and I have. I told you what I want to do and I haven't hurt myself in three days. Now the urges are getting stronger and I'm telling you that I need help."

"I have to go. I have another patient," Carson said and then just left.

I said, "Okay." But he was already gone, so I had spoken to thin air. Carson came back shortly after. The man was like a yo-yo.

"I want you to sit on the bed where I can see you," he instructed.

"Why? You can't see me from your post anyway."

"No, but when we pass by your room we can."

"How about I just go to another corner," I offered as I pointed across the room to a corner that would be seen by the doorway.

Carson said that was okay, so that's what I did.

I began passing the time by tapping musical notes into the floor with my hands. I was so mad that I wanted to kick and hit at the walls really hard just to spite Carson. Lucky for me, my better judgement stopped me. I wished that my judgement would do that more often.

Saul came in and sat on my bed. He looked down on me to where I sat on the floor.

"What's going on?" Saul asked.

"I'm angry," I replied.

"Tell me why."

"Because they stick me in this room expecting me to keep from hurting myself, but they don't provide me with the tools I need to succeed," I explained.

"You have tools."

"Like what?"

"You. Your better judgement," Saul answered.

I thought about what he said, but I disagreed. "If I were able to use that without losing control, I wouldn't be here."

"That's true."

"I try to do things to calm myself down, like tapping on the wall. It barely made a sound and Carson only heard it when he passed by my room. When he told me to stop, I asked him why? His best explanation was that we just don't do that. I asked if it was bothering anyone. He said, no, we just don't do that," I rolled my eyes. "It's like there are rules being invented just to keep me from succeeding."

"You should talk to your doctor about that tomorrow," Saul suggested. "The doctors are our bosses and we have to do what they say. Tell her that you need more than what your plan offers."

"I will, but what about tonight?" I asked. "How do I get through tonight? I'm told that I'm not even supposed to talk through a crisis. How am I supposed to get through when I can't even talk?"

I made it through that evening. Maybe it was my anger that fueled me, but mostly, I think it was because I had a friend who would talk to me no matter what Carson said the rules were.

Saturday, January 10

The next morning was my fourth day in isolation.

Dr Goodshaw came to see me early in the morning.

I told the doctor all the things that had been bothering me. I made several requests for some changes, which included having more time outside of isolation. I also asked if I could get my clothes back, or at least a bra, but I wasn't sure how much I could get away with.

Dr Goodshaw seemed receptive. "Is there anything else that you want to add to your list of requests?"

"I can have more than that?" I was surprised because the wish list I gave her was already extensive.

The doctors arms were crossed and she was holding her medical pad. "How about we add your release to the list?" she asked.

My jaw dropped.

Allowing me to leave was the last thing that I thought I would be offered. They had scared me into thinking that I was going to be there for a long, long time.

I was glad that the threat of a long stay was gone, but my emotions were on such low gear in the last few days that it was hard to simply transition into happiness. They were letting me go? After all I had been through it was hard to believe. My mind was a bit fuzzy and confused.

"I spoke with Dr Silk and we agreed that you can leave as long as you continue to go to the day hospital. Can you do that?" Dr Goodshaw asked.

"Yes," I replied immediately.

"I was expecting to come back after the weekend and find you with cuts up to here," Dr Goodshaw motioned with her hand to show me her elbow.

It turned out that being on my best behavior had saved me, and sooner than I thought it could.

I had managed to escape the psychiatric ward, but something gave me the feeling that I would be seeing it again. Somehow, I always ended up there.

I was allowed to get dressed. It felt good to be in my own clothes once again.

I walked out of the hospital with my sister. We were so relieved that I was allowed out in time to go into Quebec city and get my birth certificate and passport for the trip.

I saw my psychiatrist, Dr Silk, one last time before going to Cancun. I told her all about my doll, Assilem, and about how I was afraid of hurting my mom by missing the vacation.

We talked about how I try to protect everyone else. I protect my family, my friends, my elderly people at work, and even my doll…. but I didn't protect myself. I would hurt myself.

"I always sleep with Assilem," I told Dr Silk. "I hold her hand as I fall asleep. I don't let harm come to her. She makes me think about how ridiculous it is that I protect a doll and not myself. She makes me realize that I should care for me too. Maybe, in a way, she can watch over me like I watch over her."

"You don't want to hurt your family or your doll, but you don't care if you hurt yourself?" Dr Silk asked.

"No, I don't."

"Why?"

"Because I don't matter," I answered simply.

The doctor shrugged her shoulders. "And yet the doll does?"

I knew that it didn't make sense. I had thought a lot about it. "Yes," I answered.

"What do you think you would need for you to matter?" she asked.

"I don't know," I answered feeling perplexed. "I am responsible. I can take care of people. I do my job well. I have a family that is amazing and that I am close to. I have lots of friends. I have some talents that I love, like drawing and writing. I don't know what I need."

"Don't you think that by hurting yourself, you are saying that your father is right?" Dr Silk asked.

I was puzzled and I wondered if she was insinuating that my cutting was the same as being an alcoholic. "My cutting doesn't change my personality and make me hurt the people I love," I defended myself.

"But what does your cutting say about what he did to you?"

"Do you mean, am I saying that it was okay for my father to hurt me, because now I'm hurting me?" I asked for specification.

"Yes."

"I've thought about that," I admitted. "I've become my own monster.

"And what do you need to do to change that?"

"I don't know," I said. "I just don't think it matters. I would be so worried if someone I cared about was doing this, but when it comes to me, it just doesn't matter."

"Because that is what you learned from your father; that you don't matter," Dr Silk concluded.

"Yes," I confirmed. "I'm trash worth throwing away."

"What are you going to do to keep from hurting yourself?"

"I can write, draw, talk, walk, watch TV," I recited my usual list.

"And those things work well?"

I thought about it. "Not as well as cutting, but they help a bit."

"What is it about cutting that helps?" the doctor asked.

"The pain is a good distraction. The whole act of it is a good distraction. Cutting; metal through skin. Watching the blood run. Feeling it trickle over my skin. For a while it's like nothing else exists. It's calming."

"What about holding an ice cube or snapping a rubber band?" Dr Silk suggested. "Do those sound like things you could try?"

I knew those methods very well. I reached over and pulled at the blue rubber band on my left arm, then I let it go. The sound of the rubber snapping on my arm answered the question for me.

Dr Silk smiled as she realized my familiarity with those ideas.

I changed the subject. "I've been having to take Lorazepam before bed so that I can fall asleep. Can I also have some for my anxiety during the day?"

"We are going to lower your dose of Lorazepam," Dr Silk informed me.

I grew very worried. "But how am I going to deal with my anxiety?"

"By doing the things that you talked about, like drawing and writing."

I didn't share the doctors faith that I could manage without medicinal help. The idea of going off of Lorazepam scared me. I scared me. I still dreamt of hurting myself and the things that I wanted to do were worse than I had ever done before. I was afraid of me; Afraid of the monster in me.

I needed to behave so I would have only scars and no wounds. I wanted to be abel to draw tattoo's over my scars so I could go on the beach.

I needed to keep trying, if not for me, then for those I loved. I needed for my scars to fade and to let my past fade with them.

I knew that all the difficulties I had faced had shaped the person I was and would be. I wasn't sure what kind of potential everyone saw in me, but I couldn't wait to get there, and find out.

I'd like to offer special thanks to the people in this story who were under the pseudonyms Saul, Sylvia, and Dr Stone. Thank you for giving me all that you could. Thank you for your part in saving me from myself.

Thank you Tracy for putting up with me and helping me to edit my story.

Thank you mom for giving me confidence in what I wrote and the confidence to publish.

Thank you to my family for their loving support.

Thank you to all those who took a moment of their time to make a difference in my life.

Would you like to see your manuscript become a book?

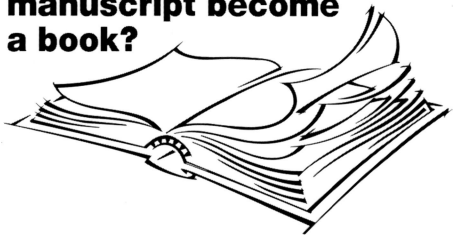

If you are interested in becoming a PublishAmerica author, please submit your manuscript for possible publication to us at:

acquisitions@publishamerica.com

You may also mail in your manuscript to:

PublishAmerica
PO Box 151
Frederick, MD 21705

www.publishamerica.com

Lightning Source UK Ltd.
Milton Keynes UK
173283UK00001BA/168/P